AF334732

ISOLATION AND ETHOS

A Study of Joseph Conrad

Wiesław Krajka

EAST EUROPEAN MONOGRAPHS, BOULDER
DISTRIBUTED BY COLUMBIA UNIVERSITY PRESS, NEW YORK

1992

EAST EUROPEAN MONOGRAPHS NO. CCCXXXIV

ISBN 0-88033-231-X
Library of Congress Catalog Card Number 91-75987

Printed in the United States of America

TABLE OF CONTENTS

Foreword

This book[1] outlines a distinct synthesis of Joseph Conrad's output, formulated in terms of its two most important and characteristic aspects: isolation and ethos, whose relationship indicates a definite manifestation of the Conradian world view. All the analytical comments are subordinated to the discussion of these problems. I decided to base my research on a thorough and intensive examination of all of Conrad's writings and tried to avoid superficialities so as to objectify interpretive judgements as much as possible. The methodological foundation of this study is the concept of the literary work of art as a structure, i.e., a set of semantically significant and dynamically interconnected elements, subordinated to organizing principles (main lines of meanings), its explication depending upon higher-level structures (literary and extraliterary contexts).[2] The interpretation of a text, which reveals its semantic and artistic uniqueness, richness, and the diversity of meanings. It was combined with synthesis, which gives an overall picture of Conrad's oeuvre while placing particular works in this picture and explaining their position in the history of literature and culture. Adoption of a synthetic perspective has resulted in the treatment of all Conrad's creations as one text of a higher order with clearly manifested parallels among them, with recurring themes and motifs that reveal the considerable uniformity of the Conradian visions of man and the world. This delineation of the diverse realizations of the crucial concepts of isolation an ethos and the abundance and productiveness of structural and semantic configurations generated by them testifies to the greatness of Conrad's masterpieces.

Part One: Isolation

The problem of isolation, central to Conrad's literary output, is usually mentioned as a typically Conradian motif. Considerations of the external determinants of his texts lead to the viewing of the various aspects of isolation. Biographers point to the estrangement of his characters as having been strongly influenced by certain facts of his life: his childhood, his school years in Kraków, his stay in Marseilles, his service in the British Merchant Navy, his settled life in England.[1] Investigations of the Conradian canon from the perspectives of the history of both literature and ideas depict detachment in terms of several factors: the transformation of the Robinson Crusoe pattern,[2] the impact of the works of Byron,[3] Melville,[4] France, Flaubert, Maupassant, Baudelaire, the influence of nineteenth-century French literature,[5] the ideology and poetics of Polish Romanticism,[6] and a significant relationship with Existentialism.[7] The treasury of Conradology comprises only a few publications that present a penetrating and thorough examination of the ways he shaped the motif of solitude and how it functioned: Baines (2:441-443), Hewitt (36: Complete Isolation from All Land Entanglements), Kennedy (205), Moser (57: 29-35), Osborn (63), Pawłow (269), Pettersson (67), Ryf (74: 40-46), Spoerri-Müller (83), Wiley (94: The Hermit. Man in the World), Urbisz (312), and especially Gillon (23). Gillon's book is undoubtedly the best-documented and most convincing treatment of this subject.

A psychological angle is conspicuous in the study by Spoerri-Müller (83). It is manifest both in the choice of categories to classify the material and in the mode of argument, i.e., in an extensive and well-exemplified discussion of the psychological laws underlying the particular kinds of loneliness. The second part of the book is more valuable: it surveys the techniques by which the theme is presented, although even here the approach is old-fashioned, and the relevance of considered literary devices to the issue of separation frequently appears to be tenuous and unconvincing. Pettersson (67) stresses that the seclusion of Conradian characters (viewed as single entities), both from the other characters and from the world to which they are opposed, typifies the general human predicament.

Isolation is, however, most often examined in terms of the relationship between an individual and a community. A treatment of this problem from a Marxist viewpoint is put forward by Pawłow (269). He deals with the alienation of the characters in *Nostromo* from the material interests they serve, with the degeneration of their spiritual selves through the desire for money and property. Osborn (63) asserts that loneliness results from conflicts with a milieu, from the failure to adjust or conform to the rules of social organization. The outcome of a character's distancing from society is ambivalent: it brings about either disasters, suffering, and death, or fruition of his ambitions and dreams. In spite of occasional interesting comments, the study by Osborn is disappointing, since he subordinates all Conradian texts to his theory, which frequently results in distorting their meanings and giving wrong interpretations.

Maladjustment to life in a community is sometimes caused by objective factors (Baines 2: 441-443): a cultural heritage (Urbisz 312: 302-303), the impossibility of fathoming the psyche of another human being (Baines 2: 441-443) (Urbisz 312: 303-304), or by nature (the sea, tropical forests). These create the conditions in which one is obliged to fulfill duties (Gillon 23: The Balance of Colossal Forces), (Hewitt 36: 8-10). A character's solitude is, however, much more frequently determined by his own conduct: conscious choices or a past guilt (Baines 2: 441-443), (Gillon 23), (Moser 57: 31-35), (Ryf 74: 40-46), (Urbisz 312), (Wiley 94: The Hermit. Man in the World). Conradians unequivocally condemn the characters who do not serve supraindividual ideals but remain egoistically separated from others and undergo a final catastrophe. Urbisz (312: 293-299) claims that such an attitude may result from a lack of social feelings, a fascination with one's own visions, immersion in dreams of greatness, or the skeptical renunciation of all positive values. This selfishness is sometimes hidden under the pretense of noble-mindedness and altruism.

Gillon (23: To Follow the Dream) combines egocentric seclusion with love entanglements–both as the partners' isolation from society and from each other. Their estrangement originates in romantic and dreamy attitudes, devotion to harmful illusions, and loss of contact with life. Gillon distinguishes and discusses numerous cases of separation caused by a character's past guilt and betrayal (Gillon 23: The Anatomy of Betrayal). He asserts that isolation nearly always brings about distressing consequences, misery, and calamity–death, suicide, madness, or at least unsettling one's system of values and emotional balance–which result both from individual activities and the cruel fate. In his words, only very few manage to overcome this tragic loneliness.

A similar viewpoint is represented by Wiley (94: The Hermit. Man in the World), who claims that separation–one of the main themes of Conrad's early creations–is caused by surrender to pernicious illusions and nonconformity to communal norms of conduct. Solitude is a manifestation of a character's weakness: it brings about his degradation, loss of good reputation, or some other kind of downfall. Hence the presentation of this motif in Conrad is colored with pessimistic reflections and an ironic, contemptuous distance. A parallel view is communicated by Kennedy (205), according to whom Conrad's treatment of estrangement emphasizes its destructive impact upon an individual and constitutes an ironic transformation of the Robinson Crusoe stereotype. The latter expresses glorification of man's detachment from his community and its culture, undermining the role of society as the foundation of life and civilization. Delineations of Conradian loneliness are nearly unanimously concluded with the thesis of needing to override this predicament by identifying with a community and accepting its ethos (see the discussion of this in the introduction to Part 2).

This part of the book deals with the concrete patterns of isolation in Conrad's entire literary output, testifying to the great range and meaningful, diverse versions of the motif: external or geographical (at sea or on land), and internal or psychological (escape into an imaginary realm, in love and marriage, and ethical–with all their manifold variants). The proposed classification is original as a total scheme. Only some of its particular categories are close to the kinds of seclusion mentioned by the other critics: imposed by nature (Gillon, Hewitt), caused by objective cultural factors (Urbisz), by love (Gillon), and by a character himself through his egoism, dreamy or skeptical disposition, betrayal or some ignoble deed in his past (Baines, Gillon, Urbisz).

Chapter 1
External (Geographical) Isolation

1. Isolation at Sea

A. Depiction

Isolation at sea is one of the most popular Conradian varieties of the motif, since in many of his works the universe of waters constitutes the shape of the fictional world. A ship and its crew are depicted as forming a closed circle, removed from the outer world.[1] This configuration si frequently created by an infinity of sea or ocean, which is abundantly exemplified in *The Nigger of the "Narcissus."* The boundless universe around the *Narcissus* is delineated by the narrator's use of phrases like "the measureless expanse of smooth water" (NN 27),[2] "the level expanse of the sea," "a vast and deserted plain" (145), "a pitiless vastness...an immensity" (99; cf. also 28, 147, 155). In *The Shadow-Line* the vessel is surrounded by the absolute emptiness of a monotonous seascape: "And but for those bits of land there was no speck on the sky, no speck on the water, no shape of vapour, no wisp of smoke, no sail, no boat, no stir of humanity, no sign of life, nothing!" (SL 196).

A similar design appears in *Chance,* where Powell is aware of the magnitude of water encircling his ship, separating it from the world:

> It was the immensity of space made visible–almost palpable. Young Powell felt it. He felt it in the sudden sense of his isolation; the trustworthy, powerful ship of his first acquaintance reduced to a speck, to something almost undistinguishable, the mere support for the soles of his two feet. (C 292-293)

In this passage the seclusion is hyperbolized by belittling the *Ferndale* and magnifying the sea space around it. A parallel contrast appears in *Cobwebs and Gossamer,* where the implied author emphasizes the weakness and fragility of rigging, masts, and sails in contrast with the water around: "For what is the array of the strongest ropes, the tallest spars, and the stoutest canvas against the mighty breath of the infinite, but thistle stalks, cobwebs, and gossamer?" (MS 37). Boundlessness also isolates mariners in smaller vessels. Marlow in *Youth* escapes from the burning *Judea* in a little craft on vastness of the ocean: "I sat steering my cockle-shell...with nothing but water and sky around me" (YNTOS 36). The boat of the *Patna* fugitives in *Lord Jim* constitutes a closed circle, detached from the world by the magnitude of the waters: according to Marlow it forms "the speck of life" amid "the solitude of the sea" (LJ 123), the "indefinite immensity" (114).

The infinity separating a crew from the world assumes sometimes the shape of a gigantic darkness. This pattern may be observed in *The Nigger of the "Narcissus"* where the space around the ship forms "the immeasurable night of an empty sea" (NN 126) or "a vast universe of night and silence" (104). In *The Shadow-Line* the nocturnal abyss is portrayed as "impenetrable blackness" (SL 108) or "a bottomless, black pit...[of] inconceivable depths" (110). Similarly, in *Typhoon* the world of waters assumes the nebulous shape of an immense gloom:

> The far-off blackness ahead of the ship was like another night seen through the starry night of the earth–the starless night of the immensities beyond the created universe, revealed in its appalling stillness through a low fissure in the glittering sphere of which the earth is the kernel. (TOS 29)
>
> A faint burst of lightning quivered all round, as it flashed into a cavern–into a black and secret chamber of the sea, with a floor of foaming crests. (40; also 39, 43, 45, 54)

The expanse of darkness isolates Lingard's brig in *The Rescue:*

> There was not a star in the sky and no gleam on the water; there was no horizon, no outline, no shape for the eye to rest upon, nothing for the hand to grasp. An obscurity that seemed without limit in space and time had submerged the universe like a destroying flood. (Re 241)

In *Chance* the seascape around the *Ferndale* is frequently portrayed as enormous murk, illuminated only by starlight (C 287-288, 408-410, or the metaphorical title of the last chapter: "A moonless night, thick with stars above, very dark on the water.") Analogous imagery appears sporadically in *Nostromo,* although it is not a sea novel: Nostromo and Decoud, escorting the treasure to the Isabels, are surrounded by thick sullenness of Golfo Placido, which favors the secrecy of their political mission (N 260-261, 263).

The elemental fury of a storm, sometimes combined with gloom, acts as another factor distancing mariners from humanity. This is well evidenced by *The Nigger of the "Narcissus"* and *Typhoon:*

> Soon the clouds closed up and the world again became a raging, blind darkness that howled, flinging at the lonely ship salt sprays and sleet....The horizon seemed to have come on all sides within arm's length of the ship. (NN 55)
> The gale howled and scuffled about gigantically in the darkness, as though the entire world were one black gully. (TOS 43)

In *Youth* the gigantic forces of nature seem to fill the space around the *Judea* completely:

> The world was nothing but an immensity of great foaming waves rushing at us, under a sky low enough to touch with the hand and dirty like a smoked ceiling....Day after day and night after night there was nothing round the ship but the howl of the wind, the tumult of the sea, the noise of water pouring over her deck. (YNTOS 10)
> There was for us no sky, there were for us no stars, no sun, no universe–nothing but angry clouds and an infuriated sea. (11)

Apart from infinity, nocturnal gloom, and the grandeur of

water, silence and immobility constitute the other determinants of the isolation of a crew. In *The Secret Sharer* the introductory descriptions of nature show that the protagonist's perception of his surroundings is of this type:

> A blue sea...itself looked solid, so still and stable did it lie below my feet; even the track of light from the westering sun shone smoothly, without that animated glitter which tells of an imperceptible ripple. (TLS 91)
> There was not a sound in her [the ship]–and around us nothing moved, nothing lived, not a canoe on the water, not a bird in the air, not a cloud in the sky. (92)

A complete lull recurs, like a leitmotiv, in the course of the story (98, 99, 123). In *The Shadow-Line* calm and windlessness imprison the vessel:

> It was impossible to distinguish land from water in the enigmatical tranquility of the immense forces of the world. (SL 76)
> A great over-heated stillness enveloped the ship and seemed to hold her motionless in a flaming ambience composed in two shades of blue. (81; also 73-74, 91, 108, 121)

The shallow sea of Carimata in *The Rescue* is shaped in a similar way:

> The sun had sunk already, leaving that evening no trace of its glory on a sky clear as crystal and on the waters without a ripple. All colour seemed to have gone out of the world...and such was the silence within the horizon that one might have fancied oneself come to the end of time. (Re 425; also 148-149)

Such a state is acutely sensed by Edith Travers, who is alien to this environment:

> And when she raised her eyes the same abysmal immobility seemed to reign over the whole sun-bathed enlargement of that lagoon which was

one of the secret places of the earth. She felt strongly her isolation. (285; also 461, 466)

Quietude and lifelessness, which seem to pervade all the universe, seclude the schooner-yacht *Hermit* and its passengers–making it impossible for them to get out of the zone of Carimata–and Lingard's brig:

> The calm was absolute, a dead, flat calm, the stillness of a dead sea and of a dead atmosphere. As far as the eye could reach there was nothing but an impressive immobility. Nothing moved on earth, on the waters, and above them in the unbroken lustre of the sky. (5)
> The calm surface of the bay reflected the glorious night sky, and the brig with the *prau* riding astern seemed to be suspended amongst the stars in a peace that was almost unearthly in the perfection of its unstirring silence. (76; also 89, 241)

Moreover, the setting of the initial phase of the *Patna*'s voyage in *Lord Jim* is created by a sense of tremendous peace and dormancy, which encircles the steamship as it steers lazily on its course:

> And under the sinister splendour of that sky the sea, blue and profound, remained still, without a stir, without a ripple, without a wrinkle–viscous, stagnant, dead. (LJ 15-16)
>
> A marvellous stillness pervaded the world, and the stars, together with the serenity of their rays, seemed to shed upon the earth the assurance of everlasting security. (17; also 19)

However, this aspect of the sea is deceptive: it weakens Jim's alertness and fills him with a blissful sense of safety (17).[3] Absolute stillness accompanies the ignoble escape of the *Patna*'s captain and his three companions (114).

The patterning of isolation may also be discerned in Conrad's other marine works: *The Nigger of the "Narcissus"* (NN 103-104, 126, 146-147), *Chance* (C 287-288, 409-410), *Youth* (YNTOS 20, 24) in which it forms the mute background for the heroic struggle of the *Judea*'s deckhands, and in *The End of the Tether* (YNTOS 317-318, 326-327), where it is the only factor determining the loneliness of the *Sofala*'s crew. The situation of separation brought about by quietude and immobility is also conveyed in the truths generalizing mariners' plight and experiences:

> At sea, you know, there is no gallery. You hear no tormenting echoes of your own littleness there, where either a great elemental voice roars defiantly under the sky or else an elemental silence seems to be part of the infinite stillness of the universe. (*Chance*, C 326)
> In my early days, starting out on a voyage was like being launched into Eternity. I say advisedly Eternity instead of Space, because of the boundless silence which swallowed up one for eighty days–for one hundred days–for even yet more days of an existence without echoes and whispers.... An enormous silence, in which there was nothing to connect one with the Universe but the incessant wheeling about of the sun and other celestial bodies... (*Well Done*, NLL 182)

Sometimes solitude amid an immensity of water is magnified through the use of the symbolism of the planets and the cosmos: portraying a craft as an autonomous heavenly body and sea as boundless space. This type of imagery is applied most consistently in *The Nigger of the "Narcissus"*:

> The passage had begun, and the ship, a fragment detached from the earth, went on lonely and swift like a small planet. Round her the abysses of sky and sea met in an unattainable frontier. (NN 29)
> Our little world went on its curved and unswerving path....And again, for long hours she remained lost in a vast universe of night and silence... (103-104)

An equivalence between the *Narcissus* and the earth is implied in the comparison of its appearance to the seasons of the year:

> In the morning the ship, beginning another day of her wandering life, had an aspect of sumptuous freshness, like the spring-time of the earth. (132)

> In the evening the cleared decks had a reposeful aspect, resembling the autumn of the earth. (31)
> On clear evenings the silent ship, under the cold sheen of the dead moon, took on a false aspect of passionless repose resembling the winter of the earth. (145)

Cosmic metaphors also concern the other vessels encountered by the crew in their peregrination (29). Such visions lead to a conception of Conradian mariners as existing beyond the pale of human life (6, 24-25). An analogous delineation of seclusion at sea appears in *The End of the Tether* (YNTOS 317-318), *Typhoon* (TOS 29, 54, 83), *The Rescue* (Re 76), *Christmas Day at Sea* (LE 33), as well as in *Lord Jim* and *The Shadow-Line:*

> The ship moved so smoothly that her onward motion was imperceptible to the senses of men, as though she had been a crowded planet speeding through the dark spaces of ether behind the swarm of suns, in the appalling and calm solitudes awaiting the breath of future creations. (LJ 21-22; also 120-121)
> My command might have been a planet flying vertiginously on its appointed path in a space of infinite silence. (SL 74; also 108)

Sometimes it assumes the form of apothegms universalizing marine lore (e.g., *Well Done,* NLL 182; *Ocean Travel,* LE 38).[4]

B. Functions

Conradian maritime isolation makes a ship the focus of a universe of water.[5] This determines the perspective from which the surrounding reality is perceived and presented. According to the narrator of *Chance,* "The solitude of the sea intensifies the thoughts and the facts of one's experience which seems to lie at the very centre of the world, as the ship which carries one always remains the centre figure of the round horizon" (C 300). Such a configuration is typified by *Typhoon,* where a subjective, centrifugal portrayal of the fury of the sea is emphasized, where nearly all the descriptions reveal the narrator's highly creative vision. This outlines the original, fantastically shaped world of the typhoon. A narrative perspective articulating the pivotal position of the crew is also found in the other works depicting detachment at sea: *The Nigger of the "Narcissus"*, *Lord Jim*, *The End of the Tether*, *Nostromo*, *The Secret Sharer*, *The Shadow-Line* and *The Rescue*. Delineations of nature–petrified in quietude and stillness–are frequently there contrasted with the characters' violent passions. This testifies to nature's indifference to human conflicts and tragedies. The relationship results in the secondary role of the marine setting and shifts the focus of presentation to the individual's psychological and ethical problems.

Seclusion at sea constitutes, however, the main factor that renders the performance of the captain's and crew's duties more difficult, to the extent that these duties frequently surpass human strength and capability. The characters have to carry on in complete separation from the rest of the world, relying exclusively on themselves and their companions. This is served mostly by the principle of hyperbole, which conditions the shaping of solitude at sea: the expanse of waters is nearly always limitless, the darkness dense and impenetrable, the silence and immobility ideal and omnipresent. Moreover, the "planetary" metaphor constitutes the extreme case of magnified marine loneliness. This technique of presentation applies the contrast between the immense power of the elemental forces of nature, which are not merely indifferent, but rather hostile to man, and the weakness of a lonely individual resisting or enduring them. Such isolation, in all its emphatic forms, implies, by exaggerating the difficulties of the seamen's profession, the glorification of these who perform them. It also lessens the blame of those who do not manage in such trying conditions (see the discussion of the marine ethos in Part 2, Chapter 4 of this book, 1-3, 5 and Conclusion).

Loneliness at sea, especially in its "planetary" shape, enriches the mariners' predicament with symbolic and universal meanings, e.g., in *The Nigger of the "Narcissus"* (Part 2, Chapter 4). The "cosmic" perspective makes it comparable to existence on land, taking in all its essential problems, dangers, and values. The seamen's experiences are ennobled, and provide material for reflections upon life in general–hence the profusion of gnomic utterances in Conrad's texts.

2. Isolation on Land

A. Representation

The most natural manifestation of a secluded realm in Conrad's works is the universe of water. However, water is not the only isolating device. The solitude of many individuals on land is analogous to that experienced at sea, since they live in areas also separated geographically from the rest of the world.

Insularity constitutes the variety of isolation on land, which is the closest to the marine configuration because of the sea's function as the separating element. This scenery appears in *The Planter of Malata,* where Renouard leads a lonely existence in his "kingdom," which is surrounded by waters. *An Anarchist* has a similar formation of the fictional world: Paul Crocodile, a convict, is confined on an islet-prison. Having escaped from there he is forced, because of his anarchist entanglements (see the discussion in Part 2, Chapter 5), to dwell on an island detached from the nearest land by "twenty miles of discoloured muddy water" (SS 137). In *Nostromo* the Great Isabel, situated between the sky and the waters, is the habitation of Martin Decoud, and later of Giorgio Viola and his daughters Linda and Giselle. Jacobus and Alice in *A Smile of Fortune* and Nelson and Freya in *Freya of the Seven Isles* also live on islands. Heyst's domain in *Victory* assumes an identical shape, and its solitary ruler is compared to one placed on the highest peak of the Himalayas (V 3-4) or on the moon. The natural, geographical seclusion of Heyst's territory is complemented by a barricade of wood, by which the Alfuro tribe distances itself from the Tropical Belt Coal Company. Heyst's and Lena's escape to the isle means renunciation of the world (78), and Mr. Jones views the arrival of his group there as a visit paid from the world.[6] A similar pattern appears in *The Rover,* where the sea and mountains separate the Hyères peninsula, on which the Escampobar Farm, the scene of most of the action, is situated (Rov 14, 30, 142). The internal ring of this secluded realm is Peyrol's room, which is compared to a lonely lighthouse (30, 34).

Isolation by sea and mountains appears in *Nostromo* and *Karain,* where a coastal region is encircled by waters and a formidable, almost impassable mass of high land. The similar topography of Sulaco, the place of action in *Nostromo,* which is a province of the state of Costaguana, is manifest at the beginning of the novel.[7] The narrator surveys Sulaco from a bird's-eye view: it is encompassed by the waters of the gulf, the masses of dense "immovable" clouds and the mighty Cordillera:

> Sulaco had found an inviolable sanctuary from the temptations of a trading world in the solemn hush of the deep Golfo Placido as if within an enormous semi-circular and unroofed temple open to the ocean, with its walls of lofty mountains hung with the mourning draperies of cloud. (N 3)
>
> Sky, land, and sea disappear together out of the world when the Placido–as the saying is–goes to sleep under its black poncho [of clouds]....The eye of God Himself–they add with grim profanity–could not find out what work a man's hand is doing in there... (6-7; also 5-6 and other excerpts)

The descriptions of this massif, which forms the land part of the geographical "insulator," articulate its inaccessibility and monumentality: "The dawn breaks high behind the towering and serrated wall of the Cordillera, a clear-cut vision of dark peaks rearing their steep slopes on a lofty pedestal of forest rising from the very edge of the shore" (5-6). A sense of the remoteness of this territory is also disclosed by the utterances of the railway board chairman from London, who comes to the place through the mountain range. Recollecting his dangerous journey along impassable routes that wind among precipices (35), he views Sulaco as completely separated by natural barriers: "But I had no notion that a place on a sea-coast could remain so isolated from the world. If it had been a thousand miles inland now–most remarkable! Has anything ever happened here for a hundred years before today?" (36) An analogous image of this region occurs in the final part of the novel, where Golfo Placido and the Great Isabel become the scene of the activities of Nostromo, enacting the drama of his vanity (536, 552; the comments on his conduct in Part 2, Chapter 5). A similar configuration of seclusion on land appears in *Karain,* where the gulf and mountains cut off the protagonist's terrain from the rest of the world. Karain "was...the master of an insignificant foothold on the earth–of a conquered foothold that, shaped like a young moon, lay ignored between the hills and the sea" (TU 4; also 7, 8).

Tropical topography where nature in a wall separates the characters' domain from the rest of the world is the most widespread version of land isolation in Conrad's works. This type of imagery is exemplified in *Lord Jim:* Patusan forms a closed area, surrounded by the highlands (LJ 228) and the jungle.[8]

> Thirty miles of forest shut it [Jim's success] off from the sight of an indifferent world, and the noise of the white surf along the coast overpowered the voice of fame. The stream of civilisation, as if divided on a headland a hundred miles north of Patusan, branches east and south-east, leaving its plains and valleys, its old trees and its old mankind neglected and isolated, such as an insignificant and crumbling islet between the two branches of a mighty, devouring stream. (226)

This specific spatial situation is sensed by Marlow, the main narrator, as he travels to this country (246), and it is emphasized later in his recollections (323). Brierly looked into Jim's case during the trial: he had advised him to "creep twenty feet underground and stay there" (202). By placing Jim in the Patusan settlement, the narrator effects Brierly's suggestions: "Once he got in, it would be for the outside world as though he had never existed. He would have nothing but the soles of his two feet to stand upon, and he would have first to find his ground at that" (232).

Detachment in the tropics appears in Conrad's other Malaya-based fiction, too. In *The Rescue* the region of Carimata, which is inhabited by natives, constitutes Lingard's secluded "kingdom." The sea, together with the adjoining land that is surrounded by forests, forms an unbreachable continuum. Thus the "kingdom" lies outside the routes of merchant ships (Re 108). The action of *Almayer's Folly* and *An Outcast of the Islands* (that together with *The Rescue* form the Malay trilogy) is located in Sambir–a land at the river Pantai, which is encircled by impenetrable vegetation in the heart of forest:

> Behind the whole group of buildings there stretched the level ground of rice-clearings, which in their turn were closed in by the wall of untouched forests with undergrowth so thick and tangled that nothing but a bullet–and that fired at pretty close range–could penetrate any distance there. (OI 98-99; also 65-67)

The "insulator" is complemented by the Pantai, along which nobody, except Lingard, is able to steer a ship to Sambir. An identical topography of isolation appears in *Because of the Dollars,* where Bamtz and Laughing Anne live in a Malay village enclosed by woods (WT 180-181). Bamtz trades at this outpost, and Davidson links it with markets for its products (these characters' performance corresponds to that of Almayer and Lingard in *Almayer' Folly* and *An Outcast of the Islands*). A solitary white colonizer figures in *The End of the Tether:* it is Mr. Van Wyk "whose feeling of outraged love was translated into a form of struggle with nature" (YNTOS 302). He has decided to devote the rest of his life to work in a corner of exotic country; he lives at a distance from other cottages in a little clearing in the jungle. His only connection with the world is Captain Whalley's ship, which comes twice a year and brings all the furniture and utensils for his house and regularly provides him with newspapers and correspondence. The protagonists of *The Lagoon,* Arsat and Diamelen, are depicted by the narrator as "the lonely man and the long-haired woman...who live together hidden by the forest–alone and feared" (TU 192).

Existence in a realm cut off by tropical nature is also in Conrad's two African stories, *Heart of Darkness* and *An Outpost of Progress*. In the first, the trading stations in the African interior are like islands in the equatorial jungle. Marlow, the narrator, following the routes of white colonizers in Africa, shares their solitary style of life. In *An Outpost of Progress* the Europeans' loneliness amid the powerful tropical vegetation is shaped identically. Kayerts and Carlier's habitation is lost in the immensity of woodland, which is surrounded by "the impenetrable bush that seems to cut off the station from the rest of the world" (TU 88). The nearest place of trade is about 300 miles distant. They experience estrangement acutely in this alien and incomprehensible environment: "They felt themselves very much alone, when suddenly left unassisted to face the wilderness: a wilderness rendered more strange, more incomprehensible by the mysterious glimpses of the vigorous life it contained" (89; also 107).[9]

The setting of a big city constitutes another factor in an individual's detachment from the world and people. Metaphors of this kind, of minor importance in Conrad, appear in *The Return, The Secret Agent, The Inheritors,* and episodically in *Lord Jim*.

B. Analogies to Isolation at Sea

All the variants of isolation on land are shown in much the same way as marine separation; in both, fundamental features common to the aspects of imagery and functions are discernible. This parallelism is most conspicuous in the case of insular configuration, where water is the isolating ring. The most characteristic of this tendency appears in *The Rover,* where the protagonist treats his life on land in terms of marine isolation: he views his room as being surrounded by the Mediterranean Sea (Rov 35), or compares the Escampobar Farm to a ship: "I am old Peyrol and this place, as lonely as a ship at sea, is like a ship to me and all in it are like shipmates" (44).

Such affinities also figure in the texts that apply the tropical version of seclusion on land. The infinity of forests (sometimes of dark hues) that enclose the characters' domain, resembles an immensity of water around a vessel. In *Lord Jim* the jungle that distances Patusan from the world is so shaped:

> They could see below them in the declining light the vast expanse of the forest country, a dark sleeping sea of sombre green undulating as far as the violet and purple range of mountains... (LJ 260)
> Below us stretched the land, the great expanse of the forests, sombre under the sunshine, rolling like a sea, with glints of winding rivers, the grey spots of villages, and here and there a clearing, like an islet of light amongst the dark waves of continuous tree-tops. (264)

In this novel limitless woodland looks like an abyss; it is similar to a vast, monotonous water universe. Metaphors of this kind are also in *Heart of Darkness* (YNTOS 86, 92) and *An Outcast of the Islands:* "The green sea of leaves–the sea that glowed shimmered, and stirred above the uniform and impenetrable gloom of the forests–the joyous sea of living green powdered with the brilliant dust of oblique sunrays." (OI 291-292).

Sometimes the stillness and immobility of the tropics isolating an individual are emphasized. This again resembles the maritime presentation, and is used in *An Outcast of the Islands* where complete tranquility fills the enormous jungle encircling Willems:

> Over the great forests, over all the innumerable people of unstirring trees–over all that living people immense, motionless, and mute–the silence, that had rushed in on the track of the passing tumult, remained suspended as deep and complete as if it had never been disturbed from the beginning of remote ages. (272)
> For a time nothing on earth stirred, seemingly, but the canoe, which glided up-stream with a motion so even and smooth that it did not convey any sense of movement. Overhead, the massed clouds appeared solid and steady as if held there in a powerful grip....Willems looked on, as motionless as everything round him and above him. (282; also 274-275)

The quietude and inactivity of the environment deepen Arsat's and Diamelen's solitude in *The Lagoon:*

> The forests, sombre and dull, stood motionless and silent on each side of the broad stream....In the stillness of the air every tree, every leaf, every bough, every tendril of creeper and every petal of minute blossoms seemed to have been bewitched into an immobility perfect and final. Nothing moved on the river but the eight paddles... (TU 187; also 193)

A similar configuration of nature appears in *Heart of Darkness* (YNTOS 93) and *An Outpost of Progress* (TU 107-108).

The parallelism between isolation in the tropics and at sea is also shown by the magnification of the power of the woods encircling a character's domain, just as the power of the surrounding waters. In both cases it is a force that seems to be tremendous when juxtaposed with human weakness. Such a vision of the jungle "insulator" appears in *Lord Jim* and *An Outpost of Progress:*

> The immovable forests rooted deep in the soil, soaring towards the sunshine, everlasting in the shadowy might of their tradition, like life itself. (LJ 243; also 415)
>
> And stretching away in all directions, surrounding the insignificant cleared spot of the trading post, immense forests, hiding fateful complications of fantastic life, lay in the eloquent silence of mute greatness. (TU 94; also 89)

In *The End of the Tether* the strength and grandeur of the woodland secluding Van Wyk's habitation are perceived by Captain Whalley from the deck of his ship, which makes regular trips to the settlement (YNTOS 257, 264-265). Similar impressions are received by the white man in *The Lagoon* as he travels in a boat toward Arsat's dwelling (TU 188-189). The contrast of powerful nature with human helplessness is introduced in *Almayer's Folly* by the metaphor of Pantai taking a tree by force (AF 4), which is a projection of the protagonist's destiny. An analogous image of this river–huge, incessantly flowing, indifferent to human joys, sufferings, and disasters–is found in *An Outcast of the Islands* (OI 214). Martin Decoud in *Nostromo,* left on the Great Isabel to guard the treasure, feels his own insignificance when confronted with the immense unconcern of the environment.

The power of tropical enclosure sometimes acquires a specific shape owing to a narrowing perspective in scenes of direct contact with the encircling jungle and to the emotions evoked by it. In *Heart of Darkness* Marlow frequently emphasizes the dynamism and magnificence of African nature, juxtaposed with his own and the other Europeans' impotence:

> All this was great, expectant, mute, while the man [brickmaker] jabbered about himself. I wondered whether the stillness on the face of the immensity looking at us two were meant as an appeal or as a menace. What were we who had strayed in here? Could we handle that dumb thing, or would it handle us? I felt how big, how confoundedly big, was that thing that couldn't talk, and perhaps was deaf as well. What was in there? (YNTOS 81)
>
> The great wall of vegetation, an exuberant and entangled mass of trunks, branches, leaves, boughs, festoons, motionless in the moonlight, was like a rioting invasion of soundless life, a rolling wave of plants, piled up, crested, ready to topple over the creek,to sweep every little man of us out of his little existence. (86; also 76, 80, 127)

He has identical reflections when navigating the vessel up the river:

> Trees, trees, millions of trees, massive, immense, running up high; and at their foot, hugging the bank against the stream, crept the little begrimed steam-boat, like a sluggish beetle crawling on the floor of a lofty portico. It made you feel very small, very lost... (95)

The contrast here is effected through the application of stylistic devices (repetition, cumulation of epithets, multiplication) that hyperbolize the might of virgin forest and belittle the ship, comparing it to a crawling beetle. Disparagement is applied to human activities as well: Marlow's steering maneuvers seem clumsy and funny, like monkey tricks (93-94), against grand woodland. In one of the phases of this journey isolation is enhanced by fog, which tightly wraps the river and the steamboat. The temporal aspect also enters here: human feebleness is compared with powerful and fathomless nature in terms of the distance between the present and the primeval epoch:

> We were wanderers on prehistoric earth, on an earth that wore the aspect of an unknown planet....The steamer toiled along slowly on the edge of a black and incomprehensible frenzy....We were cut off from the comprehension of our surroundings....We could not understand because we were too far and could not remember, because we were travelling in the night of first ages, of those ages that are gone, leaving hardly a sign–and no memories. (95-96; also 92-93)

Marlow's meditations on the loneliness of people brought into contact with the elemental force of equatorial vegetation are also stimulated by his meeting with Kurtz, the most "eminent" colonizer, which takes place against the background of the African jungle–monumental and indifferent to human plight:

> There was no sign on the face of nature of this amazing tale [about Kurtz]...The woods were unmoved, like a mask–heavy, like the closed door of a prison–they looked with their air of hidden knowledge, of patient expectation, of unapproachable silence. (129)

The same type of contact applies to the Roman commander of a trireme taking part in the conquest of the British Isles.

The contrast between an individual and nature, shown in the perspective of close, almost intimate, contact, determines the shape of tropical isolation in *An Outcast of the Islands* too. The magnitude of the forest is already indicated in one of its initial descriptions, where the narrator stresses the impossibility of penetrating the dense wall of vegetation (OI 65-67), which Willems has also failed to do. Characteristic exemplification of this kind of imagery figures in the portrayal of the forest before a rainstorm: as a "ragged barrier" and "a straight wall of formless blackness" (291, 292). The protagonist's loneliness and defenselessness in confrontation with gigantic nature–disinterested witness of his internal conflicts–is revealed right at the beginning of his stay in Sambir:

> The big trees would appear on the bank, tall, strong, indifferent in the immense solidity of their life, which endures for ages, to that short and fleeting life in the heart of the man who crept painfully amongst their shadows in search of a refuge from the unceasing reproach of his thoughts. (67)

Surrounded by a hostile jungle and the Malays, Willems lives with his mistress Aissa in a little clearing. However, she is not his support but rather a metaphorical foe, an embodiment and extension of the vegetation endangering him. Willems's helplessness reaches its apex in the final part of the novel when Lingard subjects him to the most severe punishment for steering his rival's ship to Sambir: he rejects him and deliberately leaves him in this hateful environment (274-279). Aware of his newly hopeless predicament, Willems feels his loneliness intensely and experiences his impotence in relation to powerful nature, which is unconcerned with his sufferings and tragedy and is even hostile to him:

> Above and below, the forests on his side of the river came down to the water in a serried multitude of tall, immense trees towering in a great spread of twisted boughs above the thick undergrowth; great, solid trees, looking sombre, severe, and malevolently stolid, like a giant crowd of pitiless enemies pressing round silently to witness his slow agony. He was alone, small, crushed. (329; also 327-329, other excerpts, 335-337)

The proximity of these elemental forces stirs sad reflections about the unavoidable end of his life, which will be caused by being absorbed by the exuberant, indestructible, and aggressive vegetation:

> He was not alone, he saw death looking at him from everywhere; from the bushes, from the clouds–he heard her speaking to him in the murmur of the river, filling the space, touching his heart, his brain with a cold hand....He saw the horrible form [of death] among the big trees, in the network of creepers in the fantastic outlines of leaves, of the green indented leaves that seemed to be so many enormous hands with big broad palms, with stiff fingers outspread to lay hold of him; hands gently stirring, or hands arrested in a frightful immobility, with a stillness attentive and watching for the opportunity to take him, to enlace him, to strangle him, to hold him till he died; hands that would hold him dead, that would never let go, that would cling to his body for ever till it perished–disappeared in their frantic and tenacious grasp. (330-331; also 331-332, other passages)[10]

Tropical isolation concerns natives as well, though much less frequently than whites. In *Almayer's Folly* Dain, a local nobleman and the lover of Nina, Almayer's daughter, hides in a glade encompassed by a wall of dense forest. Close confrontation with the powerful jungle strengthens his loneliness and weakness:

> [He] seemed very small and as if lost in the pale green iridescence reflected from the ground. On three sides of the clearing, appearing very far away in the deceptive light, the big trees of the forest, lashed together with manifold bonds by a mass of tangled creepers, looked down at the growing young life at their feet with the sombre resignation of giants that had lost faith in their strength. And in the midst of them the merciless creepers clung to the big trunks in cable-like coils...carried death to their victims in an exulting riot of silent destruction. (AF 165)

Marlow in *Heart of Darkness* perceives the Negroes' settlements as lost in the gigantic woodland, during the sea journey toward the outlet of the big river (YNTOS 60). Another example of this opposition may be found in *The Lagoon,* in which monumental nature, petrified in muteness, is indifferent to Arsat's dramatic and tragic experiences, thus magnifying his solitude: "A plaintive murmur rose in the night; a murmur saddening and startling, as if the great solitudes of surrounding woods had tried to whisper into his ear the wisdom of their immense and lofty indifference" (TU 194).

Analogies between tropical and marine isolation also concern the planetary imagery, emphasizing the distancing of both a ship and a land area. The cosmic hyperbole is conspicuous in *Lord Jim,* where Marlow compares Patusan to a star situated in limitless space:

> I don't suppose any of you had ever heard of Patusan?...It does not matter; there's many a heavenly body in the lot crowding upon us of a night that mankind had never heard of...the astronomers...are paid to talk learnedly about its composition, weight, path–the irregularities of its conduct, the aberrations of its light....Thus with Patusan. It was referred to knowingly in the inner government circles in Batavia, especially as to its irregularities and aberrations....Nobody, however, had been there, and I suspect no one desired to go there in person, just as an astronomer, I should fancy, would strongly object to being transported into a distant heavenly body, where, parted from his earthly emoluments, he would be bewildered by the view of an unfamiliar heavens. (LJ 218)

This presentation makes Jim's expedition there like a journey to another planet, a complete separation from the tragic entanglement of his past (see in Part 1, Chapter 2).

> I only meant you to understand [Marlow says] that had Stein arranged to send him into a star of the fifth magnitude the change could not have been greater. He left his earthly failings behind him and that sort of reputation he had, and there was a totally new set of conditions for his imaginative faculty to work upon. (218; also 232)

This type of exaggeration of tropical separation is exemplified by the description of the gulf in which the protagonists of *The Lagoon* are hidden: "In a few moments all the stars came out above the intense blackness of the earth and the great lagoon gleaming suddenly with reflected lights resembled an oval patch of night sky flung down into the hopeless and abysmal night of the wilderness" (TU 192).

Metaphors of this kind also figure in the sea-mountain variant of land isolation in *Karain:*

> The circular sheet of water reflected a luminous sky, and the shores enclosing it made an opaque ring of earth floating in an emptiness of transparent blue. (TU 5)
> There could be nothing outside. It was as if the earth had gone on spinning, and had left that crumb of its surface alone in space. He appeared utterly cut off from everything but the sunshine, and that even seemed to be made for him alone. (7-8)

The sense of separation of Karain's "state" becomes particularly strong when the narrator and his companions yield to the ruler's suggestive gesticulation and really seem to believe in its "planetary" autonomy:

> From the deck of our schooner, anchored in the middle of the bay, he indicated by a theatrical sweep of his army along the jagged outline of the hills the whole of his domain; and the ample movement seemed to drive back its limits, augmenting it suddenly into something so immense and vague that for a moment it appeared to be bounded only by the sky. And really, looking at that place, landlocked from the sea and shut off from the land by the precipitous slopes of mountains, it was difficult to believe in the existence of any neighbourhood. It was still, complete, unknown, and full of a life that went on stealthily with a troubling effect of solitude.... (4-5)[11]

The hyperbole is enhanced by the theatrical imagery depicting this "kingdom" as the place of its sovereign's acting, cut off like a stage from its environment (7-8).

These ways of shaping the relationship between man and nature are reflected in the texts using an urban setting. The characters in *The Secret Agent, The Return, The Inheritors,* and *Lord Jim* are lost in the abyss of London, an immense metropolis. Winnie Verloc in *The Secret Agent,* having murdered her husband, leaves the house and plunges into this enormous, monstrous city,[12] its mud and hopeless dark night magnify her crime in her imagination (SA 270-271). The urban colossus is indifferent to her tragedy (see the depiction of he plight in Part 1, Chapter 2 and Part 2, Chapter 5):

> Winnie Verloc turning about held him [Ossipon] by both arms, facing him under the failing mist in the darkness and solitude of Brett Place, in which all sounds of life seemed lost as if in a triangular well of asphalt and bricks, of blind houses and unfeeling stones. (276)

In *The Return* the Harvey's surroundings "proudly" display a lack of interest in their emotions and affairs:

> And right and left all the innumerable dwellings, standing shoulder to shoulder, had resisted the shock of his passion, had presented, unmoved, to the loneliness of his trouble, the grim silence of walls, the impenetrable and polished discretion of closed doors and curtained windows. (TU 145)

The same pattern of seclusion concerns the professor in *The Secret Agent* (such a presentation underlines his grotesque portrayal and the monstrosity of his intellectual, moral, and political views; see his characteristics in Part 2, Chapter 5) and the narrator of *The Inheritors* (I 46-47). The gigantic expanse of the city is directly compared to an infinity of water in *The Return* and *Lord Jim:*

> A sinister loom as of a hidden conflagration lit up faintly from below the mist, falling upon a billowy and motionless sea of tiles and bricks. At the rattle of the opened window the world seemed to leap out of the night and confront him [Hervey], while floating up to his ears there came a sound vast and faint; the deep mutter of something immense and alive. (TU 126)
>
> His [the addressee's of Marlow's letter] rooms were in the highest flat of a lofty building, and his glance could travel afar beyond the clear panes of glass, as though he were looking out of the lantern of a lighthouse. The slopes of the roofs glistened, the dark broken ridges succeeded each other without end like sombre, uncrested waves, and from the depths of the town under his feet ascended a confused and unceasing mutter. The spires of churches, numerous, scattered haphazard, uprose like beacons on a maze of shoals without a channel. (LJ 337; also 351)

The parallelism of isolation on land and at sea is manifest not only in the stratum of imagery, but also in the sphere of functions of these motifs in the structure of a literary work. It pertains to the central position of an individual, constituting the axis of a zone cut off by nature. This configuration is discernible in the texts that enforce insular detachment. In *A Smile of Fortune* the house and garden of Jacobus and his daughter Alice form the area enclosed by a wall (never crossed by Alice), on the Pearl of the Ocean surrounded by water. A similar spatial construction appears in *Victory:* Heyst and Lena make the core of a concentrically arranged fictional world, their house being inside both the ring of luxuriant tropical vegetation and the shores of the island (V 173).

The pivotal location of a character is also conspicuous in the works with the tropical version of isolation on land; the surrounding reality is shaped in them by the character's subjective perception. This may be exemplified by Kurtz's and Marlow's relationship to the presented world in *Heart of Darkness*. Kurtz considers everything around to be his property (YNTOS 116; also the depiction of his conduct as a colonizer in Part 2, Chapter 5), and his central position at the Inner Station is strengthened by the godlike homage paid to him by natives. And Marlow the narrator portrays the African locality from his point of view. A similar role is played in *An Outcast of the Islands* by the perspectives of Willems and Aissa. These constitute the axis of their miniature world, which is cut off by forest. In the majority of descriptions their creative vision is articulated; they observe the neighborhood as filtered through their emotions, which is manifest in the passages quoted before. They depict the powerful, elemental force of the jungle: it is hostile and brings death to Willems. It is shown similarly in the following presentation of nature harmonizing with Aissa's suffering and impending tragedy:

> She wrung her hands, glanced over the courtyard with that eager and distracted look that sees nothing, then looked up at the hopeless sky of livid grey and drifting black; at the unquiet mourning of the hot and brilliant heaven that had seen the beginning of her love, that had heard

> his entreaties and her answers, that had seen his desire and her fear; that had seen her joy, her surrender–and his defeat. (OI 246)

Such romantic correspondences between imagery and feelings reveal the impact of the human psyche upon its surroundings–subordinated to a focally situated individual. This configuration is clearly visible in *The Lagoon,* where the tropical setting is strongly colored by the narrator's subjective perspective:

> Suddenly the long straight reach seemed to pivot on its centre, the forests swung in a semicircle, and the slanting beams of sunset touched the broadside of the canoe with a fiery glow, throwing the slender and distorted shadows of its crew upon the streaked glitter of the river. (TU 188)
>
> The forests came out of the clear shadows of the morning, became distinct, as if they had rushed nearer–to stop short in a great stir of leaves, of nodding boughs, of swaying branches. (203; also 189)

His perceptions acquire the status of objective phenomena, thus creating the world all around. His stand-point is fixed, whereas the fictional reality is dynamic.[13] Arsat's connection with the environment is parallel to that of the narrator (the white man). Because of the silence and fixity of the surrounding nature, the addressee's attention is focused upon the Malay fugitive, which suggests the slight importance of the setting and significance of the realm of his emotional experiences, reflected in the shaping of tropical nature: the personified nibong palms lean over the hut occupied by Arsat and the dying Diamelen (189) as if expressing sad tenderness and concern, and their drooping leaves "rattle together with a mournful and expiring sound" (202), externalizing compassion.

An individual's axial place in a locality, which forms an analogy between isolation on land and at sea, acquires a higher degree of intensity when the character appears to be the ruler of a solitary domain, which is subordinated to him as a ship to its captain. Renouard, the protagonist of *The Planter of Malata,* leaseholder of the island and master of its plantation, entertains unlimited power over it, his orders being exactly fulfilled by all his dependants (WT 61); in his thoughts he frequently identifies with his "kingdom."

Such a relationship also concerns characters situated in a zone separated by sea and mountains. Karain's power, as well as the force of arms of his warriors, repelled and intimidated the invaders, thus consolidating the separation of this territory from the rest of the world (TU 14-15). The autocrat determines the lot and directs almost all the actions of his vassals:

> They were Karain's people–a devoted following. Their movements hung on his lips; they read their thoughts in his eyes; he murmured to them nonchalantly of life and death, and they accepted his words humbly, like gifts of fate. They were all free men, and when speaking to him said, 'Your slaves.' (4)
> He gave them wisdom, advice, reward, punishment, life or death, with the same serenity of attitude and voice. (8)

Under his protective reign they have forgotten the past and do not care about the future (8). The extreme subordination of the natives to Karain brings about their excessive worship of him:

> No wonder his people admired him. We saw him once walking in daylight amongst the houses of the settlement. At the doors of huts groups of women turned to look after him, warbling softly, and with gleaming eyes; armed men stood out of the way, submissive and erect; others approached from the side, bending their backs to address him humbly; an old woman stretched out a draped lean arm–'Blessings on thy head!' she cried from a dark doorway; a fiery-eyed man...bellowed out pantingly after him, 'God give victory to our master!' (15; also 6, 10, 16, 17)

The ruler becomes the embodiment of perfection and surpasses his subjects in every possible respect, which is implied, e.g., by the use of synecdochic repetition:

> He understood irrigation an the art of war–the qualities of weapons and the craft of boat-building. He could conceal his heart; had more endurance; he could swim longer, and steer a canoe better than any of his people; he could shoot straighter, and negotiate more tortuously than any man of his race I knew. (8)

He constitutes an adequate, miniature representation of the "state," its core, its basis:

> He seemed too effective, too necessary there, too much of an essential condition for the existence of his land and his people, to be destroyed by anything short of an earthquake. He summed up his race, his country, the elemental force of ardent life, of tropical nature. He had its luxuriant strength, its fascination... (7)

The complete dependence of Karain's subjects upon him increases their distance from the world, from which he has cut himself off through his sin, guilt, and expulsion (Part 1, Chapter 2).

Tropically secluded regions are entirely subjected to their masters also. In *Almayer's Folly* and *An Outcast of the Islands* Sambir forms the "kingdom" of Lingard, who has monopolized its trade as the only one able to navigate a ship there. Enjoying unlimited power over it, he treats the Pantai and the trading station as his property (OI 43); his word is the law there, and none of the inhabitants dares oppose it (see the portrayal of Lingard the colonizer in Part 2, Chapter 5). His attachment to Sambir magnifies the separation of this realm from the world: he wished "the muddy river [Pantai]...if he could help it, would carry no other craft but the 'Flash' [Lingard's brig] on its unclean and friendly surface" (200). In *The Rescue* King Tom displays an affectionate attitude toward the exotic domain of the shallow sea of Carimata, where his authority is also generally respected (Re 37). Lingard views it as his own possession. This, for example, is felt by Carter, who is sent to seek help for the passengers of the stranded schooner-yacht *Hermit* (50). Preservation of the complete separation of Carimata from the world and guarding it from intruders, is for Red-Eyed Tom the equivalent to saving all his hopes, dreams, and plans, even his identity (hence his tremendous despair, which is caused by their ultimate ruin). In *Lord Jim* the district of Patusan, which is closed off by woodlands, is entirely subjugated to Tuan. He enjoys unquestioned supremacy there (LJ 175-176, 265, 269, 274), the boundless confidence and highest esteem of the aboriginals (269, 361, 393). Like Lingard, he is protective and devoted to his people (see the description of Jim the colonizer in Part 2, Chapter 5).

Resemblances between the patterns of isolation on land and at sea and in the functions they perform are not limited to the pivotal position of an individual in a secluded territory. In the land environment, too, one undergoes a test of personality and character, especially in professional ethics (usually as a colonizer); and solitude substantially increases the hardships of this ordeal[14] (most clearly revealed in *Lord Jim, Almayer's Folly, An Outcast of the Islands, Heart of Darkness, An Outpost of Progress*). A completely lonely hero has to rely exclusively on himself when coping with mounting difficulties. The outcome of a confrontation with nature either emphasizes his ethical excellence, or partly lessens his condemnation (Part 2, Chapter 5 and Conclusion). Besides, the delineation of his plight, particularly in its "planetary" variation, stresses the autonomy of a separated realm, making it a seat of life equivalent to the earth and comprising all its essential manifestations, problems, and values in their universal aspect as well.[15]

All the analogies discussed above testify to the expansion of the sea imagery into the fictional worlds of those novels and short stories by Conrad that do not employ a marine setting. They prove the sea and land configurations to be two versions of basically the same formation: the geographical isolation imposed upon a character by his surroundings, the external world.[16]

Chapter 2
Internal (Psychological) Aspects of the Characters' Isolation

Patterns of geographically determined solitude do not comprise all possible varieties of this motif in Conrad's writings. Internal, psychological seclusion is at least equally important; it is voluntarily and consciously chosen by an individual, and results from his performance and conduct. Conradian characters frequently separate themselves from reality, trying to replace it with an illusory world, the sphere of their love feelings, or experiences of ethical dilemmas.[1] Escapism usually brings about loosening or loss of contact with the environment, leading to tragic consequences.

1. Self-Imposed Psychological Isolation as an Escape into an Imaginary Realm

A. Tokens of European Civilization

Some colonizers, feeling strange and lonely and incapable of resisting the elemental forces of tropical nature and of fulfilling the tasks entrusted to them, replace hateful actualities with dreams. Such an attitude is characteristic of Kayerts and Carlier, the protagonists of *An Outpost of Progress*.[2] Situated in an African trading station, devoid of the facilities needed to secure a peaceful and safe existence, they disclose incompetence and unpreparedness for coping unaided with their predicament and their inimical surroundings. Helpless and lost, they desperately cling to the manifestations of European culture: "In the centre of Africa they made acquaintance [through reading] of Richelieu and d'Artagnan, of Hawk's Eye and of Father Goriot, and of many other people" (TU 94). Kayerts and Carlier live in a fancied domain, peopled by characters, notions, and values from their civilization. In this way they distance themselves from the alien and incomprehensible African environment and reveal a complete lack of understanding of the events happening around them:

> They lived like blind men in a large room, aware only of what came in contact with them (and of that only imperfectly), but unable to see the general aspect of things. The river, the forest, all the great land throbbing with life, were like a great emptiness. Even the brilliant sunshine disclosed nothing intelligible. Things appeared and disappeared before their eyes in an unconnected and aimless kind of way. The river seemed to come from nowhere and flow nowhither. It flowed through a void. (92; also 92-94)

Conscious self-inflicted seclusion causes their collapse: they die, unable to stand the psychological pressure of reality (see also the delineation of Kayerts and Carlier as colonizers in Part 2, Chapter 5).

A similar course of conduct is taken by the Company's chief accountant at the outer station in *Heart of Darkness*. In this place of tremendous exploitation and suffering (Part 2, Chapter 5) amid equatorial nature, he leads the life of a European clerk: he dresses with excessive elegance, keeps his books in perfect order, goes out to get a breath of fresh air when taking shorts rests from work (YNTOS 67-68). Adopting this line of action he separates from his surroundings and becomes a thoughtless automaton fulfilling routine duties. Absorbed in labor he is entirely unconcerned with the misery of the white agents and Negro workers, who are dying in great numbers because of exhaustion and ill treatment. He loathes the climate and the conditions unfavorable to his work:

> When a truckle-bed with a sick man...was put in there, he exhibited a gentle annoyance. 'The groans of this sick person,' he said, 'distract my

> attention. And without that it is extremely difficult to guard against clerical errors in his climate.' (69)
> When one has got to make correct entries, one comes to hate those savages–hate them to the death. (70)[3]

A stubborn attachment to substitutes for civilization characterizes the protagonists' performance in *Almayer's Folly* as well. He is proud to possess the only geese in the whole coastal region, or even on the island (AF 122), and he endeavors to arrange his habitation in European style: "He called (the big room) his sitting-room, whenever, in the company of white men, he wished to assert his claims to the commonplace decencies of civilization" (90). Nevertheless, in spite of all his attempts, the appearance of the house and station reveal the futility of their owner's aspirations:

> Nobody ever sat there; there was nothing there to sit upon, for Mrs. Almayer in her savage moods, when excited by the reminiscences of the piratical period of her life, had torn off the curtains to make sarongs for the slave-girls, and had burnt the showy furniture piecemeal to cook the family rice. (90-91; also 12, 15-16, 124, 199-200, 202-203, and OI 300-301)

B. Illusions of Power or a Splendid Future

The central figure of colonial expansion presented in *Heart of Darkness* remains in a detached realm of reveries governing his psyche and activities.[4] Initially they are filled with noble ideals of civilizing Africa, and later, exclusively with insatiable instincts and ambitions of possession and unlimited power (see the portrayal of Kurtz the colonizer in Part 2, Chapter 5). These fancies shape his relationship to the other characters in *Heart of Darkness*. They prevent him from making psychological contact with the other agents, who envy and hate him, and especially with the Negroes: they are completely subjugated or treat him with godlike worship. Marlow views Kurtz's illusions as precluding the achievement of any mutual understanding between them: "I had to deal with a being to whom I could not appeal in the name of anything high or low....There was nothing either above or below him, and I knew it. He had kicked himself loose of the earth" (YNTOS 144). Lingard in the Malay trilogy, another representative of imperial power, builds the utopia of his greatness: he disregards socioeconomic realities, and desires absolute control over Sambir (*Almayer's Folly, An Outcast of the Islands*) and the region of the shallow sea of Carimata (*The Rescue*) and wants to settle all the natives' problems and conflicts.[5] But he does not achieve these goals permanently (see comments on his conduct in Part 2, Chapter 5). A parallel attitude is taken by the hero of *Karain*. Separation of his "kingdom" from the world, which is deeply rooted in his consciousness, makes him lose a sense of reality and create an overemphasized, false notion of his might. Preparing a war, Karain "in his plans displayed a sagacity that was only limited by his profound ignorance of the rest of the world. We tried to enlighten him, but our attempts to make clear the irresistible nature of the forces which he desired to arrest failed to discourage his eagerness" (TU 18). The visions he conjures up are corrected by the perspective of the white seaman, the members of the narrative situation, to whom he appears as "the ruler of three villages on a narrow plain" (4), "only a petty chief of a conveniently isolated corner of Mindanao" (7), "[an] obscure adventurer feasting like a king" (17).

Mariners' loneliness usually assumes the shape of wishful thinking about future glorious exploits and materialization of an idealistic view of their vocation. Such behavior distances the protagonist of *Lord Jim* from the environment (see also his depiction in Part 2, Chapter 4).[6] This is already manifest on the training ship, when in spite of failure, he deems himself superior to his colleagues and more capable of enacting heroic deeds at sea (LJ 8-9). He displays an identical frame of mind on the *Patna*, elevating himself over its captain and crew:

> Jim went on smiling at the retreating horizon; his heart was full of generous impulses, and his thought was contemplating his own superiority. (23)

> Those men did not belong to the world of heroic adventure; they weren't bad chaps though....The quality of these men did not matter; he rubbed shoulders with them, but they could not touch him; he shared the air they breathed, but he was different.... (24-25)

After his ignoble escape, Jim is still faithful to his fantasies, while taking jobs in various ports and in Patusan. A sublime vision of the profession is cherished by the narrators (captains) in *The Secret Sharer* and *The Shadow-Line,* and by Marlow in *Youth,* who is anxious to see the charms of the East.[7] This does not, however, stop them from overcoming difficulties and fulfilling duties (see Part 2, Chapter 4). Jasper Allen in *Freya of the Seven Isles* dreams of happiness of his "beloved" brig; and the Russian in *Heart of Darkness,* met by Marlow at the threshold of the Inner Station, expresses a naive, boundless fascination with life at sea and exotic adventurers.[8]

Almayer's performance in *Almayer's Folly* and *An Outcast of the Islands* constitutes the most typical instance of self-imposed seclusion in the sphere of reveries about a lucky future.[9] Left by Lingard at the trading station at Pantai, in the jungle, he feels as if in prison: he hates the aboriginals, treating his coexistence with them as degradation, and is aware of the grandeur, indifference, and even hostility of nature toward him. In this situation the protagonist escapes from disappointing reality into the realm of ambitions, desires, and fancies. He aims at compensating for the Sambir "exile" with his and Nina's prospective rich and happy life in Europe. His temporary stay at the trading station should allow him to accumulate the means to reach this goal: "It was for you [Nina], for your happiness I was working. I wanted to be rich; I wanted to get away from here....For that I bore patiently the burden of work, of disappointment, of humiliation amongst these savages here" (AF 101). Almayer's wishful thinking hyperbolizes these visions: he imagines the expected wealth as "great piles of shining guilders," his residence as gleaming "like a fairy palace the big mansion in Amsterdam, that earthly paradise of his dreams" (10), and Nina appears to him as the queen of the Dutch high society:

> They would live in Europe, he and his daughter. They would be rich and respected. Nobody would think of her mixed blood in the presence of her great beauty and of his immense wealth. Witnessing her triumphs he would grow young again, he would forget the twenty-five years of heart-breaking struggle on this coast where he felt like a prisoner. (3-4; also 101)

In Sambir he constantly cherishes joyful dreams of living in the Dutch metropolis:

> [He was] bent upon forgetting the hated reality of the present by absorbing himself in his work, or else by letting his imagination soar far above the tree-tops into the great white clouds away to the westward, where the paradise of Europe was awaiting the future Eastern millionaire. (63)
>
> In his mind's eye he saw the rich prize in his grasp; and, with tin spoon in his hand, he was forgetting the plateful of rice before him in the fanciful arrangement of some splendid banquet to take place on his arrival in Amsterdam. (65)

The reveries color his perception of the surroundings. For example, they are reflected in some descriptions of the river from his subjective viewpoint:

> He liked to look at it about the time of sunset; perhaps because at that time the sinking sun would spread a glowing gold tinge on the waters of the Pantai, and Almayer's thoughts were often busy with gold....(3)
>
> For many years he had listened to the passionless and soothing murmur that sometimes was the song of hope, at times the song of triumph, of encouragement. (162; also 11)

His desire to escape from Sambir is expressed by the image of a tree floating toward the sea (4). Almayer intends to get out, like the tree, to the wide world; its branch, sticking upward and "protesting" against brutal treatment by the water, resembles the hero's hopeless attempts at futile resistance to nature and his own lot.[10] In *An Outcast of the Islands,* too, Lingard's protégé regards his presence at the outpost as a displeasing necessity, as the only way of gaining resources for a magnificent life in Europe:

> And Almayer sat, his face in his hands, looking on and hating all this: the muddy river; the faded blue of the sky; the black log passing by...the green sea of leaves....He hated all this; he begrudged every day–every minute–of his life spent amongst all these things; he begrudged it bitterly, angrily, with enraged and immense regret....And yet all this was very precious to him. It was the present sign of a splendid future. (OI 291-292)

In this novel, as in *Almayer's Folly,* he is absorbed in thoughts about a better tomorrow that are centered on Nina: "Things charming and splendid passed before him in a magic unrolling of resplendent pictures; pictures of events brilliant, happy, inexpressibly glorious, that would make up her life. He would do it!" (320). These fantasies are shared by Lingard, although he builds a house of cards when daydreaming, which implies the naivete and illusory nature of these plans (194-196).

Thus Almayer's isolation is determined by the polarity of his world of gorgeous fancies and dreary actualities. Immersion in reveries separates him from the environment, which is alien, hostile, and constitutes their antithesis. Estrangement causes the loss of a sense of reality. His daughter's idealized image is at variance with her true form: as a half-caste she could never become a favorite of Amsterdam nobility. The events taking place around look unintelligible to Lingard's agent: he is not aware of Nina's love affair with Dain, of her contempt for the white race (caused by previous humiliations), of the activities of the local élite (Abdulla, Babalatchi, Lakamba, and Mrs. Almayer). All this makes him their plaything and turns his efforts into futility (cf. the comments on Almayer's conduct as a colonial in Part 2, Chapter 5). He is passive amid intrigues, and inefficient; he tries to get support from tokens of European civilization, as if they could ensure his success. In the light of this, the hope of acquiring in Sambir the wealth that would secure a proper social position in Holland for himself and Nina is entirely deceptive: "He thought so in perfect good faith, deceived by the emotional estimate of his motives, unable to see the crookedness of his ways, the unreality of his aims, the futility of his regrets" (AF 102).

Almayer's self-imposed isolation in the exotic milieu is enhanced by his views on race. Confident of white superiority, he cuts himself off from the aboriginals, regarding any ties with them as debasement and defeat. This distance and his antipathy increase during his stay in Sambir. His detestation of indigenous people is sensed, for instance, by the Dutchman pursuing Dain:

> The Malays, you understand, are not company for a white man; moreover they are not friendly; they do not understand our ways. Great rascals they are. (122)
> I had to take care of myself, and when I asked for protection I was met with threats and contempt, and had Arab slander thrown in my face. I! a white man! (138)

Lingard's agent's racial prejudice is also revealed in his contempt for his wife (40, 191), and in the evolution of his attitude toward his beloved daughter, the only person who diminishes his loneliness and functions both as a compensation for life's failures and as the projection of his dreams (3-4, 101, 190-192; OI 300, 320). Nina's repugnance to white people, as well as her father's unconcern with her affairs and problems, result in the weakening of their emotional and psychological relationship. The crucial factor in this process is her love affair with Dain, which activates her native personality, makes her renounce the past and start a new, happy life (AF 64, 152). Mrs. Almayer favors this romance and treats Dain as the ideal of a native leader and man (64). Thus Nina leaves her father, crosses the racial barrier, and takes her mother's side. The lack of understanding between the daughter and the father culminates during the dramatic meeting at Bulangi's clearing shortly before her departure with Dain. Almayer excludes any possibility of their loving each other and interprets this union entirely in terms of hurt ambition and pride:

> What made you give yourself up to that savage? For he is a savage. Between him and you there is a barrier that nothing can remove. (178)
> 'It would be too great a disgrace. I am a white man....It would be a disgrace...all over the islands...the only white man on the east coast. No, it cannot be...white men finding my daughter with this Malay. My

> daughter!' he cried aloud, with a ring of despair in his voice. (184; also 180)[11]

Nina's reaction is an outburst of hatred for the white race, in which for the first time she reveals her true self to her father, and externalizes her feelings (178-180). Almayer realizes, only under the pressure of this violent confrontation and his daughter's elopement, that the world of his aspirations, based largely on the elevated, unreal image of Nina has fallen apart (he also decides to facilitate their escape, wanting to hide this shameful relation from the whites).

The protagonist's whole Sambir story is made up of successive disappointments, disillusionments, and sufferings, making the realization of his utopia more and more unlikely. For him the major blows are the return of a humiliated Nina from Singapore, the capture of Sambir by the Dutchmen, the collapse of his hopes for getting treasure from the upper region of the Pantai, and the separation from Nina. The last is the most tragic of all and finally destroys his illusions of a wonderful future and crowns this series of calamities:

> He looked at them [Dain and Nina] embarking, and at the canoe growing smaller in the distance, with rage, despair, and regret in his heart, and on his face a peace as that of a carved image of oblivion. Inwardly he felt himself torn to pieces, but Ali who–now aroused–stood close to his master, saw on his features the blank expression of those who live in that hopeless calm which sightless eyes only can give. (194; also 162-164, 178-179, 183-184, 189-190)

Her departure makes Almayer entirely insensitive to everything around. He erases Nina's footprints and makes little graves of sand in their place, as if intending to forget dreams and wipe out her memory (195-196). Obliteration is to be enhanced by the burning of his dwelling, and by removal to a new, unfinished house which Dutch officers called "Almayer's folly." However he does not attain the mercy of forgetfulness until shortly before death.[12]

The case of Captain Hagberd, the principal character of *To-morrow,* corresponds to Almayer's voluntary psychological isolation. Hagberd remains in the domain of wishful thinking about a happy future, based on a deep-rooted belief in his son Harry's return.[13] The retired coasting skipper dreams about a tranquil life together with his son and daughter-in-law (see also the delineation of Hagberd as a seaman in Part 2, Chapter 4), about Harry's staying in his house and marriage with Bessie, the neighbor's daughter (the title emphasizes the crucial role of this vision in the semantic organization of the story). After his wife's death, having casually learned about Harry's appearance in the vicinity of Colebrook, he conducts persistent inquiries that are bound to be fruitless and testify to his insanity:

> That stranger in mourning [Captain Hagberd] had been seen exploring the country, in carts, on foot, taking every body into his confidence, visiting all the inns and alehouses for miles around, stopping people on the road with his questions, looking into the very ditches almost; first in the greatest excitement, then with a plodding sort of perseverance, growing slower and slower; and he could not even tell you plainly how his son looked. (TOS 245)

After some time, disappointed with people's reactions, Hagberd abandons attempts at finding his son, but still strongly believes in the latter's return (254). This conviction assumes the shape of an absurd waiting for the return that is to take place "to-morrow." Immersed in reveries, Hagberd postpones all plans and treats his present existence as temporary. This is demonstrated by his outward appearance (he goes about dressed in "No. 1 sail-cloth"; 244), his preferred style of living (he saves nearly all his money for the arrangement of his house, which is to be the scene of the anticipated paradise), and his attitude toward Bessie (he constantly encourages her, speaking about "to-morrow"). The results of Hagberd's futile and senseless activities are visible in his garden:

> He dug every day in his front plot. He turned it over and over several times every year, but was not going to plant anything 'just at present.'

> To Bessie Carvil he would state more explicitly: 'Not till our Harry comes home to-morrow.' And she had heard this formula of hope so often that it only awakened the vaguest pity in her heart for that hopeful old man. Eveıything was put off in that way, and everything was being prepared likewise for to-morrow. (250; also 244, 257, 260)

Unfading confidence in the fulfillment of fancies makes him a static figure, beyond the passing of time: "He appeared...like a man roughened out of granite, standing in a wilderness....A heavy figure of a man of stone" (244). Thus the captain's life is determined by two temporal categories: the provisional "today" and the expected joy, shifted into the vague future. This specific mode of existence distinguishes him from the other characters of the story, who are subjected to the laws of quasi-empirical time.

Living in the sphere of illusions of "to-morrow" does not allow Hagberd to perceive the reality in its true shapes (in this he parallels Almayer). This impossibility is stressed by comparing the captain to his blind neighbor, Bessie's father:

> Miss Carvil praised him [Hagberd] for his good sense, and he was soothed by the part she took in his hope, which had become his delusion; in that idea which blinded his mind to the truth and probability, just as the other old man in the other cottage had been made blind, by another disease, to the light and beauty of the world. (255)

Viewing the world exclusively in terms of fantasies is Hagberd's reaction to Bessie's attempt to open his eyes to the truth:

> Only once she had tried pityingly to throw some doubt on that hope doomed to disappointment, but the effect of her attempt had scared her very much. All at once over that man's face there came an expression of horror and incredulity, as though he had seen a crack open out in the firmament.
>
> 'You–you–you don't think he's drowned!'
>
> For a moment he seemed to her ready to go out of his mind, for in his ordinary state she thought him more sane than people gave him credit for....
>
> 'There's nothing to prevent him coming back....'

> His eyes began to wander.
> 'To-morrow."
> She never tried again, for fear the man should go out of his mind on the spot. (251-252)

Being discouraged, she tolerates this utopia, considers his remaining in the domain of illusions beneficial to him (263). Hagberd's continuous, senseless search of Harry, mad belief in his return, parsimony, and shabby clothes, become the targets of the local people's mockery. These ironic attitudes deflect him from making contacts with others: "Captain Hagberd lived amongst a scheme of settled notions which it pained him to feel disturbed by people's grins. Yes, people's grins were awful. They hinted at something wrong....It was bad enough on the streets, but he had never before been outraged like this" (259). He does not blame himself for his isolation:

> She [Bessie] seemed the only sensible person in the town....The rest of the town, he confided to her once, in a fit of temper, was certainly queer. The way they looked at you–the way they talked to you! He had never got on with anyone in the place. Didn't like the people. (252; also 256).

Their line of action strengthens his solitude: he responds to ridicule by increasing his distance from the milieu, by making the "insulator" stronger. The captain lets nobody into his garden and abode, which have been assiduously prepared for Harry's return. Even Bessie, his intended daughter-in-law, the only person who does not laugh at him, is not admitted there:

> For all their intimacy, which had lasted some years now, they had never talked without a fence or a railing between them. He described to her all the splendours accumulated for the setting-up of their housekeeping, but had never invited her to an inspection. No human eye was to behold them till Harry had his first look. In fact, nobody had ever been inside his cottage; he did his own housework, and he guarded his son's privilege so jealously that the small objects of domestic use he bought sometimes in the town were smuggled rapidly across the front garden under his canvas coat. (256)

The walls of the house, as well as the iron railing and wooden fence enclosing the front and back gardens, acquire the metaphorical sense of the barriers hyperbolizing the hero's separation from the world and preventing intruders from invading the "kingdom" of imaginary "to-morrow."

The apogees of Hagberd's estrangement is created by his reactions to the coming of the actual Harry. His obsession prevents him from recognizing his son, whom he does not allow into the house, taking him for a stranger trying to penetrate this "sanctuary"; he behaves aggressively when Harry attempts to force his way in (264). The son is for him only the cherished ideal, the foundation of dreams about a happy future: "Send him away, my dear [Bessie]. He's only a vagabond. What you want is a good home of your own. That chap has no home–he's not like Harry. He can't be Harry. Harry is coming to-morrow" (273-274). Hagberd's loneliness, like Almayer's, has a tragic dimension, and the misery of the captain's predicament is lessened only by his insanity, excluding comprehension of the hopelessness of his own existence.[14]

The solitude of an individual preoccupied with fancies about the future appears episodically in *Freya of the Seven Isles*. Old Nelson, Freya's father, desires to make the autumn of his life peaceful and safe, owing to good relations with the Dutch authorities; marrying his daughter off to Heemskirk is meant to serve this aim. Narrow-minded Nelson is not aware of the feelings of Freya and her lover Jasper, of their tragic plight, an of the true reasons for his daughter's death (TLS 235-238). He is a childish old man of "naturally benighted intelligence" (233) with "unintelligently furrowed, anxious forehead and...round, innocent eyes" (234), credulous and unable to perceive the truth, "the note of his personality is a profound, echoless, irresponsiveness to everything around him" (233).

C. Skepticism and Contempt for the World

Voluntary psychological isolation is sometimes brought about by assuming a skeptical attitude. Axel Heyst, the principal character in *Victory*, frequently utters maxims arguing for such an outlook: "All action is bound to be harmful. It is devilish. That is why this world is evil upon the whole. But I have done with it! I shall never lift a little finger again" (V 54); "He who forms a tie is lost" (199-200; also 174, 198-199, 203, 212). Contempt for the environment is an essential component of this standpoint: Heyst asserts the world to be "not worth touching, and perhaps not substantial enough to grasp" (176), "for the wise...nothing but an amusing spectacle" (178), and "had renounced all outside nourishment, and was sustaining itself proudly on its own contempt of the usual coarse aliments which life offers to the common appetites of men" (177). He puts these ideals into practice. After the bankruptcy of the Tropical Belt Coal Company (on Heyst the colonizer see Part 2 Chapter 5), he settles alone on the island, feeling discouragement and resentment, which are enhanced by the wrongs of Lena, who accompanies him, and Schomberg's calumnies and accusations of murder. The doubt, cynicism, and disgust with reality revealed in Heyst's appreciation of the others' actions originate from his dispositions. The Swede is permanently supercilious, which makes him lonely: always and everywhere, both on a desert island and among people (28, 90, 177). A substantial role in stimulating these inclinations was played by Heyst's father, who instilled in him the ideology of skepticism, passivity, and misanthropy (e.g., 91-92, 174-175, 195-196),[15] which, combined with subtlety and oversensitivity, induces him to exaggerate the misfortunes and problems of living and to take an attitude of despondency, apathy, and estrangement: "[He] was disenchanted with life as a whole. His scornful temperament, beguiled into action, suffered from failure in a subtle way unknown to men accustomed to grapple with the realities of common human enterprise" (65). Heyst's delicacy is manifest in his abhorrence of brutality and violence, which is embodied by "plain Mr. Jones" and his companions.[16]

In consequence of this estrangement, the inefficient leading figure of *Victory* does not control the situation on the island, which is visible, for instance, in his relations with the servant Wang. Heyst, "who plunged himself into an abyss of meditation over books" (180), does not realize that the Chinese actually rules the whole property and acts entirely according to his own will (180-184). Even in a crisis situation he does not manage to prevent Wang's theft of his revolver. Furthermore, overpowered by skepticism and passivity, he can not cope with the emergency caused by Jones's group. Facing mortal danger,he does not take energetic and decisive measures but, as before, yields to inertia and repugnance. He confesses, "They ought to have aroused my fury. But I have refined everything away by this time–anger, indignation, scorn itself. Nothing's left but disgust" (329-330). After unsuccessful negotiations with the servant over the return of the gun and failing to get any help, Heyst collapses, expecting confrontation with the invaders to end inevitably in his defeat: "Why this stupid concern for the preliminaries, since, when the issue was joined, it would find him disarmed and shrinking from the ugliness and degradation of it?" (357). The thought of struggling with bestial adversaries, of the need to deal them a mortal blow in defense of himself and Lena, fills him with abomination (360-361). He is unable to strike in the moment of Jones's weakness, originating in his misogyny (a shock from the discovery of a woman's presence on the island) (387). The protagonist's life story, like those of nearly all the Conradian characters undergoing psychological separation, is brought to a tragic conclusion. His defeat comprises not only the incapability of saving his own and his partner's lives, but also the knowledge, shortly before his death, of his mistakes: the attitude of doubt and inaction. He takes the blame for the unhappy development of events onto himself.

> Heyst bent low over her, cursing his fastidious soul, which even at that moment kept the true cry of love from his lips in its infernal mistrust of all life. (406)
>
> Ah, Davidson, woe to the man whose heart has not learned while young to hope, to love–and to put its trust in life! (410)

A parallel course of conduct constitutes an essential reason for Martin Decoud's self-imposed psychological isolation in *Nos-*

tromo (see the depiction of his political views in Part 2, Chapter 5). He is frequently aloof to the plans, intentions, and practices of others. This cynical intellectual displays an aversion to all public activities, especially the political, as miserable distortions of the ideals forming their premises. Skepticism, as well as excessive subtlety and oversensitiveness, determines Decoud's final catastrophe: he can not stand solitude on the island and commits suicide.[17] Giorgio Viola in *Nostromo* lives enveloped in the illusions of his past: he feels contempt for the political events in Costaguana, fails to perceive Nostromo's love for Giselle rather than for Linda, and shoots him in mistaking him for Ramirez.[18]

Detachment caused by scorn and detestation of reality also concerns the anarchists in *The Secret Agent, The Informer,* and *An Anarchist,* the revolutionaries and the representatives of the émigré opposition in *Under Western Eyes* (the narrator emphasizes their estrangement from the Geneva milieu), and Scevola in *The Rover* (an agent of bloody terror, both during the revolution and in postrevolutionary France; see the comments on their political attitudes in Part 2, Chapter 5). The loneliness of the terrorists does not bring about aloofness to worldly matters, passivity, and surrender, but rather activity aimed at the destruction of a ruling social order.

D. Subtle Estheticism

The count's self-inflicted psychological isolation in *Il Conde,* resembles the parallel motif in *Victory* and *Nostromo*. It originates in his delicate and emotional nature.[19] Works of art are his immediate surroundings. They harmonize with his refined estheticism. The setting of the protagonist's first conversation with the narrator is the suite containing the collection of bronzes at the National Museum in Naples. The analogy between Il Conde and the ancient Romans of the upper classes, who are shown in the exposition, enhances the portrayal of his belonging to the domain of esthetic. The count lives in an ivory tower of sublime experiences, he expresses disgust for all forms of brutality. His frame of mind is revealed, for instance, in his attitude toward art works: he dislikes the busts and statues of Roman emperors in this gallery, whose facial expressions seems to him too vigorous and pronounced (SS 270). His style of life is distinguished by his excessive concern for his health and the avoidance of physical pain (272-273); it is "correct, well ordered and conventional, undisturbed by startling events" (270). These motives make the principal character of the story renounce attempts to enlarge his property; he considers such conduct a manifestation of primitiveness, incompatible with his sense of honor:

> To be extremely rich would have appeared to him improper, outré–too blatant altogether. And obviously, too, the fortune was not of his making. The making of a fortune cannot be achieved without some roughness. It is a matter of temperament. His nature was too kindly for strife. (272)

Repugnance to violence (similar to that of Heyst's in *Victory*) is most conspicuous in Il Conde's reactions to the incident in which he becomes a victim. He suffers not so much from the assault itself, as from the insult it inflicts on his sensitivity and dignity: "He was not ashamed. He was shocked at being the selected victim, not of robbery so much as of contempt. His tranquility had been wantonly desecrated. His lifelong, kindly nicety of outlook had been defaced" (284). When attacked, he does not cry for help, to avoid commotion, because "it was in his character to shrink from scandal, much more than from mere death" (281). This event takes place in a public pleasure ground during a concert. The robber's particular moves correspond to definite sections of the performance (280-283): at the beginning of the assault "the clarionet...was finishing his solo...the band crashed *fortissimo*"; the thief's demand for the wallet is accompanied by "a slow movement of solemn braying by all the trombones, with deliberately repeated bangs of the big drum"; money is given simultaneously with "the sweet thrilling of flutes and clarionets sustained by the emotional drone of the hautboys"; the murderous push is awaited when "great waves of harmony went on flowing from the band"; and at the end of this episode, after the robber's disappearance, "the band was executing, with immense bravura, the complicated finale. It ended with a tremendous crash." The aggression inflicted upon the aristocrat is a confrontation of two opposite attitudes: subtle estheticism and brutal barbarity.[20] The music, constantly evoked, is almost physically present during this scene; it unites with the hero. This enriches the presentation, giving it a more general sense of assault upon art and appreciation of its beauty, upon the subtlety of human emotions. The bandit puts a knife to "the very spot of the human body where a Japanese gentleman begins the operations of the Hara-kiri, which is a form of suicide following upon dishonour, upon an intolerable outrage to the delicacy of one's feelings" (279-280). And in fact the protagonist commits it: after the mortification he decides to leave Naples, and the change of climate in his state of health is equivalent to passing a death sentence upon himself:

> His delicate conception of his dignity was defiled by a degrading experience. He couldn't stand that. No Japanese gentleman, outraged in his exaggerated sense of honour, could have gone about his preparations for Hara-kiri with greater resolution. To go home really amounted to suicide for the poor Count. (288)

Such meanings are suggested also by the funeral imagery used in the description of his departure. Thus the attack upon the count ruins his elevated existence, the system of values he cherishes.[21]

Stephen, the protagonist of the unfinished *The Sisters,* represents, like Il Conde, a voluntary psychological isolation in the domain of refined estheticism. He is fascinated by masterpiece of art and wants to understand the mystery of their beauty and perfection.[22] Devotion to this passion separates him from others: he is laughed at by strangers (Sis 34), he is not understood by his parents and brother (31-33, 35-38) and even within the milieu of the artistic bohemia in Paris (44-46).

The detachment of the majority of female characters (see the comments on their unfavorable portrayal Part 2, Chapter 4) corresponds to that of Il Conde and Stephen. Braving the adversities of nature and excessively difficult conditions of life (e.g., at sea), typical of males figures, is alien to Conradian women. They usually remain in an idealized and imaginary realm of subtlety and beauty, removed from harsh realities.

> It's queer how out of touch with truth women are. They live in a world of their own, and there had never been anything like it, and never can be. It is too beautiful altogether, and if they were to set it up it would go to pieces before the first sunset. Some confounded fact we men have been living contentedly with ever since the day of creation would start up and knock the whole thing over. (*Heart of Darkness,* YNTOS 59; see also *Chance,* C 93-94)

This attitude is embodied primarily by Marlow's aunt and Kurtz's Intended in *Heart of Darkness,*[23] Alice in *A Smile of Fortune,* Felicia Moorsom in *The Planter of Malata,* Edith Travers in *The Rescue,* and the mariners' wives in *Typhoon.*

E. Borderline Cases, Hereditary and Cultural Estrangement

A specific kind of loneliness is delineated by Conrad in *The Idiots, The Secret Agent,* and *Amy Foster.* It is partly self-imposed, resulting from an individual's own conduct. But unlike all the types of psychological seclusion discussed so far, it is caused by voluntary, conscious choices. In these three works it is practically independent of the characters: it is an effect of the genetic or cultural determinants of their existence.[24]

The title of *The Idiots* denotes a group of children met by the narrator during his travels in France. Weak-mindedness clearly distinguishes them from others and from nature: "They were on offense to the sunshine, a reproach to empty heaven, a blight on the concentrated and purposeful vigour of the wild landscape" (TU 58). Their lack of psychological contact with people is indicated by their outward appearance (unseeing, thoughtless eyes) and behavior (senseless loitering, rolling in the sand, not reacting to utterances). They are separated from reality in the temporal dimension as well: "Such creatures are forgotten by time, and live untouched by years till death gathers them up into its compassionate bosom" (57). Because of the key motif of the story, multiplied by repetition (four mentally deficient children), *The Idiots* is probably Conrad's most tragic text; the experiences of the title characters' parents are heart breaking: the despair of the father, unable to realize his dreams of heirs to farm his estate, and especially the mother's sufferings, directly preceding her death. They seem to pervade the surrounding nature:

> And from morning till night one could see all over the land black denuded boughs, the boughs gnarled and twisted, as if contorted with pain, swaying sadly between the wet clouds and the soaked earth. The clear and gentle streams of summer days rushed discoloured and raging at the stones that barred the way to the sea, with the fury of madness bent upon suicide. (70; also 71-72)

In *The Secret Agent* feeble-minded Stevie's detachment from his milieu is much like one described in *The Idiots*.

The culturally determined seclusion of the Carpathian emigrant Yanko Goorall in *Amy Foster* constitutes a different kind of self-inflicted isolation, only partly caused by the character himself.[25] His entirely distinct domestic ethos and tradition hinder assimilation to foreign environments. Unknown, alien reality enlivens Yanko's recollections of his motherland, enhancing his loneliness. The imagery with these connotations is conspicuous in his perception of the port in Hamburg (TOS 115-116) and the railway station in Berlin:

> There was a roof over him, which seemed made of glass, and was so high that the tallest mountain-pine he had ever seen would have had room to grow under it....People swarmed more than you can see on a feast-day round the miraculous Holy Image in the yard of the Carmelite Convent. (114-115)

The protagonist also senses poignant solitude during the sea voyage (117-118, 123-124). Settling in an English village does not alter his plight:

> It is indeed hard upon a man to find himself a lost stranger, helpless, incomprehensible, and of a mysterious origin, in some obscure corner of the earth. (113)
> He was different; innocent at heart, and full of good will, which nobody wanted, this castaway, that, like a man transplanted into another planet, was separated by an immense space from his past and by an immense ignorance from his future. (132)

Goorall's detachment is caused mainly by his style of living, which to everyone around seems queer and incompatible with the norms of conduct accepted in this milieu:

> Strangers would turn round to look after him on the road. His foreignness had a peculiar and indelible stamp. At last people became used to see him. But they never became used to him. His rapid, skimming walk; his swarthy complexion; his hat cocked on the left ear; his habit, on warm evenings, of wearing his coat over one shoulder, like a hussar's dolman; his manner of leaping over the stiles, not as a feat of agility, but in the ordinary course of progression–all these peculiarities were, as one may say, so many causes of scorn and offence to the inhabitants of the village. *They* wouldn't in their dinner hour lie flat on their backs on the grass to stare at the sky. Neither did they go about the fields screaming dismal tunes. (131-132; also 111)

Yanko's predicament is revealed during an incident in the inn, from which local notables expel him, as they have no intention of tolerating his vigorous performance of a highlander's dance (132-133, 136-137). He is generally despised and considered as one whom only dull Amy Foster can join in marriage (135-136). The expatriate keenly senses his estrangement from the English farmers. Brought up in the Catholic faith, he is unable to comprehend the essence of the Protestant religion: "He...remained for a long time surprised at the bare poverty of the churches among so much wealth. He couldn't understand either why they were kept shut up on week-days. There was nothing to steal in them. Was it to keep people from praying too often?" (131). All his surroundings seem strange and unfamiliar. This magnifies his loneliness, despair, anguish:

> There was nothing here the same as in his country! The earth and the water were different; there were no images of the Redeemer by the roadside. The very grass was different, and the trees. All the trees but the three old Norway pines on the bit of lawn before Swaffer's house, and these reminded him of his country. He had been detected once, after dusk, with his forehead against the trunk of one of them, sobbing, and talking to himself. (129)

2. Isolation in Love and Marriage

A. Lovers' (Spouses') Renunciation of the World

The self-imposed seclusion of characters frequently results from their amorous entanglements.[26] Sometimes it assumes the form of a pair's distancing themselves from their environment. An interesting example of this motif appears in *Freya of the Seven Isles* where it is combined with affection for a ship, typical of Conradian seamen. Jasper Allen desires to unite with his beloved Freya on his brig, which is to be the foundation of their lonely existence, "the fortune and the home, and the great free world for them" (TLS 156), "the only foothold of the two lives on the wide earth, the security of his passion" (218). The *Bonito* and the sweetheart constitute oneness for him–an object of worship, supreme happiness: "And then to console him he had the brig which seemed pervaded by the spirit of Freya, since whatever he did on board was always done under the supreme sanction of his love" (167; also 158, 210, 218). The partner shares her admirer's dreams about a pleasurable life together on board (162, 166-167). Attempts at accomplishing these designs lead, however, to the clash of Jasper's idealism with the brutality and force personified by Heemskirk (167)–the confrontation ending tragically for both lovers. The repulsive Dutchman, humiliated and rejected by the girl and motivated by a malicious passion for vengeance, treacherously arranges to wreck the brig.[27] This catastrophe brings about the young sailor's complete breakdown, ruins his hopes for happiness, the foundations of the life he had dreamed of: "He looked as though he would never laugh at anything in his life" (221), resembles one who got "a deadly blow into [the] heart, and...walked about with the dagger in his breast" (228), becoming a human ruin. Jasper's agony is shared by his mistress, who dies soon after this incident.

In *Chance* and *Victory* the love-based isolation springs from extracting the heroine from debasing situations.[28] After the scandalous affair and imprisonment of her rich father, Flora de Barral in *Chance* experiences numerous instances of ill-treatment: her governess displays hatred toward her, her father's cousin takes care of her, but motivated by the prospect of financial profit (C 174). Flora does not meet with friendliness and help from her protector Mrs. Fyne, who intrigues to thwart the girl's connection with her (Mrs. Fyne's) brother Roderick Anthony. In those hard, depressing times

> she had nothing to fall back upon, no experience but such as to shake her belief in every human being. She was dreadfully and pitifully forlorn. (237-238)
>
> Nothing but wretchedness, whichever way she turned in an unjust and prejudiced world. (246)

She undergoes numerous humiliations in the later years of her vagabond life as well: accompanying an old lady in Bornemouth, or having English conversations with the boys of a well-to-do family in Hamburg. Flora is not understood by her father who, released from prison, disapproves of her marriage because of his egoistic love for her. All these events and circumstances–exaggerated in a melodramatic way–produce her estrangement. The second leading figure of the novel, Captain Roderick Anthony, is also detached; he belongs to "silent solitary men, the voluntary, passionate outcasts of their kind" (331). Inclination toward a secluded life motivates his choice of the marine profession:

> Solitude had been his best friend. He wanted some place where he could sit down and be alone. And in his need his thoughts turned to the sea which had given him so much of that congenial solitude. There...he could always be as solitary as he chose. Yes. Get out to sea! (346)

Thus loneliness links both protagonists: "He had broken away from his surroundings; she stood outside the pale...those two were outside all conventions. They wold be as untrammelled in a sense as the first man and the first woman" (210). Their marriage and transfer to the ship means breaking ties with the environment inimical to the heroine, making an end of her degradation and anguish (when marrying, Anthony is motivated by both love and compassion), closing in the ivory tower of their happiness. Flora and Anthony maintain a psychological distance from the crew: even the most inquisitive mariners (Franklin, Powell) are unable, in spite of painstaking efforts, to detect the true nature of their union, and the reasons for de Barral's presence in the captain's cabin.

The voluntary isolation of the pair in *Victory* assumes a similar shape. The work of Lena, a violinist, in Zangiacomo's woman orchestra entails numerous humiliations: the conductor's tyranny, the maltreatment by his wife, and Schomberg's wooing (e.g., V 93-94). The girl's hopeless situation harmonizes with a pejorative portrayal of the band: when performing, it "was simply murdering silence with a vulgar, ferocious energy" (68); the figures of Zangiacomo, his wife, and the majority of the group's members are repulsive. The acquaintance with Heyst gives Lena a hope of ending this debasement. Motivated by an instinctive desire for safety, she begs him for help (80, 85-86, 95). The Swede fulfills Lena's expectations: yielding to an awakening feeling of love, as well as to sympathy and compassion, he flees with the girl to "his" island, which brings about their seclusion: "Nothing can break in on us here" (223); "We are two. Never were such a lonely two out of the world, my dear!" (315-316; also 190, 349). The couple's situation is enhanced by the use of biblical imagery: by comparing them to the creatures rescued from the Deluge (191) and their isle to Eden (173-174). Her desire to distance herself from the world is seen in her attempts to make herself strongly dependent on Heyst (187) and completely breaking with the past (88, 191), which she accomplishes by taking a new name (88). The idyll is terminated by the arrival of Mr. Jones, Ricardo, and Pedro (inspired by Schomberg)–the emissaries of the renounced world of lawlessness, monstrosity, and moral misrule. The brutal force personified by them penetrates from the outside and destroys the protagonists' "isolation."

Seraphina's position in *Romance* recalls the predicament of the heroines of *Chance* and *Victory*. She, too, feels completely lost and lonely when constantly threatened by O'Brien, and John Kemp is aware of having rescued her from a difficult plight: "Her father's long aloofness from life had created such an isolation round his closing years that his daughter had no one but me to turn to for protection against the plots of her own Intendente" (Rom 259). Common experiences and vicissitudes strengthen their affection and a sense of separation from reality:

> We had thought of nothing but ourselves; we had dwelt alone in our emotions, as if there had been no inhabitant of flesh and blood on the earth but we two. Our danger had been present, no doubt, in our minds, because we drew it in with every breath. It was the indispensable condition of our contact, of our words, of our thoughts; it was the atmosphere of our feelings; a something as all-pervading and impalpable as the air we drew into our lungs. (184-185)
>
> We must have been grotesque, pathetic, and lonely; like two people newly arisen from a tomb, shrinking before the strangeness of the half-forgotten face of the world...
>
> The sensation of...solitude, rolled upon our souls emerging from the darkness, overwhelmingly, like a wave of the sea. We might have been an only couple sent back from the underworld to begin another cycle of pain on a depopulated earth. (417; also 233, 365, 433-434, 440)

The shape of Seraphina's and John's isolation is determined by the conventions of the literature of adventure and melodramatic romance, dominant in this novel (exaggerating the dangers to which the lovers are exposed, their heroism, and their defiance of the entire world). Self-inflicted amorous seclusion appears as a marginal motif in another romance, *The Arrow of Gold,* in reference to George and Rita:[29]

> A thick veil of secrecy had been lowered between the world and the lovers; yet even this veil turned out not altogether impenetrable.
> He–it would be convenient to call him Monsieur George to the end–shared with Doña Rita her perfect detachment from all mundane affairs... (AG 340)

Lovers' distancing themselves from their environment–which puts an end to an ignominious predicament for one or both of them–concerns not only whites but also natives. Arsat (*The Lagoon*) decides to escape with his beloved Diamelen in order to unite with her. Before meeting Dain (*Almayer's Folly*), Nina treats life with revulsion. In Sambir she is forced to endure Mrs. Almayer's cunning and fierceness, and the machinations of her friends:

> She had breathed the atmosphere of sordid plottings for gain, of the no less disgusting intrigues and crimes for lust or money; and those things, together with the domestic quarrels, were the only events of her three years' existence....Her young mind having been unskilfully permitted to glance at better things, and then thrown back again into the hopeless quagmire of barbarism, full of strong and uncontrolled passions, had lost the power to discriminate. (AF 43)

Her father's inefficiency is as unacceptable to her as the activities of the autochthones and her mother. All of this makes the half-caste's position desperate, like that of "a captive thinking of liberty within the walls of his prison cell" (151-152). Dain liberates her from this degrading situation, changes her life in this "hopeless quagmire of barbarism" for the bliss of love:[30]

> With the coming of Dain she found the road to freedom....She understood now the reason and the aim of life; and in the triumphant unveiling of that mystery she threw away disdainfully her past with its sad thoughts, its bitter feelings and its faint affections, now withered and dead in contact with her fierce passion. (152)

> In the cold ashes of that hateful and miserable past she would find the sign of love, the fitting expression of the boundless felicity of the present, the pledge of a bright and splendid future. (72)

This salutary isolation is particularly conspicuous in the erotic scenes depicted against the setting of tropical vegetation. It functions as a barrier that tightly encloses the love-nest sanctuary, their only reality (the canoe, the fog, the river and the jungle create a concentric construction):

> To those two nothing existed then outside the gunwales of the narrow and fragile craft. It was their world, filled with their intense and all-absorbing love. They took no heed of thickening mist, or of the breeze dying away before sunrise; they forgot the existence of the great forests surrounding them, of all the tropical nature awaiting the advent of the sun in a solemn and impressive silence. (69; also 68, 71)

The couple's separation from the world is emphasized by Nina during her dramatic parting with Almayer too: "Then I found that we could see through each other's eyes: that he [Dain] saw things that nobody but myself and he could see. We entered a land where no one could follow us, and least of all you. Then I began to live" (179).

Self-imposed love isolation in *An Outcast of the Islands,* concerning, however, a native woman and a white man, is treated in much the same way as in *Almayer's Folly*. Defrauder Willems, prevented by Lingard from committing suicide and posted to Sambir, is unable to undertake the dealings that would satisfy his ambitions (see comments on Willems's ethical estrangement in Part 1, Chapter 2, and on his performance as a colonizer in Part 2, Chapter 5). There he meets Aissa, who arouses his desire, causing him to forget his past life and the humiliations he has experienced, and leading him to change his plans for the future:

> And while she was near there was nothing in the whole world–for that idle man–but her look and her smile. Nothing in the past, nothing in the future; and in the present only the luminous fact of her existence. (OI 76-77; also 74-77 other extracts, 80-81, 128-129)

Reciprocation of this passion is evident, for instance, in the musings and utterances Aissa directs at Lingard, who has arrived there in order to punish his protégé: "I live with him all the days. All the nights. I look at him; I see his every breath, every glance of his eye, every movement of his lips. I see nothing else! What else is there?" (249; also 248-250 other passages). An awareness of amorous detachment appears in Willems's dream about becoming independent of the Malays manipulating him and about prospective happiness with the beloved woman:

> And then I would have her all to myself away from her people–all to myself–under my own influence...then go away to some distant place where, far from all she knew, I would be all the world to her! All the world to her! (92; also 126-127, 151-152)

Aissa, also afraid of losing her admirer, aims at separating him from the world and the white race: "She would keep him here a slave and a master; here where he was alone with her; where he must live for her–or die. She had a right to his love....She must put between him and other white men a barrier of hate" (153). She participates in Babalatchi's intrigue, hoping to provoke a quarrel between Willems and Lingard, and treats all who come from outside as potential threats to her happiness (353). The pair's seclusion is favored by tropical nature, which forms the background to their infatuation:

> The solitary exile of the forests, great, motionless and solemn in his abandonment, left alone by the life of ages...towered high and straight above their heads...spreading his branches wide in a gesture of lofty protection, as if to hide them in the sombre shelter of innumerable leaves...to screen this struggle of two human hearts from the cold scrutiny of glittering stars. (154)

Love "insulation" of individuals belonging to different cultural traditions is manifest in *Amy Foster*. The plight of the castaway Yanko among the rural English is distressing and debasing. His desperate attempts at making contact with them are futile, since all of them regard him as a madman and a tramp, and not as a lonely human being who needs help (TOS 118-121). Goorall's inability to assimilate with the local people is the source of his sufferings:

> He remembered the pain of his wretchedness and misery, his heartbroken astonishment that it was neither seen nor understood, his dismay at finding all the men angry and all the women fierce. He had approached them as a beggar, it is true, he said; but in his country, even if they gave nothing, they spoke gently to beggars. The children in his country were not taught to throw stones at those who asked for compassion. (124)

Only Amy Foster rebels against Smith's cruel treatment of the stranger (121) and is friendly and helpful to him (124-125). Yanko realizes that the change from this hopeless situation is due to her:

> Through this act of impulsive pity he was brought back again within the pale of human relations with his new surroundings. He never forgot it–never. (125)
>
> She had been neither fierce nor angry, nor frightened. Her face he remembered as the only comprehensible face amongst all these faces that were as closed, as mysterious, and as mute as the faces of the dead who are possessed of a knowledge beyond the comprehension of the living. (129)

Their mutual liking develops into fascination and leads to matrimony, to the disapproval of the villagers, who still despise Goorall.

B. Reciprocal Detachment of Lovers (Marriage Partners) Caused by Disparate Desires and Attitudes

A couple's isolation from the world brings fruition to dreams only in *Almayer's Folly* and *Romance*. In all the other cases it modulates to a pair's estrangement from each other, leading usually to a tragic conclusion to their union; frequently only the second variation of amorous seclusion appears.[31]

Such a transformation may be noticed in *Freya of the Seven Isles*. Freya and Jasper are initially strongly linked by the desire for a happy life together on their dear ship. Yet this is only a seeming unity, concealing ambitions for dominance over the partner. The girl does not yield entirely to passion, but aims at controlling the development of their relationship. Motivated by common sense, she tones down her admirer's naive frenzy; she confesses she would never surrender to his rule (TLS 237). The sailor, on the other hand, treats his lack of supremacy over Nelson's daughter as one of the reasons for his defeat:

> If I had been a man I would have carried her off, but she made a child, a happy child, of me. Tell her that the day the only thing I had belonging to me in the world perished on this reef I discovered that I had no power over her... (236)

Both are egocentric, since love is not of the utmost importance for them: Freya prefers personal freedom, and Jasper attachment to his brig.[32] A similar development of a love plot may be discerned in *The Arrow of Gold*. George's and Rita's carefree secluded life is deprived of internal harmony: she decides to leave him and renounce her personal happiness in order to prevent a disintegration of his personality and to enable him to make a marine career. Thus the love affair ends unhappily for Rita, and less so for George: although he claims that the golden arrow presented by the mistress "surer than Mr. Blunt's bullet...has found its mark" (AG 350). Yet he quickly recovers and devotes himself to sea service.[33]

Flora de Barral and Captain Anthony in *Chance,* who cut themselves off from the "evil" world on board the ship, become largely alien to each other.[34] They are linked by protectiveness and loyalty rather than by real passion, which would reveal itself in tenderness and intimate actions. The mutual estrangement of the couple in *Victory*[35] is especially strongly emphasized: it is caused by their disparate attitudes toward reality (a fact generally noticed by Conradians). A subtle aristocrat, Heyst personifies cynicism, unconcern, and contempt for reality. Lena, on the other hand, coming from a low social class, is an allegory of the instinct for life.[36] With determination and heroism she opposes Mr. Jones and his companions and aims at saving her prospective bliss on the island:

> She...faced the danger with a passionate desire to defend her own. (V 298)
> All her energy was concentrated on the struggle that she wanted to take upon herself, in a great exaltation of love and self-sacrifice, which is woman's sublime faculty... (317)

The heroine gains a victory (hence the title), triumphing over Ricardo and breaking, at the moment of her death, the protagonist's self-inflicted skeptical detachment (405-407, 409-410).[37]

The discussed pattern of amorous isolation applies to Antonia Avellanos and Martin Decoud in *Nostromo* as well. They are separated from each other by a fundamental discrepancy in outlooks (discussed in Part 2, Chapter 5): Antonia is an ardent patriot, deeply engaged in the program and activities of the Blanco party, whereas Martin reveals a critical attitude toward both his fiancée's ideals and conduct, and all political action.[38] Reciprocal estrangement caused by disparate frames of mind is also characteristic of Kurtz and his intended (who is unaware of his true actions in Africa) in *Heart of Darkness,* Bamtz and Laughing Anne in *Because of the Dollars,* and Davidson and his wife (who misinterprets her husband's goodness and compassion toward Anne and her son) in the same story.

C. Mutual Aloofness of Lovers (Wife and Husband) Resulting from Their Belonging to Different Races and Cultures

Transformation of a pair's isolation from reality into estrangement from each other originates sometimes in a lack of uniformity in outlooks that is ethnically determined. In *An Outcast of the Islands* Willems realizes the existence of this barrier at the beginning of his acquaintance with Aissa, although his infatuation is stronger than any prejudices.[39]

> He [was] a white man....That woman was a complete savage....He seemed to be surrendering to a wild creature the unstained purity of his life, of his race, of his civilization. (OI 80)
> This manifestation of her sense of proprieties was another sign of their hopeless diversities....She was too different from him....It struck him suddenly that they had nothing in common–not a thought, not a feeling; he could not make clear to her the simplest motive of any act of his...and he could not live without her. (128; also 126-127)

The girl regards this newcomer with suspicion, characteristic of the natives' attitude toward whites (143-144). The psychological distance between them is increased by conflicting expectations connected with the attack on Almayer's habitation: Aissa wants Willems to kill him (as would become a Malay warrior), and is unable to understand why her beloved is satisfied merely with wounding his adversary's honor (which is a more subtle punishment, closer to the white man's mentality). With time Willems's adoration dies and intense racial hatred replaces affection and eroticism: "The eyes of a savage; of a damned mongrel, half-Arab, half-Malay. They hurt me!...I swear to you I can't stand this! Take me away. I am white! All white!" (271). He considers Aissa the source of all defeats, calamities, and afflictions:

> In a moment of his idleness, of suspense, of discouragement, she had come–that creature–and by the touch of her hand had destroyed his future, his dignity of a clever and civilized man; had awakened in his breast the infamous thing which had driven him to what he had done, and to end miserably in the wilderness and be forgotten, or else remembered with hate or contempt. He dared not look at her, because now whenever he looked at her his thought seemed to touch crime, like an outstretched hand. (334)

Thus Lingard's protégé becomes a double outcast: cut off both from the world of whites, and from his former sweetheart, in he case by enmity, bitterness, and reproach. She too senses the tragedy of their mutual estrangement keenly:

> She shared his torment in the poignant wonder, in the acute longing, in

> the despairing inability to understand the cause of his anger and of his repulsion; the hate of his looks; the mystery of his silence; the menace of his rare words...thrown at her with rage, with contempt, with the evident desire to hurt her... (333; also 249-252, 333-336 other extracts)

The autochthonous girl detests Willems for false worship, feels humiliated (355-359), removed "beyond the possibility of any hope, into an infinity of wrongs without any redress" (357). In *An Outcast of the Islands* the solitude of the protagonists' amorous paradise changes into profound mutual isolation based on racial animosity, and becomes excessively tragic:

> Those two, surrounded each by the impenetrable wall of their aspirations, were hopelessly alone, out of sight, out of earshot of each other; each the centre of dissimilar and distant horizons; standing each on a different earth, under a different sky. (333-334)
>
> Hate filled the world, filled the space between them–the hate of race, the hate of hopeless diversity, the hate of blood; the hate against the man born in the land of lies and of evil from which nothing but misfortune comes to those who are not white. (359; also 328, 348)

Jim's and Jewel's reciprocal detachment in *Lord Jim* assumes a similar shape. It may be represented by Marlow's vision on his way to Patusan:[40]

> There can be seen rising above the level of the forests the summits of two steep hills very close together, and separated by what looks like a deep fissure, the cleavage of some mighty stroke...the appearance from the settlement is of one irregularly conical hill split in two, and with the two halves leaning slightly apart. (LJ 220)

The lack of understanding between them results partly from the incongruity of their outlooks, but primarily from the native girl's ignorance of the secret of the protagonist's past. It creates a psychological gulf between them, causes that "his soul...remains even for her who loved him best a cruel and insoluble mystery" (393). Fearing the loss of her partner she desperately desires to get to know this mystery (308). Like Aissa, Jewel is a tragic figure: she is left by her white lover for reasons completely incomprehensible to her. That is, she cannot understand why Jim, losing ground, does not escape with her for the sake of their happiness, but stays in Patusan and chooses an honorable death. Her tragedy is the price paid for the fruition of Tuan's dreams (see also the delineation of his conduct in Part 1, Chapter 2, Part 2, Chapter 4).

A fundamental discrepancy between systems of values creates an impassable barrier between Mr. and Mrs. Almayer in *Almayer's Folly,* bringing about their mutual psychological separation.[41] Both of them reason in terms of their own races and are unable to understand each other's way of thinking. The disunion is already conspicuous during their wedding:

> While swearing fidelity, he [Almayer] was concocting plans for getting rid of the pretty Malay girl in a more or less distant future. She, however, had retained enough of conventual teaching to understand well that according to the white man's law she was going to be Almayer's companion and not his slave, and promised to herself to act accordingly. (AF 23; also 10-11)

With time it develops into hatred. Almayer treats this marriage as a manifestation of a white man's degradation and sees his autochthonous spouse, who comes from bloodthirsty Sulu pirates, as a disgrace to his honor:

> And each of these scenes was concluded by a piercing shriek, reaching him far away. 'You know, Kaspar, I am your wife! your own Christian wife after your own Blanda law!' For she knew that this was the bitterest thing of all; the greatest regret of that man's life. (40)
> Between you and my mother [Nina says] there never was any love....Then I saw that you could not understand me; for was I not part of that woman? Of her who was the regret and shame of your life? (191)

To the wife he appears the antithesis of her ideal of a warrior and a man, incapable not only of killing or intrigue, but of any effective performance: "I have cooked rice for a man who had no courage and no wisdom. Hai! I! even I, was given in gift by a chief and a warrior to a man that was neither. Hai! Hai!" (148; also 136). Motivated by repugnance against her husband and his way of living, the indigenous woman destroys in fury the tokens of white civilization in their house (26, 90-91). Mrs. Almayer also detests the Christian upbringing imposed upon her by Lingard: she misconceives it, interpreting religion exclusively on the level of superstition (22). Representing the Malay rovers' moral standards and mind set, she secretly cherishes great esteem for their bravery: "She wailed to herself softly, lamenting the lost possibilities of murder and mischief that could have fallen to her lot had she been mated with a congenial spirit" (148; also 152-153).

Substantial incongruity of mentalities and traditions determines, too, the reciprocal estrangement of the protagonists of *Amy Foster*.[42] Amy, fascinated by Yanko's unconventional character and behavior (TOS 134-136), puts an end to his loneliness and cuts herself off with him from the environment. However, in the course of married life they become more and more alien to each other. Their child is the catalyst of this process: Goorall intends to bring him up in the spirit of his own culture, whereas Amy, unable to comprehend her husband's attempts, interprets them as queer magic practices that may harm the boy:

> And she sat...with the terror, the unreasonable terror, of that man she could not understand creeping over her. She had drawn the wicker cradle close to her feet. There was nothing in her now but the maternal instinct and that unaccountable fear. (139; also 137)

Their mutual isolation culminates during the emigrant's illness: Amy gets panic-stricken at Yanko's entreaty for a drink of water, uttered in his native language, and escapes with the child. Left by those dear to him, the outcast "perished in the supreme disaster of loneliness and despair" (142).

D. Reciprocal Solitude of a Married Couple (Lovers) Determined by a Middle-Class or Bourgeois Style of Life

A pair's mutual isolation, resulting from an urban outlook, is conspicuous in the attitudes of the characters of *The Return.* Their marriage seems to bring the fruition of their hopes: Mr. Hervey is contented and achieves his ambitions, Mrs. Hervey gets an opportunity to leave the parental house and elevate and enrich her individuality by realizing philanthropic and social aspirations (TU 120-123). Yet in spite of this, their relationship lacks profound understanding and unity:

> Thus Alvan Hervey and his wife for five prosperous years lived by the side of one another. In time they came to know each other sufficiently well for all the practical purposes of such an existence, but they were no more capable of real intimacy than two animals feeding at the same manger, under the same roof, in a luxurious stable. (122)

This is chiefly caused by the egocentric behavior of both, especially Mr. Hervey:[43]

> They understood each other warily, tacitly, like a pair of cautious conspirators in a profitable plot; because they were both unable to look at a fact, a sentiment, a principle, or a belief otherwise than in the light of their own dignity, of their own glorification, of their own advantage. (123)

Their estrangement from each other is particularly clear in the crucial scene of the story, which takes place after the wife's return to the husband. Her departure originated in disappointment with the marriage, in the impossibility of achieving a genuine union with her spouse. And the homecoming constitutes one more attempt at ending the disharmony. Her effort is, however, futile because of Alvan Hervey's conduct. He views his wife's departure exclusively in terms of its social repercussions, of its injurious influence upon his position in the milieu (128-129, 132-133, 163-165).

He does not seek to terminate the crisis, but merely to satisfy his own vanity and excessive, egoistic ambition: "He yearned unaffectedly to see morality [in his person] triumphant before the world. As to her–she would be forgotten. Let her be forgotten–buried in oblivion–lost! No one would allude..." (132-133). Instead of initiating sincere communication, yielding to emotions, and trying to comprehend his partner, he considers himself flawless and takes a moralistic stance:

> His wish was to crush her by a single sentence. He was stainless. Opinion was on his side; morality, men and gods were on his side; law, conscience–all the world! (142)
>
> The walls of his house seemed to enclose the sacredness of ideals....He understood confusedly that he was part of an immense and beneficent power....He dwelt within the invincible wisdom of silence; he was protected by an indestructible faith that would last forever, that would withstand unshaken all the assaults....He represented the moral strength of a beautiful reticence that would vanquish all the deplorable crudities of life–fear, disaster, sin–even death itself. (155-156; also 140, 156-158, 164-165)

He enjoys it, is completely immersed in it (144, 149-150),[44] and does not notice his spouse's reaction: "Absorbed by the tragedy of his life he had absolutely forgotten her very existence. She stopped, and her outstretched arms fell slowly. He, with his features distorted by the bitterness of his thought, saw neither her movement nor her gesture" (153; also 141). This state of affairs makes union between them unattainable since their attitudes are so disparate. She repents, suffers, and hopes for accord, forgiveness, and help, whereas he assumes the posture of an unblemished, proud apostle of the "holy" morality of their class (censure by townspeople; see Part 2, Chapter 4). The oratorical display does not effect the slightest change in the situation: the cleavage is as great as immediately after Mrs. Hervey's arrival, when "they stood before one another, and the fragments of the torn letter lay between them–at their feet–like an insurmountable obstacle, like a sign of eternal separation!" (143). Her facial expression seems to Alvan to convey hatred, reproach, suspicion, lack of faith and love. It does not raise his expectations for an idyllic marital life (177-179, 184-186). Incapable of reconciling himself to his wife's inability to adapt to his illusions, Hervey leaves the house for good.[45] The protagonist's separation represents a more generalized phenomenon too: city dwellers' isolation and complete unconcern with others' problems. People emerging from the West End railway station into the street are depicted as "brothers, who through prudence, dignity, disgust, or foresight would resolutely ignore each other" (118), and the urban habitations as "the flimsy and inscrutable graves of the living, with the doors numbered like the doors of prison-cells, and as impenetrable as the granite of tombstones" (156; also 135-136, 180).

Another example of psychological distance between spouses caused by incompatible attitudes toward urbanites' value system may be seen in *The Rescue*.[46] Mr. Travers, acting as its representative and propagator, condemns his wife for not accepting its style of living:

> I can't credit you with the possession of feelings appropriate to your origin, social position, and the ideas of the class to which you belong. It was the heaviest disappointment of my life. (Re 267)
> You have a scorn in you for the serious side of life, for the ideas and the ambitions of the social sphere to which you belong. (268; also 267-270 other excerpts)

Edith Travers, on the other hand, assumes a posture of fascination with exotic adventure, while her husband views such behavior as eccentric and ridiculous (351-353).[47]

The motif of mutual estrangement of a middle-class married pair appears in *The Secret Agent*.[48] Mr. and Mrs. Verloc live in the insulated domains of their desires and ambitions, but they are motivated by different ethical notions. The hero's role of confidential agent, which is not known to his wife, exacerbates this predicament (see the portrayal of his political self in Part 2, Chapter 5). The heroine–entirely uninterested in her husband's concerns and never disclosing her own thoughts and dreams to him–is responsible for this situation too, and makes their union superficial:

> Their accord was perfect, but it was not precise. It was a tacit accord, congenial to Mrs. Verloc's incuriosity and to Mr. Verloc's habits of mind, which were indolent and secret. They refrained from going to the bottom of facts and motives. (SA 245)

This is sometimes emphasized ironically by the narrator, e.g., in the scene immediately after the secret agent has been murdered by his spouse:

> Except for the fact that Mrs. Verloc breathed these two would have been perfectly in accord: that accord of prudent reserve without superfluous words, and sparing of signs, which had been the foundation of their respectable home life. For it had been respectable, covering by a decent reticence the problems that may arise in the practice of a secret profession and the commerce of shady wares. To the last its decorum had remained undisturbed by unseemly shrieks and other misplaced sincerities of conduct. And after the striking of the blow, this respectability was continued in immobility and silence. (263-264)

However, their differing conduct toward Stevie, her afflicted brother, is the principal cause of the couple's estrangement from each other. The hero treats his marriage as a display of magnanimity toward his partner and her family. To his idiot brother-in-law he shows indifference close to cynicism: he does not regret his death but only the loss of the post of secret agent (235-236). Winnie's attitude toward Stevie is entirely different: a desire for protection for her handicapped brother induced her to marry Adolf, to sacrifice her personal happiness (243-244, 275-276). After this tragic death she considers herself absolved not only from her marital obligations ("There was no need for her now to stay there, in that kitchen, in that house, with that man–since the boy was gone for ever") (251), but from any ties, and is thus deprived of a sense of living: "She had become a free woman with a perfection of freedom which left her nothing to desire and absolutely nothing to do, since Stevie's urgent claim on her devotion no longer existed" (263; also 251).

The divergence of attitudes is manifest most clearly in the couple's dialogue after the tragedy (237-250). Here Winnie is absorbed in recollections of her youth and past life, and in despair over her irreparable loss. All her thoughts and feelings are focused on Stevie. This makes her fail to hear her husband, who justifies his actions, confides to her the mysteries of his secret employment, and makes optimistic plans for the future. Reciprocal detachment leads to disasterous, consequences for both Adolf and Winnie: left by all her family (the mother's departure for the Charity, the brother's and husband's deaths), "she had nothing. She was the most lonely of murderers that ever struck a mortal blow" (270). Guided by the instinct of self-preservation and by a fear of being hanged (308), the woman turns for help to Ossipon, Verloc's anarchist companion. However, she gets no support: the comrade not only mocks her (e.g., calling the beloved brother a perfect case for scientific study) (297), but perfidiously cheats her out of her money and leaves. These experiences, and in particular the heroine's resultant suicide, constitute the heart-rending epilogue of the novel (on the calamitous aftermath of anarchist activities see Part 2, Chapter 5).

The psychological separation of the Goulds in *Nostromo* (cited constantly by Conradians) is determined by Charles Gould's capitalist life style. It corresponds to the city dwellers' seclusion discussed above.[49] The San Tomé mine is the source of disharmony, since the Administrator devotes all his energy to it, even his thoughts and reveries (see the delineation of the political aspects of his performance in Part 2, Chapter 5):

> The mine had got hold of Charles Gould with a grip as deadly as ever it had laid upon his father. (N 400)
> She [Mrs. Gould] saw clearly the San Tomé mine possessing, consuming, burning up the life of the last of the Costaguana Goulds; mastering the energetic spirit of the son as it had mastered the lamentable weakness of the father. (522)

The hero's involvement in this enterprise makes him alien to his wife. Emilia Gould acutely senses this painful plight:

> It was as if the inspiration of their early years had left her heart to turn into a wall of silver-bricks, erected by the silent work of evil spirits, between her and her husband. He seemed to dwell alone within a circumvallation of precious metal, leaving her outside with her school, her hospital, the sick mothers and the feeble old men, mere insignificant vestiges of the initial inspiration. (221-222)
>
> With a prophetic vision she saw herself surviving alone the degradation of her young ideal of life, of love, of work–all alone in the Treasure House of the World. (522; also 245)

Greatly disappointed and resentful, she loathes the precious metal and does not intend to learn from the dying Nostromo where its stolen portion is hidden (557, 560); she views the mine as a monstrosity:

> She saw the San Tomé mountain hanging over the Campo, over the whole land, feared, hated, wealthy; more soulless than any tyrant, more pitiless and autocratic than the worst Government; ready to crush innumerable lives in the expansion of its greatness. (521)

Nostromo and Giselle Viola are another pair divided by the silver. Living on the Great Isabel with her father and sister, Giselle feels lonely, misunderstood; she is unable to set a permanent foundation for her happiness with her beloved. Nostromo does not tell her the secret of the treasure and the political aims accomplished by it (see his portrayal in Part 2, Chapter 5). He rejects the girl's suggestion that they leave together at once because he is unwilling to part with the hidden ingots. Capataz de Cargadores dies, having been shot accidentally by Giorgio Viola. This puts an end to his own and his sweetheart's dreams. Thus Emilia Gould and Giselle Viola love partners bewitched by the silver; the enchantment captures both men's feelings and the men themselves.[50]

3. Ethical Isolation

A. Estrangement by Guilt

Conradian loneliness frequently results from moral problems. A transgression places a hero outside the pale, his awareness of it brings about remorse and anxiety and makes a significant imprint upon his personality. He often confides his secret to somebody, trying in this way to lessen his solitude and neutralize his sufferings.[51]

A typical example of mariners' self-imposed ethical seclusion appears in *The Secret Sharer*. Already at the threshold of his sea voyage the narrator (the captain) feels alien in this environment and harbors doubts about his capability to carry out his duties:

> I knew very little of my officers....I had been appointed to the command only a fortnight before. Neither did I know much of the hands forward. All these people had been together for eighteen months or so, and my position was that of the only stranger on board. I mention this because it has some bearing on what is to follow. But what I felt most was my being a stranger to the ship; and if all the truth must be told, I was somewhat of a stranger to myself. (TLS 93; also 110)

His psychological distance from the crew is magnified by Leggatt's unexpected appearance on board and the diversity of opinions on the murder he had committed. All the subordinates definitely condemn this deed (122-123), as does the skipper of the *Sephora,* who regards him as an ordinary criminal and wants to bring him to justice. The culprit's superior does not recognize the "murderer's" crucial role in saving the ship in terrible weather, claiming it was due to providence (117-119). A different viewpoint is represented by the protagonist of *The Secret Sharer* and by the fugitive himself. A praiseworthy characterization of him is already implied in his introductory descriptions, based on first impressions (97-100). Leggatt stresses the critical situation on the *Sephora* during the gale and points out the violation of the professional ethos by both his boss and the mariner he fought and unintentionally killed while merely trying to force him to obey (see Part 2, Chapter 4). He points out their ignoble performance, and that rescuing the vessel rendered him at least partly guiltless. The hero surrenders to the fugitive's reasoning and comes to share his standpoint:

> He appealed to me as if our experiences had been as identical as our clothes. And I knew well enough the pestiferous danger of such a character [the insubordinate seaman] where there are no means of legal repression. And I knew well enough also that my double [Leggatt] there was no homicidal ruffian. (102)

Justification of this act and compassion for the offender's plight lead the principal figure of *The Secret Sharer* to ethical solidarity with him (see the comments on their attitudes in Part 2, Chapter 4). And disagreement with the crew on that matter enhances the protagonist's solitude.

His ethical isolation is magnified by his feeling of dual consciousness, articulated strongly, developing his initial sensation of strangeness toward himself and by his psychological identification with the law breaker. In the initial phase of their acquaintance the hero already views Leggatt as his own alter ego: "In a moment he had concealed his damp body in a sleeping-suit of the same grey-stripe pattern as the one I was wearing and followed me like my double on the poop" (100). Such a relationship is implied by the form of the captain's cabin (which has the shape of an "L," the initial letter of the fugitive's surname) and Leggatt's instinctively entering it in order to hide (as if it were destined for his concealment). The protagonist identifies with Leggatt while the latter relates the story of the *Sephora* and his subsequent escape:

> He was not a bit like me, really; yet, as we stood leaning over my bed-place, whispering side by side, with our dark heads together and our backs to the door, anybody bold enough to open it stealthily would have been treated to the uncanny sight of a double captain busy talking in whispers with his other self. (105)

This sense of unity is transformed into an obsession, becomes the source of his inner crisis:

> All the time the dual working of my mind distracted me almost to the point of insanity. I was constantly watching myself, my secret self, as dependent on my actions as my own personality, sleeping in that bed, behind that door which faced me as I sat at the head of the table. It was very much like being mad, only it was worse because one was aware of it. (113-114)

He experiences oneness with Leggatt during the visit of the skipper of the *Sephora* as well:

> If he had only known how afraid I was of his putting my feeling of identity with the other to the test...he was not a little disconcerted...by something in me that reminded him of the man he was seeking–suggested a mysterious similitude to the young fellow he had distrusted and disliked from the first. (120)

Attachment to the "strangler" thwarts him in the performance of his duties:

> I was not wholly alone with my command; for there was that stranger in my cabin. Or rather, I was not completely and wholly with her. Part of me was absent. That mental feeling of being in two places at once affected me physically as if the mood of secrecy had penetrated my very soul. (125)

The union of these lonely individuals constitutes the key motif of the story (highlighted, for example, in its title and conclusion) and colors all the events and the hero's reactions to them.

In consequence of ethical solidarity and psychological identification with Leggatt, the narrator assumes a line of action aiming at rescuing him. He confines the visitor in his cabin, then enables him to leave the ship by navigating it close to land to let him swim to shore. Such deeds bring the risk of discovery and disgrace and endanger his professional career: it would certainly be ruined if the "murderer" is detected or the ship is wrecked

(135).[52] The performance of both main characters brings about their separation from the environment as well; they seem to oppose all the world, people, and nature:

> The Sunday quietness of the ship was against us; the stillness of air and water around her was against us; the elements, the men were against us–everything was against us in our secret partnership; time itself–for this could not go on forever. The very trust in Providence was, I suppose, denied to his guilt. (123)

The hero is completely solitary when helping the "assassin." He regards no one among the crew worthy of sharing the secret. The subordinates, ignorant of his motivation, treat him as an eccentric:

> This was the sort of thing that made my terrifically whiskered mate tap his forehead with his forefinger. I had detected him using that gesture while talking on deck with a confidential air to the carpenter. It was too far to hear a word, but I had no doubt that this pantomime could only refer to the strange new captain. (128; also 128-129 other extracts)

Astonishment and terror on board culminate when, for completely incomprehensible reasons, he risks destruction of the craft by commanding the crew to direct it close to coast:

> At noon I gave no orders for a change of course, and the mate's whiskers became much concerned and seemed to be offering themselves unduly to my notice....The stare of extreme surprise imparted an air of ferocity also to his eyes, and he looked truly terrific for a moment. (133-134; also 133-135 other passages, 139-141)

After a short period of "symbiosis" with his protector, Leggatt reenters the world to live alone with his mystery and to receive punishment, proudly and honorably (141-143). Thus his ethical estrangement is continued after his departure from the ship: he is a typical Conradian outcast who, having committed an offense, must start a new life with the weight of guilt and tread a wanderer's path (107, 143). He aims at dignified repentance, at avoiding humiliating capture (109), and delivery to court, which he deems incompetent to judge his case (see Part 2, Chapter 4).[53]

The protagonist of *The Shadow-Line,* too, is isolated by the brand of guilt: he did not control the ship's medicine chest and ignored the doctor's warning. He hastily set out to sea, which brought about the return of his crew's illness (see also the comments on his conduct in Part 2, Chapter 4). The master constantly blames himself for the sufferings of his mariners, who fulfill their duties in spite of exhaustion:

> I had to bear within me a tumult of suffering, vitality, doubt, confusion, self-reproach, and an indefinite reluctance to meet the horrid logic of the situation. (SL 92-93)
> No confessed criminal had ever been so oppressed by his sense of guilt. (96; also 95, 98, 100, 111, 121, 125-126, 129)

The captain is the only healthy man on board (except for Ransome, the cook), which magnifies his anguish and additionally separates him from his subordinates:

> I stood amongst them like a tower of strength, impervious to disease and feeling only the sickness of my soul. I waited for some time fighting against the weight of my sins, against my sense of unworthiness... (109)
> I felt ashamed of having been passed over by the fever which had been preying on every man's strength but mine, in order that my remorse might be the more bitter, the feeling of unworthiness more poignant, and the sense of responsibility heavier to bear. (117)

The commanding officer's isolation in *The Tale* assumes a similar shape. He is unable to find out whether the steamship, which is commanded by the Northman, is immobilized because of having lost its way and having suffered damage to its engines, or whether it is trying to complete a secret warlike mission. The second possibility is suggested neither by the inspection of the craft nor by the conversation with its master (there is no irregularity within its cargo, papers, and log), although this does not put an end to the hero's doubts either: "I can't suspect him. Yet why was he lying with steam up in this fog–and then, hearing us come in, why didn't he give some sign of life? Why? Could it be anything else but a guilty conscience?" (TH 75; also 77). Convinced intuitively that the Northman is guilty, he sets a course that leads to shipwreck. Nonetheless, the protagonist is not sure whether he acted correctly: "He steamed out–ran on it–and went down. So he had spoken the truth. He did not know where he was. But it proves nothing. Nothing either way. It may have been the only truth in all his story. And yet..." (80). He feels this uncertainty all his life; it gives rise to a sense of guilt and remorse (80-81), which are particularly painful because of "his passion for truth, his horror of deceit, his humanity." (81; see too the comments on this character's attitude in Part 2, Chapter 4).[54]

Captain Whalley in *The End of the Tether* undergoes self-inflicted ethical isolation as well (see his delineation in Part 2, Chapters 4 and 5). Even the past separates him from the company of the steamship *Sofala:* he belongs to the first generation of imperial seamen, pioneers of trade and civilization. This biography is completely foreign to his subordinates, who belong to the next generation of "sea servants." His distance from the crew is determined principally by the secret of his failing eyesight, which he carefully conceals from Massy, the co-owner of the *Sofala,* and the other mariners, since he wants to keep his post until the termination of the engagement. The captain speaks openly only to Van Wyk, the only acquaintance he regards as respectable and trustworthy. Whalley, going blind and acting against the principles of professional conduct, retains the command of the vessel. He relies on intuition and experience, as well as on the Malay Serang's skill. His secret is discovered by Sterne, the mate, just before the last voyage in the contract period.

Estrangement by guilt also determines the plight of the commander-owner of the tugboat in *Falk.*[55] In a critical predicament–on a drifting steamer with no hope of rescue, and among a company tormented by hunger–Falk engaged in cannibalism (on his actions, see also Part 2, Chapter 4). This deed has left a permanent imprint upon his psyche, producing a sense of sin, pricks of conscience, and an inferiority complex. The tugboat master becomes a vegetarian, since meat dishes recall the situation on the *Borgmester Dahl* and his infamous performance. The mystery is confided to nobody, which leads to various false and unfavorable interpretations of his conduct and enhances his isolation in the marine milieu. Falk is a recluse and avoids social contacts: the narrator (commander of an iron barque) views meetings with him as the "limited intercourse of nods and grunts" (TOS 167), his "idea of...courting, seemed to consist precisely in sitting silently for hours in the vicinity of the beloved object" (201). He is unable to stand the pressure of loneliness and discloses his secret to the prospective wife and her protector Hermann. Thanks to the narrator's mediation this confession is received with understanding and does not hinder his marriage.

In Conrad's works there are other seamen estranged by former transgressions. Big Brierly–an assessor in the processing of the *Patna* fugitives in *Lord Jim*–experiences unease. Marlow speculates that the court proceedings remind him of some blemish from his own past, which makes his enjoyment of general respect unbearable (LJ 58-59; see also Part 2, Chapter 4). Davidson in *Because of the Dollars* feels responsible for the killing of Laughing Anne, who had warned him of the planned theft of the money in transit:

> And while he was rendering these last services to the dead, the desolation of that life and the atrocious wretchedness of its end cried aloud to his compassion, whispered to him in tones of self-reproach. He ought to have handled the warning she had given him in another way. (WT 207)

Bunter in *The Black Mate* is isolated by a secret: he hides his advanced age from the commander and crew–dyeing his grey hair black–and feels remorse because of this trick (TH 95-96, 109; see also Part 2, Chapter 4). The chief officer's estrangement is increased by his superior's incessant persecutions, which are aimed at getting him to believe in the existence of spirits. Running short of hair dye and being in danger of disclosure, Bunter uses his superior's obsession an attributes the sudden greying of his hair to ghosts.[56]

The voluntary ethical isolation of the protagonist of *Lord Jim*[57] resembles, in many respects, the cases of mariners' estrangement by guilt discussed above–especially the situation of the captain and Leggatt in *The Secret Sharer*. Jim's drama is initially set against the marine environment, and later, in the "kingdom" of Patusan, cut off by tropical forests. In both cases environmental isolation results. As the chief mate of the *Patna,* he indulges in reveries and proves incapable of undertaking effective, honorable action in a crisis: with the master and two engineers, he leaves the sinking steamship and her passengers (see the comments of Jim's conduct in Part 1, Chapter 2 and Part 2, Chapter 4). This act is the calamity of his life: according to Marlow, he "had indeed jumped into an everlasting deep hole. He had tumbled from a height he could never scale again" (LJ 112). It brings the runaways absolute condemnation at the trial and by the sea community, which puts them outside the pale. Such an evaluation is conveyed, for instance, in Captain O'Brien's conversation with Egström:

> Skunks! ...It's no laughing matter. It's a disgrace to human natur'–that's what it is. I would despise being seen in the same room with one of those men...and I wouldn't care to have them here myself, so you're quite safe in this room....I am going to quit. It stinks here now. (193-194)

Jim's exclusion from the seamen's world is emphasized by Marlow, who calls him "a straggler yearning inconsolably for his humble place in the ranks" (223-225). According to the French lieutenant of the gunboat that towed the *Patna* to Aden, the young culprit's tragedy consists principally in the loss of his good reputation (148). General repulsion cuts Jim off. He feels his isolation acutely during the examination of the *Patna* affair:

> While his utterance was deliberate, his mind positively flew round and round the serried circle of facts that had surged up all about him to cut him off from the rest of his kind: it was like a creature that, finding itself imprisoned within an enclosure of high stakes, dashed round and round, distracted in the night, trying to find a weak spot, a crevice, a place to

> scale, some opening through which it may squeeze itself and escape. (31)

He might have avoided turning up in court (as the other escapees did), yet he desired undergoing a public abasement as penance for his offense. He does not regard the jury as capable of passing an adequate verdict upon his actions and analyzes his transgression in his own conscience, in dialogue with himself (see Part 2, Chapter 4).

In order to lessen the anguish of solitude Jim tries to find a confidante to whom he can present his interpretation of the events. He wants understanding and at least partial justification. This role is filled by Marlow, who mistrusts the court version of the events. He treats his younger colleague with friendliness and sees him in a rather good light (on such portrayal, see in Part 2, Chapter 4). Thus Marlow's relationship to Jim is analogous to that of the captain's with Leggatt in *The Secret Sharer*. The mentor notices the "criminal's" loneliness and its possible destructive influence upon his future (174, 177); therefore he finds him a job, hoping it will turn his attention from fantastic dreams and defeats, permit his rehabilitation, and terminate his moral banishment. The law-breaker appreciates this help: "I always thought that if a fellow could begin with a clean slate....And now you...in a measure...yes...clean slate" (185). Thanks to his confrère's attitude, the hero is no longer in absolute disgrace. He regains a little of his sense of bond with people. Marlow's goodwill diminishes slightly the chasm separating him from the glorious marine fraternity from which he was dismissed so unfortunately.

Yet Jim's confidante's fellow-feeling does not eliminate his isolation. Afterwards, taking successive jobs in various places, he continues to carry the burden of his vicious behavior–the secret that cannot be imparted to or understood by anybody. For all except Marlow he remains the former chief mate of the *Patna*, one of those responsible for the disaster. The protagonist's misfortune consists mainly in the fact that wherever he settles, somebody remembers the *Patna* after a time, which makes him have to leave. Such is the end of his employment as ship chandler's water clerk in various Eastern ports (e.g., with Egström and Blake), in a rice mill, with the Yucker Brothers charterers and teak merchants in Bangkok, with De Jongh, and in other occupations (3-5, 188-189, 193-200). The past guilt repeatedly estranges Jim from honest people, follows him all his life, thwarts his attempts at regaining his honor, turns him into an outcast endeavoring ineffectively to wipe out the stain:

> When the fact broke through the incognito he would leave suddenly the seaport where he happened to be at the time and go to another–generally further east....He retreated in good order towards the rising sun, and the fact followed him casually but inevitably. (4-5)
> He was indeed unfortunate, for all his recklessness could not carry him out from under the shadow. (197)

After many failures of this kind Marlow concluded that the scandal, known to all people connected with the sea, would "capture" the culprit sooner or later in every place on the earth: "It was almost pathetic to see him go about in sunshine hugging his secret, which was known to the very up-country logs on the river" (198). He tries to prevent Jim from having even more serious troubles (200). Marlow decides to isolate him completely from mariners' society: acting on Brierly's advice and Stein's suggestion, he sends him to Patusan, an area tightly separated from the world by geographical barriers. Initially Jim, now Tuan (Lord), achieves astounding success there, fulfilling his desire to realize sublime ideals: he becomes the powerful and generally worshipped ruler of the natives (175, 269, 274; on Jim the colonial see Part 2, Chapter 5). His feat also seems to consist in overcoming his tragic destiny, in escaping from the torturing sin: "he seemed to have come very near at last to mastering his fate" (274), "at last mastered his fate" (324). It restores the hero's peace of mind and atones for his wrongdoing. In Patusan he begins to forget his distress and gets back a sense of self-worth and prestige:

> I am satisfied he [confesses)...nearly. I've got to look only at the face of the first man that comes along, to regain my confidence. (306)
> In this simple form of assent to his will lies the whole gist of the situation; their creed, his truth; and the testimony to that faithfulness which made him in his own eyes the equal of the impeccable men who never fall out of the ranks. (393; also 333)

However, in spite of these exploits and of the healing of the psychic wounds caused by the Patua disaster, the protagonist feels acute loneliness. He is cut off from his subordinates by the chasms of race, culture, mentality. Marlow's visit makes him aware of his expulsion from the freedom of the marine domain (331-333). This shows especially in the axiologically colored opposition "stagnant superheated air; the smell of mud, of marsh, the primeval smell of fecund earth, [which] seemed to sting [the] faces" of the forests, and the all-pervading freshness of the idealized sea (331). Jim's ethical seclusion in Patusan mostly involves the need to live alone with his disreputable secret. No one among the natives can become his confidante, can comprehend it: "All these people [he asserts] who would do anything for me, can never be made to understand? Never! ...And yet they can never know the real, real truth..." (305; also 306). The hero's isolation is highlighted particularly in the final, heart-rending phase of the novel:

> Loneliness was closing on him. People had trusted him with their lives–only for that; and yet they could never, as he had said, never be made to understand him. (409)
> [Brown's and his companions'] exact relation to their own white man they [the Patusan inhabitants] could never understand. Even for those simple minds poor Jim remains under a cloud. (414)

The tremendous distance from the autochthones makes Tuan's genuine communication with them impossible. This is manifest in their treatment of his as almost a god:

> I can't [Marlow says] with mere words convey to you the impression of his total and utter isolation. I know, of course, he was in every sense alone of his kind there, but the unsuspected qualities of his nature had brought him in such close touch with his surroundings that his isolation seemed only the effect of his power. His loneliness added to his stature. There was nothing within sight to compare him with, as though he had been one of those exceptional men who can be only measured by the greatness of their fame... (272)
>
> He appeared like a creature not only of another kind but of another essence. Had they not seen him come up in a canoe they might have thought he had descended upon them from the clouds. (229)

Jim does not disclose his past even to Jewel, the only person who eases his solitude (299-300, 393).[58]

Nevertheless, even in Patusan the young dreamer is overtaken by the *Patna* disgrace, which destroys his happy existence. His past sin is recalled to him by Brown, who arrives there accidentally, also dismissed from the sea brotherhood. (Having stolen a Spanish schooner, he and his accomplices escape a trial as "outcasts, men without country" 366). In dialogue with Jim the runaway constantly emphasizes their similarities. His numerous utterances seem to refer to the local ruler's infamous action:

> 'There are my men in the same boat–and, by God, I am not the sort to jump out of trouble and leave them in a d——d lurch,' I said....'Have we met to tell each other the story of our lives?' I asked him. 'Suppose you begin....Keep it to yourself. I know it is no better than mine....I won't ask you what scared you into this infernal hole... (382-383)
>
> And there ran through the rough talk a vein of subtle reference to their common blood, an assumption of common experience; a sickening suggestion of common guilt, of secret knowledge that was like a bond of their minds and of their hearts. (387; also 386-387 other excerpts)

Tuan is assured the newcomer knows his secret. He feels humiliated when such a loathsome creature appeals to him in the name of parallel transgressions. He breaks down when somebody comes reminding him of his crime and estrangement, even to this secluded realm (the "planet" of Patusan): "These were the emissaries with whom the world he had renounced was pursuing him in his retreat. White men from 'out there' where he did not think himself good enough to live" (385). There is no other place for Jim to flee from his ill fortune and self-inflicted isolation. He decides that self-sacrifice is the only way of braving his tragic destiny, of not surrendering to it. Therefore he faces Doramin, to take death honorably and to triumph over his fate (410, 415-416).[59]

There is an analogous shape to the self-imposed ethical isolation of the protagonist in *Karain,* the native lord of a geographically separated area and its tribal inhabitants.[60] Initially Karain dramatizes his life: he assumes an actor's pose (TU 4, 6), and his domain is like a stage–the setting for a performance (6-9). Nevertheless, this image of the omnipotent sovereign, playing the central role in the "theater" of the fictional world, is one-sided. The narrator frequently alludes to the hero's secret, which clearly contrasts with the splendor of his royalty:

> He was ornate and disturbing, for one could not imagine what depth of horrible void such an elaborate front could be worthy to hide. (6)
> It was only on board the schooner...that Karain seemed to forget the strange obsession that wound like a black thread through the gorgeous pomp of his public life. (12; also 8-9, 11-12)

Karain's true personality, hidden behind the mask, is frequently suggested by the mysterious figure of the sword bearer, the confidante who constantly accompanies the ruler:

> He...seemed weary, not with age, but with the possession of a burdensome secret of existence. (5)
> The old fellow, impenetrable and weary, was always there. He shared his food, his repose, and his thoughts; he knew his plans, guarded his secrets; and, impassive behind his master's agitation, without stirring the least bit, murmured above his head in a soothing tone some words difficult to catch. (12)

During his visits to the schooner the principal character is no longer the proud and majestic masters relishing infinite power, the star in the "playhouse" of his "state," but an ordinary human being, who displays common weaknesses, apprehension, and pain: "But it was at night that he talked openly, forgetting the exactions of his stage" (10; also 11). Karain's self is revealed in the second part of the story when he comes on board in panic at night during a rainstorm. Encouraged by the white mariners' kind and compassionate behavior, the protagonist lays bare his secret, the source of his unrest and fear. He tells the story of his friendship with Pata Matara, whose sister, acting against the will of her family and tribe, eloped with a Dutch trader. Matara swore to find them to take revenge on the mischief maker, and Karain decided to accompany him in his quest, which was very long and arduous, abounding in dangers, afflictions, and crises. Eventually they succeeded, but at the crucial moment the hero, under the hypnotic impact of the woman's image, unexpectedly shot not at her lover, but at Matara. This deed gave rise to a sense of guilt and pangs of conscience., to self-inflicted ethical isolation. (The importance of this deed is stressed by the subtitle, *A Memory,* which denotes not only the seamen's recollection of Karain but, above all, his remembrance of the past sin). Thus Karain's enigma accounts for his strange conduct: for his unexpected anxieties, which are incompatible with an actor's mien and a ruler's stateliness and unlimited power:

> He had a dislike of an open space behind him. It was more than a dislike–it resembled fear, a nervous preoccupation of what went on where he could not see. This, in view of the evident an fierce loyalty that surrounded him, was inexplicable...even during the most important interviews, Karain would often give a start. (11-12)

The autocrat's confession reveals great superstitiousness and dependence on fancies. At first he is a slave of Matara's sister's phantom, which enables him to retain composure and persist in the pursuit:

> She never left me [he recollects]. She shared the warmth of our fire, she sat on my couch of leaves, she swam on the sea to follow me....I saw

> her!... She gave me courage to bear weariness and hardships. Those were times of pain, and she soothed me. (34-35)

Fear of parting with this illusion becomes a direct cause of the fatal deed (37). The vision of his dead companion constantly reminds Karain of his crime and causes suffering (41-42). However, he fortunately meets the old Malay, to whom he imparts the confidential matter, and whose friendship becomes an effective therapy for his hallucinations:

> To me he was father, mother, protection, refuge and peace....He said over me words of compassion, of wisdom, of prayer. He warded from me the shade of the dead....Doubtless he could command a spirit stronger than the unrest of my dead friend, and again I had peace... (42)

The sword bearer, who accompanies the hero constantly, functions as an amulet to protect him from his recollections, anxiety, and remorse. The words muttered by the confidante, or even his mere presence act like a charm to bring back the protagonist's peace of mind (11, 17). Absolute dependence on the sovereign's mentality upon his attendant leads to a severe psychological crisis after the sword bearer's death. Unable to shake off Matara's spirit, which haunts and torments him, the terrified potentate flees onto the craft:

> Of course it had been a long swim off to the schooner; but his face showed another kind of fatigue, the tormented weariness, the anger and the fear of a struggle against a thought, an idea–against something that cannot be grappled, that never rests–a shadow, a nothing, unconquerable and immortal, that preys upon life. (23)[61]

In order to restore his self-possession, the white seamen create a fetish to neutralize the impact of the apparition. One of them, Hollis, rummages in his box, creating a unique atmosphere of suspense. The visitor is impressed and perceives the objects in the box as magical (48-49). Hollis picks from the box a Jubilee sixpence with the image of the British empress and gives it to the native, solemnly declaring it to be the talisman capable of defending him from the specter, self-reproach, and evocation of guilt. Karain, fascinated by the figure of the queen and her enormous power (12-13, 49), yields to the persuasion and trustingly accepts the gift.[62] The amelioration of the painful aftermath of his offense and the change in his mood are reflected in the aspect of nature (51).

The self-imposed ethical isolation of the principal character in *The Lagoon*–a Malay afflicted by his brother's death[63]–is analogous. Arsat imparts his secret to the white visitor; the confession coincides with is beloved's (Diamelen's) death. Arsat recalls how, fleeing their country and in danger of being caught, his brother decided to stay behind and ward off the chase to ensure the lovers' escape (it was achieved at the cost of the brother's life). The hero always remembers his brother's death cry. Still, he pushed off in the canoe and paddled away with Diamelen. Having lost his brother when he failed even to try to help, he was filled with agony and tormented by pangs of conscience and his separation from virtuous people (TU 201-204). Thus Arsat's calamity consists in the loss of both his sweetheart and his nearest relative and in his own ethical seclusion.[64]

Estrangement brought about by compunction and a sense of guilt appears in Conrad's political novels as well. Already the expository portrayal highlights the protagonist's solitude in *Under Western Eyes:*

> Officially and in fact without a family...He was as lonely in the world as a man swimming in the deep sea. The word Razumov was the mere label of a solitary individuality. There were no Razumovs belonging to him anywhere. His closest parentage was defined in the statement that he was a Russian. (UWE 10-11).

Razumov's isolation acquires, however, primarily an ethical dimension. His colleague, Victor Haldin, unexpectedly arrives in his flat after the successful attempt on the life of the President of the Repressive Commission and begs for shelter and assistance in escaping. The hero, not approving of this kind of activity faces a dilemma: to aid him or to deliver him up to the authorities.

Initially he tries to fulfill the visitor's wish, but afterwards changes his mind (partly by accident–he is unable to communicate with Ziemianitch, the sled driver Haldin asked for). The principal character is sure to act correctly from the political point of view (see the delineation of his ideology in Part 2, Chapter 5), although he does not have this conviction when evaluating his deed in moral terms. His denunciation bring on anguish and feelings of guilt; it determines his voluntary ethical isolation. He becomes incapable of living and working normally:

> He had a distinct sensation of his very existence being undermined in some mysterious manner, of his moral supports falling away from him one by one. (76-77)
>
> Whenever he went abroad he felt himself at once closely involved in the moral consequences of his act. It was there that the dark prestige of the Haldin mystery fell on him, clung to him like a poisoned robe it was impossible to fling off. (299; also 67-68)

Notes and books, so precious to him, turn out to be "a mere litter of blackened paper–dead matter–without significance or interest" (68). He is overpowered by "a strange dread of the unexpected" and annihilation of energy (72); he forfeits his self-possession during his examination by Councilor Mikulin. His suffering is worsened by the necessity of living alone with the stain; in spite of his treasonous act, his prestige in his milieu does not decline.[65]

Razumov's torments become more intense during his stay in Geneva, where he meets Haldin's sister and mother. Under compulsion by the tsarist authorities he spies on the Russian émigré opposition, which precludes his imparting the confidential matter to anyone:

> 'It's intolerable!' Razumov could only speak in gasps....
>
> He made a gesture of despair. It was not his courage that failed him. The choking fumes of falsehood had taken him by the throat–the thought of being condemned to struggle on and on in that tainted atmosphere without the hope of ever renewing his strength by a breath of fresh air. (269)

Moreover, he fails to conceal his agony and frequently shows it in his contacts with the narrator and Nathalie Haldin. She does not sense the true reason of this behavior, though she considers him "to be a man who has suffered more from his thoughts than from evil fortune" (168). He tries to break out of his loneliness by writing a diary, which realizes the inner need to disclose his mind, to make a confession:

> The perplexities and the complex terrors–I may say–of this sleeplessness are recorded in the document I was to see later–the document which is the main source of this narrative. (192)
> Mr. Razumov looked at it...as a man looks at himself in a mirror... (214)

Nevertheless, this way of externalizing his feelings does not diminish his misery. Unable to stand the psychological pressure the protagonist unburdens his conscience first to Nathalie Haldin, then to the assembly of expatriate revolutionaries. Thus, in spite of their cruel revenge (Nikita breaks his eardrums), he overcomes his psychological separation and puts an end to his inner unrest: "I made myself [Razumov says] free from falsehood, from remorse–independent of every single human being on this earth" (368).[66]

Dr. Monygham and the title figure in *Nostromo* are isolated by transgressions, too (see the depiction of their political performance in Part 2, Chapter 5). Monygham, imprisoned by the tyrant's henchmen, had broken under torture and betrayed alleged fellow conspirators (N 311-312, 370-374). Memory of this accompanies his later actions, which aim at atonement (431, 438-439, 461).[67] And Nostromo lives alone with the stolen treasure and the secret of his infamous performance.[68]

B. Ethical Separation of Characters Who Consider Themselves Guiltless

Sometimes strictures on conduct are regarded as undeserved, and neither pangs of conscience nor awareness of being at fault are revealed. In *A Smile of Fortune* the inhabitants of the Pearl of the Ocean treat Jacobus's romance with the circus woman (from which Alice was born) as a scandal, widely manifesting their indignation (TLS 37-39, 51). In this situation the heroine becomes "very helpless and condemned to moral solitude by the verdict of a respectable community" (64). Her father is a man despised by the milieu (40, 60, 75), and both are beyond the pale as

> a lonely pair of castaways, on a desert island; the girl sheltering in the house as if it were a cavern in a cliff, and Jacobus going out to pick up a living for both on the beach–exactly like two shipwrecked people who always hope for some rescuer to bring them back at last into touch with the rest of mankind. (39)

Jacobus reacts to the scorn by not having any social contacts and enclosing their garden with a wall beyond which Alice may not pass. This brings about her almost complete seclusion and inability to comprehend the events taking place outside their habitation: "The girl had learned nothing, she had never listened to a general conversation, she knew nothing, she had heard of nothing" (60). The newspapers provided for captains shape her inadequate idea of people, which is based on an image of England (the subject of many of the articles) as being the size of her island:

> As her mind could not grasp the meaning of any matters treated there...she had formed for herself a notion of the civilized world as a scene of murders, abductions, burglaries, stabbing afrays, and every sort of desperate violence....One could not make her understand that these horrors on which she fed her imagination were lost in the mass of orderly life like a few drops of blood in the ocean. (60-61)

Alice is incapable of experiencing elementary human feelings as well: "She seemed, indeed, as unaware of shame as of anything else in the world....What could she know of death–she who knew nothing of life?" (67). She is in a state of lethargy and does not react to others' actions or outside stimuli. The narrator (captain) fails in his attempts at making psychological contact with her and putting an end to her solitude.

Willems, in *An Outcast of the Islands,* is depicted as self-confident, vain, and egocentric. He does not feel responsible for his own estrangement either (OI 3-5).[69] Consequence to some fraud he loses his job and is expelled from the house by his wife (the boss's illegitimate child), and faces the necessity of changing his environment and starting a new life:

> And now the work of long years was destroyed utterly. What would become of him? ...His past was so utterly gone from him... (23)
> It was some other man. Another man was coming back. A man without a past, without a future, yet full of pain and shame and anger....Would he ever sleep, and where? He felt as if he was the outcast of all mankind... (30)

He considers his own position uncensurable–he does not feel guilty. He complains about his misfortune, and resents his family and master (22-23, 266-267). The protagonist's suicidal desperation is ended by Lingard, who sends him to Sambir and gives him a chance to rehabilitate himself. But the newcomer is isolated; he cannot find a place in this settlement pulsing with life and activity (65; see too the portrayal of Willems the colonizer in Part 2, Chapter 5):

> [He] felt a bitter and savage rage at the cruel consciousness of his superfluity, of his uselessness....He heard the reproach of his idleness in the murmurs of the river, in the unceasing whisper of the great forests. Round him everything stirred, moved, swept by in a rush; the earth under his feet and the heavens above his head. The very savages around him strove....And it was only himself that seemed to be left outside the scheme of creation in a hopeless immobility filled with tormenting anger and with ever-stinging regret. (65)

In Sambir his humiliating experiences and a sense of loneliness permanently dominate his thoughts. He separates himself from the whites, because he is deeply convinced of his innocence: " 'I shall never return,' interrupted Willems. 'I have done with my people. I am a man without brothers. Injustice destroys fidelity' " (131). Renunciation of his own race facilitates his contact with a native woman, Aissa, which evolves first into amorous passion, then into mutual enmity. The betrayal of his protector's interests distances the protagonist from his sole friend and helper, the only link with the white world. It increases his self-inflicted ethical isolation:

> On Lingard's departure solitude and silence closed round Willems; the cruel solitude of one abandoned by men; the reproachful silence which surrounds an outcast ejected by his kind, the silence unbroken by the slightest whisper of hope; an immense and impenetrable silence that swallows up without echo the murmur of regret and the cry of revolt. (327)

He does not feel responsible for the self-evident wrong done to "Rajah-Laut" by piloting Abdulla's ship into Sambir (269-270). In the epilogue of his story, as well as in its earlier parts, the principal character does not repent, a fact which is ironically commented on by the narrator:[70]

> The bitter peace of the abandoned clearings entered his heart, in which nothing could live now but the memory and hate of his past. Not remorse. In the breast of a man possessed by the masterful consciousness of his individuality with its desires and its rights; by the immovable conviction of his own importance, of an importance so indisputable and final that it clothes all his wishes, endeavours, and mistakes with the dignity of unavoidable fate, where there could be no place for such a feeling as that of remorse. (327)

In Conrad's works there are also others who are isolated by transgressions without feeling at fault: James Wait and Donkin in *The Nigger of the "Narcissus,"*[71] Brown and the *Patna* fugitives (except Jim) in *Lord Jim,* Paul Crocodile in *An Anarchist,* Tomassov in *The Warrior's Soul,* and John Kemp in *Romance* (see their portrayal in Part 2, Chapters 4 and 5). Evaluation of the characters' guiltless stance is ambivalent: sometimes the narrator undermines by means of irony a character's conviction of his own virtue (Willems, James Wait, Brown, and the *Patna* culprits), whereas in other cases (Jacobus and Alice, Paul Crocodile, Tomassov, John Kemp) he views their censure as unjust.

C. Confidantes' Loneliness

Self-imposed ethical isolation affects those who share others' mysteries as well. This is best exemplified by Marlow, the narrator in *Heart of Darkness,* who alone arrives at the accurate perception of Kurtz's and his fellow colonizers' practices (see the comments on them in Part 2, Chapter 5). Marlow's loneliness is emphasized constantly in the course of his journey. He already senses it on the ship heading for Africa (YNTOS 61), and especially at the outer and Central Stations, where nobody (except for the Swedish captain) shares his evaluation of the surrounding reality, his comprehension of the Europeans' repulsive activity. The steamship commander's solitude is enhanced by his awareness of human insignificance in confrontation with mighty equatorial nature. He has to overcome by himself all the difficulties that crop up in the course of the expedition (the damaged steamship, the fainting companion, the Negro carriers' rebellion), and especially when navigating among shallows (see Part 2, Chapter 4). The pilgrims on board display enmity, suspecting him of liking Kurtz and wanting to thwart their exploitation of the natives; the voyage has for them a goal different from his (95). He reciprocates the pilgrims' contempt by calling their excited conversations "immense jabber, silly, atrocious, sordid, savage, or simply mean, without any kind of sense" (115). He solitarily cherishes his disapproval of Kurtz's activities, even though the agent's infamous conduct is censured neither by the other colonizers (who view him as a rival in getting maximum profit at all costs), nor by his companion the Russian, who worships him as much as the Africans do.

Marlow becomes Kurtz's sole loyal friend. He is entrusted with the care of the packet of papers and the report for the guidance of the International Society for the Suppression of

Savage Customs with the postscript "Exterminate all the brutes!"; the publication of its "corrected" version would damage the author's reputation. Marlow keeps his word: he neither discloses this disgraceful text nor imparts any materials to the representatives of the company. Such behavior is motivated by his aversion to the colonizers and respect for the "most outstanding" agent, who shortly before his death expresses contempt for his own life. Marlow does not open his mind even to Kurtz's Intended, thus preserving her illusion of the beloved's magnanimous, sublime conduct (115, 158-162).[72]

Marlow's voluntary ethical isolation in *Lord Jim* assumes an analogous shape. Initially he is the only one dissatisfied with the official, court version of the *Patna* story. As a result, he is the one to whom Jim unburdens his conscience, presenting his interpretation of the events as well as the thoughts and feelings accompanying them. Later Marlow shares this knowledge and concern for the young culprit with Stein.

Other Conradian isolated confidantes are the narrator (captain) in *Falk,* the recipient of the title character's confession; the protagonist in *The Secret Sharer,* who becomes familiar with the mystery of Leggatt's guilt; the sword bearer in *Karain,* who is the sovereign's mentor and protector; Captain MacWhirr in *Typhoon,* who alone faces the necessity of settling the conflict among the Chinamen; Linda Viola in *Nostromo,* who is filled with envy when she becomes aware of her fiancé's (Capataz de Cagadores) unfaithfulness.

Chapter 3
The Rings of Isolation

1. Interrelationships of Types of Isolation

The multifarious manifestations of Conradian isolation discussed heretofore[1] form configurations of varied complexity. Among them are the simplistic situations, in which only one variant of this motif is applied: at sea, on land, escape into an imaginary realm, in love and marriage, ethical. They are illustrated by the following diagrams:[2]

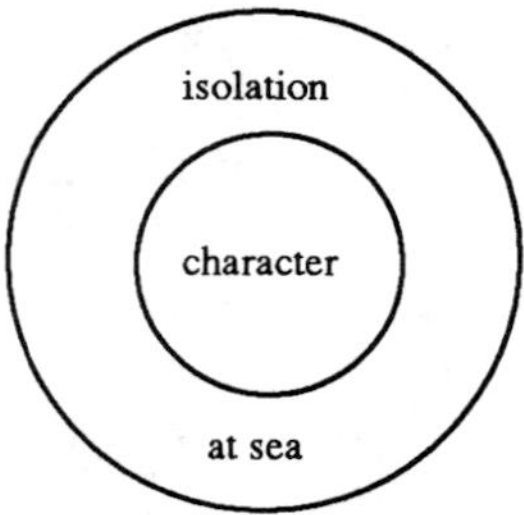

Diagram 1. The crews in *The Nigger of the "Narcissus," Lord Jim, Youth, The End of the Tether, Typhoon, The Secret Sharer, Chance, The Shadow-Line, The Rescue,* the passengers of the schooner-yacht *Hermit* in *The Rescue,* the implied author in *Cobwebs and Gossamer, Well Done, Ocean Travel* and *Christmas Day at Sea.*

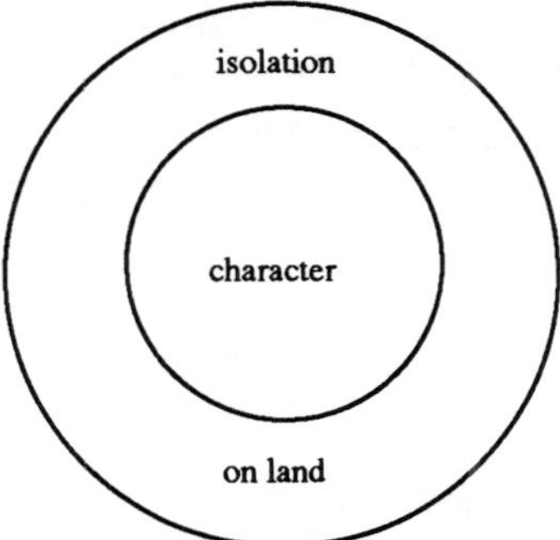

Diagram 2. The Sambir dwellers in *Almayer's Folly* and *An Outcast of the Islands,* the sovereign's subordinates in *Karain,* the people of Patusan and the addressee of Marlow's letter in *Lord Jim,* Mr. Van Wyk in *The End of the Tether,* the characters in *Nostromo* and *The Secret Agent,* Renouard in *The Planter of Malata,* the Carimata autochthones in *The Rescue,* Peyrol and the inhabitants of the Escampobar Farm in *The Rover,* the narrator in *The Inheritors.*

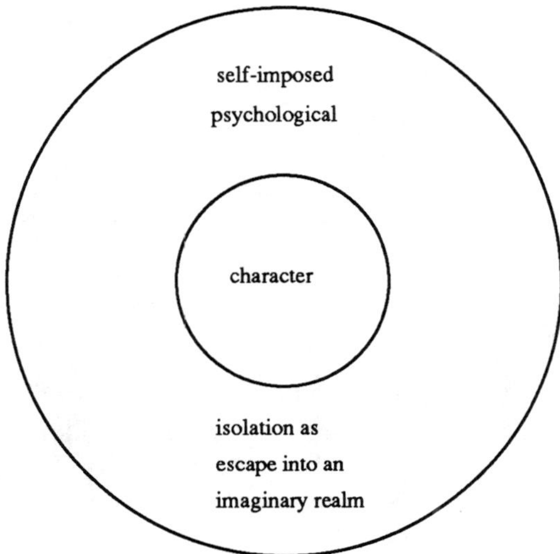

Diagram 3. Lingard in *Almayer's Folly* and *An Outcast of the Islands,* the mentally deficient children in *The Idiots,* Captain

Hagberd in *To-morrow,* the anarchists in *The Informer* and *An Anarchist,* the Count in *Il Conde,* the revolutionaries and the representatives of the émigré opposition in *Under Western Eyes,* Stephen in *The Sisters,* and many female characters.

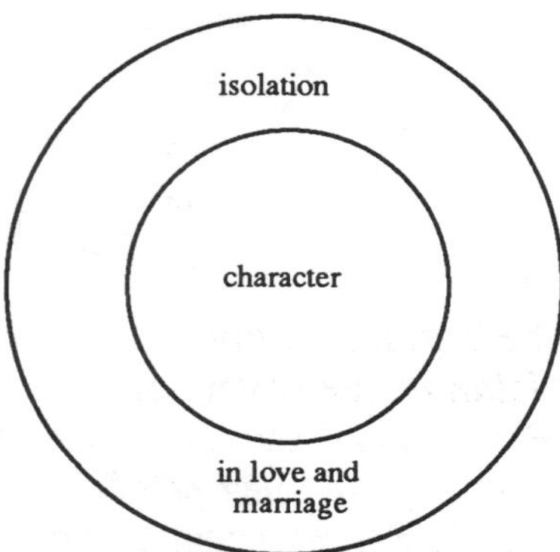

Diagram 4. Amy in *Amy Foster,* Davidson's wife in *Because of the Dollars,* Rita and George in *The Arrow of Gold,* Seraphina in *Romance.*

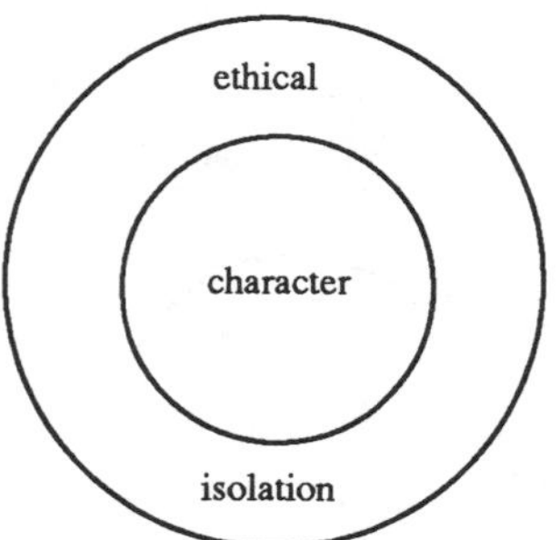

Diagram 5. Marlow, Brierly, and Brown in *Lord Jim,* the narrator (captain of an iron barque) and the commander of the tugboat in *Falk,* Razumov in *Under Western Eyes,* Bunter in *The Black Mate,* Tomassov in *The Warrior's Soul,* the narrator (commanding officer) in *The Tale.*

Numerous other occurrences of this motif display a more elaborate construction, combining external (at sea or on land) with internal distancing (escape into an imaginary realm, in love and marriage, ethical) into two man-centered concentric circles. The particular varieties of this pattern are represented as follows:

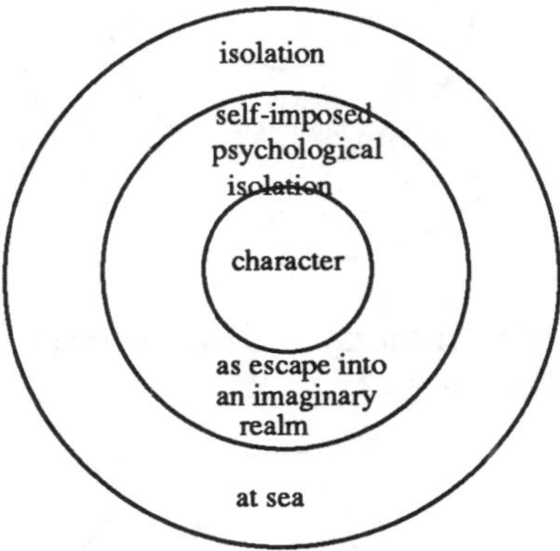

Diagram 6. Marlow in *Youth.*

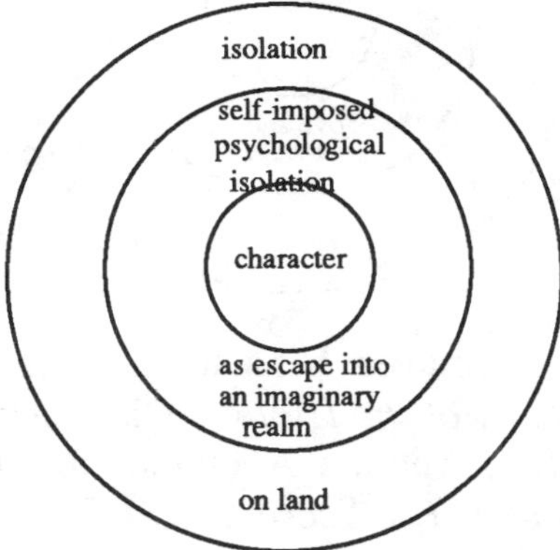

Diagram 7. Kayerts and Carlier in *An Outpost of Progress,* the Russian, the Company's chief accountant, and the other colonizers (except for Kurtz) in *Heart of Darkness,* Giorgio Viola in *Nostromo,* the anarchists and Stevie in *The Secret Agent,* Nelson in *Freya of the Seven Isles,* Scevola in *The Rover.*

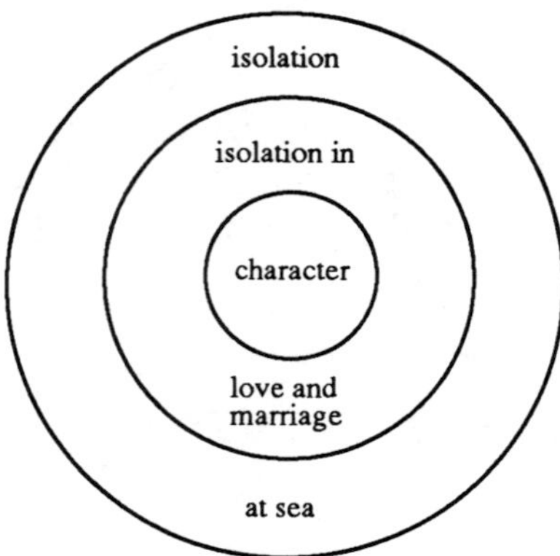

Diagram 8. Captain Anthony and Flora de Barral in *Chance,* Mr. Travers in *The Rescue.*

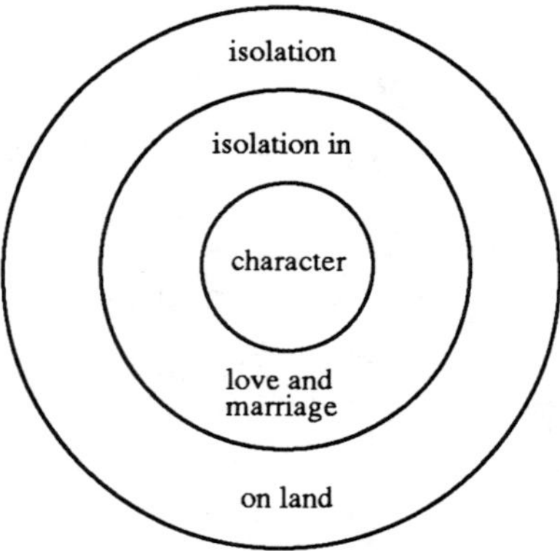

Diagram 9. Mrs. Almayer, Nina and Dain in *Almayer's Folly,* Aissa in *An Outcast of the Islands,* Diamelen in *The Lagoon,* Jewel in *Lord Jim,* Antonia Avellanos and Giselle Viola in *Nostromo,* Winnie in *The Secret Agent,* Freya in *Freya of the Seven Isles,* Lena in *Victory,* Laughing Anne and Bamtz in *Because of the Dollars,* the Herveys in *The Return,* and the Goulds in *Nostromo.*

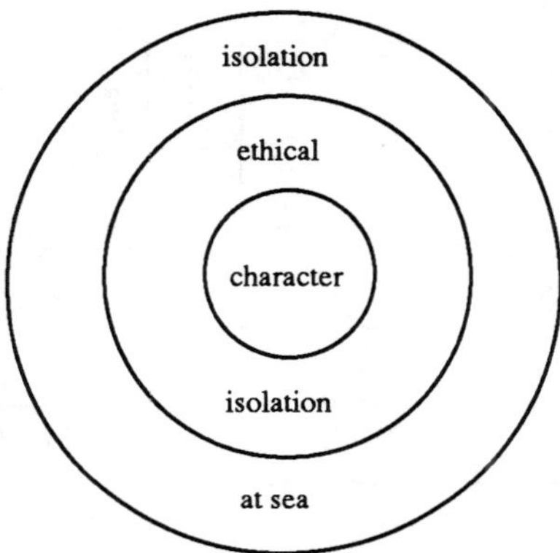

Diagram 10. James Wait and Donkin in *The Nigger of the "Narcissus,"* the *Patna* fugitives in *Lord Jim,* Captain Whalley in *The End of the Tether,* Captain MacWhirr in *Typhoon,* Leggatt in *The Secret Sharer.*

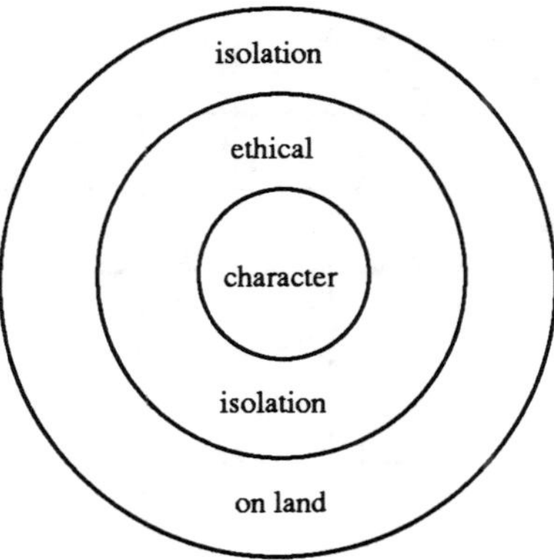

Diagram 11. The sword bearer in *Karain,* Arsat in *The Lagoon,* Marlow in *Heart of Darkness,* Dr. Monygham and Linda Viola in *Nostromo,* Paul Crocodile in *An Anarchist,* Jacobus in *A Smile of Fortune.*

The two-level formations attain still greater intricacy through the coalescence of the several types of geographical, and especially psychological, seclusion. These most complex situations may be tabulated.[3]

Character	Isolation at sea	Isolation on land	Self-imposed psychological isolation as an escape into an imaginary realm	Isolation in love and marriage	Ethical Isolation
Almayer in *Almayer's Folly* and *An Outcast of the Islands*		+	+[4] +	+	
Willems in *An Outcast of the Islands*		+		+	+
Karain in *Karain*		+	+		+
Arsat in *The Lagoon*		+		+	+
Jim in *Lord Jim*	+[5]	+[6]	+	+	+
Kurtz in *Heart of Darkness*		+	+	+	
Kurtz's Intended in *Heart of Darkness*			+	+	
Yanko in *Amy Foster*			+	+	
Martin Decoud in *Nostromo*	+	+	+	+	
Nostromo in *Nostromo*	+	+		+	+
Verloc in *The Secret Agent*		+	+	+	
Alice in *A Smile of Fortune*		+	+		+
Narrator (captain) in *The Secret Sharer*	+		+		+ +[7]
Jasper Allen in *Freya of the Seven Isles*			+	+	
Heyst in *Victory*		+	+	+	
Davidson in *Because of the Dollars*				+	+
Narrator (captain) in *The Shadow-Line*	+		+		+
Edith Travers in *The Rescue*			+	+	
Lingard in *The Rescue*	+	+	+		
John Kemp in *Romance*				+	+

2. Narrators' Penetration to the Truth About Characters and Their Loneliness

Concentric patterning of a fictional world entails specific shaping of the narration. Getting to know an individual, who is situated in the center of such a configuration, requires that the "insulators" separating him from the environment be passed. Such attempts, which constitute one of the most significant aspects of Conradian narration, are stressed in many of his novels and short stories.[8]

The quest for truth about a hero and the essence of his detachment is most prominent in *Lord Jim*. The trial aims exclusively at the reconstruction of events. This is evident both in the witnesses' testimony (e.g., in the report of the commander of the French gunboat that towed the *Patna* to Aden) and in the pronouncements of the judges: "They wanted facts. Facts! They demanded facts...as if facts could explain anything!" (LJ 29). Marlow emphasizes the futility of these proceedings; they are incapable of properly treating the offense and assigning a penalty (see Part 2, Chapter 4, too):[9]

> The examination of the only man able and willing to face it was beating futilely round the well-known fact, and the play of questions upon it was as instructive as the tapping with a hammer on an iron box, were the object to find out what's inside. However, an official inquiry could not be any other thing. Its object was not the fundamental why, but the superficial how, of this affair.
> The young chap could have told them, and, though that very thing was the thing that interested the audience, the questions put to him necessarily led him away from what to me, for instance, would have been the only truth worth knowing. (56; also 56-57 the following passage)

He decides to get to the core of the matter on his own, devoting himself completely to this pursuit.[10] He relies on an intuitive conviction that the protagonist is superior to the other *Patna* escapees, that he does not deserve such a severe verdict and condemnation by the sea community, that his weakness was natural and could befall anyone (42-43, 50-51; see also on Jim and his portrayal by Marlow in Part 2, Chapter 4). The private investigation commences with an examination of the young lawbreaker. His account is regarded as subjective and one-sided, though more trustworthy than the official version, because it comprises not only the culprit's presentation of the events, but his thoughts and feelings as well. These are crucial for a correct explication of the motives of his conduct (113-114, 120-121). The story-teller is not satisfied with the dreamer's account and desires to speak with others involved in the scandal: "The thing was always with me, I was always eager to take opinion on it, as though it had not been practically settled" (159; also 50-51). He interviews the *Patna*'s chief engineer in the hospital, but considers the information obtained completely useless (49-55); he meets the French lieutenant (a boarding officer from the gunboat), and regards his version as tendentious, though valuable in its factual aspect.

Marlow's investigation pertains not only to the leading character's involvement in the *Patna* affair, but also to his subsequent career. A letter from the rice mill owner provides information about the outlaw's performance and departure (187-189), and Egström–about his work in Egström and Blake's firm (192-196). The description of the hero's arrival in Patusan is based on what was related by the elderly headman of a fishing village who piloted him up the river (242-243), and by Tuan himself (chapters 24-25). Jim, too, narrates the story of his stay in the settlement. Some of its parts are expanded and complemented by Jewel and by natives' accounts (transportation of guns up the hill) (266), and the attack upon Sherif Ali's dwelling (269-270). In order to obtain the closest possible approximation to the truth about the tragic conclusion of Jim's rule in Patusan, he interviews many who participated in these events: Jewel and Tamb' Itam, the Malay who brought them to Samarang, the Bugis accompanying Tamb' Itam, and Brown. His own interpretation is built on the basis of the knowledge collected and conveyed in the form of an epistolary confession to one who had listened to the earlier yarn: "I put it down here for you as though I had been an eyewitness. My information was fragmentary, but

I've fitted the pieces together, and there is enough of them to make an intelligible picture" (343).

The plot-constructor is nevertheless aware that, in spite of his zealous and painstaking efforts, he is unable to depict the young dreamer's character and life story in an entirely impartial way:

> I don't pretend I understood him. The views he let me have of himself were like those glimpses through the shifting rents in a thick fog–bits of vivid and vanishing detail, giving no connected idea of the general aspect of a country. They fed one's curiosity without satisfying it; they were no good for purposes of orientation. Upon the whole he was misleading. (76)
>
> It is impossible to see him clearly–especially as it is through the eyes of others that we take our last look at him. (339)
>
> It is when we try to grapple with another man's intimate need that we perceive how incomprehensible, wavering, and misty are the beings that share with us the sight of the stars and the warmth of the sun. It is as if loneliness were a hard and absolute condition of existence... (179-180; also 79, 197, 216, 221, 241, 323, 416)[11]

His constant apologies for the limited reliability of the presentation are not merely a display of the "told-tale" rhetoric, but also of his conviction of the impossibility of fully comprehending another human being's mentality.[12]

Marlow's role in *Chance*–another novel with intricate narration–is analogous to his in *Lord Jim*. He frequently asserts he has founded the story on others' recollections (mostly Powell's), and has built these partial accounts into the ultimate version (C 222, 325-326). This attitude is echoed in *Heart of Darkness*,[13] where the story-teller's journey to the African interior, which constitutes the compositional axis of the plot, is undertaken to penetrate to the essence of Kurtz's isolation and the colonizer's conduct (see on them in Part 2, Chapter 5).[14]

There are also the other Conradian narrators endeavoring to obtain veracity, to accumulate the greatest possible knowledge about characters by passing through the rings insulating them. In *Amy Foster* a country doctor named Kennedy inquires into Yanko's life: his Carpathian experiences and travel, his loneliness on English soil, and his tragic death. His relation of the happenings prior to Yanko's landing, as well as of the periods of courtship and marriage, is based mainly on Goorall's own confession:

> I have been telling you more or less in my own words what I learned fragmentarily in the course of two or three years, during which I seldom missed an opportunity of a friendly chat with him. He told me this story of his adventure... (TOS 117; also 117-118; other extracts)

Yanko's futile attempts to make contact with the locals emerge from their reports and from the opinions circulating in that milieu:

> The next thing we know of him for certain is that he had been hiding in Hammond's pig-pound....Through the rumors of the country-side, which lasted for a good many days after his arrival, we know that the fishermen of West Colebrook had been disturbed and startled by heavy knocks....The driver of Mr. Bradley's milk-cart made no secret of it that he had lashed with his whip at a hairy sort of gypsy fellow....Also three boys confessed afterwards to throwing stones at a funny tramp....All this was the talk of three villages for days; but we have Mrs. Finn's (the wife of Smith's waggoner) unimpeachable testimony....There is no doubt after this of what happened to him. All is certain now: Mrs. Smith's intense terror; Amy Foster's solid conviction....Smith's exasperation... (118-119)

Kennedy plays a crucial role in giving the final shape to the story. He replaces the simple reconstruction of events with his own conjectures and interpretations whenever he is short of reliable information–e.g., when telling about the castaway's first experiences on the land, or about the circumstances that made possible his rescue from the sinking vessel:

> It is possible that a man (supposing he happened to be on deck at the time of the accident) might have floated ashore on that hencoop. He might. I admit it is improbable, but there was the man....This looks as if he had been on deck some time during that night. (123)

The narrative strategy of a search for facts and speculation is combined with sententious utterances generalizing Yanko's and Amy's predicament, since Kennedy's "intelligence is of a scientific order, of an investigating habit, and of that unappeasable curiosity which believes that there is a particle of a general truth in every mystery" (106).

A parallel method is applied in *The Idiots,* where the tragic history of the Bacadou couple and their four mentally deficient offspring is composed from information given by the inhabitants of the neighboring villages:

> I saw them [the idiot children] many times in my wandering about the country....In time the story of their parents shaped itself before me out of the listless answers to my questions, out of the indifferent words heard in wayside inns or on the very road those idiots haunted. Some of it was told by an emaciated and sceptical old fellow with a tremendous whip, while we trudged together over the sands by the side of a two-wheeled cart loaded with dripping seaweed. Then at other times other people confirmed and completed the story: till it stood at last before me, a tale formidable and simple... (TU 58)

The narrator (a teacher of languages in Geneva) in *Under Western Eyes* meets Razumov on frequent occasions, tries to fathom his psyche and way of thinking, and gets access to his diary–the fullest and most reliable source of information, the basis of the communicated version of his life story:

> I turn over for the hundredth time the leaves of Mr. Razumov's record, I lay it aside, I take up the pen–and the pen being ready for its office of setting down black on white I hesitate. (UWE 67)
> These sentiments stand confessed in Mr. Razumov's memorandum of his first interview with Madame de S———. The very words I use in my narrative are written where their sincerity cannot be suspected. (214; also 24, 88, 192, 214 other passages)

The commentator is nevertheless aware of revealing only partial truth about the protagonist. He constantly asserts his inability to comprehend the Eurasian imperial power (impossible for an average European like himself): its tradition, culture, and political mentality, as represented by Razumov and the other Russian characters.

The captain in *A Smile of Fortune* passes through the wall of social prejudices that cause Jacobus's isolation among the inhabitants of the Pearl of the Ocean; he collects abundant evidence, making possible a just evaluation of his conduct, and endeavors to penetrate the mystery of Alice's estrangement and to make contact with her. Davidson in *Victory* investigates the facts concerning the detached pair: in particular he inquires of Schomberg and his guests about the hotel occurrences (the stay of Zangiacomo's band, Lena's and Heyst's escape), and witnesses the heroine's tragic death (the main narrator frequently refers to Davidson's account). The story-teller in *An Anarchist* constantly recollects his own travels to the places in which the reported events happened, and claims to have based his account on verified data:

> I have checked the facts as far as possible. I have turned up the files of French newspapers, and I have also talked with the officer who commands the military guard on the Ile Royale, when in the course of my travels I have reached Cayenne. I believe the story to be in the main true. It is the sort of story that no man, I think, would ever invent about himself... (SS 136)

He relies on Paul Crocodile's report as well, convinced of its veracity: "From personal inquiry I can vouch that the story of the convict mutiny was in every particular as stated by him" (161).[15]

Sometimes information about characters and their solitude is obtained by confidantes taking a passive attitude: in such cases a narrative situation becomes a situation of confession.[16] This method is manifest in *Karain:* the native ruler lets the white mariners know the source of his agony and asks for protection from the phantom persecuting him–this exposure is not directly quoted but related by the plot-constructor; in *The Lagoon,* the white man is told of Arsat's anguish, feelings of guilt and self-imposed ethical separation; in *Il Conde* the count communicates his experiences. In *The Warrior's Soul* Tomassov's revelation constitutes the foundation of the account:

> It was then that I heard most of that–you can't call it a story. The story I have in my mind is not in that. Outpourings, let us call them.
> I would sit quite content to hold my peace, a whole hour perhaps, while Tomassov talked with exaltation. And when he was done I would still hold my peace. (TH 8; also 7-8 other extracts)

In the epilogue it is asserted that it lays bare the real motives for the shooting of De Castel and falsifying the public version, so that the young Russian is condemned for murdering the captive in cold blood. In *The Secret Sharer* and *Falk* the essence of the suffering and moral distancing is disclosed to the narrators, who have not sought such confidence. Thus the captain in *The Secret Sharer* is the only one who learns the entire truth about Leggatt's deed–this makes him evaluate it more adequately. The story teller in *Falk* is the sole figure who understands the tugboat commander's aversion to meat dishes and notices the absurdity of the superficial and biased interpretations of his behavior.

Penetration to the essence of seclusion (mostly ethical) is one of the principal methods of portraying characters in Conrad's literary output. It constitutes a realization of his artistic manifesto, which highlights the reflection of the truth of life as a fundamental task of literary creativity (see "Preface" to *The Nigger of the "Narcissus"*; and *Books,* NLL 6-7; *Alphonse Daudet,* NLL 24; *Stephen Crane,* NLL 50).

Part Two: Ethos

The above considerations evince that estrangement from a milieu, the opposition to its norms and laws–echoing Byron's writings and the creations of Polish Romanticism–constitutes an essential trait of the Conradian hero. He feels powerless, lost in the surrounding nature or society, and maintains a profound conviction of the absurdity and lack of ethical goals in the universe. Yet he must exist under such circumstances, preserve his dignity, and remain faithful to his principles.[1] Nevertheless, this formulation does not imply an extremely pessimistic ideology in the author of *Victory,* a total negation of the sense of living. It treats isolation, experienced by a large majority of Conrad's primary characters, as a natural element of the human predicament,[2] but it admits a possibility of overcoming this situation, or at least of alleviating an all-but-hopeless plight.[3] This is possible through realizing a definite ethos[4] of collective values, through renouncing egoistic contemplation of solitude and getting involved in social matters and community service.[5] Detached characters engage in such performances, mostly in critical situations that demand maximum concentration, effort, and heroism.[6] Some manage to master loneliness and to accomplish supraindividual ideals,[7] whereas others fail.[8] For many the outcome of such attempts is ambiguous.

The Conradian ethos assumes multifarious and meaningful forms with varying degrees of complexity, though all of them are situated on two distinct strata: they comprise respectively the courses of conduct in sea or land communities.[9] The present analysis focuses on attempts to transform detachment into devotion to collective values.[10] It studies whether the attempts succeed, to what degree, and why. In the end, this leads to a clearer understanding of the ideology of the Conrad canon.

Chapter 4
The Ethos ofFellowship at Sea

Isolation is an inherent element of the marine vocation (Part 1, Chapter 1). Conradian heroes, lonely amid infinity, silence, darkness, and the power of elemental forces (sometimes separated from one another), brave difficulties. They are constantly subjected to tests of professional efficiency and character,[1] "of manliness, of temperament, of courage and fidelity–and of love" (*The Shadow-Line,* SL 40). Events and experiences at sea "show in the light o day the inner worth of a man, the edge of his temper, and the fibre of his stuff; that reveal the quality of his resistance and the secret truth of his pretences, not only to others but also to himself" (*Lord Jim,* LJ 10).

The protagonist in *The Secret Sharer* acutely senses detachment in such circumstances: "And then I was left alone with my ship, anchored at the head of the gulf of Siam...far from all human eyes, with only sky and sea for spectators and for judges" (TLS 92). This emotion is enhanced by distancing from the ship and deckhands (93), and most of all by his psychoethical identification with Leggatt. The secluded hero's struggle with the silence of the watery universe that immobilizes the vessel with a sick crew on board is frequently emphasized in *The Shadow-Line*–e.g., "The intense loneliness of the sea acted like poison on my brain" (SL 92). *Heart of Darkness* portrays Marlow's loneliness in steering a steamboat up the hardly navigable big river; he receives no help from the accompanying pilgrims and feels powerless in confronting the tropics. In *The End of the Tether* Captain Whalley, going blind, is assisted only by his Malay Serang. Adversities are overcome in solitude by the narrator (the commander of an iron barque) in *Falk* (TOS 154-156, 189) and the captain in *A Smile of Fortune*. The shipmaster's estrangement is a consequence of his post and its responsibility:[2]

> Jukes was uncritically glad to have his captain at hand. It relieved him as though that man had, by simply coming on deck, taken most of the gale's weight upon his shoulders. Such is the prestige, the privilege, and the burden of command. (*Typhoon*, TOS 39)
>
> My sensations could not be like those of any other man on board. In that community I stood, like a king in his country, in a class all by myself....I was brought there to rule by an agency as remote from the people and as inscrutable almost to them as the Grace of God. (*The Shadow-Line*, SL 62; also 53, and *Chance*, C 288)

Seamen, too, have to perform their tasks in isolation: "He [Ransom] was alone, I [the protagonist] was alone, every man was alone where he stood" (*The Shadow-Line*, SL 113). In analogous situations they endure the pressure of threatening elements in *The Nigger of the "Narcissus," Youth*, and *Typhoon*: "[The *Narcissus*] drifted, bearing their patience and their suffering, through the stormy solitude of the sea. Huddled close to one another, they fancied themselves utterly alone" (*The Nigger of the "Narcissus,"* NN 82). The estranged protagonist of *Lord Jim* experiences perplexity before the fatal jump from the sinking *Patna*. Performance of professional duties in separation from the world is emphasized as well by sententious utterances in *Overdue and Missing* (MS 62) and *Chance* (C 326). Estrangement amid immensity of water often coexists with psychological detachment (Part 1, Chapter 3).

Conradian sea characters try to end isolation by compliance with the definite norms of conduct that make sense of their lives. They struggle primarily against the forces of nature and adversities, exhibiting labor, conscientiousness, solidarity, love for ships and the sea. Heroism constitutes the foundation of this axiology, since fulfillment of the glorious marine ethos by lonely human beings, insignificant against the environment, demands acts of bravery.

1. Blameworthy Seamen

A. Nonconformity to the Dictates of Struggle, Work, and Duty

Many Conradian mariners are definitely censurable: they violate the basic principles of professional morality and are the antithesis of the glorious ethos. Some of them do not fight the storms or cope with other obstacles and difficulties, others avoid toil and everyday duties.

The skipper of the *Sephora* in *The Secret Sharer* does not rise to the occasion during a storm. According to Leggatt, he is unable to mobilize the deckhands to effective action, displays cowardice and inefficiency:

> He was afraid of the men, and also of that old second mate of his....Devil only knows what the skipper wasn't afraid of (all his nerve went to pieces altogether in that hellish spell of bad weather we had)... (TLS 107)
>
> The man told you he hardly dared to give the order....I assure you he never gave the order. He may think he did, but he never gave it. He stood there with me on the break of the poop after the maintopsail blew away, and whimpered about our last hope–positively whimpered about it and nothing else–and the night coming on! To hear one's skipper go on like that in such weather was enough to drive any fellow out of his mind. (124)

The unfavorable depiction of Captain Archbold is underlined by the ironic distance of the protagonist, sympathizing and identifying with the escapee. This is revealed in his attitude toward the *Sephora*'s commander during his visit on board (pretending deafness, ostentatious demonstration of all the nooks and crannies of the captain's cabin), and in the descriptions of his posture, implying an ignoble nature:

> He was not exactly a showy figure...his stature but middling–one leg slightly more bandy than the other....A spiritless tenacity was his main characteristic, I judged....Perhaps he was shy. He mumbled to me as if he were ashamed of what he was saying... (116; also 116 other excerpts)

Such an image contrasts sharply with Archbold's self-esteem, which is based on his long sea service and blameless reputation in the fellowship (117, 118-119).

The subordinate accidentally strangled by Leggatt behaves as shamefully as his master under those critical circumstances. He does not obey orders, and thwarts the setting of a reefed foresail, which is crucial to saving the vessel. According to the "murderer"

> he was one of those creatures that are just simmering all the time with a silly sort of wickedness. Miserable devils that have no business to live at all. He wouldn't do his duty and wouldn't let anybody else do theirs. But what's the good of talking! You know well enough the sort of ill-conditioned snarling cur———. (101)

In *The Nigger of the "Narcissus,"* too, James Wait's behavior during a gale does not become a sailor: he is lazy and pretends sickness to avoid work (see also on his voluntary ethical isolation in Part 1, Chapter 2). Jim throws off his mask e.g. in the dialogue with Donkin:

> 'I know all about yer....You 'aven't the bloomin' nerve–so you inventyd this 'ere dodge....Yer ain't sick–are yer?'
> 'No,' said Jimmy, firmly....'Ye 'ave done this afore 'aven'tchee? ...Last ship–yes....' 'I am as well as ever,' he said....In course, he said, profoundly, 'any one can see that.' 'They don't,' said Jimmy... (NN 111)

In these moments of greatest danger his shamming impedes the crew, which is defying the elemental fury. He makes his "illness" a nuisance to this colleagues, demands constant service and numerous sacrifices. The mariners, as well as the narrator speaking for them, despise the "black fraud" (41), and call his conduct "shamming sick" (72), "unmanly lie" (73), "brazen lies," "transparent deceptions" (134), "falsehood," "untruthful attitude" (138), "sentimental lie" (155). Nevertheless they go along with all his caprices. Wait, on the other hand, not only does not express gratitude, but even reciprocates with contempt and complains about being treated with insufficient care (72, 105-106, 141).

Donkin also does not join the deck hands wrestling heroically with the tempest and is unwilling to fulfill his obligations.[3] His introduction already reveals his attitude:

> This clean white forecastle was his refuge; the place where he could be lazy; where he could wallow; and lie and eat–and curse the food he ate; where he could display his talents for shirking work, for cheating, for cadging; where he could find surely some one to wheedle and some one to bully–and where he would be paid for doing all this....They all knew him! He was the man that cannot steer, that cannot splice, that dodges the work on dark nights; that, aloft, holds on frantically with both arms and legs, and swears at the wind, the sleet, the darkness; the man who curses the sea while others work. The man who is the last out and the first in when all hands are called. The man who can't do most things and won't do the rest....The sympathetic and deserving creature that knows all about his rights, but knows nothing of courage, of endurance, and of the unexpressed faith, of the unspoken loyalty that knits together a ship's company. (10-11)

Donkin constantly avoids toil (40, 96) and hides in Jim's cabin in most difficult situations: "Nothing could keep him away from the pious work of visiting the sick, especially when there was some heavy hauling to be done on deck" (102-103). His performance provokes scorn from the crew:

> Donkin's position in the forecastle was distinguished but unsafe. He stood on the bad eminence of a general dislike....Donkin's insolence to long-suffering Mr. Baker became at least intolerable to us, and we rejoiced when the mate, one dark night, tamed him for good. (40; also 10-11, 64, 100-102, 143-144, 170)

Donkin is not content just with evading marine duties but also tries to convince others to behave the same way. Even a slight instance of confusion and disturbances in the friendly atmosphere on board makes him glad. This is manifest, e.g., in his reaction to the theft of the officers' Sunday fruit pie (38). He constantly incites the crew to rebellion, to cutting the masts (60), to disobeying the chief mate's orders (76). He convinces the sailors that they are exploited by their superiors and are underpaid for hard, dangerous work (100-102). Donkin makes them believe the captain's decision unjust in a malingerer's case (120-121), and manages to provoke a short-lived mutiny.[4] Donkin's treatment of his ally Jim is reprehensible: he robs him of personal belongings during his pre-death weakness. The monstrosity of this deed is magnified by comparing the thief to a vulture (128), which accords with the persistent naturalistic depiction of his hideous outward appearance.

Condemnable behavior in a situation of crisis is also exemplified in *Typhoon* by the second mate of *Nan-Shan,* who is eliminated from the struggle with elemental forces at the very outset, and by a part of the crew:

> Directly the full force of the hurricane had struck the ship, every part of her deck became untenable; and the sailors, dazed and dismayed, took shelter in the port alleyway under the bridge....The boatswain had been keeping up a gruff talk, but a more unreasonable lot of men, he said afterwards, he had never been with. They were snug enough there, out of harm's way, and not wanted to do anything, either; and yet they did nothing but grumble and complain peevishly like so many sick kids. (TOS 53-54)

Some other Conradian seamen violate the dictates of work, struggle, and duty when facing other perils and problems. In *Lord Jim* the captain, the chief mate, and two engineers ingloriously leave in a boat, running for their lives and abandoning the sinking ship and its 800 passengers.[5] This deed is unanimously censured by the marine community (see also Part 1, Chapter 2): "There was something abject [in it] which made the isolation more complete–there was a villainy of circumstances that cut these men off more completely from the rest of mankind... (LJ 121). Marlow shares this opinion, though he treats one of the escapees, Jim, much less severely: he calls pushing a boat into the sea "a bit of fooling...fit for knockabout clowns in a farce" (104), and depicts the others–the chief and second engineers–as drunkards and degenerates (22-26, 49-50, 54). He treats the

Patna's commander with supreme contempt for both this act and his later behavior: for failing to acknowledge his own viciousness and for regarding the resultant scorn as unjust (41-42). This is conspicuous, too, in highly ironic descriptions of this figure, implying his inadequacy for the post:

> I spotted the jolly skipper of the "Patna" at the first glance: the fattest man in the whole blessed tropical belt clear round that good old earth of ours....He made me think of a trained baby elephant walking on hind-legs...something round and enormous, resembling a sixteen-hundred-weight sugar-hogshead wrapped in striped flannellette, up-ended in the middle of the large floor space in the office. He [Ruthvell] declares he was so taken aback that for quite an appreciable time he did not realise the thing was alive, and sat still wandering for what purpose and by what means that object had been transported in front of his desk. (36-38; also 21, 23-24, 36-38 other passages, 42)

In emergency the shipmaster and crew in *Falk* do not rise to the occasion either.[6] The mariners are apathetic, undisciplined, quarrelsome and demoralized. Their superior does not care about preserving the remaining food and fails to evacuate his people in proper time to another craft. He is unable to maintain order and stop the complete disintegration of life on board (TOS 228-231).

Mr. Travers, the sailing master of the schooner-yacht *Hermit* in *The Rescue,* also acts ignominiously in a *Grenzsituation*. He does not keep the vessel from running aground on an outlying shoal, and then does not aid attempts by Lingard (acting under a threat from hostile natives) to set its passengers at liberty. Travers completely misunderstands the events taking place around him (Re 145, 356-357), and basing his view of reality on some publication about this exotic area: "What's up? Are the natives unfriendly? My book says–'Natives friendly all along this coast!'" (134). This attitude is ironically commented upon by Carter, the chief mate: "'You go down into the pantry, where you belong, Skipper,and read that bit about the natives over again,' he said to his superior officer, with savage contempt. 'I'll be hanged if some of them ain't coming aboard now to eat you–book and all" (134).

In Conrad there are also characters who never experience emergency, never have a chance to display their professional qualifications fully, and prove themselves full-fledged sea servants, for instance, ship conductor Hermann in *Falk*. His *Diana* was never subjected to the crucial test of enduring the fury of the elements, "was world proof" (TOS 156), "was a most innocent old ship, [which] seemed to know nothing of the wicked sea" (149), on board of which "apparently no whisper of the world's iniquities had ever penetrated" (156; also 153). Therefore he is unable to comprehend the crew's cannibalism on the steamer *Borgmester Dahl,* who were guided by self-preservation:

> According to his ideas no circumstances could excuse a crime–and certainly not such a crime....The duty of a human being was to starve. Falk therefore was a beast, an animal; base, low, vile, despicable, shameless, and deceitful....He would have preferred not to know that such an unclean creature had been in the habit of caressing his children...no decent housewifely girl would think of marrying him. At least he [Hermann] could not conceive how any girl could....Horrible! Horrible! (221-222; also 218-219, 237-238)

Apart from individuals who fail the marine ordeal, the group of unworthy seamen includes those who do not do their everyday duties. The story told by the chief mate Burns in *The Shadow-Line* gives such an image of the protagonist's predecessor:

> He was a peculiar man....He used to keep the ship loafing at sea for inscrutable reasons. Would come on deck at night sometimes, take some sail off her, God only knows why or wherefore, then go below, shut himself up in his cabin, and play on the violin for hours–till daybreak perhaps....The mere getting clear of the land took two days, and somehow or other they bumped slightly on a reef...[a monsoon] blowed away sails, strained the spars, exhausted the crew–nearly maddened by the absolute conviction that the attempt was impossible and was bound to end in some catastrophe.

> Meantime the captain, shut up in his cabin and wedged in a corner of his settee against the crazy bounding of the ship, played the violin.... It was like fighting desperately towards destruction for the ship and the men....
> The old man [the captain] gave him [Burns] a look of savage spite, and said these atrocious words in deadly, slow tones:
> 'If I had my wish, neither the ship nor any of you would ever reach a port. And I hope you won't....
> He didn't care for business, or freights, or for making a passage–or anything. He meant to have gone wandering about the world till he lost her with all hands. (SL 58-62)

He even becomes a potential murderer: by selling the ship's supply of quinine (as Burns claims), he deprives the sick crew of medicine. The narrator (the captain) essentially shares in the disapproval of his antecedent's conduct, calling it "a complete act of treason, the betrayal of a tradition which seemed...as imperative as any guide on earth could be" (62).

However, the chief officer is not spotless either. His constant nonsensical twaddle about the influence of the inefficient commander's ghost upon this critical situation does not fortify him in grappling with adversities (86, 92-93, 102). When coming close to the place where the demonic captain was buried at sea, Burns obstructs the heroic efforts of his superior and the exhausted mariners (115-120).[7] The second mate, too, is unfavorably different from the valiant, suffering sailors: "I would find him sitting on the skylight half-senseless, as it were, and with an idiotic gaze fastened on some object near by....That young man was rather troublesome. He remained cubbish in his sufferings. He seemed to have become completely imbecile..." (99; also 104).

In *Falk* the plight of the narrator (commander of an iron barque) is analogous to that of the principal character in *The Shadow-Line:* his predecessor is viewed as not having performed his tasks properly, as neglecting the vessel and wasting its resources:

> [He] had died suddenly, leaving for the guidance of his successor some suspiciously unreceipted bills, a few dry-dock estimates hinting at

> bribery, and a quantity of vouchers for three years' extravagant expenditure....I found besides a large account-book, which, when opened, hopefully turned out to my infinite consternation to be filled with verses–page after page of rhymed doggerel of a jovial and improper character, written in the neatest minute hand I ever did see...of the two last freights the ship had indubitably earned of late, there were not even the husks left. It was impossible to say where all the money had gone to. It wasn't on board. It had not been remitted home; for a letter from the owners, preserved in a desk evidently by the merest accident, complained mildly enough that they had not been favoured by a scratch of the pen for the last eighteen months. There were next to no stores on board, not an inch of spare rope or a yard of canvas. The ship had been run bare, and I foresaw no end of difficulties before I could get her ready for sea. (TOS 153-154)

The crew does not support the captain in braving hardships: the chief mate reveals his dislike for him, the second is "the stupidest man he had ever seen on board ship," and the steward's Chinese successor–"the only decent person at the after end of the ship"–steals the savings he had reserved for extreme need (154-156).

Captain Johns in *The Black Mate* also does not perform his professional duties. His wrong attitude toward the ship's company comes largely from fanatical spiritualism and intrusive endeavors to convince others (the protagonist included) of the existence of ghosts:

> He had the reputation of being an uncomfortable commander, meticulous in trifles, always nursing a grievance of some sort and incessantly nagging. He was not a man to kick up a row with you and be done with it, but to say nasty things in a whinning voice; a man capable of making one's life a perfect misery if he took a dislike to an officer. (TH 91)

Captain Williams in *Romance* largely ignores his obligations to the *Lion* and his subordinates, and indulges primarily in sprees.

B. Noncompliance with the Call of Solidarity, Love for Ships, Sea, and Existence at Sea

Improper performance–fecklessness, laziness, lack of conscientiousness, etc.–in confronting storms or other adversities determines censure. All are violations of the fundamental principle of the Conradian marine ethos: unity in work and struggle. Not identifying with a crew, aiming exclusively at personal advancement in one's profession, constitutes another violation of this principle. Such an action is committed by the officer of the *Sofala* in *The End of the Tether:*

> Always–as he [Sterne] was ready to confess–on the lookout for an opening to get on, it had become an instinct with him to watch the conduct of his immediate superiors for something 'that one could lay hold of' ...whenever he joined a ship the intention of ousting his commander out of the berth and taking his place was always present at the back of his head, as a matter of course. It filled the leisure of his waking hours with the reveries of careful plans and compromising discoveries–the dreams of his sleep with images of lucky turns and favourable accidents...nowadays, professional merit alone does not take a man along fast enough. A chap must have some push in him, and must keep his wits at work, too, to help him forward. (YNTOS 239-240; also 238-240 other extracts)

He tries to use the discovery of his superior's blindness to achieve his dreams. He first attempts to communicate with Massy, the co-owner of the steamer: he intends to get a promise for the ship's command in exchange for disclosing the master's secret. Failing in this, Sterne does his utmost to make Mr. Van Wyk persuade Captain Whalley to leave the *Sofala* and transfer the appointment to him.

In *The Rescue* Shaw, the chief mate, is full of the same ambitions. He notices the mutual antipathy between captains Lingard and Travers and tries to associate himself with the sailing master against his superior: "Perhaps–it flashed upon him–the yacht's gentry will hear I stood up for them. This could conceivably be of advantage to a man who wanted a lift in the world" (Re 190). But his actual performance does not validate his aspirations. Shaw is an incompetent officer: he fails to notice the approach of Carter's gig in time and shows a lack of understanding of the intricate situation created in the zone of Carimata by the appearance of the *Hermit*. Lingard dislikes his chief mate for disobeying orders, loses confidence in him, and entrusts the command not to him but to Carter. Ultimately Show is thrown off the *Lightning* for insubordination and demoralizing the sailors (426-427).

Careerists appear in *The Shadow-Line* too. Hamilton views himself as a prospective shipmaster. His helper, the chief steward, does not tell the protagonist about the official communication form the Harbour Office, since it may be connected with the nomination. But this intrigue, unraveled by Captain Giles, does not bring the result expected by the conspirators. Mr. Burns reveals an identical desire by overemphasizing a reprehensible image of the former master, in order to highlight his own merits in saving the ship an crew from the dangers caused by the boss's irresponsible, incompetent, and malicious activities (SL 62-63). After the captain's death the chief mate openly tries for the appointment:[8]

> He took the ship to a port where he expected to be confirmed in his temporary command from lack of a qualified master to put over his head....But his naive reasoning forgot to take into account the telegraph cable reposing on the bottom of the very Gulf up which he had turned that ship which he imagined himself to have saved from destruction. Hence the bitter flavour of our interview. I tasted it more and more distinctly–and it was less and less to my taste. (63)

Chief Engineer Massy in *The End of the Tether* personifies a special case of violating professional solidarity: unintelligent, impulsive, conceited, pathologically misanthropic–an individual of nasty temper, incapable of living in harmony with his fellow mariners:

> Clearly a mutinous sort of chap...a perfect nuisance, everlastingly shipped and unshipped, unable to keep a berth very long; pretty nigh went through every engine-room afloat belonging to the colony. (YNTOS 204)
>
> As a shipowner everyone had conspired to make him a nobody...as the difficulties of his improvident ambition gathered thicker round him, he really came to hate everybody he had ever come in contact with. A temper naturally irritable and an amazing sensitiveness to the claims of his own personality had ended by making of life for him a sort of inferno–a place where his lost soul had been given up to the torment of savage brooding. (269; also 205-208)

This unlovely portrait is complemented by his attitude toward the steamer co-owned with Captain Whalley. He does not carry out vital repairs on it, and wastes money on the Manila lottery, his great obsession (207, 265-266). Finally Massy deliberately engineers the sinking of the *Sofala,* because he wants the insurance money for gambling. He packs the pockets of his coat with pieces of iron and hangs it beside the compass, which deflects the magnetic needle, causing the ship to go off course and into catastrophe. By the criteria of the maritime ethos this action is an offense against the vessel, which makes Massy a kind of murderer:

> In his cabin he perceived that his hands were all red–red with rust. It disconcerted him, as though he had found them covered with blood: he looked himself over hastily. Why, his trousers, too! He had been rubbing his rusty palms on his legs. He...brushed his coat, washed his hands. Then the air of guilt left him... (322)[9]

Cloete, in *The Partner,* is similarly motivated, and he counts on indemnity. He persuades George Dunbar to founder his brother's (Harry's) craft willfully and hires Stafford to execute this plan, who accepts the proposal without scruples. Nevertheless, the intrigue takes a course different from the one devised by its maker and ends in complete failure.

An analogous "crime" is committed by Heemskirk in *Freya of the Seven Isles*. Insinuations that Jasper Allen's activities are hostile to the Dutch authorities serve him as a pretext for treacherously wrecking his rival's brig. The narrator condemns not only this deed but the entire conduct of the gunboat commander–a malevolent, common naval officer, "of no particular connections or ability to boast of" (TLS 159). In *The Rescue* an identical transgression by the Dutchman perfidiously destroys Dawson's schooner (Re 101).

Other seamen, too, are reprehended for wrongful treatment of ships. Kennedy in *Amy Foster* disapproves of the master and crew of the craft that rams amidships the German vessel transporting emigrants, sinks it, and goes on unseen (TOS 122). The implied author in *On the North Sea Outrage* expresses extreme indignation at the performance of the Russian squadron that goes through a group of fishing boats and sinks some of them. He treats this as a violation of the generally accepted norm, according to which smacks at sea should be circumnavigated. In *Lord Jim* Brown and his companions steal a Spanish schooner to flee on it, for which they are chased (see also on his ethical isolation in Part 1, Chapter 2).

Unworthy Conradian mariners also comprise those who evince hatred of or disgust with the maritime life. Captain Hagberd in *To-morrow* exemplifies such:

> Many sailors feel and profess a rational dislike for the sea, but his was a profound and emotional animosity–as if the love of the stabler element had been bred into him through many generations. 'People did not know what they let their boys in for when they let them go to sea,' he expounded to Bessie. 'As soon make convicts of them at once.' He did not believe you ever got used to it. (TOS 249)

His fear and repugnance of the trackless deep are ironically commented upon by the narrator and his own son Harry:

> Captain Hagberd had been one of those sailors that pursue their calling within sight of land...he had been apprenticed hurriedly to a coasting skipper, and had remained on the coast all his sea life....One might have thought him weary of distant voyages; and the longest he had ever made had lasted a fortnight, of which the most part had been spent at anchor,

> sheltering from the weather...he threw up his command of an East-coast collier with a feeling as though he had escaped from the galleys. After all these years he might have counted on the fingers of his two hands all the days he had been out of sight of England. He had never known what it was to be out of soundings. (249-250)
>
> He used to go about looking very sick for three days before he had to leave home on one of his trips to South Shields for coal. (265)

Aversion to toil at sea is also characteristic of Donkin in *The Nigger of the "Narcissus,"* who is portrayed as "the independent offspring of the ignoble freedom of the slums full of disdain and hate for the austere servitude of the sea" (NN 11), of Willems in *An Outcast of the Islands* ("The boy was hopelessly at variance with the spirit of the sea. He had an instinctive contempt for the honest simplicity of that work which led to nothing he cared for") (OI 17), and of vagabonds: Harry in *To-morrow,* unable to persevere in maritime service (TOS 245, 268), and Ricardo in *Victory,* who escapes together with Mr. Jones from a ship, having robbed its master of money. Laziness, distaste for work, and the lack of conscientiousness are traced in Hamilton's behavior in *The Shadow-Line* where he permanently stays in the Officers' Sailors' Home, taken under its roof out of pity; and in degenerate Stafford's in *The Partner*–kicked off a ship, sponging upon a widow boarding-house keeper (WT 103-105).[10]

C. Ties with a Woman or Land as Forming These Censurable Attitudes

Connections with women who adversely influence the characters' conduct are an essential reason for the hostile delineation of these men in light of the marine ethos. The cowardice of the skipper of the *Sephora* in *The Secret Sharer* comes in some degree from his wife's presence on board (TLS 107). Captain Williams's inefficiency in *Romance* is caused mostly by his many amours and rakishness (Rom 450-451). According to the chief mate in *The Shadow-Line*, the former commander's love affair in Haiphong influences his professional duties badly (SL

59). In *Freya of the Seven Isles* a similar liaison brings about Heemskirk's departure from the principles of the maritime ethos: he wrecks the *Bonito* out of envy of Jasper Allen. Generally, the unfavorable impact of women upon shipmasters[11] gives rise to the frequently expressed conviction that seamen should not marry.[12]

The company of the captain's whole family is as disadvantageous to him as his wife, as the narrator in *Falk* argues, treating Hermann somewhat scornfully. In his opinion the German captain, never having experienced a critical situation at sea, has not become a full-fledged master mariner. His *Diana* is like a village cottage transferred from the land:

> She was heavy, strong, blunt-bowed affair...of a rustic and homely nature. The extraordinary timber projections which I have seen in no other vessel made her square stern resemble the tail end of a miller's waggon. But the four stern ports of her cabin, glazed with six little greenish panes each, and framed in wooden sashes painted brown, might have been the windows of a cottage in the country. The tiny white curtains and greenery of flower pots behind the glass completed the resemblance. (TOS 148)
>
> And the sentiments she suggested were unexceptionally and mainly of a domestic order. She was a home. All these dear children had learned to walk on her roomy quarter-deck....Their teeth, I should judge, they cut on the ends of her running gear. (149-150)

The portrait of Hermann is in tune with that of the ship: his appearance, habits and manner are peculiar to settled people:

> He...had the simple, heavy appearance of a well-to-do farmer, combined with the good-natured shrewdness of a small shopkeeper. With his shaven chin, round limbs, and heavy eyelids he did not look like a toiler, and even less like an adventurer of the sea. Still, he toiled upon the seas, in his own way, much as a shopkeeper works behind his counter. (147-148)
>
> He resembled curiously a caricature of a shopkeeping citizen in one of his own German comic papers. (181-182; also 168)

A land-bound style of living is clearly preferred by Hagberd–a retired coasting skipper–in *To-morrow*. He manifests both hatred for the sea and fondness of a comfortable life:

> And there was nothing like home–a fireside–a good roof: no turning out of your warm bed in all sorts of weather...his affection turned to the land, with its innumerable houses, with its quiet lives gathered round its firesides. (TOS 249)

At all costs, Hagberd wants to prevent his son Harry from becoming a mariner (266). Harry nevertheless despises his father's predilections, calling his dwelling a "dead-alive place" (263) and "a rabbit hutch" (268). Irony is also evident in the narrator's depictions of his senseless activities in the garden (see too on his self-imposed psychological isolation in Part 1, Chapter 2). He is, for example, compared with the lord of the seas and oceans holding his attribute of power: "Captain Hagberd, amongst the mounds of turned-up earth, chuckled. With his maritime rig, his weather-beaten face, his beard of Father Neptune, he resembled a deposed sea-god who had exchanged the trident for a spade" (253).

The burgher mentality and manners make Mr. Travers in *The Rescue* an unworthy captain. During the cruise he cares chiefly about his own and his friends' comfort, indulges in gossip, and lacks awareness of the threat to the passengers from the natives.[13]

2. Praiseworthy Seamen: The Ethos of Struggle, Work and Duty

The Conradian ideal of captain, mate, and crew member, personifies numerous qualities, principally discipline (*The Nigger of the "Narcissus,"* NN 16), conscientiousness (*The Shadow-Line,* SL 53 and *Well Done,* NLL 191-192), strong character, courage, endurance, loyalty (*The Nigger of the "Narcissus,"* NN 11,25). These virtues enable them to fulfill their professional obligations. Grappling with the elements, overcoming adversities, and dealing with everyday exertions on board are inherent in the marine vocation:

> They must without pause justify their life to the eternal pity that commands toil to be hard and unceasing... (*The Nigger of the "Narcissus,"* NN 90)
> The difficulties, the dangers, the problems of a ship at sea must be met on deck. (*The Shadow-Line*, SL 89)
> They can be best defined as men who lived under the command to do well, or perish utterly. (*Well Done*, NLL 182; also *Protection of Ocean Liners*, NLL 251; *Chance*, C 431)

The slogan "Do or die" written on the stern of the *Judea* in *Youth* is a concise formulation of the inevitability of such conduct. *The Fine Art* presents an argument for regarding struggle, labor, and compliance as the fundamental values of the maritime life:

> Now, the moral side of an industry...is the attainment and preservation of the highest possible skill on the part of the craftsmen. Such skill, the skill of technique, is more than honesty; it is something wider, embracing honesty and grace and rule in an elevated and clear sentiment, not altogether utilitarian, which may be called the honour of labor...
> This is why the attainment of proficiency, the pushing of your skill with attention to the most delicate shades of excellence, is a matter of vital concern. (MS 24)

A. Heroism of Mariners Braving a Storm

The Conradian model of a seaman is most conspicuous in particularly hard and dangerous circumstances that demand the maximum commitment of the entire personality. Threat from the water creates the most critical situation and requires the straining of all human powers to face it and survive.

The plot of *The Nigger of the "Narcissus,"* Conrad's first sea novel, consists nearly exclusively of episodes of fighting a hurricane. The narrator consistently describes the ship's company in heroic terms, e.g., when resisting waves on deck:[14]

> They gripped rails, they had wound ropes'-ends under their arms; they clutched ringbolts, they crawled in heaps where there was foothold; they held on with both arms, hooked themselves to anything to

> windward with elbows, with chins, almost with their teeth: and some, unable to crawl away from where they had been flung, felt the sea leap up, striking against their backs as they struggled upwards. (NN 59-60; also 49-50)

Under such conditions they carry out their tasks with extraordinary devotion, e.g. when setting or furling sails:

> They went up the rigging with faltering and desperate efforts. Their heads swam as they shifted their hold, stepped blindly on the yards like men in the dark; or trusted themselves to the first rope at hand with the negligence of exhausted strength...the wind filled their eyes with tears, and with heavy gusts tried to push them off from where they swayed in insecure positions. With streaming faces and blowing hair they flew up and down between sky and water, bestriding the ends of yard-arms, crouching on foot-ropes, embracing lifts to have their hands free, or standing up against chain ties. Their thoughts floated vaguely between the desire of rest and the desire of life, while their stiffened fingers cast off head-earrings, fumbled for knives, or held with tenacious grip against the violent shocks of beating canvas. They glared savagely at one another, made frantic signs with one hand while they held their life in the other....Their lips moved, their eyes started, furious and eager with the desire to be understood....In an unendurable and unending strain they worked like men driven by a merciless dream to toil in an atmosphere of ice or flame. They burnt and shivered in turns. Their eyeballs smarted as if in the smoke of a conflagration; their heads were ready to burst with every shout. (92-93; also 55, 85)

The *Narcissus* seamen are most often portrayed collectively in their duel with the raging waters. Nevertheless the narrator sometimes focuses upon particular mariners' activities:

> The sailmaker, with his bald head bared, worked feverishly, forgetting his intimacy with so many admirals. The boatswain, climbing up with marlinspikes and bunches of spunyarn rovings, or kneeling on the yard and ready to take a turn with the midship-stop, had acute and fleeting visions... (93)

First and foremost he distinguishes Singleton from this community (the name emphasizes individualization): he stands for more than thirty hours at the helm and keeps the course:

> Singleton had stuck to the wheel. His hair flew out in the wind; the gale seemed to take its life-long adversary by the beard and shake his old head. He wouldn't let go, and, with his knees forced between the spokes, flew up and down like a man on a bough. (60; also 89)[15]

The cook endeavors to match the valiant sailors: he makes hot coffee in spite of the ship heeling over (81-84) and is determined to remain at his post to the end (81).

The officers' performance during the gale is as heroic as that of the crew. Mr. Baker, the model chief mate[16] (166-167), is devoted to his duties; he spurs the men to permanent exertion:

> Mr. Baker, feeling very weak, tottered here and there, grunting and inflexible, like a man of iron....He ordered, encouraged, scolded....No rest till the work is done. Work till you drop. That's what you're here for. (93; also 31, 79)

The shipmaster proves equal to his task as well:

> The captain, with a round turn of a rope on his wrest, and kneeling on one knee, swung with a face cold and stiff; but with living eyes he was still holding the ship up, heeding no one, as if lost in the unearthly effort of that endeavour. (74)

The encounter with the storm is made more difficult by the need to get Jim out of the "house." An added trouble to the sailors, he demands care and assistance in emergencies on board. The meaning of his shammng is stressed by the surname "Wait," equivalent phonetically to "weight,"[17] and his being called by the narrator (a spokesman for the crew) as a "hateful burden" (72) or "unfair burden" (160). Nevertheless, the seamen do not complain, but zealously try to free their colleague (65-72), seeing this action in terms of professional honor, as codetermining success in the confronting the forces of nature (72).

Struggling with the wild expanse of water is the principal theme of *Typhoon,* as well. Glorification of the intrepid members of the *Nan-Shan* crew[18] focuses mainly on Jukes, whose perspective is most frequently assumed by the narrator:

> This [extremely bad weather] was so much beyond his powers of fancy that it appeared incompatible with the existence of any ship whatever...[he was] so harassed by the necessity of exerting a wrestling effort against a force trying to tear him away from his hold. Moreover, the conviction of not being utterly destroyed returned to him through the sensations of being half-drowned, bestially shaken, and partly choked.
>
> It seemed to him he remained there precariously alone with the stanchion for a long, long time. The rain poured on him, flowed, drove in sheets. He breathed in gasps; and sometimes the water he swallowed was fresh and sometimes it was salt. For the most part he kept his eyes shut tight, as if suspecting his sight might be destroyed in the immense flurry of the elements. (TOS 41)

Sometimes the chief mate and the commander are shown together, resisting at the attack of the elements: "They stood clasped thus in the blind night, bracing each other against the wind, cheek to cheek and lip to ear, in the manner of two hulks lashed stem to stern together" (45-46; also 42, 47). In this story, as in *The Nigger of the "Narcissus,"* the helmsman's (Hackett's) feat of valor is appreciated; he sticks to his post in spite of exhaustion:

> God knows how long he had been left there to steer, as if forgotten by all his shipmates. The bells had not been struck; there had been no reliefs; the ship's routine had gone down wind; but he was trying to keep her head north-north-east....He was anxious not to get muddled and lose control of her head....He suffered from mental stress. He was horribly afraid, also, of the wheelhouse going. (64; also 87)

In *Typhoon* the seamen's meritorious behavior forms a mere background for the exploits of their admirable skipper: "Every ship Captain MacWhirr commanded was the floating abode of harmony and peace" (4). His performance during and after the hurricane confirms this. He rejects intricate nautical strategies designed to dodge dirty weather, which are recommended in books and by Captain Wilson. Guided by instinct, he decides to face the gale (32-35, 87-89). His valiance is magnified by the contrast between the force of nature and his insignificance as a human being:

> The hurricane, with its power to madden the seas, to sink ships, to uproot trees, to overturn strong walls and dash the very birds of the air to the ground, had found this taciturn man in its path, and, doing its utmost, had managed to wring out a few words. (90)

Captain MacWhirr's duel with the raging waters is depicted in terms of battle metaphors: he calls to mind a swordsman in his fighting panoply (36-37), and his adversary the typhoon is like an army: "There was the throb as of many drums in it, a vicious rushing note, and like the chant of a trampling multitude" (90; also 40, 66, 83, 86, 36-37 and 89-90 other excerpts). The commander's courageous conduct heartens the crew and strengthens their faith in the possibility of riding out the storm (39, 45-46, 88-89).

Additional difficulty is created by the turmoil among the Chinese coolies in the fore 'tween-deck, returning to their home villages with their savings of a few years' labor. The violent movements of the steamer break their chests loose. They bounce around and open and their money falls out of them and mixes. Attempts to retrieve it all brings on a melee, which is as dynamic and vehement as the gale:

> When the boatswain threw open the door it seemed that an eddy of the hurricane, stealing through the iron sides of the ship, had set all these bodies whirling like dust: there came to them a confused uproar, a tempestuous tumult, a fierce mutter, gusts of screams dying away, and the trampling of feet mingling with the blows of the sea. (77; also 72)

The crew's efforts to calm the Chinamen are an integral aspect of braving the elements:

> When the wash of water rolling on the deck died away for a moment, it seemed to Jukes, yet quivering from his exertions, that in his mad struggle down there he had overcome the wind somehow: that a silence had fallen upon the ship, a silence in which the sea struck thunderously at her sides. (79)

The organic unity of the typhoon and the human uproar is also confirmed by the coincidence of the separation of the fighters, the pacifying and managing of the situation in the foredeck, with the subsidence of the hurricane.

Grappling with the forces of nature is also depicted in *Youth.* The apotheosis of the *Judea*'s company is manifest in their victories during the first gale, especially when righting the barque (YNTOS 6-7), as well as in their devoted struggle to save it from sinking in the second encounter with rough weather:

> We pumped all night, all day, all the week–watch and watch. She was working herself loose, and leaked badly–not enough to drown us at once, but enough to kill us with the work at the pumps.... And we pumped....We pumped watch and watch, for dear life; and it seemed to last for months, for years, for all eternity, as though we had been dead and gone to a hell for sailors. We forgot the day of the week, the name of the month, what year it was, and whether we had ever been ashore....We turned those handles...we turned, we turned incessantly, with the water to our waists, to our necks, over our heads. It was all one. We had forgotten how it felt to be dry...we were pumping on, deafened with the wind, and without spirit enough in us to wish ourselves dead... (11-12; also 10)

Getting the cook out of the swept away deckhouse testifies to the seamen's bravery too (13-14); and they resist the elements on the return journey to England (14). The motif of withstanding a storm appears episodically in *The Secret Sharer,* where the *Sephora*'s crew, particularly Leggatt, display fearlessness (see on him in Part 1, Chapter 2 and Part 2, Chapter 4).

The bravery of those opposing the elements is suggested indirectly as well in all the cases outlined above by emphasizing the gigantic power of nature, the adversary of a handful of weak people:[19]

> A big, foaming sea came out of the mist; it made for the ship, roaring wildly, and in its rush it looked as mischievous and discomposing as a madman with an axe....It towered close-to and high, like a wall of green glass topped with snow. (*The Nigger of the "Narcissus,"* NN 57; also 55-56)
>
> At certain moments the air streamed against the ship as if sucked through a tunnel with a concentrated solid force of impact that seemed to lift her clean out of the water and keep her up for an instant with only a quiver running through her from end to end. And then she would begin her tumbling again as if dropped back into a boiling cauldron. (*Typhoon,* TOS 43; also 36-37, 44, 46-47, 53-54, 63, 74; *Youth,* YNTOS 6, 10-11)

B. Valiant Victory over Other Difficulties

Portraits of meritorious seamen are revealed not only in fighting a storm. In *Youth* the fight is merely the initial stage of desperate attempts to rescue the *Judea.* Later, too, the crew behaves courageously: during the fire fought with much effort (YNTOS 21-22), after the explosion of coal dust (25), when furling sails (28), when attempting, in peril of their lives, to save gear from the burning barque (30-31). Finally they overcome exhaustion and weakness, reaching land after the craft sinks.

> I need not tell you what it is to be knocking about in an open boat. I remember nights and days of calm, when we pulled, we pulled, and the boat seemed to stand still....I remember the heat, the deluge of rain-squalls that kept us bailing for dear life...and I remember sixteen hours on end with a mouth dry as a cinder and a steering-oar over the stern to keep my first command head on to a breaking sea. I did not know how good a man I was till then. I remember the drawn faces, the dejected figures of my two men... (36; also 37)[20]

The apotheosis of the sailors managing a critical situation caused by the fever epidemic on board is the theme of *The Shadow-Line:*[21]

> The fact was that disease played with us capriciously very much as the winds did. It would go from one man to another with a lighter or heavier touch, which always left its mark behind, staggering some, knocking others over for a time, leaving this one, returning to another, so that all of them had now an invalidish aspect and a hunted, apprehensive look in their eyes....It was a double fight. The adverse weather held us in front and the disease pressed on our rear. (SL 85)

The mariners gallantly endure sickness both before making for the open sea (66) and in the course of the voyage, when their agonies cannot be eased because of the lack of quinine (99-100). Performing tasks in spite of ill health and adverse weather, they are conscientious and devoted:

> They were all so reduced by sickness that no watches could be kept. Those who were able to walk remained all the time on duty, lying about in the shadows of the main deck, till my voice raised for an order would bring them to their enfeebled feet, a tottering little group, moving patiently about the ship, with hardly a murmur, a whisper amongst them all. (98)
>
> Those men were the ghosts of themselves, and their weight on a rope could be no more than the weight of a bunch of ghosts....They wandered feebly after me from rope to rope, stumbling and panting. They toiled like Titans....When the last leech-line was made fast, my eyes, accustomed to the darkness, made out the shapes of exhausted men drooping over the rails, collapsed on hatches. One hung over the after-capstan, sobbing for breath... (109; also 85, 87-88, 107)

The men's performance arouses their commander's supreme admiration: they are "worthy of his undying regard" (100, and the motto).[22]

In *The Shadow-Line*, as in *The Nigger of the "Narcissus,"* the ship's company is glorified as a whole: the narrator rarely emphasizes the heroism of its particular members, as for instance, in the case of Frenchy (100) and Gambril sticking with the helm (110-112). The exceedingly devoted Ransome is the only figure clearly singled out. Although the excessive exertions of this man with heart disease may end tragically, he not only carries out his duties as cook but helps the captain in many other ways: "That man noticed everything, attended to everything, shed comfort around him as he moved" (121; also 104, 112). Ransome's assistance makes attempts to set the sails successful. The protagonist speaks about him with extraordinary respect:

> Ransome and I rushed along the decks letting go all the sheets and halliards by the run....I could hear him panting close to me and I avoided turning my eyes his way for fear of seeing him fall down and expire in the act of putting out his strength....Every effort, every movement was an act of consistent heroism. It was not for me to look at a man thus inspired. (126; also 122)

Such judgement of the cook's conduct is in harmony with his overall characteristics, stressing positive features of his personality: an intelligent glance, well-bred face, nice watchful smile, cheerful frame of mind, grace, pleasant voice, etc.

Many commanders cope with hardships that crop up in the course of service. In *Youth,* Captain Beard's conduct evokes respect and is in tune with the crew's zeal: he persistently takes the barque to the end of its journey, in spite of obstacles:[23]

> His only thought was to get that miserable, stripped, undecked, smouldering shell of a ship back again with her head pointing at her port of destination. Bankok! That's what he was after. I tell you this quiet, bowed, bandy-legged, almost deformed little man was immense in the singleness of his idea... (YNTOS 25)

The principal characters in *A Smile of Fortune* and *Falk* rise to the occasion under difficult conditions, though only partly because of their devotion and fortitude. The narrator (the captain) in *A Smile of Fortune* is expected to be equal to the shipmaster's duties on a voyage to the Pearl of the Ocean, and to represent his shipowner's mecantile interests properly (TLS 6-7). He encounters serious troubles when fulfilling these obligations. His attempt to establish contact with Jacobus, the appointed business partner, is futile. His connection with Alice and her father (Jacobus's brother), ostracized by all the island community (see Part 1, Chapter 2), stirs up dislike of him. His inability to get a sufficient number of bags makes completion of the ship's loading impossible. Finally, the protagonist manages to overcome all these adversities, and the purchase of potatoes, forced upon him, brings an unexpectedly large profit and commercial success (the "smile of fortune") and completes the tasks entrusted to him. However, this is achieved mainly through the intrigues of Alice's father, who views him as a prospective son-in-law an uses his trade contacts to accomplish the advantageous transaction.

The leading figure in *Falk* also undergoes many hardships after getting his captaincy:

> The crew was sickly, the cargo was coming very slow; I foresaw I would have lots of trouble with the charterers, and doubted whether they would advance me enough money for the ship's expenses. Their attitude towards me was unfriendly. Altogether I was not getting on. (TOS 155)

He lacks the necessary support of his subordinates in the critical situation. The greatest obstacle is posed by the sole tugboat owner, who for incomprehensible reasons refuses to tow his iron barque out of port. Attempts to put an end to these unfavorable conditions prove unsuccessful (e.g., the refusals to help from Siegers and Johnson, who have been bribed by Falk). It is only a sincere talk with his persecutor that breaks the impasse and dissipates his suspicions and prejudices. Thus the protagonist passes a test of professional competence, owing not to his assiduity and bravery but to characteristics atypical of Conradian master mariners–"diplomatic dealing" and clearing up a misunderstanding.

The shipmasters Allistoun in *The Nigger of the "Narcissus"* and MacWhirr in *Typhoon* not only struggle heroically against the fury of the elements, like their subordinates, but also overcome the extra hardships created by human relationships on board. The *Narcissus*'s commander makes the correct decision about Jim: as the storm passes, he forbids the malingerer any work in order to refuse him payment after the voyage. Allistoun copes with the mutiny of his simple-hearted mariners, who want to defend their companion, by keeping them busy all the time to absorb their attention and to manifest his grip on the situation. He publicly humiliates Donkin, who threw a pin at him to provoke rebellion: he compels the agitator to put it back where it was taken from. Thus Allistoun proves the validity of the opinion that "he was one of those commanders who speak little, seem to hear nothing, look at no one–and know everything, hear every whisper, see every fleeting shadow of their ship's life" (NN 125).[24] MacWhirr, on the other hand, not only gets the *Nan-Shan* through the typhoon, but also solves the difficult problem posed by the coolies. To restore peace on the steamer, he orders the suppression of the Chinamen's brawl and the collection of their scattered money, which he later shares out equally, assuming that their earnings were all nearly the same (TOS 101). This move is approved of by the crew members Jukes and Rout.[25]

High qualifications are displayed as well by helmsmen steering ships in adverse conditions. In *Heart of Darkness,* Marlow's navigation of the ship is seriously hampered by extensive shallows, which are impossible to recognize, and by a complete lack of navigation marks:

> The broadening waters flowed through a mob of wooded islands; you lost your way on that river as you would in a desert, and butted all day long against shoals, trying to find the channel....I had to keep guessing at the channel; I had to discern, mostly by inspiration, the signs of hidden banks; I watched for sunken stones; I was learning to clap my teeth smartly before my heart flew out, when I shaved by a fluke some infernal sly old snag that would have ripped the life out of the tin-pot steamboat and drowned all the pilgrims... (YNTOS 93)

He compares his performance to that of "a blindfolded man set to drive a van over a bad road" (94). The voyage is trammeled in its final phase by fog and the natives' attack, during which Marlow has to retain his presence of mind, keep on course, and correct the errors committed by the Negro helmsman, who unconsciously yields to the instinct to fight. Masterly seamanship is also shown by Lingard in the Malay trilogy:

> For the next hour he handled his little vessel in the intricate and narrow channel with careless certitude, as if every stone, every grain of sand upon the treacherous bottom has been plainly disclosed to his sight. He had handled her in the fitful and unsteady breeze with a matter-of-fact audacity that made Shaw, forward at his station, gasp in sheer alarm. (*The Rescue,* Re 53-54)

These exceptional abilities make him the absolute ruler of the shallow sea of Carimata in *The Rescue,* and Sambir in *Almayer's Folly* and *An Outcast of the Islands,* as the only man able to direct a craft into these areas[26] (Part 1, Chapters 1 and 2), Part 2, Chapter 5 also). Efficiency at sea is revealed by the title character in *Nostromo* as well (his outward appearance and way of speaking are depicted as typical of a Mediterranean sailor). In spite of bad weather, he and Decoud run the leaky lighter with treasure to the Great Isabel (on the political significance of this and other actions of Nostromo, see Part 2, Chapter 5): "There was certainly something almost miraculous in the way the Capataz made the cove with nothing but the shadowy hint of the island's shape and the vague gleam of a small sandy strip for a guide" (N 295).

A separate group of praiseworthy marines includes those who devotedly take care of a ship in spite of the absence or incompetence of the commander. The crew of the French gunboat in *Lord Jim* successfully completes the difficult towing of the damaged *Patna* and its 800 passengers to Aden. Remarkable bravery is displayed by Marlow's interlocutor, the boarding officer, who stays for thirty hours on the imperiled steamer.[27] Carter, in *The Rescue,* is persistently portrayed as a model mate and is clearly opposed to Travers, the inefficient commander of the schooner-yacht *Hermit:* he "showed the minuteness of...observation, the clear vision of a seaman able to master quickly the aspect of a strange land and of a strange sea" (Re 33). Carter notices the landmarks made by Lingard that indicate his "private" sailing route in the shallow sea of Carimata (33-34). The King of the Sea entrusts him with the temporary command of his brig, *Lightning,* and the schooner, *Emma,* which is loaded with ammunition (231-232). Carter carries out the task admirably, protecting both vessels from attack by the threatening aboriginals (424-425). In *Romance* the narrator favourably presents the chief mate Sebright, who "conducted their [Mr. and Mrs. William's] affairs, as...a trustworthy and experienced old nurse rules the infinite perplexities of a room full of children" (Rom 338; also 338-339 other excerpts).

C. Coping with Adversities at Sea as Professional Initiation

Wrestling with the forces of nature or other hardships, which reveals exemplary realization of the principles of the marine ethos, is for some captains and crew members the first or a particularly demanding test. Braving the fury of the elements by both principal characters in *Typhoon* is their real baptism of fire. In the course of long-standing service as a shipmaster, MacWhirr has never experienced such a herculean task as during the hurricane:

> The sea itself...had never put itself out to startle the silent man....Dirty weather he had known, of course. He had been made wet, uncomfortable, tired in the usual way, felt at the time and presently forgotten....But he had never been given a glimpse of immeasurable strength and of immoderate wrath, the wrath that pauses exhausted but never appeased–the wrath and fury of the passionate sea. He knew it existed, as we know that crime and abominations exist; he had heard of it as a peaceable citizen in a town hears of battles, famines, and floods, and yet knows nothing of what these things mean... (TOS 18-19)

He passes the real trial of seamanship when grappling with the typhoon (and not during the theoretical examination by a maritime board). Jukes is a young officer of "no wide experience of men or storms" (51), for whom resisting the raging gale on the *Nan-Shan* is a true ordeal, an initiation into life at sea.[28] Carter in *The Rescue* undergoes the same in a critical situation. Acting in Lingard's stead on the *Lightning* brings him experience: "His days of responsibility amongst the Shoals of the Shore of Refuge had matured his view of the external world and of his own place therein" (Re 423; also 425-426, 452). The ordeals of the commander of an iron barque in *Falk* and Marlow in *Youth* (who makes his debut as a second mate during the *Judea*'s voyage) (YNTOS 3-4) have similar significance.[29] He constantly emphasizes his youthful inexperience, most conspicuous in confrontation with the veteran seamen Beard, Mahon, and Jermyn (4-6).[30]

Mariners' heroism and maturity revealed on the threshold of a career or in the first instance of emergency or uncommon hardships, i.e., with mostly minimum professional skills and experience, highlight laudable characteristics. Only passing such a test produces a full-fledged mariner; and those who never were confronted with it are treated with condescension and irony (e.g., the shipmasters Brierly in *Lord Jim* or Hermann in *Falk*).

D. Glorification of English Seamen

Conrad's presentation of encounters with inclement weather or other obstacles is sometimes tinged with anglophilism (on this tendency see also Part 2, Chapters 4 and 5). The narrator in *Youth,* admiring the *Judea*'s crews exploits, shows such a predilection:

> To an onlooker they would be a lot of profane scallywags without a redeeming point. What made them do it–what made them obey me....They had no professional reputation–no examples, no praise. It wasn't a sense of duty...it was something in them, something inborn and subtle and everlasting. I don't say positively that the crew of a French or German merchantman wouldn't have done it, but I doubt whether it would have been done in the same way. There was a completeness in it, something solid like aprinciple, and masterful like an instinct–a disclosure of something secret–of that hidden something, that gift of good or evil that makes racial difference, that shapes the fate of nations. (YNTOS 28-29; also 3)

The anglophilic apotheosis of seamen is conveyed as well in *The*

Rover, where Peyrol expresses the highest esteem for his British companions:

> Amongst the members of the Brotherhood it was the Englishmen whom he preferred. He had also found amongst them that particular and loyal appreciation, which a Frenchman of character and ability will receive from Englishmen sooner than from any other nation....The lead [of the brotherhood] used to fall to him mostly at a time of crisis of some sort; and when he had got the lead it was on the Englishmen that he used to depend most. (Rov 133; also 110)

It is in *Rulers of East and West,* idolizing indirectly the courageous English mariners:

> North Atlantic is the heart of a great empire. It is the part of the West Wind's dominions most thickly populated with generations of fine ships and hardy men. Heroic deeds and adventurous exploits have been performed there, within the very stronghold of his sway. The best sailors in the world have been born and bred under the shadow of this sceptre....Reckless adventurers, toiling fishermen, admirals as wise and brave as the world has ever known have waited upon the signs of his Westerly sky. (MS 94)

It is seen in *Well Done* and *Tradition,* which extol the valor of the crews who perfectly fulfilled professional and patriotic obligations in both peace and war: "I can safely affirm [Conrad writes] that I have never, never seen British seamen refuse any risk, any exertion, any effort of spirit or body up to the extremest demands of their calling." *Tradition* (NLL 198). See *The Unlighted Coast* and *The Dover Patrol,* in which laudable actions during World War I are depicted, and in *The Loss of the "Dalgonar,"* which describes commendable performance in a collision of vessels. This theme appears in the ending of *The Nigger of the "Narcissus,"* too, where these brave people's homeland, resisting the ocean from time immemorial, takes on the metaphorical form of a ship braving storms (NN 162-163).[31]

E. Commonplace Characteristics of Sea Heroes

Conradian mariners do not personify unattainable, unrealizable ideals; they are simple, ordinary characters.[32] Such people are most conspicuous in *The Nigger of the "Narcissus,"* where the episodes of resistance to the elements are interwoven with abundant descriptions of the seamen: realistic and occasionally naturalistic, detailed, provoking impressions of authenticity and ordinariness. They are shown as such in their introductory delineation (4-9, 19-20) and in short pauses between the particular phases of the sea ordeal (32-34, 61-63, 94-96, 108-109). Valiant sailors of the *Narcissus* appear as average figures also after the termination of the voyage, when they disembark, get payed, part with one another, and disappear in the urban crowd (165-172). The *Judea* company in *Youth* are depicted similarly as "Liverpool hard cases" (YNTOS 25) with "dark stolid souls" (25), as "a lot of profane scallywags" (28).

Similar methods are applied to the portrayal of the shipmasters in *The Nigger of the "Narcissus"* (N 30-31) and *Typhoon:* Captain MacWhirr's physiognomy "had no pronounced characteristics whatever; it was simply ordinary, irresponsive, unruffled" (TOS 3). This presentation is, however, evidently overemphasized through persistent articulation of his low intelligence:[38]

> Having just enough imagination to carry him through each successive day, and no more, he was tranquilly sure of himself... (4)
> I believe he hasn't brains enough to enjoy kicking up a row....Outside the routine of duty he doesn't seem to understand more than half of what you tell him. (17; also 10, 12, 22, 98, 102)

The heroism and commendable characteristics of the mariners may be attained by every human being. The clear nature and accessibility of these ideals determine the democratic character of the Conradian ethos,[34] the humanism of his canon.

F. The Universal Aspect of the Ethos of Struggle, Work and Duty

The gallant braving of gales or adversities, testifying to the admirable execution of professional obligations, has wider significance. It means passing a test of virtue and inner fortitude, triumphing over evil forces of the external world and over human weakness. The global sense of situations at sea and psychomoral problems revealed in them is regarded as Conrad's substantial contribution to world marine literature.[35]

The all-embracing importance of the ethos of bravery, diligence, and conscientiousness is conspicuous in *The Nigger of the "Narcissus":* its characters endeavor both to face a storm and to overcome their own imperfections. Donkin and Jim, the unambiguous examples of marine antiheroes, embody metaphorically the definite vices of the hardy sailors. Donkin represents a natural inclination to shirking and to self-pity.[36] This is generalized to many people in various milieux: "They all knew him. Is there a spot on earth where such a man is unknown, an ominous survival testifying to the eternal fitness of lies and impudence?" (NN 10). Donkin exerts considerable influence on the crew, who temporarily yield to his instigations and faults and rebel against the captain.

James Wait's deficiencies also represent a seaman's improper urges, his supraindividual status is stressed mainly at the close of the novel, where he proves to be an unreal creature, deprived of any ties with the world and people (169). The significance of the "nigger" is determined mostly by his connection with the symbolic darkness, denoting, for instance, danger, threat, and evil, allied to the tempest and death lying in wait for the mariners, keeping them in its grip.[37] The Negro nearly always appears in the murk (e.g., 104-105)–indistinguishable from it, belonging to it because of his black skin; sometimes powerful sullenness, as if issuing from him, seems even to dim a feeble brightness of the day:

> He seemed to hasten the retreat of departing light by his very presence;

> the setting sun dipped sharply, as though fleeing before our nigger; a black mist emanated from him; a subtle and dismal influence; a something cold and gloomy that floated out and settled on all the faces like a mourning veil. (34)

This type of imagery is in harmony with the frequent presentation of Jim in terms of corpse metaphors: his imprisonment in the house, a result of the ship's listing, is like entombment in a coffin, a grave (66, 69); he looks like a dead person or a specter when awaiting the end of life in the cabin (122, 139, 149, 151, 152). This depiction turns him into a personification of death endangering the *Narcussus's* company, arousing their justifiable fear:[38]

> They...hated to hear, that idea of a stalking death, thrust at them many times a day like a boast and like a menace by this obnoxious nigger. He seemed to take a pride in that death which, so far, had attended only upon the ease of his life; he was overbearing about it, as if no one else in the world had ever been intimate with such a companion; he paraded it unceasingly before us with an affectionate persistence that made its presence indubitable, and at the same time incredible. No man could be suspected of such monstrous friendship! Was he a reality–or was he a sham–this ever-expected visitor of Jimmy's? ...On the slightest provocation, he shook before our eyes the bones of his bothersome and infamous skeleton. He was forever trotting him out. He would talk of that coming death...as if it had sat by his side at every meal. It interfered daily with our occupations, with our leisure, with our amusements...(we all lovingly called him Jimmy, to conceal our hate of his accomplice)... (36)

Wait and his "comrade" influence the seamen's psyche and temper considerably:[39]

> Jimmy's hateful accomplice seemed to have blown with his impure breath undreamt-of subtleties into our hearts. (41)
> At every insignificant turn of our humble life we met Jimmy overbearing and blocking the way, arm-in-arm with his awful and veiled familiar. It was a weird servitude. (43; also 33-34)

This impact is visible in their compliance with all the malingerer's caprices, rebellion against the captain included (36-37, 46-47, 105, 138-140)–the very attitude censured at the end of the voyage (138, 155-156, 161).[40] Human imperfections embodied by the title character[41] are organically combined with the inimical forces of nature: Singleton asserts that "Jimmy was the cause of head winds" (142), "the universe conspired with James Wait" (143). A favorable wind comes only after disposing of his body, which enables the ship to sail to the land (160-161).

The ending of Wait's life implies that the same fate might befall any of the shipboard community who assume an attitude of passivity, idleness (his surname), and of surrendering to panic and their own faults. The mariners' status as potential victims of death is suggested by the application of the imagery relating to death's semantic field (as in the case of Jim).[42] The crew's cabin is called a gloomy crypt (129), "as quiet as a sepulchre" (24), the berths placed there "narrow niches for coffins in a whitewashed and lighted mortuary" (8) or "graves tenanted by uneasy corpses" (22). Captain Allistoun resembles a phantom appearing above a grave (30), and the chief mate Baker "some carnivorous animal prowling amongst corpses" (78). The sailors sleeping on the deck are depicted as "shapeless dark mounds that had the appearance of neglected graves" (155).

All the exploits of the *Narcissus*'s crew may be interpreted as manifestations of the symbolic struggle between life (work) and death (passivity),[43] between threats from the outside (the storm) and threats from the inside (the grave faults embodied by Jim and Donkin, which weaken their commitment to duty):[44]

> They could not spare a moment or a thought from the great mental occupation of wishing to live. And the desire of life kept them alive, apathetic and enduring, under the cruel persistence of wind and cold... (82)
>
> Life seemed an indestructible thing. It went on in darkness, in sunshine, in sleep; tireless, it hovered affectionately round the imposture of his ready death. (105; also 92)

The seamen triumph in this confrontation, display an exemplary attitude, overcome deficiencies, and valiantly endure all the hardships of the voyage. Their ultimate victory coincides with Wait's death and funeral, after which the ship is no longer wrapped in darkness (161-162). The final landfall takes place in the light. The mariners' performance acquires extraprofessional significance and leads to a special catharsis by putting an end to jeopardy and overcoming human flaws (31, 49), which confirms the universal aspect of the maritime ethos presented in this novel.

The general significance of virtues displayed in the face of bad, heavy weather is manifest in *Typhoon,* too, where the mariners' fight against the fury of the elements takes place in gloom (TOS 40, 43, 83, 89-90), which signifies destruction and death and is allied to the hurricane. A human being, Captain MacWhirr, is shown as representing the good, facing the forces of evil and not yielding to the powers of darkness and inimical nature:[45]

> And Jukes heard the voice of his commander...bearing that strange effect of quietness like the serene glow of a halo. (46)
> A man's voice...indomitable sound that can be made to carry an infinity of thought, resolution and purpose...shall be pronouncing confident words–on the last day, when heavens fall, and justice is done... (44)

The universal aspect of the courageous seamen carrying out their tasks in adverse conditions is also evoked in *The Shadow-Line:* the helmsman's hands were "grasping the spokes of the wheel...like a symbol of mankind's claim to the direction of its own fate" (SL 76).

The professional initiation of mariners acquires wider importance by denoting a baptism into life.[46] The narrator in *Youth* (Marlow) recollects his *Judea* voyage to the East as the beginning not only of his maritime career, but also of his adult existence. Hence his story abounds in apostrophes and apothegms that typify and generalize the experiences of those days: e.g. "O youth! The strength of it, the faith of it, the imagination of it! To me she was not an old rattle-trap...to me she was the endeavour, the test, the trial of life" (YNTOS 12). A similar universalization appears in *The Shadow-Line,* mainly in the following expository utterance:

> Only the young have such moments....It is the privilege of early youth to live in advance of its days in all the beautiful continuity of hope which knows no pauses and no introspection.
> One closes behind one the little gate of mere boyishness–and enters an enchanted garden. Its very shades glow with promise. Every turn of the path has its seduction. And it isn't because it is an undiscovered country. One knows well enough that all mankind had streamed that way. It is the charm of universal experience from which one expects an uncommon or personal sensation–a bit of one's own....Yes. One goes on. And the time, too, goes on–till one perceives ahead a shadow-line warning one that the region of early youth, too, must be left behind. (SL 3)[47]

Parallelism between a seaman's baptism of fire and initiation into life is mentioned in *Typhoon* (TOS 19); and *Romance* applies a related realization of this motif: attaining maturity through undergoing many perilous adventures (Rom 203).

The overall aspect of human attitudes and virtues embodied by them is most conspicuous in the cases discussed above, though it pertains to Conrad's entire marine output. The valiant fulfillment of duties by Conradian captains, mates, and their subordinates discloses the moral values that bring success in work, not only at sea. This universalization, however, concerns not only the sphere of axiology, but the entire multifarious and rich ethos of this fellowship, which is representative of manifestations of human life: "Everything can be found at sea, according to the spirt of your quest–strife, peace, romance, naturalism of the most pronounced kind, ideals, boredom, disgust, inspiration–and every conceivable opportunity" (*A Personal Record,* PR 109). This equivalence is suggested particularly by the "planetary" isolation of a ship in the immensity of water, much as the earth is suspended in the cosmos (Part 1, Chapter 1). Such a conception of the maritime existence serves Conrad as the basis for existential reflections based on his observation of sea and the events there, which results in a profusion of sententious utterances, especially in *Lord Jim, Youth,* and *Chance.*[48]

3. Praiseworthy Seamen: The Ethos of Solidarity, Love for Ships, the Sea, and the Maritime Existence

A. Solidarity Manifested in Attitudes and Utterances

Success in the struggle against a storm or in other hardships is determined chiefly by one's character traits, but also by one's relationship to the surrounding world: one's fellow mariners, the vessels, and the water. Unity with companions and awareness of a profound bond with them bring a happy outcome to such situations. They lead to a mastery of the isolation inherent in life at sea, and the weakness that comes in confrontation with the fury of the elements.[49]

The importance of solidarity among mariners is particularly stressed in *The Nigger of the "Narcissus," The Shadow-Line,* and *Youth.* The *Narcissus*'s company desperately tries to get James Wait out of his confinement in the "house" during the gale, in spite of his malingering. They also lend a hand to the second outsider, Donkin, fitting him out. In *The Shadow-Line* the men support their ship's master in critical moments: they do not, for example, reproach him for the lack of quinine but display understanding (SL 96-97), and, in spite of exhaustion, they perform indispensable actions on board and work towards controlling a difficult situation. In *Youth,* the entire crew withstands all the perils threatening its craft.

Grappling with rough weather and overcoming obstacles bind seamen together:

> Youthful faces, bearded faces, dark faces: faces serene, or faces moody, but all akin with the brotherhood of the sea; all with the same attentive expression of eyes, carefully watching the compass or the sails. (*The Nigger of the "Narcissus,"* NN 30; also 173; *Youth,* YNTOS 21)

Marlow in *Heart of Darkness* becomes aware of the bond born in shipboard cooperation:

> I missed my late helmsman awfully,–I missed him even while his body was still lying in the pilot-house...he had done something, he had steered; for months I had him at my back–a help–an instrument. It was a kind of partnership...a subtle bond had been created, of which I only became aware when it was suddenly broken. And the intimate profundity of that look he gave me when he received his hurt remains to this day in my memory–like a claim of distant kinship affirmed in a supreme moment. (YNTOS 119)

The behavior of the narrator (the captain) toward Leggatt in *The Secret Sharer* and Marlow toward Jim in *Lord Jim* bears the stamp of solidarity as well (Part 1, Chapter 2 and Part 2, Chapter 4). A sense of union of maritime fraternity is expressed by many gnomic "sea truths," too, e.g.:

> Woe to the stragglers! We exist only in so far as we hang together. (*Lord Jim*, LJ 223)
> The mysteriously born tradition of sea-craft commands unity in a body of workers engaged in an occupation in which men have to depend upon each other. (*Well Done*, NLL 183; also *The Nigger of the "Narcissus,"* NN 11; *Lord Jim*, LJ, 128-129; *Victory*, V 29)

B. Fellowship in Mariners' Experiences

The bond of community is created by the professional wisdom and knowledge of the mysteries of the sea. These include common perils, hardships, obligations, and experiences. Communicated by universal "sea truths,"[50] this constitutes a significant aspect of Conrad's texts and indicates the essential foundations of the brotherhood's manner of living.

A number of maxims concern obligations (e.g., they stress the need to brave all adversity and react properly and unfailingly to real circumstances):

> There are to a seaman certain words, gestures, that should in given

> conditions come as naturally, as instinctively as the winking of a menaced eye. A certain order should spring on to his lips without thinking; a certain sign should get itself made, so to speak, without reflection. (*The Secret Sharer,* TLS 126)

Other "sea truths" pass on detailed information about the service and customs on ships: e.g. they deal with the chief mate's duties in *The Nigger of the "Narcissus"* (NN 28), *Emblems of Hope* (MS 17), *The Faithful River* (MS 108-109); the men's attitude to their ship master in *A Smile of Fortune* (TLS 8); or the position of a young novice among experienced companions in *Chance* (C 286). Seamen's feelings, tempers, and conduct are similarly generalized through, e.g., inactivity and stoicism in *Typhoon* (TOS 51-52); joy in setting out on a voyage in *Chance* (C 31-32). Sententious utterances pertaining to hardships shared by mariners are connected with ugly weather in *Typhoon* (TOS 20) or difficulties in manoeuring ships in *The Brute* (SS 111-112), *Falk* (TOS 189), etc. They articulate loneliness, which is typical of the marine existence, against the fury and the infinity of water.

Apothegms codetermining the ethos of the sea fraternity refer to other aspects of life as well: celibacy in *Youth* (YNTOS 9), *Nostromo* (N 344), *A Smile of Fortune* (TLS 17) and *Chance* e.g. (C 31, 300-303), where the misogynist Franklin persistently communicates such opinions combined with the glorification of manly friendship born from solidarity; difficulties in obtaining a command (an autobiographical motif), or a place on an English ship in *The Nigger of the "Narcissus"* (NN 167), *The End of the Tether* (YNTOS 186), *The Shadow-Line* (SL 39-40), *Chance* (C 6, 22), *The Black Mate* (TH 88, 117); and the crucial role of professional practice in becoming a full-fledged seaman in *Chance* (C 6). Other such expressed thoughts deal with attachment to a vessel (a home on a voyage), or with important episodes in maritime life: a landfall in *Lord Jim* (LJ 221-222), *A Smile of Fortune* (TLS 5), *Victory* (V 23); a death in *Lord Jim* (LJ 176), *Landfalls and Departures* (MS 10, 12-13), *Chance* (C 52), *The Shadow-Line* (SL 92), *The Rover* (Rov 279), *The Tale* (TH 63-64), and, in particular, *The Nigger of the "Narcissus"* (NN 130, 142, 156).

Gnomic utterances evoking experiences that unite sailors form a kind of popular presentation of the marine ethos–a transmission of basic information about it. This is revealed first and foremost in *The Mirror of the Sea*–a collection of essays abounding in such remarks, illustrated with many digressions that introduce the elements of autobiography and reminiscence.[51] They discuss the beginning and end of a voyage, everyday service on board ship ("*Landfalls and Departures*"); the anchor and how it is used ("Emblems of Hope"); kinds of sailing vessels, techniques of manoeuvring them, and the old generation of mariners ("*The Fine Art*"); masts and sails ("*Cobwebs and Gossamer*"); and cargo loading ("*The Weight of the Burden*"). These are obligations toward a ship ("*The Weight of the Burden,*" "*The Grip of the Land,*" "*Initiation*"); ships not arriving when expected ("*Overdue and Missing*"); shallows ("*The Grip of the Land*"); storms and ways of dealing with them ("*The Character of the Foe*"); winds ("*Rulers of East and West*"), river estuaries ("*The Faithful River*"); the docks, mooring, and transshipment in the Port of London ("*The Faithful River,*" "*In Captivity*"); raging elements and the dangers posed by them ("*Initiation*"); and traditions ("*The Nursery of the Craft*"). Analogous treatment of elements in this ethos are in "*The Silence of the Sea*" from *Last Essays* (comments about late and lost ships and the feelings about waiting for them, about the power and mystery of the watery expanse an the threats inherent in it), in *Lord Jim* (LJ 3-4), *The End of the Tether* (YNTOS 195, 250), and *Chance* (C 316).

C. Ethos of Solidarity and Narrative Stylization in Seamen's Yarns

Mariners' tales cement and demonstrate their fellowship. *Lord Jim* is the clearest instance of shaping the narration by the conventions of the "told-tale."[52] The entire story, except for four initial and ten final chapters, is produced in a precisely delineated narrative situation:

> And later on, many times, in distant parts of the world, Marlow showed himself willing to remember Jim, to remember him at length, in detail

> and audibly. Perhaps it would be after dinner, on a verandah draped in motionless foliage and crowned with flowers, in the deep dusk speckled by fiery cigar-ends. The elongated bulk of each cane-chair harboured a silent listener. Now and then a small red glow would move abruptly, and expanding light up the fingers of a languid hand, part of a face in profound repose, or flash a crimson gleam into a pair of pensive eyes overshadowed by a fragment of an unruffled forehead; and with the very first word uttered Marlow's body, extended at rest in the seat, would become very still, as though his spirit had winged its way back into the lapse of time and were speaking through his lips from the past. (LJ 33; also 34-35, 320, 337)

Marlow is turned into a yarner by his repeated tellings of Jim's adventures in the maritime milieu: this makes *Lord Jim* resemble a sea narrative.

Affinities with "told-tales" are also manifest in Marlow's direct addresses to his listeners. Many of them are extended digressions in which he evokes fundamental principles of the maritime ethos, the experiences common to the whole family of seagoers (43-46, 128-129, 159, 221-22, 223-225), or recollects the figures popular in this social environment. They are Ruthvell and Elliot (37-39), Brierly (57-66), Matherson (64), Bob Stanton (149-151), and Brown (352-354).[53] Jim's adventures are known to this community as well (35-36, 137-138, 197-198). Marlow strengthens this fellowship by appealing to universal problems and values (42-43, 80, 143, 176-177, 313, 320).

Other works by Conrad model narration upon the conventions of the sailor's yarn–this enforces the professional solidarity. But this method achieves in none of them such intensity as in *Lord Jim*. The textual frames of *Youth, Heart of Darkness, Falk, The Brute,*[54] *The Black Mate, Chance,* and *Because of the Dollars* are built by the natural conversations of the seamen, in which references are made to the experiences and lore of the fellowship, e.g.:[55]

> We all began life in the merchant service. Between the five of us there was the strong bond of the sea, and also the fellowship of the craft... (*Youth*, YNTOS 3; also 42)

> Several of us, all more or less connected with the sea, were dining... That flavour of salt-water which for so many of us had been the very water of life permeated our talk....So, comparatively empty, but upon the whole fairly happy, we sat back and told our artless tales. We talked of the sea and all its works....And we talked of old ships, of sea-accidents, of break-downs, dismastings; and of a man who brought his ship safe to Liverpool all the way from the River Plate under a jury rudder. We talked of wrecks, of short rations and of heroism–or at least of what the newspapers would have called heroism at sea. (*Falk*, TOS 145-146)[56]

Narrators and listeners recall characters and events of this milieu. There are, for instance, Captain Harry Dunbar in *The Partner* (WT 89, 128); or the legend about a "murderous" ship in *The Brute* (SS, especially 113-114). Occasionally traces of narration resembling the sea yarn may be noticed in *Nostromo:* Captain Mitchell's story about Sulaco revolutions and coups d'état (N 10-14, 323-326, 473-489); *The Rescue* with Lingard's account (passed to casual listeners) of his acquaintance with Hassim (Re 78); the first-person-plural account in *Victory;* in *The Nigger of the "Narcissus"* with the seamen's freely talking about their experiences and various events (NN 107-108, 161); *Typhoon* with the famous battle between the *Nan-Shan*'s crew and the elements (TOS Author's Note, V-VI); the portrayal of Nelson and his daughter in *Freya of the Seven Isles* (TLS 147-148, 232).[57]

D. Bond of Union with the Professional Tradition

Identification with the heritage of previous generations and the dictate to continue it codetermine and reinforce a sense of oneness in the maritime fraternity.[58] The protagonist in *The Shadow-Line,* having obtained a command, reflects upon his predecessors and his affinities with them:

> I sat down in the arm-chair at the head of the table–the captain's chair... A succession of men had sat in that chair. I became aware of that thought suddenly, vividly, as though each had left a little of himself between the

> soul four walls of these ornate bulkheads; as if a sort of composite soul, the of command, had whispered suddenly to mine of long days at sea and of anxious moments....And I stared back at myself with...some sympathy for this latest representative of what for all intents and purposes was a dynasty; continuous not in blood, indeed, but in its experience, in its training, in its conception of duty, and in the blessed simplicity of its traditional point of view on life. (SL 52-53)

The significance of this treasury of values is also stressed in *The Nursery of the Craft* (MS 148-149), *Well Done* (NLL 183-184), *Tradition* (NLL 196-197, 201), and *Geography and Some Explorers* (LE 17-18). It indicates the foundations of the ethos of the community:

> All ideals are built on the ground of social achievement, which in a given profession creates in the course of time a certain tradition, or, in other words, a standard of conduct. The existence of a standard of conduct in its turn makes the most improbable achievement possible, by augmenting the power of endurance and of self-sacrifice amongst men who look to the past for their lessons and for their inspiration. (*The Dover Patrol*, LE 58)

Such perfection is embodied in the eulogized mariners of the older generation. Singleton in *The Nigger of the "Narcissus"* distinguishes himself by exceptional valor; his entire life is filled with faithful service:

> Through half a century [he] had measured his strength against the favours and the rages of the sea. He had never given a thought to his mortal self. He lived unscathed, as though he had been indestructible, surrendering to all the temptations, weathering many gales. (NN 98-99; also 172)

Veneration of this figure, described as "a statue of heroic size" (129), pertains, through synecdoche, to the whole generation represented by him:

> Yet he was only a child of time, a lonely relic of a devoured and

> forgotten generation....The men who could understand his silence were gone–those men who knew how to exist beyond the pale of life and within sight of eternity. They had been strong, as those are strong who know neither doubts nor hopes. They had been impatient and enduring, turbulent an devoted, unruly and faithful...knew toil, privation, violence, debauchery–but knew not fear, and had no desire of spite in their hearts. Men hard to manage, but easy to inspire; voiceless men–but men enough to scorn in their hearts the sentimental voices that bewailed the hardness of their fate. It was a fate unique an their own; the capacity to bear it appeared to them the privilege of the chosen! Their generation lived inarticulate an indispensable, without knowing the sweetness of affections or the refuge of a home–and died free from the dark menace of a narrow grave...[they] were strong and mute; they were effaced, bowed and enduring, like stone caryatides that hold up in the night the lighted halls of a resplendent and glorious edifice. (24-25)

When predicting Jim's fate Singleton becomes a deliverer of the immemorial laws of the sea: "The wisdom of half a century spent in listening to the thunder of the waves had spoken unconsciously through his old lips" (24; also 6, 14, 42-43, 129-130, 142). Captain Whalley in *The End of the Tether* (see on him in Part 1, Chapter 2 and Part 2, Chapters 4 and 5), and Mr. Stonor, who appears episodically in *The Brute* (SS 106-107), are the other admired seamen of this age group.

The exaltation of tradition results frequently from an evaluative juxtaposition of the past and present. According to the narrator in *An Outcast of the Islands,* it pertains to the former, glamorous, romantic image of the sea, as opposed to the latter–which is one of serving trade (OI 12-13). The protagonist in *A Smile of Fortune* expresses a similar dislike of turning the marine vocation mercantile (TLS 6-7). In other texts–especially *Youth, Heart of Darkness, The Mirror of the Sea, Freya of the Seven Isles, The Shadow-Line, Notes on Life and Letters*–this idea takes the form of contrast between sailing ships, which belong to the previous epoch, and steamers. Sometimes it concerns the eulogized marines of bygone times and their successors who do not live up to them as in *The Nigger of the "Narcissus"* (NN 24-25). Glorifying sea voyages in the past is most conspicuous in Conrad's nonfictional prose: *The Fine Art* (MS 31), *Poland Revisited* (NLL 161-162), *Outside Literature* (LE 42), *Ocean Travel* (LE 35-38) and *Legends* (LE 46-47).[59]

E. Ethos of Devotion to Ships

A vessel, like professional solidarity, is a crucial means of multiplying human powers and counteracting loneliness, a mainstay in everyday confrontations with the immensity of water, "the closest partner of [man's] toil and courage"–*Well Done* (NLL 188-189). Many seamen treat their craft as a basis of existence: Morrison in *Victory* (V 14), Captain Harry Dunbar in *The Partner* (WT 113), Tom Lingard in *The Rescue* (Re 10, 229), and most of all Jasper Allen in *Freya of the Seven Isles* (TLS 152, 156, 210, 218; also on his love isolation in Part 1, Chapter 2).

Anthropomorphized craft[60] actively participate in wrestling with the powerful, infinite elements.[61] Their "heroism" is prominent in *The Nigger of the "Narcissus"*:

> Before the strong breath of westerly squalls the ship...lay slowly over, obstinate and yielding. She drove to and fro in the unceasing endeavour to fight her way through the invisible violence of the winds....Enduring and valiant, she answered to the call of men... (NN 49)
> And devastated, battered, and wounded she drove foaming to the northward, as though inspired by the courage of a high endeavour...

Typhoon portrays the same:

> Her middle structure was like a half-tide rock awash upon a coast. It was like an outlying rock with the water boiling up, streaming over, pouring off, beating round–like a rock in the surf to which shipwrecked people cling before they let go–only it rose, it sank, it rolled continuously, without respite and rest, like a rock that should have miraculously struck adrift from a coast and gone wallowing upon the sea. (TOS 43-44; also 91)

Vessels are also praised because they carry out their duties and the commanders' orders and give gallant service.[62] The *Lightning* in *The Rescue* "put forth all her qualities and her power, to repay his exacting affection by a faithfulness tried to the very utmost limit of endurance" (Re 54); the *Sofala* in *The End of the Tether* "could always be depended upon to make her courses. Her compasses were never out. She was no trouble at all to take about" (YNTOS 166; also 326); the steamer in *The Shadow-Line* "I [was] a most excellent Scottish ship–for she was that from the keel up–excellent sea-boat, easy to keep clean, most handy in every way" (SL 5). The craft in *Initiation* (MS 128-129, 136, 146-147), *The "Tremolino"* (MS 161), and *Youth* (YNTOS 35) perform equally admirably.

The virtuous "attitude" of a ship, the people's brave partner in struggle and work, makes them admire it.[63] Red-Eyed Tom's relation to the *Lightning* in *The Rescue* is the most characteristic instance of this frame of mind:[64]

> Every flutter of the sails flew down from afloat along the taut leeches, to enter his heart in a sense of acute delight; and the gentle murmur of water alongside...was to him more precious and inspiring than the soft whisper of tender words would have been to another man. It was in such moments that he lived intensely, in a flush of strong feeling that made him long to press his little vessel to his breast. She was his perfect world full of trustworthy joy. (Re 54)
>
> There's nothing in the world I love so much [Lingard says] as this brig....Nothing in the world. If I lost her I would have no standing room on the earth for my feet. (229; also 10, 203; *An Outcast of the Islands*, OI 45)

Other of Conrad's captains treat their ships with profound affection as well: Allistoun in *The Nigger of the "Narcissus"* (NN 30-31, 91), Marlow in *Heart of Darkness* (YNTOS 85), MacWhirr in *Typhoon* (TOS 90), the protagonist and *Hilda*'s commander in *A Smile of Fortune* (TLS 18-19, 87), Gasper Allen in *Freya of the Sevn Isles* (TLS 156, 158), Anthony in *Chance* (C 346), Morrison in *Victory* (V 14), and Harry Dunbar in *The Partner* (WT 102).[65]

Mates' behavior is like that of their superiors. Baker in *The Nigger of the "Narcissus"* persuades his subordinates that care for the ship belongs to their most important duties (NN 79), and unwillingly parts with the *Narcissus* after the voyage is over (166-167). Marlow in *Youth* nostalgically recollects the *Judea,* the place of his maritime baptism with fire: "I think of her with pleasure, with affection, with regret–as you would think of someone dead you have loved. I shall never forget her...." (YNTOS 12; also 15). In *Chance,* Powell's first contact with the *Ferndale* stirs his respect and confidence (C 29). Ordinary seamen, too, express affection for the vessels on which they work, e.g., Franklin in *Chance* (287) or Singleton in *The Nigger of the "Narcissus,"* who treats his craft cordially:

> 'Steers...like a little boat,' he said, at last, with hoarse tenderness,' (NN 91; also 26)
> We all watched her. She was beautiful and had a weakness. We loved her no less for that. We admired her qualities aloud, we boasted of them to one another, as though they had been our own....Less perfect than many perhaps, but she was ours, and, consequently, incomparable. We were proud of her....We knew she was the most magnificent sea-boat ever launched. (50-51)

The anthropomorphism of a ship serves the occasional expression of her psychophysical oneness with the seamen. The vessel's equipment in *The Nigger of the "Narcissus"* constitutes a part of Singleton's body (26); Captain Allistoun feels united with it as well (50). In *Freya of the Seven Isles* "Jasper felt as if, together with the command of the brig, his very heart were being taken out of his breast" (TLS 216), and when Heemskirk wrecks her it is a deadly blow to him (228-229). An organic tie is accented in *Chance* as well, where Captain Anthony treats the *Ferndale* as a part of his own self (C 346), in *The Rescue* (Re 11, 92, 226-227) and takes a sententious form in *Cobwebs and Gossamer:* "Such is the intimacy with which a seaman had to live with his ship of yesterday that his senses were like her senses, that the stress upon his body made him judge of the strain upon the ship's masts" (MS 38).[66]

Mariners' enchantment with ships (in British English this noun is often of feminine gender) displays affinities with man's adoration of woman.[67] Such is revealed by the ship's master Lingard–"to him she [the brig] was always precious–like old love; always desirable–like a strange woman; always tender–like a mother; always faithful–like the favourite daughter of a man's heart *The Rescue* (Re 10). The same is found in *An Outcast of the Islands* (OI 173), with Allistoun in *The Nigger of the "Narcissus"* (NN 50), Jasper Allen in *Freya of the Seven Isles* (TLS 157), the *Hilda*'s captain in *A Smile of Fortune* (TLS 18-19), the crews in *The Nigger of the "Narcissus"* (NN 85), *Typhoon* (TOS 7),[68] and by the implied author's maxims in *The Mirror of the Sea:*

> Men shall learn to know [the ship] with an intimacy surpassing the intimacy of man with man, to love with a love nearly as great as that of man for woman, and often as blind in its infatuated disregard of defects. (*Overdue and Missing,* MS 58; also *Emblems of Hope,* MS 19-20; *Initiation,* MS 132)[69]

A passion for the vessels is revealed in articulating their extraordinary aesthetic qualities:[70] their "grace" and "elegance" are emphasized by nearly all of Conrad's sea stories, in particular *The Nigger of the "Narcissus"* (NN 132-133, 145), *Typhoon* (TOS 7), *The Secret Sharer* (TLS 95-96), *Freya of the Seven Isles* (TLS 157-158, 165, 211), *The Shadow-Line* (SL 49-50), *The Rescue* (Re 45, 146, 203), and *The Rover* (Rov 251-252). Infatuation with their charm combined with a use of highly poetic images is, however, most conspicuous in *The Mirror of the Sea* in *Embles of Hope* (MS 21); *In Captivity* (MS 116-117); and *Initiation* (MS 129-131),[71] where the metaphorical descriptions of particular pieces of equipment and actions performed (see the titles of some essays) imply beauty and eulogy. A ship's beauty occasionally resembles a lady's, e.g., in *The Tale* (TH 63) or *Freya of the Seven Isles:* "Like some fair women of adventurous life famous in history, [the brig] seemed to have the secret of perpetual youth.... Jasper Allen...clothed her in many coats of the very best white paint" (TLS 157).

The intensity of such declarations depends upon the kind of craft. Those moved by wind are clearly preferred and treated with stronger affection than those propelled by steam,[72] as in *The Shadow-Line* (SL 4, 30) or *The End of the Tether* (YNTOS 214). In *Freya of the Seven Isles* the comparison, tendentiously colored, of the brig and the gunboat magnifies the contrast between the dreamer Jasper Allen an his rival, the brutal and repulsive Dutchman Heemskirk:

> The smoke belching out suddenly from her [the *Neptune*'s] short black funnel rolled between the masts of the "Bonito," obscuring for a moment the sunlit whiteness of her sails, consecrated to the service of love. (TLS 208)
> The brig, with her fine lines and her white sails, looked vaporous and sylph-like in the moonlight. The gunboat, short, squat, with her stumpy dark spars naked like dead trees, raised against the luminous sky of that resplendent night, threw a heavy shadow on the lane of water between the two ships. (211)

Analogous juxtapositions are evident in the collections of nonfictional prose: *The Mirror of the Sea, Notes on Life and Letters,* and *Last Essays:*

> Cargo steam vessels have reached by this time a height of utilitarian ugliness....These dismal creations look still uglier at sea than in port, and with an added touch of the ridiculous. Their rolling waddle...so unlike the soaring lift and swing of a craft under sail, have in them something caricatural, a suggestion of a low parody directed at noble predecessors by an improved generation of dull, mechanical toilers, conceited and without grace. (*Poland Revisited,* NLL 161; also *The Fine Art,* MS 30-31; *The "Torrens": A Personal Tribute,* LE 25-26)

A profound conviction about devotion to ships is a natural outcome of this attachment to them:[73]

> What awakens the seaman's sense of duty, what lays that impalpable constraint upon the strength of his manliness, what commands his not always dumb if always dogged devotion, is not the spirit of the sea but something that in his eyes has a body, a character, a fascination, and almost a soul–it is his ship. (*Well Done,* NLL 191; also 188-189)

The implied author of *The Mirror of the Sea* argues that the craft will reward those who are dutiful towards it:

> You must treat with an understanding consideration the mysteries of her...nature, and then she will stand by you faithfully in the unceasing struggle with forces wherein defeat is no shame...she will sail, stay, run for you as long as she is able, or, like a sea-bird going to rest upon the angry waves, she will lay out the heaviest gale that ever made you doubt living long enough to see another sunrise. (*The Weight of the Burden,* MS 56)

Such service requires the exertion of all the seamen's powers and capabilities:

> A ship is not a slave. You must make her easy in a seaway, you must never forget that you owe her the fullest share of your thought, of your skill, of your self-love. (*The Weight of the Burden,* MS 56; also 51-52; *The Fine Art,* MS 29-30; *The Nigger of the "Narcissus,"* NN79; *Well Done,* NLL 188-189)

The painful consequences of failing to observe this are told by the implied author in *The Mirror of the Sea,* "No seaman can feel comfortable in body or mind when he has made his ship uneasy," or in *The Weight of the Burden* (MS 53) and *Overdue and Missing* (MS 64), as well as by Marlow in *Heart of Darkness:* "After all, for a seaman, to scrape the bottom of the thing that's supposed to float all the time under his care is the unpardonable sin. No one may know of it, but you never forget the thump–eh? A blow on the very heart" (YNTOS 94). Loss of a beloved ship is a tragedy for Conradian captains. Look at Dawson in *The Rescue,* committing suicide after the treacherous foundering of the craft under his command (Re 101) or Jasper Allen in *Freya of the Seven Isles,* who grieves about his separation from the *Bonito* (TLS 214-218), and later despairs over the wreck:

> Reaching the point of land opposite that part of the reef on which his brig lay stranded, [he would] look steadily across the water at her beloved form, once the home of a exulting hope, and now, in her

> inclined, desolated immobility, towering above the lonely sea-horizon, a symbol of despair. (229)

Harry Dunbar in *The Partner* found that

> it was a great trial to lose the ship....If she must be left on the rocks–why, she must....Suddenly his voice breaks, and he squeezes Cloete's arm: It seems as if I couldn't leave her, he whispers. (WT 112-113)

F. Ethos of Love for the Sea and the Maritime Manner of Living

Affection for the ship constitutes one aspect of a wider and laudable attitude: admiration for the sea and life on it. This frame of mind is embodied in the principal character of the Malay trilogy–a man of long-time service on board, and a representative of the former generation of romantic mariners:

> Tom Lingard was a master, a lover, a servant of the sea....He loved it with the ardent affection of a lover, he made light of it with the assurance of perfect mastery, he feared it with the wise fear of a brave man, and he took liberties with it as a spoiled child might do with a paternal and good-natured ogre. He was grateful to it, with the gratitude of an honest heart. (*An Outcast of the Islands,* OI 13)

The vast waters reciprocate this intimate, passionate behavior:

> The sea woke up under the push of the sharp cutwater, and whispered softly to the gliding craft in that tender and rippling murmur in which it speaks sometimes to those it nurses and loves. Lingard stood by the taff-rail listening, with a pleased smile till the 'Flash' began to draw close to the only other vessel in the anchorage. (44)

Love for the sea is characteristic of young mariners too; it assumes the shape of a romantic vision of this vocation, governing their performance, aspirations, and dreams. It is personified principally in the protagonist of *Youth,* Marlow, who perceives reality through an ecstatic representation of the marine existence, and is as well manifest in the hyperbolic glorification of the *Judea*'s crew's activities. Marlow also feels enthusiasm and exultation when commanding a boat after the sinking of the barque (YNTOS 34), and when cherishing an idealized image of the East–the goal of the voyage–conjured up as a realm of perfect happiness (15, 36-38, 40-42). Getting there is a grand experience for him, and fascination with adventure is a significant element of his mind set.[74] Young Marlow's perspective bears upon the entire narration on all its levels (see the descriptions of weather; 10, 20).[75]

The captain narrator in *A Smile of Fortune* is enraptured by the magnificence of the mariner's profession, he extols it and expresses aversion to its becoming commercial:

> Ah! These commercial interests–spoiling the finest life under the sun. Why must the sea be used for trade–and for war as well? Why kill and traffic on it, pursuing selfish aims of no great importance after all? It would have been so much nicer just to sail about with here and there a port and a bit of land to stretch one's legs on, buy a few books and get a change of cooking for a while. (TLS 6)

This in tune with his elation, shown, for instance, in his perception of Jacobus's and Alice's isolation (39), their garden (42-43), and their habitation–the Pearl of the Ocean (3, 74).[76]

A mature person's perspective (most evident in *Youth,* but also in *Lord Jim, The Mirror of the Sea, Chance,* and *The Shadow-Line*) frequently combines with worship of the sea and highlights the splendor of a maritime youth through nostalgic reminiscence. This occasionally evokes disappointment and regret that the marine existence departs so markedly from juvenile reveries: "In no other kind of life is the illusion more wide of reality–in no other is the beginning all illusion–the disenchantment more swift–the subjugation more complete" (*Lord Jim,* LJ 129).

Seamen are not the only group of characters fascinated by the watery expanse. This emotion is sometimes connected with a desire for liberty, for putting an end to a hopeless, tragic life on land, as for example, in the attitudes of Dain and Nina in

Almayer's Folly who leave Sambir to escape from the Dutchman ("Yes, when the next day broke, they would be together on the great blue sea that was like life–away from the forests that were like death") (AF 169), Jim in the Patusan part of *Lord Jim* (LJ 331-332), or Giorgio Viola in *Nostromo* who dreams of true democracy and freedom in Costaguana (on *Nostromo* as a political novel, see Part 2, Chapter 5), enslaved by despotism and harassed by coups d'état ("All the earth made by God is holy; but the sea, which knows nothing of kings and priests and tyrants, is the holiest of all....The spirit of liberty is upon the waters...." (N 341). Flora de Barral in *Chance* is anxious to "sail away from this abominable world of treacheries, and scorns and envies and lies, away, away over the blue sea, the sure, the inaccessible, the uncontaminated and spacious refuge for wounded souls" (C 364-365), and Freya in *Freya of the Seven Isles* dreams about happiness with Jasper on his brig (on the amorous isolation of Flora, Freya, and their lovers see Part 1, Chapter 2).

Such conduct is representative of the mentality of all worthy Conradian sea characters, which is confirmed by statements for the entire community:

> There is such magnificent vagueness in the expectations that had driven each of us to sea, such a glorious indefiniteness, such a beautiful greed of adventures that are their own and only reward!...Can one of us restrain a smile? (*Lord Jim*, LJ 129; also 128-129 other passages)
>
> They [Marlow's companions] agreed that the happiest time in their lives was as youngsters in good ships....They agreed also as to the proudest moment they had known in that calling which is never embraced on rational and practical grounds, because of the glamour of its romantic associations. (*Chance*, C 4; also *Well Done*, NLL 183-184)

Eulogizing the maritime ethos is universalized in *The Mirror of the Sea,* where particular elements of reality assume metaphorical shapes (see especially *Rulers of East and West,* and *The Fine Art,* in which a mariner fulfilling his task is compared to an artist, and the result of his toil to a masterpiece). Conrad occasionally limits this praise to the previous generation of romantic sailors.

It is also frequently based upon a judgmental opposition between life at sea and on land. The tendency is subject to even greater generalization, as a glorification of an idealistic outlook of life, most visible in *Youth* (owing to Marlow's plentiful gnomic apostrophes), *Lord Jim* (see Part 2, Chapter 4), and *Within the Tides* (WT Author's Note VII-VIII).

G. Autobiographical and Anglophilic Perspectives

Adoration of the sea and the heroic vision of the marine vocation have obvious personal undertones in Conrad's texts. Many characters represent the standpoint of the author himself (chiefly Marlow, as evidenced, e.g., by "Author's Note" to *Youth: A Narrative and Two Other Stories,* YNTOS XI). In the autobiographical works the writer directly communicates his passion for the sea:

> My relation with the sea, which beginning mysteriously, like any great passion...went on unreasoning and invincible, surviving the test of disillusion, defying the disenchantment [and] went on full of love's delight and love's anguish, facing them in open-eyed exultation, without bitterness and without repining, from the first hour to the last....I surrendered my being to that passion...for twenty years I had lived like a hermit with my passion! Beyond the line of the sea horizon the world for me did not exist....
>
> This perhaps is enough to me to say on this particular occasion about these, my parting words, about...my great passion for the sea. I call it great because it was great to me....But whatever it may be the fact remains that it was something too great for words. (*The Mirror of the Sea,* MS Author's Note IX-X; also other passages in this preface and *A Personal Record,* PR 110; *The Arrow of Gold,* AG 88, 123, 242, 351)

Conrad's nostalgic homage to the universe of water, the mariners and the vessels of his life is expressed in *The "Torrens": A Personal Tribute*–in the reminiscences of his service on the craft of this name, and first and foremost in *The Mirror of the Sea,* which is pervaded by the particularly significant thread of private memories, experiences and sensations:

> Within these pages I make a full confession not of my sins but of my emotions. It is the best tribute my piety can offer to the ultimate shapers of my character, convictions, and, in a sense, destiny–to the imperishable sea, to the ships that are no more, and to the simple men who have had their day. (*The Mirror of the Sea,* MS Author's Note XI-XII; also *A Personal Record,* PR A Familiar Preface XVI-XVII)

In *The "Tremolino"* the implied author recollects with greatest esteem the ship that woke his love for the water, on which he underwent his baptism. After it founders in the Mediterranean he feels a despair analogous to the reactions of many captains in Conrad's novels and short stories: "This shipwreck lies upon my soul with the dread and horror of a homicide, with the unforgettable remorse of having crushed a living, faithful heart at a single blow" (MS 179; also *The Arrow of Gold,* AG 290-291).

Other elements of the maritime ethos show direct autobiographical references too. The author himself took part in the production of seamen's tales, later treating them as the prototypes of his fiction. Veneration for the past, as conveyed in his essays, mostly concerns the nostalgic recollection of Conrad's juvenile years and adult life at sea. Personal aspects are also inherent in dreams of adventure (*Geography and Some Explorers, The "Tremolino,"* and *The Arrow of Gold,* in which the Carlist episode of Conrad's life is presented as motivated exclusively by such aspirations), and escape to realize these desires (*A Personal Record,* PR 35-36), yearning for youth, and disappointment caused by the discrepancy between reality and its ideal image (*Initiation,* MS 141-142, 148).

Conrad's celebration of existence at sea occasionally takes on anglophilic overtones (on other manifestations of such see Part 2, Chapters 4 and 5). In "Author's Note" to *Youth: A Narrative and Two Other Stories,* he considers himself fortunate to be an adopted child of this nation (YNTOS, Author's Note X), and in *A Personal Record* he stresses his youthful determination: if to become a mariner–only an English one (PR 119, 122).[77] This is evident in the presentation of the professional tradition too: British seamen are said to zealously serve their country at all times (*Tradition,* NLL 196-198) and Britain's commercial shipping formed the foundation of an empire based on the marine trade and transportation and secured supremacy on the oceans (*Confidence*). Conrad evokes visions of the earliest expeditions in *The Nigger of the "Narcissus"* (NN 172) and *The Faithful River* (MS 112-113), and of the Napoleonic period, which was particularly glorious, combined with hero-worship of Admiral Nelson (*The Heroic Age)*. This same frame of mind is externalized in his admiration for the esthetic qualities of British vessels with *The Nigger of the "Narcissus"* (NN 50-51), *The Faithful River* (MS 110), *In Captivity* (MS 117, 119-121), *The Black Mate* (TH 85), and the masterly skill of their builders in, again, *The Nigger of the "Narcissus"* (NN 50, 68), *In Captivity* (MS 117), and in articulating the glamor of port of London and the Thames with *The Faithful River* (MS 111-113) and *Chance* (C 276-277), as well as in the eulogy of maritime institutions with *Protection of Ocean Liners* and *A Friendly Place*. Anglophilism is in *Romance* in the views of Don Carlos and Seraphina (Rom 150-151, 165-166), and in emphasizing John Kemp's noble-minded, chivalrous conduct, misunderstood by Latin Americans, in his duels with O'Brien and his henchmen (304-306, 492).

4. Superiority of Life at Sea over Life on Land

A. Mariners' Contempt for Life and Work on Land

Praise of the maritime ethos results in a persistent argument for its superiority to a settled life.[78] The particularly difficult conditions at sea demand uncommon fortitude and personal ruggedness. This opinion is stated by an old sailor and Marlow in *Chance:*

> If we at sea...went about our work as people ashore high and low go about theirs we should never make a living. No one would employ us. And moreover no ship navigated and sailed in the happy-go-lucky manner people conduct their business on shore would ever arrive into port...[since] the exacting life of the sea has this advantage over the life of the earth, that its claims are simple and cannot be evaded. (C 3-4, 32)

Marlow in *Lord Jim* contrasts Jim-mariner and his family in England "peopling that quiet corner of the world as free of danger or strife as a tomb, and breathing equally the air of undisturbed rectitude....Nothing ever came to them; they would never be taken unawares, and never be called upon to grapple with the fate" (LJ 342). Such a view is shared also by a crew member in *The Nigger of the "Narcissus"*: "It is...bloomin' easy to be a gentleman when you have a clean job for life" (NN 32).

A judgmental antithesis between sea and land people is suggested by the scornful "landlubbers" (especially in *The Mirror of the Sea, Chance, The Rover,* and *Last Essays*). The juxtaposition of characters from both these spheres implies the mariners' higher quality. This is expressed tellingly by the ending of *The Nigger of the "Narcissus"*:[79]

> Singleton has no doubt taken with him the long record of his faithful work into the peaceful depths of an hospitable sea. And Donkin, who never did a decent day's work in his life, no doubt earns his living by discoursing with filthy eloquence upon the right of labour to live. So be it! Let the earth and the sea each have its own. (NN 172; also 169-170)[80]

Land dwellers are treated with scorn by seamen in *Chance,* who are convinced of the excellence of their ethos. Captain Anthony

> went on speaking of himself as a confirmed enemy of life on shore–a perfect terror to a simple man, what with the fads and proprieties and the ceremonies and affectations. He hated all that. He wasn't fit for it. There was no rest and peace and security but on the sea. (C 221; also 270-271)

He is seconded by Marlow, the narrator (326), and Franklin, the chief mate of the *Ferndale,* who remains impressed by his superior's speech "upon the wickedness of the solid world surrounded by the salt, uncorruptible waters on which he and his captain had dwelt all their lives in happy innocence" (271). In *Heart of Darkness,* on the other hand, Marlow asserts that the expanse of water, unlike the rest of the world, is for seamen the only reality that is mysterious and worthy of cognition (YNTOS 48). For some characters, staying on land is equivalent to slavery or humiliation, and the sea appears a realm of freedom and happiness.[81]

Mariners' aversion to life on land makes them want to remain there as briefly as possible in an anxious wait to set out to sea (especially Anthony and Marlow in *Chance,* Marlow and the *Judea*'s company in *Youth,* the protagonist of *The Shadow-Line*). Too close a relationship with the earth exerts adverse or even fatal influences upon seamen. This pertains to vessels as well, making them "dead" or "enslaved:"[82]

> Brick walls rose high above the water–soulless walls, staring through hundreds of windows as troubled and dull as the eyes of over-fed brutes. At their base monstrous iron cranes crouched, with chains hanging from their long necks, balancing cruel-looking hooks over the decks of lifeless ships....Between high buildings the dust of all the continents scared in short flights; and a penetrating smell of perfumes and dirt, of spices and hides, of things costly and of things filthy, pervaded the space, made for it an atmosphere precious and disgusting. The 'Narcissus' came gently into her berth; the shadows of soulless walls fell upon her, the dust of all the continents leaped up on her deck, and a swarm of strange men, clambering up her sides, took possession of her in the name of the sordid earth. She had ceased to live. (*The Nigger of the "Narcissus,"* NN 164-165)
>
> A ship in dock, surrounded by quays and the walls of warehouses, has the appearance of a prisoner meditating upon freedom in the sadness of a free spirit put under restraint. Chain cables and stout ropes keep her bound to stone posts...a ship lying passive and still and safe, as if lost in deep regrets of her days of liberty and danger on the sea. (*In Captivity,* MS 115; also 115-116 other excerpts; *The Faithful River,* MS 110-111)

Land-dwelling businessmen profane the briny deep and the glorious ethos of the maritime fraternity. Motivated by cupidity, they subordinate the sea to commercial activities:

> The hand of the engineer tore down the veil of the terrible beauty in order that greedy and faithless landlubbers might pocket dividends....The

> once loving and devoted servants went out armed with fire and iron, and conquering the fear of their own hearts became a calculating crowd of cold and exacting masters....The sea of to-day is a used-up drudge, wrinkled and defaced by the churned-up wakes of brutal propellers, robbed of the enslaving charm of its vastness, stripped of its beauty, of its mystery and of its promise. (*An Outcast of the Islands,* OI 12-13)

A similar view is voiced by the captain in *A Smile of Fortune,* who treats mercantile dealings superciliously, as an occupation unfit for a ship's master. Refer also to the implied author of the polemical *Some Reflections on the Loss of the "Titanic,"* who claims that the construction of the liner made it resemble a huge, luxurious hotel, which identifies as one of the main reasons for the catastrophe.

B. Censure of Clerks and Institutions

Sailors are convinced about the exceptionally great value of their toil. According to the implied author in *Memorandum on the Scheme for Fitting Out a Sailing Ship,* "Seamen's work was never looked upon or had the character of mere slavish toil, as some branches of labour on shore tend to become" (LE 71). What seamen express an especially strong contempt for is clerical work. In *The Nigger of the "Narcissus"* the narrator ironically compares the shipping office clerks to caged birds (NN 167-168, 170). Mockery appears even more clearly in the description of the quill driver in *Chance* as

> a plump, little man was writing hard, his nose very near the desk. His head was perfectly bald and about the same drab tint as the papers. He appeared pretty dusty too.
>
> I didn't notice whether there were any cobwebs on him, but I shouldn't wonder if there were because he looked as though he had been imprisoned for years in that little hole...his dungeon was hot and musty; it smelt of gas and mushrooms, and seemed to be somewhere 120 feet below the ground....One couldn't imagine why the Marine Board should keep that bald, fat creature slaving down there. (C 11)

Marine officials are portrayed in a similar vein. The narrator in *The Shadow-Line* sarcastically calls Marine Superintendent Captain Ellis "the deputy-Neptune" (SL 29-30, 130), whereas Captain Eliott, the Master Attendant in *The End of the Tether,* is "a man...with round legs, round arms, a round body, a round face–generally producing the effect of his short figure having been distended by means of an air-pump as much as the seams of his clothing would stand" (YNTOS 195). Unflattering comments about scribblers are in *Karain* (TU 19), *Lord Jim* (LJ 278-279), *Heart of Darkness* (YNTOS 56, 57), *Chance* (C 338-339), *The Shadow-Line* (SL 29, 34), *The Rover* (Rov 3-5), and *Some Reflections on the Loss of the "Titanic"* (NLL 216-217).

This attitude determines the mariner's distrust of land institutions and his power to ensure realization of definite ethical principles. It is particularly clear in *Lord Jim,* in the persistently stated conviction about the incompetence of the jury in reaching a just verdict on the *Patna* incident. Jim emphasizes that those who could assess his guilt had to have experienced his ordeal: "Let them go through the kind of thing before they talk. Just let them–and do better–that's all" (LJ 106). Marlow shares Jim's conviction about the impossibility of an adequate investigation and a reasonable verdict at this trial (see also Part 1, Chapters 2 and 3 and Part 2, Chapter 4):

> You can't expect the constituted authorities to inquire into the state of a man's soul....Their business was to come down upon the consequences, and frankly, a casual police magistrate and two nautical assessors are not much good for anything else. (56-57; also 56-57; other extracts)

The official investigation is opposed to the private one–to Jim's "dialogue" with his conscience:

> He was not speaking to me [Marlow], he was only speaking before me, in a dispute with an invisible personality, an antagonistic and inseparable partner of his existence–another possessor of his soul. These were issues beyond the competency of a court of inquiry: it was a subtle and

> momentous quarrel as to the true essence of life, and did not want a judge. (93)
> For days, for many days, he had spoken to no one, but had held silent, incoherent, and endless converse with himself, like a prisoner alone in his cell or like a wayfarer lost in the wilderness. (33; also 28)

Marlow's belief influences his sardonic presentation of the officers administering justice:

> The pious sailing-ship skipper appeared excited and made uneasy movements, as if restraining with difficulty an impulse to stand up and exhort us earnestly to prayer and repentance. The head of the magistrate, delicately pale under the neatly arranged hair, resembled the head of a hopeless invalid after he has been washed and brushed and propped up in bed. (158)[83]

Jim's father, a country parson, represents another branch of institutionalized ethics (religious). He is unable to judge the protagonist properly either: "In the inviolable shelter of his book-lined, faded, and comfortable study...for forty years he had conscientiously gone over and over again the round of his little thoughts about faith and virtue" (341). He can not comprehend his son's deed (79), and limits himself exclusively to banal moralizing (341-342).[84]

The conviction that land ethics are insufficient for an appreciation of seamen's conduct in a crisis situation at sea is conveyed in *The Secret Sharer*.[85] The *Sephora*'s chief mate, who killed an insubordinate mariner in a tussle during a furious gale, emphasizes that a jury is not the right body to evaluate his deed and the extent of his offense (TLS 101, 131-132; also the portrayal of Leggatt and the protagonist in Part 1, Chapter 2 and Part 2, Chapter 4):

> You don't suppose I am afraid of what can be done to me? Prison or gallows or whatever they may please. But you don't see me coming back to explain such things to an old fellow in a wig and twelve respectable tradesmen, do you? What can they know whether I am guilty or not–or of *what* I am guilty, either? (131-132; also 101)

The validity of Leggatt's view is confirmed indirectly by the grotesque portrayal of his superior, who, assuming the role of a representative of the law, trembles with fear (107) and looks like "a criminal making a reluctant and doleful confession" (116). The same kind of censure appears episodically in *The End of the Tether,* where the official inquiry does not discover the true causes of Whalley's death on the sinking *Sofala* (YNTOS 336), and in *Some Reflections on the Loss of the "Titanic"* and *Certain Aspects of Admirable Inquiry,* which argue that hasty opinions about the tragedy wrong the liner's crew.[86]

The scorn for offices acquires a more general significance: the rejection of institutionally organized life on land. These institutions guarantee ease and security but, at the same time, kill individuality, and make one incapable of facing a critical situation. Kayerts and Carlier in *An Outpost of Progress* feel completely lost in the equatorial jungle; see about their isolation in Part 1, Chapter 2 and their performance as agents in Part 2, Chapter 5. They fall victims to this system:

> Society, not from any tenderness, but because of its strange needs, had taken care of those two men, forbidding them all independent thought, all initiative, all departure from routine; and forbidding it under pain of death. They could only live on condition of being machines. And now, released from the fostering care of men with pens behind the ears, or of men with gold lace on the sleeves, they were like those lifelong prisoners who, liberated after many years, do not know what use to make of their freedom. They did not know what use to make of their faculties, being both, through want of practice, incapable of independent thought. (TU 91; also 89)

Marlow as narrator expresses identically motivated contempt for terrestrial living in *Chance* (C4) and *Heart of Darkness* (YNTOS 114, 116), where he stresses his superiority over town dwellers, whose comfortable and carefree existence deprives them of the possibility of attaining such profound self-understanding as he achieved in the course of his African journey (116, 152 on Marlow's ethical estrangement refer to Part 1, Chapter 2, and on the colonizers' activities in *Heart of Darkness,* Part 2, Chapter 5):.

> They [the inhabitants of the sepulchral city] were intruders whose knowledge of life was to me an irritating pretence, because I felt so sure they could not possibly know the things I knew. Their bearing, which was simply the bearing of commonplace individuals going about their business in the assurance of prefect safety, was offensive to me like the outrageous flauntings of folly in the face of a danger it is unable to comprehend. I had no particular desire to enlighten them, but I had some difficulty in restraining myself from laughing in their faces, so full of stupid importance. (152; also 116)

C. Unflattering Presentation of Town Dwellers and Aristocracy

Contempt for life on land is frequently aimed at burghers or nobles. The strictures on city dwellers' mentality and ethos are realized most fully in *The Return* with the Herveys, who are presented as average, typical representatives of this social sphere (TU 119, 124-125).[87] This portrayal is highlighted by the multiplication of the central character's figure in mirrors:

> And like real people who are slaves of common thoughts, that are not even their own, they affected a shadowy independence by the superficial variety of their movements....And like the men he respected they could be trusted to do nothing individual, original, or startling–nothing unforeseen and nothing improper. (124-125)

Mrs. Alvan Hervey is described as "having not a thought of her own in her head" (120). The narrator's utterance about a society paper is in tune with this mode of presentation: this "wholly scandalous publication, redeemed by excessive dullness...contained no new thought, as it never by any chance had a flash of wit, satire, or indignation in its pages" (121). The Herveys live in a routine, conventional way. They are incapable of experiencing authentic passions; they are motivated exclusively by egoism and cupidity. Their feelings are limited to just the simplest impressions:

> They moved...amongst...men and women who feared emotion, enthusiasm, or failure, more than fire, war, or mortal disease; who tolerated only the commonest formulas of commonest thoughts, and recognized only profitable facts. It was an extremely charming sphere, the abode of all the virtues, where nothing is realized and where all joys and sorrows are cautiously toned down into the pleasures and annoyances...where noble sentiments are cultivated in sufficient profusion to conceal the pitiless materialism of thoughts and aspirations.... (120-121)

This existence brings mutual psychological estrangement to the Herveys (Part 1, Chapter 2).

Censure of this same social class appears in *The Rescue*. The stiff and conventional manners of the *Hermit*'s passengers in the tropical zone of Carimata, Lingard's "property," is contrasted with his authentic, adventurous existence. Edith Travers feels this opposition acutely: the new situation brings her disappointment with her life and its bourgeois customs and morality, and arouses her admiration for the King of the Sea and his native friends (Re 140-141, 152-153, 162-163, 165). Edith's fascination with the exotic realm manifested in the way she views all characters and events as fancied, unreal, and fantastic (247-248, 288-289, 300), or in the perceptions typical of her sphere: everything is seen in terms of a theatrical spectacle or painting (282, 295, 297, 300, 343, 366-367, 369). Travers, on the other hand, like Alvan Hervey in *The Return,* acts as a guardian of the forms and rituals of this ethos and repeatedly reproves his wife for lacking the attitudes and aspirations proper to their class (267-270, 347, 351-354; see also on their reciprocal psychological isolation in Part 1, Chapter 2).

Condemnation of townspeople is a significant, though episodic, motif in *The Secret Agent,*[88] *A Smile of Fortune, Chance,* and *The Sisters*. In the first novel it is evident in the damning presentation of Verloc (Part 2, Chapter 5) and his relationship with his wife, which is based on superficial understanding (on their marital estrangement see Part 1, Chapter 2). In *A Smile of Fortune* the inhabitants of the Pearl of the Ocean (descendants of the old colonists) lead "a narrow domestic life in dull, dignified decay" and "the emptiness of their existence passes belief" (TLS 34-35). Motivated by hypocritical lower-middle-class morality, they treat Jacobus's love affair as a scandal and cut him off in the milieu (Part 1, Chapter 2), which produces the narrator's antipathy for them. In *Chance* the contempt for land dwellers is not only a matter of the dislike that Captain Anthony, Flora, and Marlow have for the settled life, but is mostly about de Barral, who finances absurd enterprises, and the naive, obsessed people who yield to his propaganda and are ruined (C 69-70, 74-75, 78-82, 85). A pejorative portrayal of this world figures in *The Sisters* too:

> The peaceful conditions of middle life, the conventions resembling virtues, made for Rita as if a shelter behind a respectable curtain that separated her from the real existence of passions. The pretty assumptions of selfish quietude gave to events an aspect of general benevolence, a polished surface of easy curves hiding the resounding emptiness of thoughts, the deadly fear of sincerity, the cherished unreality of emotions. It went on as a tale made up of charming but meaningless sentences, flowing with gentle ease through a succession of serene days. In the shallow stream Rita was carried away from year to year; listened to the soothing imbecility of its babble. (Sis 67)

The aversion to the land and its inhabitants occasionally applies to the aristocracy. Caricatured representatives of this class (Part 2, Chapter 5) include Michaelis' patroness in *The Secret Agent* (SA 109-111), Mr. X and Lady Amateur of anarchism in *The Informer,* Madame de S———— in *Under Western Eyes* (the owner of Château Borel and the patron of the Russian émigré opposition), Mrs. Blunt in *The Arrow of Gold* (AG 184-185), the heroine's aunt (of the Grangers of Etchingham) in *The Inheritors* (I 113-114) and the people from her circles (133-134), Felicia Moorsom in *The Planter of Malata* (her quest after her fiancé is motivated not by sincere feeling but by caprices and attitudinizing) (WT 40-41) and her aunt in the same story, who is inclined to exaggeration, excitability and mawkishness (58-59, 66-67). The nobles' comfortable life is based upon the institutional organization of society, evident in the conduct of Felicia's aunt in *The Planter of Malata:* "That maiden lady in her wonderful preservation reminded Renouard somehow of a wax flower under glass. There were no traces of the dust of life's battles on her anywhere" (44), and of the protagonist in *Il Conde* "Probably...had never had any grave affairs to attend to in his life. It was a kindly existence...ruled by the prescribed usages of good society and protected by the State" (SS 272; cf. too on his self-imposed psychological seclusion in Part 1, Chapter 2). Conrad criticizes the aristocracy for upholding an anachronistic order (*Suspense,* S 105, 114-115, 149), and stresses that the prominence of this élite belongs to the past (*The Planter of Malata,* WT 76-77; *The Inheritors,* I 132).[89]

Antipathy toward those on land is evident in his theses about women. They are separated from reality and exist in fanciful realms full of trivia (on the female characters' psychological detachment, see Part 1, Chapter 2). Furthermore, their safety is guaranteed by the high level of civilization.

Conradian seamen treat such a way of life with scorn and cherish their convictions about the greater worth of the maritime ethos, which is full of toil and devotion (*Heart of Darkness,* YNTOS 59, 115; *Typhoon,* TOS 93-96; *Chance,* C 93-94; *A Happy Wanderer,* NLL 63).

5. Ambivalent Seamen

A. Admirable Characters with a Flaw

The motives for the actions of many Conradian sea people in complex situations are manifold, and their attitude to the fundamental ideals of their fellowship ambiguous.[90] However, they deserve favorable evaluation in spite of transgressions. Positive traits prevail in their characters, they follow most of the principles of the maritime ethos, or they desperately attempt to rise from moral degradation and redeem themselves.[91] Conrad's implied authors have a liking and compassion for such individuals, and try to understand and explain their conduct away–at least partly.

Faults are noticeable even when the code of maritime values is observed in exemplary fashion. The ship's company in *The Nigger of the "Narcissus,"* while heroically braving the gale and being perfectly dutiful, show weaknesses (except for Singleton): fear of death, laziness, and insubordination. At Donkin's instigation, they temporarily are convinced that they are exploited by their superiors, and are thus about to mutiny. This state of mind is ironically commented on by the narrator:

> They found comfort of a gloomy kind in an interminable and conscientious analysis of their unappreciated worth; and inspired by Donkin's hopeful doctrines they dreamed enthusiastically of the time when every lonely ship would travel over a serene sea, manned by a wealthy and well-fed crew of satisfied skippers. (NN 103)
>
> There were words of reproach, encouragement, unbelief, execration. The elder seamen, bewildered and angry, growled their determination to go through with something or other; but the younger school of advanced thought exposed their and Jimmy's wrongs with confused shouts, arguing amongst themselves. (122)

Eventually they win a double victory: over the fury of the elements and the frailties of their own nature.

Big Brierly, an assessor in *Lord Jim,* is also a seemingly unimpeachable figure. He enjoys the approbation of the mariners' ideal: "He had never in his life made a mistake...seemed to be one of those lucky fellows who know nothing of indecision, much less of self-mistrust" (LJ 57). However, he has not experienced an emergency at sea, which is the real test of professional competence; he has "never had an accident, never a mishap, never a check in his steady rise" (57). According to Marlow, Brierly's participation in Jim's trial probably reminds him of his own malpractice and makes his further enjoyment of general respect impossible (on his ethical seclusion see Part 1, Chapter 2):

> He was probably holding silent inquiry into his own case. The verdict must have been of unmitigated guilt, and he took the secret of the evidence with him in that leap into the sea. If I understand anything of

> men, the matter was no doubt of the gravest import...[arousing] some thought with which a man unused to such a companionship finds it impossible to live. (58-59)

This deed is clearly ambivalent and may be interpreted both as Brierly's own dignified imposition of death, as punishment for a former transgression, and as a capitulation, evading the moral unease caused by his pangs of conscience.

Jasper Allen in *Freya of the Seven Isles* appears to be a model seaman too, and his attachment to his ship seems an ideal realization of the Conradian maritime ethos. Nevertheless, an excessively dreamy disposition and naiveté make him weak and helpless:

> 'The sooner you [Freya] are on board to look after the man [Jasper] and the brig the better,' I said seriously. 'They need you to steady them both a bit....He's in a state of perpetual elation which almost frightens me.' (TLS 162-163)
>
> It is very fine and romantic to posses for your very own a finely tempered and trusty sword-blade, but whether it is the best weapon to counter with the common cudgel-play of Fate–that's another question. (167)

He becomes incapable of effecting his and Freya's plans for the future, and Heemskirk's successful revenge brings about their ultimate defeat and tragedy.

Native mariners' performance also seems worthy of emulation. In *Heart of Darkness* the Negro deckhands contribute to the successful navigation of the steamboat through the many shallows of the big river; for this Marlow regards them with respect (YNTOS 94), particularly the helmsman (119-120). The Malay Serangs–Haji Wasub of the brig *Lightning* in *The Rescue* (Re 16, 197-198) and Whalley's helper in *The End of the Tether*–perform their duties impeccably. The *Patna*'s Malay helmsman in *Lord Jim* display conscientious loyalty to their superiors, as well.

But these seamen's discipline is unreflective, since they carry out their tasks like thoughtless automata:[92]

> Not in the least wonder...to my mind, is the behaviour of the two helmsmen....I remember perfectly Brierly asking him, through the interpreter, what he thought of it at the time, and the interpreter, after a short colloquy, turning to the court with an important air–'He says he thought nothing.'
>
> The other...explained that he had a knowledge of some evil thing befalling the ship, but there had been no order; he could not remember an order; why should he leave the helm? ...So these two lascars stuck to the helm of that ship without steerage-way, where death would have found them if such had been their destiny. (*Lord Jim*, LJ 98-99).
>
> His [the Serang's] placid mind had remained as incapable of penetrating the simplest motives of those he served....But he had no doubt whatever that the "Sofala" was out of the proper track for crossing the bar at Batu Beru....He was not troubled by any intellectual mistrust of his senses. If his captain chose to stir the mud it was well. (*The End of the Tether*, YNTOS 228-229)

Haji Wasub is labeled as "a slave of duty" (Re 16), "symbolic of blind trust in [Lingard's] strength, of an unlimited obedience to his will" (198), and Marlow's black assistant as "a second-rate helmsman," whose work requires supervision (YNTOS 119-120).

Apart from the seemingly spotless characters Conrad portrays the mariners who follow the maritime community's ethos equivocally. Their departures from its principles are excused by important circumstances. Falk, in the story with the same title, is the chief mate of the *Borgmester Dahl*. He bears partial responsibility for the negligence that has led to the desperate plight of the ship's company. But he is primarily guilty of committing cannibalism, which is a violation of the principle of maritime solidarity. On the other hand, impossible conditions alleviate his crime. It was not he but his adversary who initiated the mortal combat; of the crew driven by hunger Falk was not the sole man eater (and such deeds were not a rarity in nineteenth-century sea voyages); faced with imminent death, he yielded to the fundamental instinct of self-preservation, suppressing other feelings. Afterward, he does not conceal this offense but tries to absolve himself by disclosing it to his intended spouse (on Falk's conduct see also Part 1, Chapter 2 and Part 2, Chapter 4).

In *The Tale* the commanding officer's decision is ambivalent: he directs a steamer lying in the fog to destruction, uncertain whether it had been replenishing the stores of enemy submarines, or whether, as its captain claims it was lost because of engine trouble. Such behavior is neither dutiful nor in violation of maritime solidarity. The uncertainty that follow this moral ambiguity gives rise to the hero's remorse and self-imposed ethical isolation (see Part 1, Chapter 2):

> Yes, I gave that course to him. It seemed to me a supreme test. I believe–no, I don't believe. I don't know. All the time I was certain. They all went down; and I don't know whether I have done stern retribution–or murder; whether I have added to the corpses that litter the bed of the unreadable sea the bodies of men completely innocent or basely guilty. I don't know. I shall never know. (TH 80)

Jörgenson in *The Rescue* is attached to his ships. He twice faces a choice of loyalties: to the ships or to other obligations, and decides with extreme regret to sacrifice them to carry out more important tasks (the implied author approves of this course of conduct). Jörgenson, in the first incident, sets his ship on fire, to prevent it being taken by the Dutchman (Re 100-101). Later, unable to defend the *Emma,* entrusted to him by Lingard, from the natives' attack, he blows it up, killing himself and Lingard's friends and enemies, but preventing the attackers from seizing Red-Eyed Tom's arsenal.[93] Of course, he had been an admirable commander of both ships (116).

Many seamen expiate their guilt and censurable or ambivalent performance by the ethos of the maritime fraternity. Bunter's deed in *The Black Mate* may be interpreted in such terms (see on his isolation in Part 1, Chapter 2); tries to evade the regulations forbidding work on board ship for men over a certain age. He asserts that this is motivated principally by a desire to provide for his wife (TH 117-118). The *Sapphire*'s mate atones for his transgression with exemplary performance: he serves unimpeachably on board, and is a man of stainless character and reputation at sea (95-96).

Peyrol, the chief character in *The Rover,* has practiced piracy and bloodshed nearly all his life. However, the ethos of the rovers' fellowship, the Brotherhood of the Coast, of which Peyrol was a member and temporarily its leader, lived by many noble principles, including solidarity and mutual help in danger (Rov 4-5, 131-132, 134). The protagonist atones for his ignoble past by a magnanimous deed at the close of his life. Because of his fondness for Arlette, who wants to be free of nightmarish reminiscences of the Toulon massacre (on the revolutionaries' activties see Part 2, Chapter 5), he decides to deliver false dispatches and letters to the Englishmen. Thus he saves Lieutenant Réal from the task and for the girl, and secures her happiness at the cost of his own life.[94] To achieve this he fakes an escape and lets himself be caught by the commander of a corvette patrolling the coast in the vicinity of Escampobar. He thus displays heroism and consummate seamanship, which were also shown when he brought his ship to the port of Toulon through the blockade. (1)

Great professional experience and long observation of the English vessel enable him to anticipate its movements (70). All of Peyrol's maneuvers performed once at sea are to mislead the English Captain Vincent, to prove superiority. Accomplishment of this plan gives Peyrol great satisfaction (262-268), which is magnified by his knowing that he had a chance to escape the English (264). His bravery and extraordinary skill at sailing his tartane arouse his adversaries' respect:

> I thought [Captain Vincent says] that your lordship [Admiral Nelson] would perhaps like to see a 40-ton lateen craft which has led such a chase to, I daresay, the fastest sloop in his Majesty's service...the old man [Peyrol] had given...proofs of his seamanship and determination...at the very moment he had the 'Amelia' alongside of him he still made a most clever attempt to prolong the chase....I cannot refuse them my admiration and especially to the white-haired man. (273-274)

They pay tribute to the crew with an honorable burial:

> His ship makes a very good coffin for a seaman, and those men deserve better than to be thrown overboard to roll on the waves. Let them rest quietly at the bottom of the sea in the craft to which they had stuck so well....After all they never surrendered and, by heavens, gentlemen, we will let them go down with their colours flying. (279-280)

Captain Whalley in *The End of the Tether* violates the dictates of the maritime ethos for love of his daughter, who needs financial help:[95] he risks catastrophe by captaining the *Sofala* in spite of intensifying blindness. He makes a tragic choice by deciding to act against the moral norms of the sea community, which he values highly, and against the principles of dignity and honesty[96] (see Part 1, Chapter 2 on Whalley's voluntary isolation):

> He had nothing of his own–even his own past of honour, of truth, of just pride, was gone. All his spotless life had fallen into the abyss. He had said his last good-byes to it. (YNTOS 319)
> The necessity of every moment brought home to Captain Whalley's heart the humiliation of his falsehood. He had drifted into it from paternal love, from incredulity, from boundless trust in divine justice meted out to men's feelings on this earth. (324; also 302, 333)

The commander bravely faces all adversities, carries out his duties desperately, and overcomes his infirmity by sheer willpower; he desires, at all costs, to keep his post till the termination of his contract. The attitude of the ship's co-owner and chief engineer Massy poses additional difficulties: he constantly complains against the master and wrongfully demands funds for repairs of the steamer. Whalley displays heroism at the end of this last voyage, remaining on the sinking vessel of his own free will, and in this way atoning for his sin.

The severity of the protagonist's offense is also abated in some measure by his past at sea, from which an extremely praiseworthy image of his appears:

> In those bygone days...he had attended faithfully, as by law a shipmaster is expected to do, to the conflicting interests of owners, charterers,

> and underwriters. He had never lost a ship or consented to a shady transaction.... (168)
>
> Conscious of his worth, and firm in his rectitude, there had remained to him, like the heritage of departed prosperity, the tranquil bearing of a man who had proved himself fit in every sort of way for the life of his choice. (187)

Whalley belongs to the earlier, glorious generation of seamen, the pioneers of civilization and imperial expansion, who traced new routes for shipping (see Part 2, Chapter 5). At the close of his career he acts nobly and honorably too: motivated by self-esteem, he refuses work offered out of compassion for his weakness, and is eager to accept only a ship's command (185-186). Such a frame of mind harmonizes with his outward appearance: monumental, majestic, and dignified. He shows a strong attachment to the sea and to vessels (170), as becomes a good captain, a romantic sailor of the old school. Whalley feels affection for the barque *Fair Maid,* and despairs over the necessity of selling it (184-185, 189-190). In his old age, his tragic blindness, the *Sofala* becomes his best friend (327)–the old steamship whose "great age had given her knowledge, wisdom, and steadiness" (166); they become as one, experiencing the final decline together.[97]

Leggatt in *The Secret Sharer,* the chief mate of the *Sephora,* turns law breaker by killing a seaman in the course of service, and becomes ethically estranged from the maritime milieu. There are, however, important extenuating circumstances in his case: the crime is committed unintentionally, during a struggle in which he tries to force his subordinate into obedience. Leggatt does atone for his wrongdoing: irritated by the commander's cowardice and lack of skill, he takes the initiative and sets the foksail, which saves the storm-tossed ship (TLS 118, 124).[98] Leggatt is convinced that a court would be incompetent to judge the essence of such a transgression. Therefore he leaves the *Sephora,* preferring drowning to yielding to a humiliating judicial procedure. He regards only an "investigation" of his own conscience as competent to evaluate his deed. After a period on board the protagonist's ship, he dooms himself to a vagrant life of guilt but also of self-respect:

> The 'brand of Cain' business....I was ready enough to go off wandering on the face of the earth–and that was price enough to pay for an Abel of that sort. (107)
> [He has] gone from the ship, to be hidden for ever from all friendly faces, to be a fugitive and vagabond on the earth, with no brand of the curse of his sane forehead to stay a slaying hand...too proud to explain...the secret sharer of my cabin and of my thoughts...had lowered himself into the water to take his punishment: a free man, a proud swimmer striking out for a new destiny. (142-143; also 131-132)

Leggatt's guilt is in some measure shared by the young shipmaster (on their isolation, ethical solidarity and psychological identification, see Part 1, Chapter 2), who has violated the law by not delivering the criminal to justice. Such is simultaneously an act of solidarity to help a mariner in a difficulty and the realization of a desire to see an honorable punishment. In spite of being absorbed with Leggatt's case and the difficulties of hiding him on board, the principal character of *The Secret Sharer* passes a test of professional competence, which is particularly laudable because it is on his first voyage as a commander (93). He manages the critical situation caused by Leggatt's arrival; he balances his solidarity with the fugitive with his loyalty to ship and crew and does not allow too great a weakening of the latter, primary loyalty. Throughout it all, he navigates the ship skillfully and shows particular deftness in navigating near the hill of Koh-ring to allow Leggatt to swim ashore.[99]

The narrator is attached to his vessel, and treats it as the partner and friend who is to help him perform his duties:

> In this breathless pause at the threshold of a long passage we seemed to be measuring our fitness for a long and arduous enterprise, the appointed task of both our existences to be carried out....I lingered yet, my hand resting lightly on my ship's rail as if on the shoulder of a trusted friend. (92; also 95)

Nevertheless, he does not unite with the ship completely until Leggatt leaves and they sail away from Koh-ring:

> Already the ship was drawing ahead. And I was alone with her. Nothing! no one in the world should stand now between us, throwing a shadow on the way of silent knowledge and mute affection, the perfect communion of a seaman with his first command. (143)

This sense of symbiosis with his craft is in tune with his great affection for the sea and the sublime vision of the maritime vocation:

> And suddenly I rejoiced in the great security of the sea as compared with the unrest of the land, in my choice of that untempted life presenting no disquieting problems, invested with an elementary moral beauty by the absolute straightforwardness of its appeal and by the singleness of its purpose. (96; also 94)

The young commander in *The Shadow-Line* also lives with a brand: he ignores the doctor's warnings that setting out immediately would bring about a recurrence of disease among his convalescent crew (SL 80). In the course of the voyage he is shocked to discover that there is no quinine in the ship's medicine chest; he blames himself for not checking its contents, even though that was not his direct responsibility, and for causing sufferings (on his self-inflicted isolation, see Part 1, Chapter 2). Later, however, the narrator-captain fully atones for this fault by acting by the principles of the maritime ethos.[100] He tries to make use of the slightest breeze when the vessel is becalmed for a long time: "I had been living on deck practically night and day so as to take advantage of every chance to get my ship a little more to the southward" (85). He works zealously for the execution of indispensable actions on board in spite of the sickness of nearly every deckhand (97-99, 128); he also has to cope with the extra difficulty posed by the chief officer's (Mr. Burns's) superstitiousness. The protagonist's extraordinary devotion and efforts to save the ship deserve special praise because of his youth and minimal professional experience. The story depicts the process by which he crosses the "shadow-line" between carefree, idealistic youth and maturity (SL Author's Note 55, 106, 129, 131-132).[101]

The principal character in *The Shadow-Line* shows awareness of the marine tradition (52-53), and a particularly strong bond with his craft:

> A ship! My ship! She was mine, more absolutely mine for possession and care than anything in the world; an object of responsibility and devotion...and yet we were indissolubly united for a certain portion of our future, to sink or swim together! (40)
>
> In all the ports of the world washed by navigable waters our relation to each other would be the same–and more intimate than there are words to express in the language. (50; also 46-47, 70)

This emotion is enhanced by idealization of the ship through fairy-tale imagery (39-40) and comparison to a charming young lady: "like some rare women, she was one of those creatures whose mere existence is enough to awaken an unselfish delight. One feels that it is good to be in the world in which she has her being" (49). Stepping foot on the vessel's deck for the first time, he experiences an unequaled feeling of deep physical satisfaction (50). The captain's attachment to his vessel is combined with a sublime vision of life and work at sea (48).

B. Jim

The title character of *Lord Jim* is the most culpable among Conrad's morally ambivalent seamen: with the captain and two engineers, he deserts the sinking *Patna* with 800 passengers still on board. The maritime fellowship unanimously condemns the fugitives, both in the trial verdict and the opinions of those interested in the case (on Jim's self-imposed ethical isolation, see Part 1, Chapter 2).

Jim also sins in excessive daydreaming, egoistic absorption in illusions, and in striving uncompromisingly for their materialization, irrespective of the interests of the communities to which he is obliged. These fancies result from his idealistic and heroic vision of the marine vocation.[102] It implies that he will carry out exploits similar to those in fiction:

> [Jim's] station was in the fore-top, and often from there he looked down, with the contempt of a man destinied to shine in the midst of dangers....He could see...the hazy splendour of the sea in the distance, and the hope of a stirring life in the world of adventure.
> On the lower deck in the babel of two hundred voices he would forget himself, and beforehand live in his mind the sea-life of light adventure. He saw himself saving people from sinking ships...confronted savages on tropical shores, quelled mutinies on the high seas, and in a small boat upon the ocean kept up the hearts of despairing men–always an example of devotion to duty, and as unflinching as a hero in a book. (LJ 6; also 94-95)

Jim can not adjust himself to the maritime service, characterized by "monotony of existence between sky and water," "the exactions of the sea, and the prosaic severity of the daily task" (10). Complete immersion in reveries isolates him from his environment (Part 1, Chapter 2), blocks fulfillment of his duties, and makes proper action impossible at a crucial moment. Even on the training ship he proves incapable of prompt and suitable reaction to a similar situation: this turns him into an outsider instead of a hero. Nevertheless, he still proudly believes that he had not been involved in a true emergency and that his colleagues' bravery was slight. Thus he remains strongly convinced of his unique abilities to cope with real danger. This evokes ironic comment from the narrator:

> He could affront greater perils. He would do so–better than anybody....The gale had ministered to a heroism as spurious as its own pretence of terror....When all men flinched, then–he felt sure–he alone would know how to deal with the spurious menace of wind and seas...he exulted with fresh certitude in his avidity for adventure, and in a sense of many-sided courage. (8-9)

Jim behaves identically on the *Patna,* he is isolated in a realm of wishful thinking about courageous actions:

> his thoughts would be full of valorous deeds: he loved these dreams and the success of his imaginary achievements. They were the best parts of life, its secret truth, its hidden reality. They had a gorgeous virility, the charm of vagueness, they passed before him with a heroic thread; they carried his soul away with them and made it drunk with the divine philtre of an unbounded confidence in itself. There was nothing he could not face. (20; also 23, 24-25)

Here the training ship emergency is repeated: his indulgence in reveries and the paralysis of his will preclude effective performance in the face of tragedy:[103]

> There was no help. He imagined what would happen perfectly; he went through it all motionless by the hatchway with the lamp in his hand–he went through it to the very last harrowing detail....'I saw [Jim confesses] as clearly as I see you now that there was nothing I could do. It seemed to take all life out of my limbs....Something held his arms down along his sides. He was not afraid–oh no! only he just couldn't–that's all....His confounded imagination had evoked for him all the horrors of panic, the trampling rush, the pitiful screams, boats swamped–all the appalling incidents of a disaster at sea he had ever heard of. (86-88; also 95-97, 113-114; 86-88 other passages)

With extreme selfishness, Jim regrets leaving the steamer merely as a lost opportunity for heroic deeds (83-84). In spite of both failures he persists on this destructive path. His voluntary death seems to bring the superb realization of his ambition:

> He passes away under a cloud, inscrutable at heart, forgotten, unforgiven, and excessively romantic. Not in the wildest days of his boyish visions could he have seen the alluring shape of such an extraordinary success! For it may very well be that in the short moment of his last proud and unflinching glance, he had beheld the face of that opportunity which, like an Eastern bride, had come veiled to his side. (416)

But it is simultaneously a manifestation of self-centeredness, since he achieves what he craves at the cost of distressing Jewel (on their love-based isolation see Part 1, Chapter 2):

> But we can see him, an obscure conqueror of fame, tearing himself out of the arms of a jealous love at the sign, at the call of his exalted egoism. He goes away from a living woman to celebrate his pitiless wedding with a shadowy ideal of conduct. (416)[104]

Marlow criticizes Jim's overactive imagination and his belief in his capacity to carry out exceptional tasks; these are the convictions that make him swagger (197, 235-236).[105] Nevertheless, the narrator is far from condemning his younger fellow mariner. He does not consider the other fugitives Jim's equal; nor does he share the general opinion of the maritime community, as confirmed by the court sentence (on the main narrator's actions toward Jim, see Part 1, Chapter 3). His stance with Jim is tutelary and permeated with compassion. Moreover, his description of the protagonist brings his laudable traits into prominence, which prevail over his censurable traits and partly redeem his faults.

This is achieved principally by the persistent depiction of Jim as an extraordinarily noble-minded man of honor, who acutely feels the painful consequences of his misfortunes and works hard to reestablish his good name. It is in his favor that he is the only one of the accused who turns up in court:

> the inquiry was a severe punishment to that Jim [and] his facing it–practically of his own free will–was a redeeming feature in his abominable case. (68)
>
> 'I couldn't clear out,' Jim began. 'The skipper did–that's all very well for him. I couldn't, and I wouldn't. They all got out of it in one way or another, but it wouldn't do for me. (79; also 66-67)

He rejects Brierly's advice to escape (152-154), treating his public abasement as a self-inflicted punishment, in accordance with his ethics. He takes his subsequent tragic experiences with dignity. His voluntary isolation from the community of seamen, the numerous humiliations he endures, the impossibility of finding a job that might give him a chance to attain full rehabilitation, the need to forsake this milieu and settle in geographically secluded Patusan–all of these successive failures are borne nobly and patiently, painfully but resolutely. He takes lowly jobs (151), hoping to accomplish his ideals, at least in part (179, 197, 201-202, 235-236), and he does not surrender in Patusan, even though the realization of his dreams (see Part 2, Chapter 5) is followed by the catastrophe of Brown's intervention. He proudly submits to execution by Doramin, triumphing in this way over a fatal destiny.[106] The protagonist's admirable qualities are implied in descriptions of his appearance (3, 40, 43, 78, 198), and the passages connecting him metaphorically with light, connoting positive values (229, 336, 393).

Jim's conduct is justified as that of an average man who experiences universal moral dilemmas.[107] Marlow consistently calls the outsider "one of us" (Conrad himself calls him so in "Author's Note"; IX). All this suggests that he belongs to the maritime community, that he is under an obligation of solidarity and mutual aid, that he is united to it by the glorious ethos, common experiences, and idealistic vision of the profession.

> Hadn't we all commenced with the same desire, ended with the same knowledge, carried the memory of the same cherished glamour through the sordid days of imprecation? What wonder that when some heavy prod gets home the bond is found to be close; that besides the fellowship of the craft there is felt the strength of a wider feeling.... (129; also 129 other excerpts)

Marlow, aware of this bond, feels responsible for the transgressor and regards Jim as still a member of the fraternity, in spite of his having been excluded from it:

> He was a youngster of the sort you like to see about you; of the sort you like to imagine yourself to have been; of the sort whose appearance claims the fellowship of these illusions you had thought gone out, extinct, cold, and which, as if rekindled at the approach of another flame, give a flutter deep, deep down somewhere, give a flutter of light...of heat.... (128)

The narrator is "one of us," a representative of humanity:

> He stood there for all the parentage of his kind, for men and women by no means clever or amusing, but whose very existence is based upon honest faith, and upon the instinct of courage. (43)
> He appealed to all sides at once–to the side turned perpetually to the light of day, and to that side of us which, like the other hemisphere of the moon, exists stealthily in perpetual darkness, with only a fearful ashy light falling at times on the edge...he was one of us.... (93; also 93; other extracts)

This portrayal mitigates his sin by putting it in the realm of the possible for everyone.[108]

> Nothing more awful than to watch a man who has been found out, not in a crime but in a more than criminal weakness. The commonest sort of fortitude prevents us from becoming criminals in a legal sense; it is from weakness unknown...from weakness that may lie hidden [that] not one of us is safe. (42-43)
> [Jim's] appearance alone added a touch of personal concern to the thoughts suggested by the knowledge of his weakness–made it a thing of mystery and terror–like a hint of a destructive fate ready for us all whose youth–in its day–had resembled his youth? (51)

Jim's frame of mind on the sinking *Patna* is described as typical, common:

> He might have been resigned to die but I suspect he wanted to die without added terrors, quietly, in a sort of peaceful trance...the desire of peace waxes stronger as hope declines, till at last it conquers the very desire of life. Which of us here has not observed this, or maybe experienced something of that feeling in his own person–this extreme weariness of emotions, the vanity of effort, the yearning for rest? (88)[109]

Marlow's evaluation is largely shared by the French lieutenant, who views Jim's conduct as motivated by fear–common to all people:

> 'One is always afraid....'The fear, the fear–look you–it is always there...'. He touched his breast near a brass button on the very spot where Jim had given a thump to his own when protesting that there was nothing the matter with his heart....an honest man–*bien entendu*–would confess that there is a point–there is a point–for the best of us–there is somewhere a point when you let go everything....And you have got to live with that truth–do you see? Given a certain combination of circumstances, fear is sure to come....And even for those who do not believe this truth there is fear all the same–the fear of themselves. Absolutely so....Man is born a coward.... (146-147)

The case is generalized by the description of Jim as Man defenseless in confrontation with Fate. The *Patna* disgrace makes him Fate's plaything. His misfortune is caused by "a sham...planned by the tremendous disdain of the Dark Powers" (121), by surrendering to "the infernal powers who had selected hm for the victim of their practical joke" (108; also 121). The encounter with Brown (the embodiment of evil and the ally of those "Dark Powers") brings an attempt to overcome destiny: "the conversation of these two across the creek appears now as the deadliest kind of duel on which Fate looked on with her cold-eyed knowledge of the end" (385). Voluntary acceptance of his end becomes Tuan's (Jim's) ultimate triumph; by surrendering to the death sentence, "He was going to prove his power...and conquer the fatal destiny itself" (410). Jim's being predestined is universalized many times by Marlow as a conviction of the whole human predicament (51, 186, 320-321, 411).

The attitude of idealism, of cherishing sublime illusions, is generalized and presented in a favorable light.[110] Many utterances (mostly Stein's) suggest that it is innate, inherent in human nature, and therefore worthy:

> This magnificent butterfly finds a little heap of dirt and sits still on it; but man he will never on his heap of mud keep still. He want to be so, and again he want to be so...every time he shuts his eyes he sees himself as a very fine fellow–so fine as he can never be....In a dream.... (213)
> A man that is born falls into a dream like a man who falls into the sea. If he tries to climb out into the air as inexperienced people endeavour

> to do, he drowns–*nicht war?*...The way is to the destructive element submit yourself, and with the exertions of your hands and feet in the water make the deep, deep sea keep you up. (214)[111]

However these opinions are only in some measure to Jim's advantage, since his fancifulness is excessive, harmful, egoistic, and detached from reality. Marlow even shows his protégé's preference for illusions at the cost of forsaking Jewel as motivated by a natural desire to realize his hopes.[112] But Marlow does not express a clear approval of Jim's performance:

> She said he had been driven away from her by a dream...there seemed to be no forgiveness for such a transgression. And yet is not mankind itself, pushing on its blind way, driven by a dream of its greatness and its power upon the dark paths of excessive cruelty and of excessive devotion? And what is the pursuit of truth, after all? (349-350)

Broadening the significance of the hero's case suits the narrator: he is particularly keen to insert apothegms into his narration. This aspect of Jim's life story justifies Marlow's persistent attempts at understanding not only the psyche of a single human being, but also some universal patterns of behavior that Jim exemplifies:

> the mystery of his attitude got hold of me as though he had been an individual in the forefront of his kind, as if the obscure truth involved were momentous enough to affect mankind's conception of itself.... (93)
>
> I don't know why he should always have appeared to me symbolic. Perhaps this is the real cause of my interest in his fate. (265)[113]

The fundamental goal of Marlow's narrative strategies is to present the young sinner as admirably as possible. He also achieves this through a contrapuntal technique. Jim is juxtaposed with other characters and secondary narrators. Their relations not only introduce diverse perspectives and evaluations, but also serve as a pretext for disclosing the speakers' personalities and attitudes. Thus they form the contexts for the appreciation of Jim.[114] The first and most important of these confrontations concerns the *Patna*'s chief mate and the other runaways (see on them in Part 2, Chapter 4). It reveals a substantial difference between the principal character of the novel, who is motivated by a sublime vision of the sailor's vocation, and the caricatured figures of his accomplices,[115] e.g., the loathsome skipper who "fixed [himself] in his [Jim's] memory for ever as the incarnation of everything vile and base that lurks in the world we love" (21). Unlike his partners, Jim neither planned nor prepared his escape, and his jump was purely accidental and instinctive. Once in the boat, he felt an impulse to return and join the passengers on the sinking steamer (113-114). As the only accused present, however, he alone bears the brand of infamy for the misdeed.

A parallel that brings out Jim's favorable traits involves Captain Brierly[116] (see on him in Part 1, Chapter 2 and Part 2, Chapter 4). The hero proudly rejects Brierly's suggestion to escape further examination in court, and later this crack ship commander and assessor commits suicide. This is probably caused by the impossibility of absolving himself from some past transgression, a fact he realizes under the impact of the trial (58-59). Brierly's suicide exonerates to some extent the young culprit: it turns out that even the assessor, who enjoys the reputation of the marine ideal (57-58), finds a moral flaw in his own life, which disturbs his peace of mind and self-complacency.

Chester and Robinson are the other characters contrasted with the principal figure of the novel.[117] The first of them is Jim's antithesis, embodying a pragmatism devoid of any dreamy quality:

> He looked knowingly after Jim. 'Takes it to heart?' he asked, scornfully, 'Very much,' I said. 'Then he's no good,' he opined....That never yet made a man. You must see things exactly as they are....Look at me. I made it a practice never to take anything to heart.' (161-162)

He entirely approves of Robinson's cannibalism. Marlow's judgement is strengthened by presenting them in comic or even caricatured fashion, mainly because of Chester's exaggerated fascination with his nonsensical plans for the plantation (163-169), and Robinson's ghastly, grotesque appearance (163, 165, 166, 168-169). Jim is also shown as superior to the Malay helmsmen of the *Patna:* they are just the unthinking slaves of duty.

The character of Stein, another idealist and dreamer, is closely parallel to Jim's.[118] The portrait is sketched by the old man's life story, which stresses the romantic traits of his personality and conduct (his participation in the revolutionary movement of 1848 and in the struggles of his friend Bonso for local power). Marlow depicts the old visionary's life as "begun in humble surroundings, rich in generous enthusiasms, in friendship, love, war–in all the exalted elements of romance" (217). Their encounter also reveals the psychology of this enthusiastic butterfly collector. His philosophy of life is expressed by one of the best known quotations from *Lord Jim:* "In the destructive element immerse....That was the way. To follow the dream, and again to follow the dream–and so–*ewig–usque ad fine....*" (214-215). Marlow commends this approach. Analogy to the unambiguously positive figure of Stein enhances the praiseworthy description of Jim.[119] But the picture is tempered because the old man, unlike the young myth maker, personifies a moderate romanticism that is suited to the realities of life.[120]

Marlow sets off the hero's laudable traits in the final part of the novel, juxtaposing his noble-mindedness with the abjectness and unscrupulousness of Cornelius and Brown, whose intrigue causes Jim's final catastrophe. Stein's agent, Cornelius, is consistently depicted as an abominable creature[121] (285, 323-324; Part 2, Chapter 5). Brown, his accomplice, is not only a blameworthy seaman (after all, he stole a Spanish schooner) but also, and principally, an embodiment of savagery and brutality:

> There was in the broken, violent speech of that man...an undisguised ruthlessness of purpose, a strange vengeful attitude towards his own past, and a blind belief in the righteousness of his will against all mankind, something of that feeling which could induce the leader of a

> horde of wandering cut-throats to call himself proudly the Scourge of God. No doubt the natural senseless ferocity which is the basis of such a character was exasperated by failure...what he had really desired...was to play havoc with that jungle town which had defied him, to see it strewn over with corpses and enveloped in flames. Listening to his pitiless, panting voice, I could imagine how he must have looked at it from the hillock, peopling it with images of murder and rapine. (370; also 344-345, 404)

This puts him in complete opposition to Jim;[122] according to the main narrator, "those two men...[were] standing on the opposite poles of that conception of life which includes all mankind" (380-381). A sharp contrast of their mentalities is reflected also in the vagabond's utterances directed to Jim and Marlow:

> you talk as if you were one of those people that should have wings so as to go about without touching the dirty earth. Well–it is dirty. I haven't got any wings. (383)
> He [Jim] a man! Hell! He was a hollow sham. As if he couldn't have said straight out, 'Hands off my plunder!' blast him! That would have been like a man! Rot his superior soul! He had me there–but he hadn't devil enough in him to make an end of me. Not he! A thing like that letting me off as if I wasn't worth a kick! (344)

Brown appears to personify the evil allied to the tragic destiny persecuting the *Patna*'s deserter (344, 385).[123] This disparateness is strengthened by superficial similarities in their biographies: both are outcasts from the marine community, having violated its ethical code (see incomer's speech directed to the lord of Patusan, abounding with allusions to his past; 381-383, 386-387).

The series of confrontations implying value judgement is concluded by opposing Jim to the Malay, Doramin. The young escapist, voluntarily submitting to capital punishment, radiates dignity: "They say that the white man sent right and left at all those faces a proud and unflinching glance. Then with his hand over his lips he fell forward, dead" (416; also 410). The descriptions of the *nakhoda,* on the other hand, stress his uncivilized aspect, and animality, particularly when he gives way to despair over his son's corpse when he "let out one great fierce cry, deep from the chest, a roar of pain and fury, as mighty as the bellow of a wounded bull" (411), and again immediately before he kills Tuan (Jim): "The unwieldy old man, lowered his big forehead like an ox under a yoke....From his throat came gurgling, choking, inhuman sounds...his little eyes stared with an expression of mad pain, of rage" (415). So the Patusan ruler is defeated not by chivalrous adversaries but by Cornelius's mean intrigues and Brown's bloodthirstiness. Moreover, the death sentence is executed by Dain Waris's father in a mad rage.

The contrapuntal technique entails the application of numerous extensive digressions that contain stories by secondary narrators.[124] The digressions' aim is not so much to communicate events as to evoke a definite appreciation of the leading figure, both directly and indirectly–by comparing him with the speakers themselves. Therefore each narrative sequence is suddenly broken off and replaced by Marlow's commentary or another narrator's report. This results in an overall pattern of discontinuous narration, innumerable time shifts, and multifarious points of view, and it creates a "chaotic" composition. The narration in *Lord Jim,* digressive, extremely intricate, and stylized in a "told-tale," does not constitute merely a realization of impressionistic patterns,[125] but also has deeper semantic significance.

Marlow's strategies of presentation–direct and indirect depiction, generalization, juxtaposition suggesting valuation–indicate that the narration in *Lord Jim* is not only a matter of conveying a variety of viewpoints, as many Conradians claim, of the young wrongdoer,[126] but also of bringing out the laudable traits of his personality and conduct and showing that they prevail over his faults.[127] This makes *Lord Jim* not only a novel about a quest for elusive and complex psychomoral truth, but also about proving the validity of Marlow's vision of the hero.[128] His frequent complaints about Jim's enigmatic nature come from his conviction that it is impossible to penetrate fully another human being's mentality. They also demonstrate his care in passing judgments and his desire to make his version of the story as objective and credible as possible.

Chapter 5
The Ethos of Communities on Land

In Conrad the terrestrial existence of individuals, like the maritime, is largely determined by isolation: external (imposed by the environment), or internal (brought about by voluntary distancing from it). Solitude forces them to grapple alone with difficulties, to fulfill tasks following from assumed or imposed social roles, to pass a test of personality. It can be overcome through realizing a definite social code of values; the way of effecting these values constitutes the principal criterion of judgement. Characters separated by powerful tropical nature either accomplish or fail to accomplish colonizers' ideals of serving conquered peoples, of contributing to their material and spiritual advancement. And those leading settled lives in highly organized communities frequently experience separation by sea and mountains or in town, as well as varied forms of psychological isolation, and strive to practice definite types of a political ethos through activities aimed at introducing better, more just–according to them–principles of social order.

1. The Colonizers' Ethos

A. Idealistic Pioneers of Civilization

The completion of the white race's glorious mission in exotic countries is in Conrad a significant criterion of a characters' stature. Those who consider the treatment of "the white man's burden" in his writing express two opposite standpoints. Lee stresses the beneficial effects of imperial expansion. He claims that the English were devoted to their task and displayed courage, honesty, fair-mindedness, dignity, responsibility, altruism, and trust. They had a beneficial impact upon the colonized, bettering their social and individual lives.[1] Fleishman takes a contrary stand: he asserts that Conrad's answer to the propaganda of empire was entirely critical. He argues that the expansion of civilization brought about a worsening of indigenous peoples' plights and turned their primitive collective order into anarchy–which resulted in the moral deterioration of the invaders themselves. The generally unfavorable consequences of colonial performance, according to Fleishman, are due to the colonizers' loss of organic ties with European communities. Fleishman maintains that all Conrad's characters exemplify pejorative aspects of the Rajah Brooke myth (instead of raising autochthonous communities he came down to their level).[2] Both Lee and Fleishman agree that such dealings are highly independent, personal, and individualistic.[3] The interpretation of the Conradian vision of bearing "the white man's burden" presented here mediates between these two extremes: a number of either censurable or ambivalent colonizers are seen, but even the ambivalent ones are positive rather than negative.

A group of English seamen, representatives of the old generation of romantic voyagers, from the times of hard physical labor on ships (see Part 2, Chapter 4), make a particularly great contribution to the realization of these sublime imperial ideals. Risking their lives, they travel to remote corners of the earth, bringing civilization and increased possibilities for trade. They include whites operating in the region of Macassar and combining business with adventure (*Almayer's Folly,* AF 6-8), mariners constantly exposed to dangers in exotic regions (*Lord Jim,* LJ 12-13), pioneers of the pepper trade, venturing their lives for a single bag of the spice (226-227), first comers to the Shore of Refuge (*The Rescue,* Re 4).

Lingard is a representative of this group: a true disinterested adventurer, "a man of high mind and of pure heart" (*The Rescue,* Re 4), who is "always in search of new markets for his cargoes–not so much for profit as for the pleasure of finding them" (*An Outcast of the Islands,* OI 14). As the King of the Sea, he is generally considered the principal figure in his milieu. The power exerted by his mercantile monopoly over the Pantai and the inaccessible region adjoining it distinguishes him from a mob of common adventurers. The "Rajah-Laut" brings civilization into the areas under his control by putting an end to bloody wars among the local inhabitants and converting them to peaceful and industrious lives.[4]

Captain Whalley in *The End of the Tether* is another typical specimen of this generation of romantic precursors of civilization and commercial intercourse (see Part 1, Chapters 2 and Part 2, Chapter 4):

> [He] had served famous firms...had sailed famous ships...had made famous passages, had been the pioneer of new routes and new trades; ...had steered across the unsurveyed tracts of the South Seas, and had seen the sun rise on uncharted islands. Fifty years at sea...had made him honourably known to a generation of shipowners and merchants in all the ports from Bombay clear over to where the East merges into the West upon the coast of the two Americas. (YNTOS 167-168)

He contributes significantly to the development of the Far East trade by discovering a sea route that "reduced the average time of a southern passage by eleven days for more than half a year" (286). An island, a reef, and a route from China to Australia are named after him to commemorate these achievements (168). A similar contribution is made by Evans, who appears episodically in the same text as the founder of "the first patent slip for repairing small ships" (194) in this part of the world. His invention leads to the creation of the Consolidated Docks Company. Other forerunners of economic expansion in these territories are Morrison in *Victory:* "Most of the places he traded with were unknown not only to geography but also to the traders' special lore which is transmitted by word of mouth" (V 11), and Nelson in *Freya of the Seven Isles:*

> He had come out East long before the advent of telegraph cables...trading and sailing in all directions through the Eastern Archipelago....There was no nook or cranny of these tropical waters that the enterprise of old

> Nelson (or Nielsen) had not penetrated in an eminently pacific way. (TLS 147)

White settlers, whose hard work contributes to development and progress in exotic regions, constitute another category of those bearing "the white man's burden" admirably. Mr. Van Wyk in *The End of the Tether* dwells in a glade wrested from the jungle in the secluded Batu Beru area (on his tropical isolation, see Part 1, Chapter 1). After many years of toil he turns it into a prosperous tobacco-growing district (YNTOS 277). He civilizes the locals employed on his plantations, leads them to quiet, hard-working lives. The beneficial influence of honest and well-conducted colonizing activity upon aborigines is generalized by Sterne and the narrator:

> It did one's heart good to see him [the headman of a coast village]–to hear that man speak. He might have been a ferocious savage once. What men wanted was to be checked by superior intelligence, by superior knowledge, by superior force, too–yes, by force held in trust from God and sanctified by its use in accordance with His declared will. (288-289)
>
> These natives, sir, as long as they have a white man close at the back, will go on doing the right thing most surprisingly well–even if left quite to themselves. Only the white man must be of the sort to put starch into them.... (309)

Heyst, the director of the Tropical Belt Coal Company in Samburan, is concerned not with profit but only with advancement of business, with making "a great stride forward for these regions" (V 6). He shows extraordinary enthusiasm and devotion:[5]

> He was rushing all over the Archipelago, jumping in and out of local mail-packets as if they had been tram-cars, here, there, and everywhere–organizing with all his might....And this sudden display of purposeful energy shook the incredulity of the most sceptical more than any scientific demonstration of the value of these coal outcrops could have done. (25)

Honest and friendly behavior toward aboriginals, gaining their trust, and enabling mutual understanding and cooperation are significant elements of the colonial ethos:

> There are those who say that a native will not speak to a white man. Error. No man will speak to his master: but to a wanderer and a friend, to him who does not come to touch or to rule, to him who asks for nothing and accepts all things...words are spoken that take no account of race or colour. (*Karain*, TU 26)

Those who do not swagger but regard autochthones with respect include Jim in *Lord Jim* (Dain Waris's bosom friend; LJ 261-262), Lingard in *The Rescue* (Hassim's and Immada's protector), the narrator and his companions in *Karain* (the Malay ruler's confidantes, who restore his psychological balance), and the Spaniard Cabeza de Vaca, mentioned in *Geography and Some Explorers* (LE 4). Such treatment of local inhabitants is accompanied by narrators' frequent emphasis on their full humanity, and their lives that equal the scope and profundity of white people's experiences[6] (see the native characters in *Almayer's Folly, An Outcast of the Islands, The Rescue, Karain, An Outpost of Progress, The Lagoon, Lord Jim, Heart of Darkness*.

Sometimes this attitude is transmuted into philanthropy and assiduous service for the natives' good. Such performance is exemplified by the title character in *Lord Jim*.[7] Before his arrival, Patusan was convulsed by domestic struggles for power and plundered by Rajah Allang (LJ 228, 256-257). Jim's daring moves–mounting guns for the defense of Doramin's residence against Sherif Ali's attack, his defeat of the enemy and capture of their fortress–make *nakhoda's* party victorious. By this, he gains respect and ascendency over the autochthons. He even becomes their lord: "there could be no question that Jim had the power; in his new sphere there did not seem to be anything that was not his to hold or to give" (274; also 175, 246-247, 265). His subordinates regard him with worshipful esteem, as Marlow notices:

> The time was coming when I should see him loved, trusted, admired, with a legend of strength and prowess forming round his name as though he had been the stuff of a hero....He captured much honour and an Arcadian happiness. (175)
> [Jim had] the reputation of invincible, supernatural power [and] was...the visible, tangible incarnation of unfailing truth and of unfailing victory...was invulnerable.... (361; also 229)

Tuan's control of the settlement has a benign influence on it: he introduces peace and safety and puts an end to internal conflicts, quarrels, and lawlessness.[8] As the white master he lives up to the expectations of the Patusan inhabitants by ruling justly and being tremendously attached to them:

> He looked with an owner's eye at the peace of the evening, at the river, at the houses, at the everlasting life of the forests, at the life of the old mankind, at the secrets of the land, at the pride of his own heart: but it was they that possessed him and made him their own to the innermost thought, to the slightest stir of blood, to his last breath...he seemed to love the land and the people with a sort of fierce egoism, with a contemptuous tenderness. (247-248)
> 'I am responsible for every life in the land,' he said....'There's no sleep for us, old girl,' he said, 'while our people are in danger.' (394)

All this brings the hero happiness, satisfaction, and the accomplishment of his lofty, romantic ideal of a person. It restores his psychological balance and wipes out the *Patna* mishap (see on his detachment and conduct in Part 1, Chapters 1 and 2, and Part 2, Chapter 4). He is magnanimous to enemies as well, although they do not reciprocate: he spares Allang's life, lets Brown and his accomplices out of Patusan, and does not take revenge on Cornelius for his intrigues.

The ideal philanthropic colonizer is also embodied by Lingard in the Malay trilogy.[9] In *Almayer's Folly* and *An Outcast of the Islands* he is the protector of Sambir, situated in jungle at the Pantai. The "Rajah-Laut" is not motivated by a desire to amass riches, to gain power or influence, but merely to ensure social order in this district:

> He would make them happy whether or no, he said, and he meant it. His trade brought prosperity to the young state, and the fear of his heavy hand secured its internal peace for many years. (*An Outcast of the Islands,* OI 200).
> I composed their quarrels [Lingard says] and saw them grow under my eyes. There's peace and happiness there. (45)

He regards Sambir principally as a source of satisfaction and joy, his exclusive property, and bestows profound affection on it:

> He looked proudly upon his work. With every passing year he loved more the land, the people, the muddy river....He loved it all: the landscape....He loved the very scents of blossoms and black earth....He loved the narrow and sombre creeks....He liked even the troops of sorrowful-faced monkeys....He loved everything there, animated or inanimated.... (200-201)

Such a frame of mind is also revealed in his reaction to the defeat brought about by Babalatchi's intrigue (202).

Red-Eyed Tom's attitude toward the inhabitants of the Shore of Refuge in *The Rescue* is likewise tutelary, unselfish, and permeated with attachment:

> [He] lay the foundation of a flourishing state on the ideas of pity and justice. He recognized chivalrously the claims of the conquered...and the reward of his noble instincts is in the veneration with which a strange and faithful race cherish his memory....the glory of his achievement has vindicated the purity of his motives. (Re 4)

Lingard, King of the Sea, means to prevent anyone else's intrusion, by trying, for example, to liberate the stranded schooner-yacht *Hermit* by himself (on his isolation, see Part 1, Chapter 1 and 2):

> He could not sacrifice his intention...the intention of his life; he could no more part with it and exist than he could cut out his heart and live. The adventurer held fast to his adventure which made him in his own sight exactly what he was. (219; also 37-39)[10]

Jörgenson resembles Lingard to some extent. He wins the Malay's esteem and gratitude by long-standing devoted activities: "[He] was faithful [to them] with his strength, with his courage, with his wisdom. A great man. He had great riches but a greater heart" (111-112). He views his past excellence as comparable with that of the *Lightning*'s commander (100). Then there are other philanthropic Conradian colonizers: Jasper Allen in *Freya of the Seven Isles,* who provides the starving natives with food (TLS 213-214), and Morrison in *Victory,* who gives out food to indigenous peoples.[11]

However, the characters discussed above, in spite of their impressive discharge of "the white man's burden," cannot be classified as entirely commendable, with the possible exception of Van Wyk and those who only episodically act along these lines–i.e., Jasper Allen, Cabeza de Vaca, and Heyst (even Heyst's practices are treated with a tinge of irony). Conradian pioneers of trade and civilization quickly lose–mostly through their own fault–their leading positions, influence, power, and wealth, and lower themselves in the Malays' esteem. The legendary Whalley desperately strives to provide for himself and his daughter. Old Evans dies in poverty (YNTOS 193-194). Nelson turns out to be helpless and humiliatingly dependent upon the authorities (on his self-imposed psychological isolation see Part 1, Chapter 2). Jörgenson degenerates and at last loses his livelihood, as emphasized both by the narrator incessantly calling him "a ghost," "a skeleton," "the wreck of an adventurer," and by himself saying, "Some of them [natives] give a plate of rice and a bit of fish to the white man. That's all I get–after thirty-five years–given up to them" (Re 100; also 103-104).

Jim's rule and success in Patusan are short-lived. Lingard's philanthropy ends in a multiple failure, too, since he loses authority over Sambir and the Shore of Refuge and is let down by all his protégés, who leave him, betray him, or disappoint his hopes.[12] And Morrison constitutes a humorous parallel to Lingard's excessive naiveté and benevolence, because he spoils trade in the area by providing natives with rice and never taking payment (V 10-12). This altruism, aggravated by intrigues of the Portuguese colonial authorities bankrupts him.

B. Colonizers' Deplorable Performances

Many of Conrad's characters clearly violate the sublime ideals of "the white man's burden." Some are censurable for their inability to carry out their mission or to handle the situation on a trading station. Such ineptness is exemplified by Kayerts and Carlier in *An Outpost of Progress:*

> They lived like blind men in a large room, aware only of what came in contact with them [and of that only imperfectly], but unable to see the general aspect of things. The river, the forest, all the great land throbbing with life, were like a great emptiness. Even the brilliant sunshine disclosed nothing intelligible. Things appeared and disappeared before their eyes in an unconnected and aimless kind of way. The river seemed to come from nowhere and flow nowhither. It flowed through a void. (TU 92)
> The two men understood nothing, cared for nothing but for the passage of days that separated them from the steamer's return. (94)

They become entirely cut off from the African reality (see Part 1, Chapters 1 and 2), they have no hold over their black workers (100-101), they do not prevent Makola's selling station hands for six tusks of ivory, and they hate the natives: "Carlier had a fit of rage...and talked about the necessity of exterminating all the niggers" (108; also 93). This adverse description is magnified by the discrepancy between the glorious principles they claim to have served and their actual activities: "the two men got on well together in the fellowship of their stupidity and laziness. Together they did nothing, absolutely nothing, and enjoyed the sense of idleness for which they were paid" (92; cf. also 94). The narrative's judgement of the main characters' behavior adds an ironic tinge to the title, to calling them "pioneers of trade and progress" (93), and to their self-esteem:

> [A paper read by them] spoke much of the rights and duties of civilization, of the sacredness of the civilizing work, and extolled the merits of those who went about bringing light, faith and commerce to the dark places of the world. Carlier and Kayerts read, wondered, and

> began to think better of themselves. Carlier said one evening.... 'In a hundred years, there will be perhaps a town here....Civilization...and all. And then, chaps will read that two good fellows, Kayerts and Carlier, were the first civilized men to live in this very spot!' (94-95)

The inefficient protagonists are gradually absorbed by the elemental forces of tropical nature:

> Something from within them was gone, something that worked for their safety, and had kept the wilderness from interfering with their hearts....And out of the great silence of the surrounding wilderness, its very hopelessness and savagery seemed to approach them nearer, to draw them gently, to look upon them, to envelop them with a solicitude irresistible, familiar and disgusting. (107-108)

Their growing submission to the pressure of the environment leads to a tragic epilogue: their quarrel, revealing their depression, ends in Kayerts shooting Carlier casually; later he commits suicide.[13]

The protagonist of *Almayer's Folly*, who represents Lingard's interests and influence in Sambir, also conforms to the pattern of the feckless colonizer.[14] Almayer fails to make real contact with the natives: he despises them, as manifested especially in his relationship to his wife, (Part 1, Chapter 2), and isolates himself by escaping into the realm of illusions about a glorious future (Part 1, Chapter 2). He loses control of the station and botches his job:

> Almayer went on struggling desperately, but with a feebleness of purpose depriving him of all chance of success against men so unscrupulous and resolute as his rivals the Arabs. The trade fell away from the large godowns, and the godowns themselves rotted piecemeal. (AF 25)

Lingard's agent is completely unaware of the local "politicians'" ambitions and intrigues: Lakamba and Babalatchi are trying to gain power over the settlement and get gold from a mine up the Pantai; Abdulla wants to bring his ship to Sambir and replaces the Rajah-Laut's trading monopoly there with his own. The daydreamer trusts Dain Maroola and does not suspect that his promises of help in organizing an expedition to find this wealth are false, and that the latter visits the settlement only to deal secretly with Lakamba and meet Nina. "Walking amongst pitfalls, with his head in the clouds, weak, irresolute, and unhappy" (42), the white man does not realize the extent to which he is beset by enemies, who deal with him only as the one who knows where the old is (27, 39-40). The pitiful results of Almayer's actions are reflected metaphorically in the deplorable appearance of his "office"–"The very dust and bones of a dead and gone business" (199)–whose furniture was destroyed by his Malay spouse in her fits of fury (90-91), where "A general air of squalid neglect pervaded the place" (16), where all is covered with a thick coat of dust, and dirty account books and heaps of yellowish paper are lying about (199-200).

He unconsciously plays the role dictated by Babalatchi, whose motive is to save Dain. This is the most typical instance of Almayer's lack of control over the situation. Lakamba's adviser uses the ignorant protagonist's real despair over Maroola's feigned death to deceive the Dutch into stopping searching for the "dead" man. Thus Babalatchi makes Almayer an object of ridicule, a pawn in the intrigue intended to effect his master's aims. Almayer also does not realize that his wife and the one-eyed statesman plan to help Nina and her lover to escape.

The protagonist is treated with particular contempt by the seamen who arrive in Sambir. They jeer at his naiveté:

> Almayer...opened his heart before the sympathizing strangers, unaware of the amusement the recital of his many misfortunes caused to those future admirals. (35)
>
> The black forest...woke up [after their departure] that night to the ringing laughter in the small flotilla provoked by some reminiscence of Almayer's lamentable narrative. Salt-water jests at the poor man's expense were passed from boat to boat.... (36; also 36-37 other excerpts)

According to the lieutenant commanding the frigate, sent in search of Dain, Almayer "seems more of a fool than a knave"

(121). His obtuseness is illustrated by his public expression of pro-British sentiments in a time of Dutch expansion in the area (83). His attitude is also emphasized by the name "Almayer's Folly" (suggesting a lack of caution, *folie de grandeur*) given to the house he built to receive Englishmen.[15]

His pitiful image recurs in *An Outcast of the Islands:*

> In his exultation of an empty-headed quill-driver he thought himself, by the virtue of that furniture, at the head of a serious business....He found out very soon that trade in Sambir meant something entirely different. He could not guide Patalolo, control the irrepressible old Sahamin, or restrain the youthful vagaries of the fierce Bahassoen with pen, ink, and paper. He found no successful magic in the blank pages of his ledgers: and gradually he lost his old point of view in the saner appreciation of his situation. (OI 300; also 93)

Lingard's deputy does not comprehend the reasons for his defeats. He fails to detect the enemy's intrigues, and mistakenly assesses his own position (93). His incapacity is shown principally in his reactions to Willems's deeds under Babalatchi's direction, which culminates in Almayer's humiliation by Aissa's admirer (181-186, 207). Nina's father misunderstands all his own conduct and tragic lot, from his arrival in Sambir until his death. Almayer's failure to bear "the white man's burden" is the principal reason for Lingard's loss of power over Sambir, the change that will diminish trade an the welfare and happiness of its inhabitants.

Lingard is also disappointed with Willems the embezzler, whom he sends to Sambir to help Almayer in the business. Willems wants to make himself and his sweetheart independent of the locals' machinations, but he lacks the means (i.e., Nina's father's help and understanding). Eventually he becomes a puppet in Babalatchi's plot against the King of the Sea. The one-eyed diplomatist, using the newcomer's love for Aissa, forces him to steer Abdulla's (the Rajah-Laut's rival) ship up the Pantai to Sambir. Having accomplished this, he tries to focus Lingard's anger on Almayer but the proud philanthropist does not yield to these suggestions. He claims that he will never be manipulated by Malays (240). The outcast's story, like Kayerts's and Carlier's, may as well be seen as a parable about a white man's growing submission to the human and natural forces of an exotic environment:[16]

> And in that atmosphere of Nature's workshop Willems felt soothed and lulled into forgetfulness of his past, into indifference as to his future. The recollections of his triumphs, of his wrongs and of his ambition vanished in that warmth, which seemed to melt all regrets, all hope, all anger, all strength out of his heart. (74-75)

In the outcast's frame of mind consciousness of degradation is combined with hatred for the natives who enslave him (151-152; on his isolation and conduct, see Part 1, Chapters 1 and 2).

Cornelius in *Lord Jim* is another colonizer who falls short of expectations. For the sake of his wife, Stein appoints him the agent in Patusan, but Cornelius abuses his master's confidence and appropriates the trading company's goods for himself (LJ 289).[17] "The white man's burden" is also perverted by the performance of the Rumanian scholar who appears episodically in *Almayer's Folly* and *An Outcast of the Islands*.

> There was a scientific explorer here a year or more ago. He lived in my [Almayer's] house: drank from morning to night. He lived joyously for a few months, and when the liquor he brought with him was gone he returned to Batavia with a report on the mineral wealth of the interior. (AF 122; also OI 360-361, 365, 367)

Another miscreant is Bamtz in *Because of the Dollars*:[18]

> A unique loafer. He made a fine art of it, or rather a sort of craft and mystery....He would arrive in some settlement up a river...posing mysteriously as a very special trader. He would spin them no end of yarns, live on the fat of the land for a while, and then do some mean swindle or other–or else they would get tired of him and ask him to quit. And he would go off meekly with an air of injured innocence. (WT 177-178)

However, the unflattering presentation of these characters is slightly varied: Cornelius's, Bamtz's, and Almayer's downfalls are shown to be due entirely to their own incompetence, whereas those of Willems, Kayerts, and Carlier are caused partly by external forces. The reasons for Willems's defeat are not so much inherent in his character as in his love affair, his overpowering passion:

> With his returning wits came [after the first encounter with Aissa] the fear of something unknown that had taken possession of his heart, of something inarticulate and masterful which could not speak and would be obeyed. (OI 72)
> he stood still [on his way to her], with a look of strained attention on his face as if listening to a far-off voice of his fate. (79-80)

The amorous attachment is mostly a manifestation of the white man's subjection to the exotic environment, since Aissa is depicted as "The very spirit of that land of mysterious forests," an "enchanting, subduing, beautiful" secret of tropical life (70), a personification of mighty nature:[19]

> the slender spikes of pale green orchids streamed down from amongst the boughs and mingled with the black hair that framed her face, as if all those plants claimed her for their own–the animated and brilliant flower of all that exuberant life which, born in gloom, struggles for ever towards the sunshine. (76)

In *An Outpost of Progress* the narrator largely blames European civilization for Kayerts's and Carlier's tragedy, since it deprived them of individuality, initiative, and fortitude, did not prepare them for the adversities of the jungle (Part 2, Chapter 4).[20] Nevertheless, this only partly explains their conduct, since culture makes the rulers superior to the natives, who frequently view them as godlike creatures (see the attitude of Gobila, the chief of neighboring villages). This greatly facilitates their resistance to the pressure of the wilderness and the execution of their mission.

Conrad's colonizers sometimes act senselessly or preach "the white man's burden" while sweating and robbing autochthones. Mrs. Almayer recollects the whites who "come...to trade, with prayers on their lips and loaded guns in their hands" (AF 153), Karain mentions the Europeans who "came in boats full of soldiers to talk...of protection and peace" (TU 28). Belarab and Daman in *The Rescue* evaluate the newcomers' performance similarly on behalf of the local community:

> Eyes do not kill, nor angry words; and curses have no power, else the Dutch would not grow fat living on our land, and I would not be alive tonight. (Re 112-113)
>
> [The whites] are sent by rulers to examine the aspects of far-off countries and talk of peace and make treaties. Such is the beginning of great sorrows. (223)

Mr. Travers in *The Rescue* and Duc de Mersch in *The Inheritors* represent the other side in such confrontations. They regard the newcomers' conduct as proper and argue for the necessity of exploiting the aborigines:

> And if the inferior race must perish, it is a gain, a step toward the perfecting of society which is the aim of progress. (Re 148)
>
> that sort of native exists...to be rooted out by men of good-will, with careers to make. (I 110)

De Mersch's activities result in the horrible abuse of the natives: they are maltreated and killed; they suffer from famine, illnesses, and crime (162, 183-185). This stands in clear contrast to the ideals professed in de Mersch's pompous public declarations:[21]

> Progress, improvement, civilisation, a little less evil in the world–more light! It was our duty not to count the cost of humanising a lower race. (81)
>
> He wished to build up a model state, *the* model protectorate of the world, a place where perfect equality shall obtain for all races, all creeds, and all colours. (92)

The narrator emphasizes this discrepancy between appearances and reality:

> But more revolting to see without a mask was that falsehood which had been hiding under the words that for ages had spurred men to noble deeds, to self-sacrifice, to heroism. What was appalling was the sudden perception that all the traditional ideals of honour, glory, conscience, had been committed to the upholding of a gigantic and atrocious fraud. The falsehood had spread stealthily, had eaten into the very heart of creeds and convictions that we lean upon on our passages between the past and the future. (184-185)

C. "Heart of Darkness" of European Colonial Expansion

All the aspects of the miscarriage of "the white man's burden" discussed here (incompetence, failure to function efficiently and firmly in a tropical environment, surrender to the pressure of the wilderness, nonsensical activities, exploitation under philanthropic pretences) appear in *Heart of Darkness,* the most comprehensive and profound expression of Conrad's condemnation of colonialism. Marlow is both protagonist and narrator, as well as the writer's mouthpiece here. His journey up the big river into the Dark Continent[22] reveals the actual performance of the envoys of civilization. He is shocked by instances of heartless exploitation. At the outer station gaunt, wretched natives are easily subjugated and forced into slave labor:

> Six black men advanced in a file, toiling up the path....I could see every rib, the joints of their limbs were like knots in a rope; each had an iron collar on his neck, and all were connected together with a chain whose bights swung between them, rhythmically clinking....All their meagre breasts panted together, the violently dilated nostrils quivered, the eyes stared stonily up-hill...with...a glance at his charge, [their guardian] seemed to take me into partnership in his exalted trust. (YNTOS 64-65)

The most impressive instance of ruthless treatment is disclosed by descriptions of the Negroes in the grove of death, where they suffer and die from sickness and misery:

> It seemed to me I had stepped into the gloomy circle of some Inferno....Black shapes crouched, lay, sat between the trees leaning against the trunks...in all the attitudes of pain, abandonment, and despair....They were dying slowly–it was very clear...they were nothing...but black shadows of disease and starvation, lying confusedly in the greenish gloom. Brought from all the recesses of the coast in all the legality of the time contracts, lost in uncongenial surroundings, fed on unfamiliar food, they sickened, became inefficient, and were then allowed to crawl away and rest. (66)

The victims' plight does not concern the whites, neither those at the trading posts, nor the pilgrims on board the steamboat. The whites at the post have a purely racist attitude toward the blacks, whom they look upon as subhumans, and the pilgrims traveling upriver with Marlow shoot at the black people, who are mourning Kurtz's departure (146-147).

The colonizers' indifference to their inferiors' afflictions result in good part from an eagerness to maximize profits, which is their main reason for being in Africa.[23] In pursuit of wealth, position, and advancement they intrigue and are wicked (78). The station manager, pretending to care for Kurtz, deliberately delays the aid expedition, which he hopes will arrive too late and find Kurtz dead–and thus he will be rid of his most outstanding agent and chief rival.[24] Insatiable greed may be detected in the actions of nearly all the whites:

> A taint of imbecile rapacity blew through it all, like a whiff from some corpse. (76)
>
> It [the agents' plotting] was as unreal as everything else–as the philanthropic pretence of the whole concern, as their talk, as their government, as their show of work. The only real feeling was a desire to get appointed to a trading-post where ivory was to be had, so that they could earn percentages. (78)

Marlow further stresses it in his presentation of the following group:

> Five such instalments came, with their absurd air of disorderly flight with the loot of innumerable outfit shops and provision stores, that, one would think, they were lugging, after a raid, into the wilderness for equitable division. It was an inextricable mess of things decent in themselves but that human folly made look like spoils of thieving. This devoted band called itself the Eldorado Exploring Expedition....there was not an atom of foresight or of serious intention in the whole batch of them....To tear treasure out of the bowels of the land was their desire, with no more moral purpose at the back of it than there is in burglars breaking into a safe. (87)[25]

The invaders' conduct testifies to their complete lack of principles or humanity. The Central Station Manager's credo that, to survive in the equatorial zone, one should be extraordinarily immune against diseases, "should have no entrails" (74), implies hollowness at the core. This imagery is used in Marlow's descriptions of the manager's nephew and plotting partner: "it seemed to me that if I tried I could poke my forefinger through him, and would find nothing inside but a little loose dirt, maybe" (81). Continual references to the Europeans as "pilgrims" acquire obvious ironic overtones in this context.[26]

Colonizing activity, advertised as the glorious civilizing mission of the white race in Africa, is viewed by Marlow with sarcastic detachment, for instance, in commentaries on his own travel there and to Kurtz's practices:

> I had been represented...as an exceptional and gifted creature–a piece of good fortune for the Company....It appeared, however, I was also one of the Workers, with a capital–you know. Something like an emissary of light, something like a lower sort of apostle. There had been a lot of such rot let loose in print and talk just about that time, and the excellent woman, living right in the rush of all that humbug, got carried off her feet. (59)
>
> 'He is an emissary of pity, and science, and progress, and devil knows what else. We want,' he began to desclaim suddenly, 'for the guidance of the cause intrusted to us by Europe, so to speak, higher intelligence, wide sympathies, a singleness of purpose.' 'Who says that?' I asked. 'Lots of them,' he replied. (79)

All this is clear from his ironic remarks about his predecessor, who was killed in a quarrel with natives:

> Freesleven...thought himself wronged somehow in the bargain, so he went ashore and started to hammer the chief of the village with a stick....he had been a couple of years already out there engaged in the noble cause, you know, and he probably felt the need at last of asserting his self-respect in some way. Therefore he whacked the old nigger mercilessly...till...the chief's son–in desperation at hearing the old chap yell, made a tentative jab with a spear at the white man–and of course it went quite easy between the shoulder-blades....What became of the hens I don't know either. I should think the cause of progress got them, anyhow. (54)

Such disparity is generalized in the narrator's gnomic utterance:

> The conquest of the earth, which mostly means the taking it away from those who have a different complexion or slightly flatter noses than ourselves, is not a pretty thing when you look into it too much. What redeems it is the idea only. An idea at the back of it; not a sentimental pretence but an idea; and an unselfish belief in the idea–something you can set up, and bow down before, and offer a sacrifice to.... (50-51)

The incongruity between the professed and actual images of colonialism is emphasized by the picture of the entirely futile and absurd performance of the representatives of colonial power.[28] Marlow sees this during his sea journey to Africa:

> We...landed custom-house clerks to levy toll in what looked like a God-forsaken wilderness...landed more soldiers–to take care of the custom-house clerks, presumably. (60)
>
> In the empty immensity of the earth, sky, and water, there she [a man-of-war] was, incomprehensible, firing into a continent...a small flame would dart and vanish, a little white smoke would disappear, a tiny projectile would give a feeble screech–and nothing happened. Nothing could happen. There was a touch of insanity in the proceeding, a sense of lugubrious drollery.... (61-62; also 61 other excerpts)

During his stay at the Outer station and the Central station Marlow repeatedly encounters preposterous undertakings and regulations. For example, he notices "a vast artificial hole somebody had been digging on the slope, the purpose of which he found it impossible to divine....It might have been connected with the philanthropic desire of giving the criminals something to do" (65). He witnesses the purposeless blasting of a cliff that was not in the path of a railway (64); he meets a uniformed white man with an armed escort of Negroes who claims to be guarding the nonexistent wilderness roads (71); he espies a man trying to put out a fire by using a pail with a hole in its bottom (76); he comes upon the central station Manager's nephew, who doesn't work:

> The business intrusted to this fellow was the making of bricks–so I had been informed; but there wasn't a fragment of a brick anywhere in the station, and he had been there more than a year–waiting. It seems he could not make bricks without something, I don't know what–straw maybe....it did not appear clear to me what he was waiting for. An act of special creation perhaps. (77)

The narrator's conviction about the pointlessness of these activities is strengthened by numerous instances of thriftlessness: a boiler abandoned in the grass, a railway car lying on its back, pieces of decaying machinery, a pile of rusty pails (63-64), broken drain pipes thrown into a ravine (65-66). He is further taken by the fact that the black members of the steamboat crew are rewarded for their work with pieces of brass wire–as they are on board continually, they could not buy provisions with this (104).

The persistent emphasis on the whites' pointless activity is enhanced by their appearance as invaders who look ridiculous in Africa[29] (62; see on their tropical isolation Part 1, Chapter 1). "We called at some more places...all along the formless coast bordered by dangerous surf, as if Nature herself had tried to ward off intruders" (62), whereas the natives are organically at one with their environment:

> Now and then a boat from the shore gave one a momentary contact with reality. It was paddled by black fellows....they had bone, muscle, a wild vitality, an intense energy of movement, that was as natural and true as the surf along their coast. They wanted no excuse for being there....For a time I would feel I belong still to a world of straightforward facts.... (61)

Reflections on the colonizers' incompatibility with equatorial nature are in tune with frequent allusions to death, which foreshadow the conclusion of this invasion.[30] Mourning imagery is used already in the relation of events preceding Marlow's expedition: Brussels appears to be a city of graves, of the deceased (55, 57, 152, 155), of "a whited sepulchre," the mortal big river is compared to a snake swallowing its victims (56), the women in the outer room of the company's office are "guarding the door of Darkness, knitting black wool as for a warm pall" (57), the doctor measures–in the interest of science–the crania of agents going to the Congo who are never to return (57-58). Analogous motifs appear in profusion in subsequent parts of *Heart of Darkness:*

> We called at some more places with farcical names, where the merry dance of death and trade goes on in a still and earthy atmosphere as of an overheated catacomb...in and out of rivers, streams of death in life. (62)

Kurtz is singled out as an unrivaled colonizer and main object of the narrator's interest (88, 90). Marlow is, however, disappointed, having found him to be the embodiment of the most abominable executor of "the white man's burden," whose sad memory should be laid "for an everlasting rest in the dust-bin of progress, amongst all the sweepings and, figuratively speaking, all the dead cats of civilisation" (119; also 116, 149). As the ruler of the Inner Station he surpasses everybody in looting: he sends out as much ivory as all the other agents together (69). This shameful preeminence is commented on sarcastically by the narrator:

> Ivory? I should think so. Heaps of it, stacks of it....You would think there was not a single tusk left either above or below the ground in the whole country....It appears these niggers do bury the tusks sometimes–but evidently they couldn't bury this parcel deep enough to save the gifted Mr. Kurtz from his fate. (115-116; also 129-130)

Calling him "an animated image of death carved out of old ivory" (134), with a head like a ball of the same (115), suggests that greed is the essence of Kurtz's character.[31]

Close contact with primeval forests and primitive people activates elemental, unquenchable, irresistible instincts of cupidity and domination in Kurtz (see more in Part 1, Chapters 1 and 2):

> The wilderness had patted him on the head...it had caressed him, and–lo!–he had withered; it had taken him, loved him, embraced him, got into his veins, consumed his flesh, and sealed his soul to its own by the inconceivable ceremonies of some devilish initiation. (115)
> I tried to break the spell–the heavy, mute spell of the wilderness–that seemed to draw him to its pitiless breast by the awakening of forgotten and brutal instincts, by the memory of gratified and monstrous passions. (144; also 116)

The matchless colonizer's extraordinarily strong attachment to the overpowering elemental force (largely resembling Willems's predicament in *An Outcast of the Islands*) renders it impossible for him to renounce his accustomed way of living:

> He hated all this, and somehow he couldn't get away. When I had a chance I begged him to try and leave while there was time; I offered to go back with him. And he would say yes, and then he would remain; go off on another ivory hunt; disappear for weeks; forget himself amongst these people. (129)

Therefore, in order to ward off the pilgrims' expedition from the Inner Station, Kurtz commands his followers to attack the steamer, and later, being taken on board, he tries to escape to his subordinates.[32]

Equipped with the attributes and power of European civilization, he seems to the Negroes a supernatural being, and is deified: they perform dances and rites (117-118), crawl before him (131-132), and obey all his demands–which include human sacrifice (Marlow notices heads on the stakes around Kurtz's cottage) (130-131).[33] Using this position to accumulate ever-increasing supplies of ivory is loathsome (127-128), and continues to satisfy his unchecked greed for wealth and power. "Mr. Kurtz lacked restraint in the gratification of his various lusts" (131), and "knew no restraint, no faith, and no fear" (145), which is confirmed by the harlequin's confession:

> he wanted to shoot me, too, one day....I had a small lot of ivory the chief of that village near my house gave me....Well, he [Kurtz] wanted it, and wouldn't hear reason. He declared he would shoot me unless I gave him the ivory and then cleared out of the country, because he could do so, and had a fancy for it, and there was nothing on earth to prevent him killing whom he jolly well pleased. (128)[34]

Yielding to insatiable passions is a gross violation of a fundamental rule of Conrad's colonial ethos, formulated in the narrator's sententious statements:

> He [a white man] must meet that truth [the natives'] with his own true stuff–with his own inborn strength. Principles won't do. Acquisitions, clothes, pretty rags–rags that would fly off at the first good shake. (97)
> you must fall back upon your own innate strength, upon your own capacity for faithfulness....And there, don't you see? your strength comes in...your power of devotion, not to yourself, but to an obscure, back-breaking business. And that's difficult enough. (116-117)

Kurtz illustrates the utter contradiction between a colonizer's laudable intentions and degenerate implementation. This specimen of the white race, overwhelmed by a desire to get rich and ruthlessly abusing the natives, still is able to discourse persuasively upon the mission to civilize them: "It [his voice] survived his strength to hide in the magnificent folds of eloquence the barren darkness of his heart" (147; also 131). This extreme disparity appears most distinctly in the report for the guidance of the International Society for the Suppression of Savage Customs. This paper abounds in transcendent, generous ideals appealing to the altruism of those carrying "the white man's burden,"[35] with the postscript appended in Africa: "Exterminate all the brutes!" This contrast reappears during Marlow's visit to Kurtz's Intended: "He lived then before me; he lived as much as he had ever lived–a shadow insatiable of splendid appearances, of frightful realities...and draped nobly in the folds of a gorgeous eloquence" (155).

In spite of his extreme degradation, Kurtz is (like Willems, Kayerts, and Carlier) partly exonerated.[36] The paper he composed on the threshold of his career is an authentic expression of his initial idealism, of his belief in "the white man's burden." This distinguishes him from the other colonial types in *Heart of Darkness*. On his deathbed he reveals his understanding of the evil of his actions. Marlow notices

> on that ivory face the expression of sombre pride, of ruthless power, of craven terror–of an intense and hopeless despair. Did he live his life again in every detail of desire, temptation, and surrender during that supreme moment of complete knowledge? He cried in a whisper.... 'The horror! The horror!' (149)

The final outcry constitutes "a judgement upon the adventures of his soul on this earth," "the appalling face of a glimpsed truth," "a moral victory paid for by innumerable defeats" (150-151). This self-condemnation evokes the story teller's respect, engages him in the deceased's cause, and induces him to defend Kurtz's good name–he does not deliver the packet of private papers to the company representatives. He also discloses to Kurtz's Intended neither the truth about his record nor the real sense of his final confession. Thus a perfect image of Kurtz remains in her memory[37] (see also on Marlow's ethical isolation as confidante in Part 1, Chapter 2).

Kurtz's bearing of "the white man's burden" also has a universal dimension in symbolizing the colonial expansion of those times. In fact, "All Europe contributed to the making of

Kurtz....The International Society for the Suppression of Savage Customs had intrusted him with the making of a report, for its future guidance" (117). In this perspective the downfall of the Inner Station sovereign, depicted as an epitome of nineteenth-century colonialism, implies a degeneracy in the progression of the entire imperial ideology.[38] His "biography" illustrates the increasing psychomoral depravity of civilized man, the barbarous instincts that under certain conditions dominate his personality. Marlow's expedition to Africa may thus be interpreted as a voyage penetrating the deepest layers of human nature.[39] The supraindividual aspect of this story is shown in the narrator's comments on the last moments of Kurtz's life: "No eloquence could have been so withering to one's belief in mankind as his final burst of sincerity" (145).

The universalization of ideas achieved in this story is mostly indirect: it comes via the key motif of darkness (which consistently accompanies the presentation of events) that symbolizes the colonizers' atrocities–the white man's corruption.[40] Blackness engulfs the Central Station (74) and the whole country, which, owing to European conquests "had ceased to be a blank space of delightful mystery–a white patch for a boy to dream gloriously over. It had become a place of darkness" (52). The densest gloom came to pervade the Inner Station. Marlow's voyage to it is like a penetration "deeper and deeper into the heart of darkness" (95); the atmosphere on this outpost was "the unseen presence of victorious corruption, the darkness of an impenetrable night" (138); the inimitable agent's words "the deceitful flow from the heart of an impenetrable darkness" (114). The low instincts and passions that overwhelmed his soul were "powers of darkness" (116), "the barren darkness of his heart" (147). The dying Kurtz is the man in "an impenetrable darkness...at the bottom of a precipice where the sun never shines" (149). He does not notice the lamplight beside him (149), and is the image of the raider evoked during the meeting with his Intended–"a shadow darker than the shadow of the night" (155). A sullenness therefore threatens to overpower this woman's personality, to destroy her sublime illusions:

> But with every word spoken [the story teller claims] the room was growing darker, and only her forehead smooth and white, remain illumined by the unextinguishable light of belief and love....I listened. The darkness deepened. (158)
>
> I...bowed my head before the faith that was in her, before that great and saving illusion that shone with an unearthly glow in the darkness, in the triumphant darkness from which I could not have defended her–from which I could not even defend myself. (159; also 157-161 other passages)

Such imagery pertains as well to Brussels (55), and the pejorative implications of the title motif are broadened to embrace Belgian colonial policies. Further, a murk surrounds the cruising yawl *Nellie* on the Thames with the narrator and his listeners on board:

> The air was dark above Gravesend, and further back still seemed condensed into a mournful gloom, brooding motionless over the biggest, and the greatest, town on earth. (45)
>
> And farther west on the upper reaches the place of the monstrous town was still marked ominously on the sky, a brooding glooming sunshine, a lurid glare under the stars. (48)

This picture of London, combined with reflections about age-old British expansion (46-47), brings the meanings of the crucial symbol to the representatives of even this nation.

The narrative situation generalizes the message of *Heart of Darkness* on a temporal level as well.[41] The plot constructor evokes the remote times when England was the "darkness"–a field for Rome's expansion done in the name of civilization, and he sketches a portrait of the commander of a trireme whose experiences are exactly parallel to Kurtz's. They comprise a voyage inland through marshes and forests inhabited by savage people, which is motivated by dreams for his career or amassing riches (his powerful countrymen are censured for robbery and violence on a grand scale), a stay at distant outposts under constant menace from an alien environment ("cold, fog, tempests, disease, exile, and death"), a final surrender, and moral degeneration (49-50). This analogy is not merely an anticipation, but primarily a universalization, of the Inner Station sovereign's life story.[42] Thus the colonizers' abominable and barbaric behavior in *Heart of Darkness* constitutes a symbolic representation of the Belgian, English, and ancient Roman expansions at their worst; it is characteristic of all imperial conquests.[43]

The Conradian colonizers' ethos is tinged with Anglophilism[44] (on other manifestations of such, see Part 2, Chapters 4 and 5). "The white man's burden" is nearly always perverted by white men of the Continent: the Dutch[45] (Heemskirk in *Freya of the Seven Isles,* Almayer in *Almayer's Folly* and *An Outcast of the Islands,* Willems in *An Outcast of the Islands,* Bamtz in *Because of the Dollars*), the Portuguese (Cornelius in *Lord Jim*), the Belgians (Kayerts and Carlier in *An Outpost of Progress,* the agents in *Heart of Darkness*) and Kurtz, "a citizen of Europe" (YNTOS 117). Such direct judgments are conveyed in *Heart of Darkness* (50-51, 55) and *An Observer in Malaya,* where the British are praised for their unimpeachable intentions and attachment to the native peoples, who regard them with respect (NLL 58-59).

2. The Political Ethos

A. Autobiographical Perspectives

The profound humanism of Conrad's oeuvre is codetermined by its political ideas, and their proper interpretation should be conditioned by taking the writer's life into account. The Polish heritage of this son of an exiled champion of the national cause, this world famous author who grew up in nineteenth-century Poland in the atmosphere of struggle for independence, explains his profound antipathy to Russia. Anti-Russian sentiments are manifested primarily in *The Secret Agent, Under Western Eyes, The Crime of Partition,* and *Autocracy and War.* In *A Personal Record* the writer gives vent to rancor caused by wrongs to his parents and himself by the tsarist authorities:

> Without wishing to treat with levity the just timidities of Imperialists all the world over, I may allow myself the reflection that a woman, practically condemned by the doctors, and a small boy not quite six years old could not be regarded as seriously dangerous even for the largest of conceivable empires saddled with the most sacred of responsibilities. (PR 65)

Conrad's heritage accounts for his contempt for Germany as well. His anti-German sentiments are most conspicuous in *Autocracy and War,* where he emphasizes Teutonic ruthlessness and lust for territory (NLL 94-96, 104-106, 112-114); and in *Poland Revisited*:[46]

> I had never lingered in that land which, on the whole, is so singularly barren of memorable manifestations of generous sympathies and magnanimous impulses. An ineradicable, invincible provincialism of envy and vanity clings to the forms of its thought like a frowsy garment. (NLL 164)
>
> German genius has a hypnotising power over half-baked souls and half-lighted minds. There is an immense force of suggestion in highly organised mediocrity. Had it not hypnotised half Europe? (159; also 146-147, 157-159; other excerpts)

Conrad's writings reveal his Polish patriotism directly.[47] Peyrol in *The Rover* personifies the writer's yearning for his motherland, his desire to return there.[48] *Amy Foster* depicts the miserable plight of (Polish) Carpathian emigrants (see also on Yanko's estrangement in Part 1, Chapter 2), and the ignominy of confidence men cheating naive villagers:

> A few months later we could read in the papers the accounts of the bogus 'Emigration Agencies' among the Sclavonian peasantry in the more remote provinces of Austria. The object of these scoundrels was to get hold of the poor ignorant people's homesteads, and they were in league with the local usurers. (TOS 121; also 116-117)

And *Prince Roman* pays tribute to the nineteenth-century uprisings, the struggles for the independence of the Polish nation, which was

> not so much alive as surviving, which persists in thinking, breathing, speaking, hoping, and suffering in its grave, railed in by a million of bayonets and triple-sealed with the seals of three great empires. (TH 29)
> That country which demands to be loved as no other country has ever been loved, with the mournful affection one bears to the unforgotten dead and with the unextinguishable fire of a hopeless passion which only a living, breathing, warm ideal can kindle in our breasts for our pride, for our weariness, for our exultation, for our undoing. (51)

Prince Roman's life story displays exemplary patriotism. After his wife's death he subordinates all his actions to the good of the country. He serves in the ranks voluntarily, in spite of his aristocratic parentage. He takes part in the insurrection and distinguishes himself by

> Resourcefulness and courage. It was not the reckless courage of a desperate man; it was a self-possessed, as if conscientious, valour which nothing could dismay; a boundless but equable devotion, unaffected by time, by reverses, by the discouragement of endless retreats, by the bitterness of waning hopes and the horrors of pestilence added to the toils and perils of war. (46)

In captivity Prince Roman renounces the chance to exculpate himself; returning from banishment, he helps neighbors and other former exiles.[49] His ordeal in war exemplifies the tragedies and sufferings of the entire nation. A deep love for the homeland is also cherished by the Jewish innkeeper Yankel (39) and Francis, Master of the Horse of the Princes S———. Their conduct is shaped by the principle of typicality governing the creation of characters in this story: the narrator gives the political reasons for the partitioned nation (Poland), Francis represents the old-fashioned gentry (41-42), and Prince John and Yankel are modeled upon figures common to the Polish reality of the nineteenth century.[50]

The writer's attitude toward his fatherland is also revealed in his nonfictional prose. *The Crime of Partition* glorifies Poland and its cultural and political traditions. He argues that it had never been aggressive toward neighboring states, that it has been famous for tolerance and liberty, and that in the eighteenth century it was a center of liberal and progressive ideas. Its downfall was the price paid for the realization of these ideas in other countries. The Polish nation preserved its identity in spite of numerous disasters, and its meritorious history made it deserving of the restoration of its independence after World War I. A similar plea is made in *Note on the Polish Problem*. *A Personal Record* highlights the admirable elements of the Polish ethos: chivalry, liberalism, the cult of freedom, and respect for individual rights (PR Author's Note VIII-IX). *Amy Foster, Prince Roman*, and the above-mentioned essays prove the groundlessness of the accusations that Conrad betrayed his native land.

Political Anglophilism reinforces the writer's outlook (Part 2, Chapters 4 and 5 with the portrayal of marines and colonizers in accordance with this attitude). He reveres the traditional love of freedom in his adopted country (*Nostromo*, N 30-31; *Suspense*, S 11) and its veneration of human rights, democracy, and law-abiding conduct (*The Secret Agent*, SA 29, 75). It is significant that the caricatured champions of anarchism in *The Secret Agent* and *An Anarchist* are not of this nationality.[51]

Political themes appear in many other works by Conrad. They form the historical setting in *Gaspar Ruiz, The Duel, The Arrow of Gold, The Rover, Suspense, The Warrior's Soul, The Sisters*, and *Romance*.[52] In *Almayer's Folly, An Outcast of the Islands*, the Patusan part of *Lord Jim*, and in *The Rescue* the natives' local intrigues are aimed at gaining power and influence. They are all politically colored, especially those of Babalatchi, who is ironically referred to as "that potentate's [Lakamba's] prime minister, harbour master, financial adviser, and general factotum" (*Almayer's Folly*, AF 38):

> He had all a true vagabond's pliability to circumstances and adaptiveness to momentary surroundings. In his readiness to learn from experience that contempt for early principles so necessary to a true statesman, he equalled the most successful politicians of any age....(*An Outcast of the Islands*, OI 56)

Politics play the most important part in *Nostromo, The Secret Agent,* and *Under Western Eyes,* which are generally regarded as masterpieces of the fictional treatment of ideas. It dominates the shaping of characters and action, largely adventurous. It motivates the narration in *Nostromo* (the interwoven plots digress from one another, which portray a diverse panorama of the characters' different viewpoints and activities) and in *The Secret Agent* and *Under Western Eyes* (largely ironic presentation of structured tendencies).

B. Censure of Anarchism

Condemnation of anarchism–the movement that flourished in Western Europe in the late nineteenth and early twentieth centuries, which aimed at annihilating the social and political order–is the principal theme of *The Secret Agent.*[53] Anarchists are caricatured, and do not fit stereotypes of this ideology. Michaelis's obesity, for instance, is compatible with neither misery nor the activity of fighters for the rights of the wronged:

> The ticket-of-leave apostle, was speaking in...a voice that wheezed as if deadened and oppressed by the layer of fat on his chest...round like a tub, with an enormous stomach and distended cheeks...as though for fifteen years the servants of an outraged society had made a point of stuffing him with fattening foods in a damp and lightless cellar. (SA 41; also 50-51, 107, 113)

Unlike a typical agitator, he feels an extremely strong need to be well cared for (it is supplied by his patroness) and is lazy: sent to the patroness's cottage in the country, "the ex-prisoner could moon about the shady lanes for days together in a delicious and humanitarian idleness" (53). His performance turns out to be ineffectual: "Michaelis was a humanitarian sentimentalist, a little mad, but upon the whole incapable of hurting a fly intentionally" (110). The portrayal of Karl Yundt is similar in the grotesque exaggeration of his helplessness:

> His little bald head quivered, imparting a comical vibration to the wisp of white goatee....His worn-out passion, resembling in its impotent fierceness the excitement of a senile sensualist, was badly served by a dried throat and toothless gums.... (42-43)
> The all but moribund veteran of dynamite wars had been a great actor in his time....he took the part of an insolent and venomous evoker of sinister impulses....The shadow of his evil gift clung to him yet like the smell of a deadly drug in an old vial of poison, emptied now, useless, ready to be thrown away upon the rubbish-heap of things that had served their time. (48; also 42; other excerpts, 52)

The conduct of the hypocritical Ossipon does not serve the realization of seditious urges: he treats the movement exclusively as a source of personal profit. He is actually a loafer who lives on naive women. For example, in the epilogue of the novel, he intends to seize Winnie's husband's funds and shop through a love affair with her. His timidity, particularly revealed in his reactions to the deaths of Stevie and Verloc (290-291), and to Winnie's suicide (307), is incompatible with his role. The narrator's strongly emphasized derisive distance from this figure is shown in the periphrastic descriptions of Ossipon's fear (272), double-dealing, and mercenary motives:

> by a sudden inspiration [he] uttered an 'Unhappy woman!' of lofty commiseration instead of the more familiar 'Poor darling!' of his usual practice....He felt conscious of something abnormal going on, while he never lost sight of the greatness of the stake. 'Unhappy, brave woman!' He was glad to have discovered that variation.... (276-77; also 273-274)

Comments on erudition apply this narrative technique most clearly:

> Comrade Alexander Ossipon–nicknamed the Doctor, ex-medical student without a degree; afterwards wandering lecturer to working-men's associations upon the socialistic aspects of hygiene; author of a popular quasi-medical study...turned...that glance of insufferable, hopelessly dense sufficiency which nothing but the frequentation of science can give to the dullness of common mortals. (46; also 296-297)

The image of the learned anarchist, "marching in the gutter as if in training for the task of an inevitable future" (311), crowns this grotesque portrayal.

The Professor, another champion of subversive ideology, is clearly despicable, and distinguished by slovenliness (61-62, 94, 310). Furthermore, he easily gets into conflicts with people:

> [he was] once assistant demonstrator in chemistry at some technical institute. He quarrelled with the authorities upon a question of unfair treatment. Afterwards he obtained a post in the laboratory of a manufactory of dyes. There, too, he had been treated with revolting injustice. His struggles, his privations, his hard work to raise himself in the social scale, had filled him with such an exalted conviction of his merits that it was extremely difficult for the world to treat him with justice....The Professor had genius, but lacked the great social virtue of resignation. (75)

His obsessive fear of the crowd is out of keeping with his professed terrorism:

> after a while he became disagreeably affected by the sight of the roadway thronged with vehicles and of the pavement crowded with men and women....with severe exultation the Professor thought of the refuge of his room. (81-82)
>
> The contemplation of the multitudes thronging the pavements extinguished his assurance under a load of doubt and uneasiness which he could shake off after a period of seclusion in the room. (305)

Verloc, the protagonist of *The Secret Agent,* is a collection of many negative features and the antithesis of a true anarchist. He displays extraordinary sloth: "The fellow was unexpectedly vulgar, heavy, and impudently unintelligent" (27). He, "the embodiment of fraudulent laziness and incompetency" (27), "the domestic dog having a nightmare on the hearthrug" (34) is incapable of following others' utterances (34). His mental languor, combined with corpulence (13, 19), testifies to laziness and gluttony. Together they form a caricature of a champion of subversion: he is called a "rusty," i.e., inactive, representative of this movement. The narrator comments sarcastically on Verloc's sluggishness.

> His idleness was not hygienic, but it suited him very well. He was in a manner devoted to it with a sort of inert fanaticism, or perhaps rather with a fanatical inertness....he had embraced indolence from an impulse as profound as unexplicable and as imperious as the impulse which directs a man's preference for one particular woman in a given thousand. He was too lazy even for a mere demagogue....He required a more perfect form of ease; or it might have been that he was the victim of a philosophical unbelief in the effectiveness of every human effort. (12)

Such disposition is given as typical of anarchists:

> [he revealed] dislike of all kinds of recognized labour–a temperamental defect which he shared with a large proportion of revolutionary reformers of a given social state....The majority of revolutionists are the enemies of discipline and fatigue mostly. There are natures, too, to whose sense of justice the price exacted looms up monstrously enormous, odious, oppressive, worrying, humiliating, extortionate, intolerable. Those are the fanatics. The remaining portion of social rebels is accounted for by vanity, the mother of all noble and vile illusions, the companion of poets, reformers, charlatans, prophets, and incendiaries. (53)

Verloc becomes a nihilist. He serves three masters simultaneously: the agents of sedition, the police, and a foreign embassy: "the practice of his life...had consisted precisely in betraying the secret and unlawful proceedings of his fellow-men. Anarchists or diplomats were all one to him....His scorn was equally distributed over the whole field of his operations" (245). The protagonist's performance is also criticized by Ossipon, his comrade:

> Prominent. No, not exactly....More useful than important. Man of no ideas. Years ago he used to speak at meetings....Not very well, though....The only talent he showed really was his ability to elude the attentions of the police somehow. (74)[54]

Narrative irony magnifies the unfavorable depiction:

> Mr. Verloc would have rubbed his hands with satisfaction had he not been constitutionally averse from every superfluous exertion. (12)
> Like a peripatetic philosopher, Mr. Verloc, strolling along the streets of London, had modified Stevie's view of the police by conversations full of subtle reasonings. Never had a sage a more attentive and admiring disciple. (230; also 5, 13-14, 37, 180)

Similar implications are carried on by calling the secret agent "the tried revolutionist," "the humble guardian of society," "a servant of law and order, faithful, trusted, accurate, admirable," (288) or by strongly periphrastic communication of events immediately preceding his death:

> Mr. Verloc had the misfortune not to be in accord with his audience [Winnie]. (250)
> The waves of air of the proper length, propagated in accordance with correct mathematical formulas [his utterances], flowed around all the inanimate things in the room, lapped against Mrs. Verloc's head as if it had been a head of stone. (260)

Descriptions of his murdered body apply an identical method:

> Mr. Verloc lay very still meanwhile, simulating sleep for reasons of his own....Black, and rim upward, [the hat] lay on the floor before the couch as if prepared to receive the contributions of pence from people who would come presently to behold Mr. Verloc in the fullness of his domestic ease reposing on a sofa. (285)
> the cracked bell clattered behind the closed door in the empty shop, as if trying in vain to warn the reposing Mr. Verloc of the final departure of his wife–accompanied by his friend. (292; also 264-265)[55]

The pejorative characterization is in tune with the description of his immediate neighborhood in repulsive, naturalistic colors: the sordid shop (3), the quarter of the town (56, 150), Mrs. Neale the charwoman (180, 184-185).[56]

The narrative censure of the anarchists' ethos includes bringing their illogical and absurd views into prominence. They place them beyond the pale and define their self-imposed psychological estrangement (Part 1, Chapter 2). Michaelis, for instance, supports an extreme formulation of the theory of matter dominating spirit:

> He made again the confession of his faith, mastering him irresistible and complete like an act of grace; the secret of fate discovered in the material side of life; the economic condition of the world responsible for the past and shaping the future; the source of all history, of all ideas, guiding the mental development of mankind and the very impulses of their passion–. (45)

He renounces endeavors to make human existence sublime: "All idealization makes life poorer. To beautify it is to take away its character of complexity–it is to destroy it" (41). He regards the capitalistic principle of competition as the source of evil in public life (43, 49), and predicts an unavoidable revolution and the abolition of private property (43). Michaelis's vision of the future is unreal–and even pathological. It springs from an obsessive need to be taken care of, and consists of "the idea of a world planned out like an immense and nice hospital, with gardens and flowers, in which the strong are to devote themselves to the nursing of the weak" (303). The stricture of his ideas is accentuated by Conrad's sarcastic comments about his style of work: this "ticket-of-leave apostle of humanitarian hopes" (104), "grotesque incarnation of humanitarian passion" (108), the author of "a book of Revelation in the history of mankind" (120) conceives a concept of posterity in complete isolation from the actual world. It is but the product of prison meditations: "secret ways [of the future]...revealed to him within the four walls of a well-known penitentiary" (107; also 44-45). He is unable to present his theses rationally:

> He was no good in discussion, not because any amount of argument could shake his faith, but because the mere fact of hearing another voice disconcerted him painfully, confusing his thoughts at once.... (45)
>
> He was like those saintly men whose personality is lost in the contemplation of their faith. His ideas were not in the nature of convictions.

> They were inaccessible to reasoning. They formed in all their contradictions and obscurities an invincible and humanitarian creed, which he confessed rather than preached....the sight of faces troubled his inspiration developed in solitude. (107)

Even Michaelis's comrades disapprove of his philosophy: the Professor–"The poverty of reasoning [in his body] is astonishing. He has no logic. He can't think consecutively" (303); and Ossipon–"It [the book] will be a ghastly failure. He has lost the habit of consecutive thinking in prison, you know" (76-77).

The Professor also preaches an incoherent and ludicrous ideology. His permanent sense of having been wronged turns him into a champion of total destruction. He eulogizes devastation and death as paving the way for the freedom and development of humanity:

> To break up the superstition and worship of legality should be our aim....You plan the future, you lose yourselves in reveries of economical systems derived from what is; whereas what's wanted is a clean sweep and a clear start for a new conception of life....Therefore I would shovel my stuff in heaps at the corners of the streets if I had enough for that.... (73)
>
> I dreamt of a world like shambles, where the weak would be taken in hand for utter extermination....Exterminate, exterminate! That is the only way of progress....First the great multitude of the weak must go, then the only relatively strong....Every taint, every vice, every prejudice, every convention must meet its doom. (303; also 67-68, 71-72, 81, 306, 309, 311)[57]

Karl Yundt represents a corresponding viewpoint:

> 'I have always dreamed,' he mouthed, fiercely, 'of a band of men absolute in their resolve to discard all scruples in the choice of means, strong enough to give themselves frankly the name of destroyers, and free from the taint of that resigned pessimism which rots the world. No pity for anything on earth, including themselves, and death enlisted for good and all in the service of humanity–that's what I would have liked to see.' (42)

Ossipon sketches a vision of a future dominated by medicine: "In two hundred years doctors will rule the world. Science reigns already....And all science must culminate at last in the science of healing" (305). Its senselessness is succinctly articulated by the Professor: "But you are funny. Your notion of humanity universally putting out the tongue and taking the pill from pole to pole at the bidding of a few solemn jokers is worthy of the prophet" (306).

In *The Secret Agent* the depiction of anarchism is combined with a censure of those social forces and institutions that provoke its existence and flourishing, and do not oppose it but treat it leniently. Michaelis's nonsense appeals to many people: "The public has a sort of sentimental regard for that fellow....What he would say would be utter bosh, but he has a turn of talk that makes it go down all the same" (77-78). The aristocratic patroness considers him a saintly, inspired prophet (109-111) and is fascinated by the predications he makes against the current public order:

> She had come to believe almost his theory of the future, since it was not repugnant to her prejudices. She disliked the new element of plutocracy in the social compound, and industrialism as a method of human development appeared to her singularly repulsive in its mechanical and unfeeling character. The humanitarian hopes of the mild Michaelis tended not towards utter destruction, but merely towards the complete economic ruin of the system. And she did not really see where was the moral harm of it. It would do away with all the multitude of the 'parvenus,' whom she disliked and mistrusted....With the annihilation of all capital they would vanish, too; but universal ruin (providing it was universal, as it was revealed to Michaelis) would leave the social values untouched. The disappearance of the last piece of money could not affect people of position. (111)

The representatives of authority are corrupt, their treatment of the subversives is too tolerant.[58] Inspector Heat does not intend to discover the real perpetrator of the explosion. Instead, he intends to turn Michaelis into a scapegoat in order to save Verloc (his agent) and to keep off the Professor, determined, in any emergency, to blow himself up along with his captors. Assistant Commissioner, too, does not want to find the real culprit. He wishes only to defend Michaelis, whose patroness remains on friendly relations with his wife.[59] The action taken by prominent members of English society against sedition imply pessimism for its future.[60]

The forces directly inspiring anarchism are largely responsible for its existence. In *The Secret Agent* they are personified by Vladimir, the first secretary of an embassy in London, who entrusts Verloc with the bombing of the Greenwich Observatory–a mission he himself considers preposterous:

> But what is one to say to an act of destructive ferocity so absurd as to be incomprehensible, inexplicable, almost unthinkable; in fact, mad? ...The attack must have all the shocking senselessness of gratuitous blasphemy. (33)
> Such an outrage combines the greatest possible regard for humanity with the most alarming display of ferocious imbecility. I defy the ingenuity of journalists to persuade their public that any given member of the proletariat can have a personal grievance against astronomy. Starvation itself could hardly be dragged in there————eh? (34-35)

The instigator is a representative of autocracy–he "Descended from generations victimized by the instruments of an arbitrary power" (224) constituting the foundation of the policy of his state. By encouraging subversive activities he intends to make the English authorities introduce repressive legislation that will bring the governmental system of England closer to the tsarist model. Clearly ironic undertones may be detected in the narrative presentation of the First Secretary's political mentality: "The general leniency of the judicial procedure here, and the utter absence of all repressive measures, are a scandal to Europe" (17); "England lags. This country is absurd with its sentimental regard for individual liberty" (29). The narrow limits of his conceptions are in tune with his outward appearance: "he had with his smooth and rosy countenance the air of a preternaturally thriving baby" (19); and his savagery, so alien to European political culture: "These people are too impossible. What do they mean by importing their methods of Crim-Tartary here? A Turk would have more decency" (138; also 36).

Apart from the ironies of its existence, anarchism is also condemned by the human tragedies it causes. Carrying out Vladimir's order is the immediate cause of the Verloc family's calamity (on their marital isolation see Part 1, Chapter 2). At his wit's end, the secret agent decides to entrust this task to the mentally deficient Stevie, who is particularly sensitive to wrongs and suffering (157-158, 167-168, 170-172), impressed by exhortations about social injustice (49, 51, 60) and dreams about destroying its institutional roots. He is blown to pieces by a premature explosion on the way to the observatory. Thus his mother's self-sacrifice–she has gone to the Charity to ease the burden on her son-in-law Verloc, hoping this would induce him to increase his care for the weak-minded Stevie–is rendered futile. Winnie, subordinating all her life to securing protection for her handicapped brother, is the most miserable figure of this novel: in despair she puts an end to her husband and herself.

The criticisms of the subversive ethos sketched above are echoed in *The Informer, An Anarchist,*[61] and *The Inheritors.* Horne, the guiding spirit of the conspirators in *The Informer* is "a fanatic of social revolution" (SS 83), "haggard and bearded, like an inspired denunciatory prophet from a wilderness" (96), "savage, tyrannical, pitiless...a good social rebel of the extreme type" (101). The Professor reappears in this story, depicted identically as in *The Secret Agent.* He is absorbed in perfecting detonators and is ready to blow himself up in case of discovery (88). The characters in *The Informer* and *An Anarchist* are incompatible with stereotypical advocates of annihilating the existing political system; they abandon their professed principles. Mr. X, a prominent destructive publicist who inspires seditious activities by preaching revolt and violence to the starving proletariat of Europe, lives a luxurious life (*The Informer,* SS 75-77). The heroes of *An Anarchist* practice downright burglary under the pretext of redressing wrongs: "Most of them were neither more nor less than house-breakers....They robbed the rich; they were only getting back their own, they said"

(SS 149). In both these texts anarchists preach totally absurd views. The narrator in *The Informer* observes that the plotters' publications "were...beyond all bounds of reason and decency. One of them preached the dissolution of all social and domestic ties; the other advocated systematic murder" (SS 89). The outlook of the champion of total nihilism and negation of tradition in *The Inheritors* is also preposterous (I 12-13, 53).

In *The Informer,* as in *The Secret Agent,* condemnation of anarchism is connected with criticism of the aristocracy that is in some measure responsible for this movement.[62] Mr. X animates terrorist activities and ideology. Other members of this social group are naively fascinated by it:

> [This] idle and selfish class loves to see mischief being made, even if it is made at its own expense. Its own life being all a matter of pose and gesture, it is unable to realize the power and the danger of a real movement and of words that have no sham meanings...a demagogue has only to shout loud enough and long enough to find some backing in the very class he is shouting at. (SS 78)

The hypocrisy of such opinions is illustrated in *The Informer* by the heroine's conduct: she behaves conventionally at most times and participates in sedition for fun, to satisfy her vanity:

> To...personal charm...she added the seductive appearance of enthusiasm, of independence, of courageous thought. I suppose she put on these appearances as she put on her picturesque dresses and for the same reason: to assert her individuality at any cost....She had acquired all the appropriate gestures of revolutionary convictions–the gestures of pity, of anger, of indignation against the anti-humanitarian vices of the social class to which she belonged herself. (80-81; also 84-86)

Her attitudinizing is also revealed in her reaction to the unmasking of Sevrin (97-98) and in her manners after she gives up the conspiracy (101).

In *An Anarchist* condemnation of seditious practices is achieved principally through a presentation of the tragic experiences of their victims (as in *The Secret Agent* again). The envenomed Paul

Crocodile publicly utters shouts of indignation at the existing order and provokes a scuffle. The dishonest careerist lawyer uses this case for his own ends. When Paul is released from prison, he bears the brand of an anarchist, which isolates him from people (see Part 1, Chapter 2) and makes it impossible to get a job. Those forcing him into participating in raids take unfair advantage of his situation. The hero confesses himself embittered:

> I remember their lies, their promises, their menaces, and all my days of misery. Why could they not have left me alone after I came out of prison? I looked at them and thought that while they lived I could never be free. Never. Neither I nor others like me with warm hearts and weak heads. (SS 158)

Later Crocodile is blackmailed and victimized by Harry Gee (the manager of a B.O.S. Co. Ltd. cattle station), who by making known his alleged past deliberately estranges him from the society: "He meant to keep him–out of a sense of duty to the company–and the name he had given him would prevent the fellow from obtaining employment anywhere in Horta" (143). Gee then "hires" Paul to work as a slave, without wages.[63]

C. The Strictures of Autocracy and Revolutionism

The condemnation of tsarist tyranny, implicit in *The Secret Agent,* is developed in *Under Western Eyes:* here the implied author portrays it as the entirely dehumanized antithesis of its exalted intentions and splendid achievements, the source of "the moral corruption of an oppressed society where the noblest aspirations of humanity, the desire of freedom, an ardent patriotism, the love of justice, the sense of pity, and even the fidelity of simple minds are prostituted to the lusts of hate and fear, the inseparable companions of an uneasy despotism" (UWE 7). The champions of tsarism are particularly resolved to consider any attempts at rebellion as perverse and unnatural and as justifying cruel reaction:

> Mr. de P——— [was] the President of the notorious Repressive Commission...the Minister of State invested with extraordinary powers....In his mystic acceptance of the principle of autocracy he was bent on extirpating from the land every vestige of anything that resembled freedom in public institutions; and in his ruthless persecution of the rising generation he seemed to aim at the destruction of the very hope of liberty itself. (7-8)

When putting this political theory into practice they treat their opponents ruthlessly: imprisonment, torture, exile to Siberia, and murder are regarded as reasonable. Government officials are corrupt and servile. They evoke the prestige of the Supreme Being when arguing for the validity of their ideology:

> the thought of liberty has never existed in the Act of the Creator. From the multitude of men's counsel nothing could come but revolt and disorder; and revolt and disorder in a world created for obedience and stability is sin. It was not Reason but Authority which expressed the Divine Intention. God was the Autocrat of the Universe.... (8)

The Russian Orthodox Church contributes to the suppression of rebellious tendencies, holding the society on a leash:

> The old priest of the village came...to confess that he...had been ordered to watch and ascertain in other ways too (such as using his spiritual power with the servants) all that was going on in the house [of Mrs. Haldin], and especially in respect of the visitors these ladies received, who they were, the length of their stay, whether any of them were strangers to that part of the country, and so on. (139)
>
> I could not go to the Church [Tekla says] where the priests of the system exhorted such unconsidered vermin as I to resignation.... (263)

Repression gives birth to radical conspiracies that are no more than desperate attempts to defend against tyranny: "The ferocity and imbecility of an autocratic rule rejecting all legality and in fact basing itself upon complete moral anarchism provokes the no less imbecile and atrocious answer of a purely Utopian revolutionism" (UWE Author's Note X). The ethos of this movement is clearly damned,[64] in spite of an emphasis on the generous intentions of many of its participants: "at any rate, that life now ended [Haldin's] had been sincere, and perhaps its thoughts might have been lofty, its moral sufferings profound, its last act a true sacrifice" (UWE 164). The narrator highlights the revolutionaries' political program as vague, concerning, e.g., "Liberty that means nothing precise. Liberty in whose name crimes are committed" (50); illusory, as Haldin and his comrades reveal "the dream-intoxication of the idealist incapable of perceiving the reason of things, and the true character of men...a sort of terrible childishness" (31); harmful to society, as "Visionaries work everlasting evil on earth. Their Utopias inspire in the mass of mediocre minds a disgust of reality and a contempt for the secular logic of human development" (95); and nonsensical, producing only murders and destruction: "And what can you people do by scattering a few drops of blood on the snow? On this Immensity." (61) (See also 33-34; see Part 1, Chapter 2 on the plotters' psychological separation from reality.) Another point Conrad stresses is that even the success of such activities would not effect their professed ideals:

> in a real revolution the best characters do not come to the front. A violent revolution falls into the hands of narrow-minded fanatics and of tyrannical hypocrites at first. Afterwards comes the turn of all the pretentious intellectual failures of the time....The scrupulous and the just, the noble, humane, and devoted natures; the unselfish and the intelligent may begin a movement–but it passes away from them. They are not the leaders of a revolution. They are its victims: the victims of disgust, of disenchantment–often of remorse. Hopes grotesquely betrayed, ideals caricatured–that is the definition of revolutionary success. (134-135)
>
> Utopian revolutionism encompasses destruction by the first means to hand, in the strange conviction that a fundamental change of hearts must follow the downfall of any given human institutions. These people are unable to see that all they can effect is merely a change of names. (UWE Author's Note X)

Condemnation of this trend is manifest in the depiction of the

Geneva group. Its main émigré center is at their seat Château Borel, called a "house of folly, of blindness, of villainy and crime" (UWE 248-249), of "the visionary and criminal babble of revolutionists" (248). The leader of the conspiracy, Peter Ivanovitch, evidently does not befit his role. His political orations are often transformed into eulogies of women (119).[65] His conduct is hypocritical, since the respect he declares is in glaring contradiction to the way he treats his female subordinates, e.g., Tekla. Some members of this group are caricatured by their disgusting appearance,[66] which is typical of *schwarzcharaktere*. The pamphleeter, revolutionary newspaper editor Julius Laspara, is "like a reduction of an ordinary-sized man" hinting at the dwarfed nature of his outlook (285-286). Nikita, the executioner of revolutionary verdicts, is a "creature, so grotesque as to set town dogs barking at its mere sight" (267), an abominable beast with a huge belly and high-pitched voice, burning with the desire to kill (380-381). Tekla's hatred for tsarist institutions is the most characteristic example of absurd seditious views:

> The Ministry of Finances! What a grotesque horror it is! What does the starving, ignorant people want with a Ministry of Finances? ...there isn't much that one can do in there [in Russia]. No, indeed–at least as long as there are Ministries of Finances and such like grotesque horrors to stand in the way....There was a lot of people put into prison....The Ministry of Finances again! ...Upon my word, I would think that finances and all the rest of it are an invention of the devil....Hatred and contempt hissed in her utterance of the word 'finances'.... (150-151)
> The people living round us were all starving and drunken. They were the victims of the Ministry of Finances. (153)
> I live in hopes of seeing all the Ministries destroyed, finances and all. (155)

The boundless fascination of radicals with the masses, which is disclosed in utterances by Victor Haldin and the head of the conspiracy, is equally senseless:

> It's extraordinary what a sense of the necessity of freedom there is in that man [Ziemianitch]. And he has sayings too–simple, to the point, such

> as only the people can invent in their rough sagacity....And, you see, the guests for the feast of freedom must be sought for in byways and hedges. (56)
>
> In Russia it is different....We have only an unclean bureaucracy in the face of a people as great and incorruptible as the ocean. (119)

As in *The Secret Agent,* the patron of the champions of subversion in *Under Western Eyes* is made ridiculous. This is the aristocrat Madame de S———, who aids the circle financially (on the other adverse criticisms of this class, see Part 2, Chapter 4). Her creed, derived from séances–"In matters of politics she is a supernaturalist" (222)–is imbecilic: "'As to extirpating,' she croaked...'there is only one class in Russia which must be extirpated. Only one. And that class consists of only one family. You understand me? That one family must be extirpated'" (222). This repulsive figure acquires a ghastly aspect: she is "like a galvanized corpse out of some Hoffman's Tale" (215). Descriptions of her palace, which stress its ugliness and neglected condition, accord with the portrayal of the owner (147, 212, 216).

The condemnation of autocracy and revolutionism is also achieved through their distressing influence on individuals. In *Under Western Eyes* the tyrannized Russians live in poverty (245, 272-273) and abasement.[67] Their efforts to throw off the yoke ("I would take liberty from any hand as a hungry man would snatch a piece of bread," confesses Miss Haldin in the motto) display "the fierceness of thwarted desire" (164). The characters' predicaments illustrate the destructive impact of the tsarist system. Tekla, when in Russia, cares for the persecuted lithographer with whom she lives in poverty. At the end of the novel she nurses the maimed protagonist there. Mrs. Haldin suffers the cruelty of tyrants (318, 335). She grieves over the loss of her son (338-339), whose noble intentions and self-sacrifice are ill spent. Razumov gets entangled in political machinations and falls victim to them[69] (on his ethical isolation see Part 1, Chapter 2). Kirylo Sidorovitch gets involved in Victor Haldin's case, and government officials use this to turn him into their agent; they order him to spy on the émigré opposition. His subordination to the civil service ruins his career and his dreams for a happy future with Nathalie. The confession of his secret results in the plotters' revenge.[69] The terrorist's sister, shocked by this disclosure, returns to her native land and devotes herself to helping the downtrodden: "She lived in a town 'in the center,' [of Russia] sharing her compassionate labours between the horrors of over-crowded jails, and the heartrending misery of bereaved homes. She did not spare herself in good service" (378).

In both the novel and the "Author's Note" criticism of despotism is occasionally broadened to include the Russian mentality and political tradition. These are said to determine the essence of the centuries-old Russian autocracy:[70]

> freedom looks [there] like a form of debauch, and the Christian virtues themselves appear actually indecent.... (67)
>
> Whenever two Russians come together, the shadow of autocracy is with them, tinging their thoughts, their views, their most intimate feelings, their private life, their public utterances–haunting the secret of their silences. (107; also 34, 318)

The image of this vast, winter-bound country forms an allegorical vision of thraldom (32-33, 66). Some of the oppressed Russian people respond to tyranny by submission, with concomitant heavy drinking, which is an attempt to suppress the sense of injury (see the performance of Ziemianitch and his milieu, 27-31). Others respond by pursuing terrorist activities based upon utopian ideology. Neither of these "solutions" improves their lot:

> Between the two he [Razumov] was done for. Between the drunkenness of the peasant incapable of action and the dream-intoxication of the idealist incapable of perceiving the reason of things, and the true character of men. It was a sort of terrible childishness. (31)
>
> we Russians are a drunken lot. Intoxication of some sort we must have: to get ourselves wild with sorrow or maudlin with resignation; to lie inert like a log or set fire to the house. (96)

Students are particularly susceptible to such extremes. Typical among them is Kostia, who oscillates between revolutionary enthusiasm and revelry, which disgusts him. Renunciation of both these options leaves only the possibility of cooperation with the detestable authorities. The narrator, who represents the Western mentality, often articulates the morbidity of this situation. In fact, the Russian political reality is quite incomprehensible to him:[71]

> this is a Russian story for Western ears, which, as I have observed already, are not attuned to certain tones of cynicism and cruelty, of moral negation, and even of moral distress already silenced at our end of Europe. (163-164)
>
> It is strange to think that, I won't say liberty, but the mere liberalism of outlook which for us is a matter of words, of ambitions, of votes (and if of feeling at all, then of the sort of feeling which leaves our deepest affections untouched) may be for other beings very much like ourselves and living under the same sky, a heavy trial of fortitude, a matter of tears and anguish and blood. (318; also 24-25, 104-105, 109, 381)

Razumov and Nathalie contradict the caricatured representatives of the ethos of autocracy and the ethos of revolution, since positive traits predominate in their portrayal. Denouncing a colleague is a sin that brings the protagonist unrest and pangs of conscience. Razumov is partly exculpated by the terrorist's intrusion into his life (it destroys his dreams and annihilates his chance to study and make a career), and by his real attempt to come into contact with the appointed man. Razumov's deed is, however, explained first and foremost by deep ideological motivations. He shuns politics, is not involved in student conspiracies, and devotes himself to his education and his future prosperity.[72] He supports not seditious activities but absolutism and the theory of progress through evolution of the existing system. He asserts that terrorism

> means disruption. Better that thousands should suffer than that a people should become a disintegrated mass, helpless like dust in the wind. Obscurantism is better than the light of incendiary torches. The seed ger-

> minates in the night. Out of the dark soil springs the perfect plant. But a volcanic eruption is sterile, the ruin of the fertile ground. (34)
> Of course he was far from being a moss-grown reactionary. Everything was not for the best. Despotic bureaucracy...abuses...corruption...and so on....But absolute power should be preserved–the tool ready for the man–for the great autocrat of the future. Razumov believed in him. The logic of history made him unavoidable. The state of the people demanded him. What else?..could move all that mass in one direction?...Nothing but a single will. (35; also 21, 71, 358)

A succinct formulation of Kirylo Sidorovitch's outlook is conveyed in his preference for history, patriotism, evolution, direction, and unity to theory, internationalism, revolution, destruction, and disruption (66). The narrator approves of this attitude, especially when compared to the blinded plotters and their ideology. Razumov's name (with is connotations of reason, intellect) stresses the rationality of his viewpoint.

Miss Haldin becomes a target of Peter Ivanovitch's intrigue when he tries to turn this idealistic, open-hearted, inexperienced girl into a fanatical devotee of the Geneva group. His designs are, however, thwarted by her friends: the narrator, Razumov, and Tekla. She retains her independence because she believes it will be possible to achieve a general reconciliation of all social classes in Russia, leading to united, peaceful toil for a better future:

> There is too much hate and revenge in that work [the émigré oppositon activities]....Destruction is the work of anger. Let the tyrants and the slayers be forgotten together, and only the reconstructors be remembered. (331)
> I shall never give up looking forward to the day when all discord shall be silenced. Try to imagine its dawn! The tempest of blows and of excretions is over; all is still; the new sun is rising, and the weary men united at last, taking count in their conscience of the ended contest, feel saddened by their victory, because so many ideas have perished for the triumph of one....They feel alone on the earth and gather close together....But at last the anguish of hearts shall be extinguished in love. (376-377; also 353)

Miss Haldin's slightly naive faith is presented with a tinge of irony. Still, she appears in a rather favorable light, especially when contrasted with the extremists and their ideology.[73]

Condemnation of tyranny and radicalism appears in *The Rover* as well, but in reference to the French Revolution.[74] The hero calls its adherents and participants "boastful and declamatory beggars" (Rov 2), "a drunken crew of scallywags...a lot of bloodthirsty landlubbers" (76). An identical appreciation is conveyed by a contrast between the pirates (the title character included) and the terrorists:

> 'Have you ever carried [Arlette asks] a woman's head on a pike?' Peyrol, who had seen fights, massacres on land and sea, towns taken by assault by savage warriors, who had killed men in attack and defence, found himself at first bereft of speech by this simple question.... (22) [He] was neither a hypocrite nor a fool. When he robbed or killed it was not in the name of the sacred revolutionary principles or for the love of humanity. (209; also 4-5, 86-87)

Oxymorons demonstrate the discrepancy between the ideals and the reality: "Everything was going to be changed. Everybody was going to tie up his dog with a string of sausages for the sake of principles" (95); Peyrol "had heard of a Revolution in France and of certain Immortal Principles causing the death of many people" (25). The incongruity is enhanced when the name of "patriots" is given to the murdering champions of the new order.

Adverse commentary on the French Revolution are achieved principally through the grotesque portrayal of Scevola. Before the upheaval he was an object of ridicule to all the girls in the countryside (92); during the revolution he became a wild, obsessed murderer, a furious participant in the Toulon massacre:

> He first became busy purveying the guillotine when they were purify ing the town from all aristocrats.After the English got driven out of there was more of that work than the guillotine could do. They had to kill traitors in the streets, in cellars, in their beds. The corpses of men

> and women were lying in heaps along the quays. There were a good many of his sort that got the name of drinkers of blood. Well, he was one of the best of them. (20)
> ex-orator in the sections, leader of red-capped mobs, hunter of the ci-devants and priests, purveyor of the guillotine, in short a blood drinker. (26; also 48, 243)

Later, during peacetime, the mania for killing overcomes this sans-culotte (40-42). His cruelty is revealed in his hostile intentions toward and his moves against Réal, Peyrol, and Arlette (183), as well as in his attempts on the lives of Michel (184-185) and Symons (194-197). He regrets that this radical sociopolitical change was not completely successful (see Part 1, Chapter 2 on his psychological isolation):

> There was a time when civic virtue flourished, but now it has got to hide its head. And I will tell you why: there has not been enough killing. (27)
> We patriots held our hand too soon. All the children of the ci-devants and all the children of traitors should have been killed together with their fathers and mothers. Contempt for civic virtues and love of tyranny were inborn in them all. They grew up and trample on all the sacred principles....The work of the Terror is undone! (166)

In *The Rover* the unfriendly view of agents of subversion is also presented in the disastrous impact of their activities upon the characters' lives. During the Toulon massacre Arlette loses her parents and is forced to participate in the slaughter, which leaves an imprint on her soul (48-49). Love gives her a chance to rally her spirits, and she avails herself of it owing to Peyrol's saving her beloved's life by carrying out his mission. The other victims of bloodshed include Catherine, who suffered her brother's death and endured her unhappy love for a priest, and Réal, who was orphaned.

Censure of the antifeudal upheaval in France appears sporadically as a theme in *Autocracy and War*, where it is shown to cause the degradation of the ideals of freedom and justice (NLL 85-86) and in *Suspense*, with the butchery of aristocrats and rulers (S 20-21, 104).

D. Condemnation of Tyranny, Military Coups d'état, and Revolutions

The political visions of *Nostromo*–an intricate novel that depicts the activities of a wide range of characters engaged in public matters–are close to the message of *Under Western Eyes* and *The Rover*, where criticism of autocracy and revolution concern tsarist Russia and Jacobin France. But *Nostromo* is set in an isolated fictional world of imprecise historical and geographical location,[75] (Part 1, Chapter 1) which makes the criticism of the sociopolitical phenomena in this novel more universal.[76]

From the *Vorgeschichte* Costaguana appears to be a state with a tradition of despotic governments and upheavals,[77] in which "the military band plays sometimes in the evenings between the revolutions" (N 11). They cause many sufferings:

> the continuous political changes, the constant 'saving of the country'...seemed [to Doña Emilia] a puerile and bloodthirsty game of murder and rapine played with terrible earnestness by depraved children. (49)
>
> In all these households she could hear stories of political outrage; friends, relatives, ruined, imprisoned, killed in the battles of senseless civil wars, barbarously executed in ferocious proscriptions, as though the government of the country had been a struggle of lust between bands of absurd devils let loose upon the land with sabres and uniforms and grandiloquent phrases. And on all the lips she found a weary desire for peace, the dread of officialdom with its nightmarish parody of administration without law, without security, and without justice. (88)

Parallel judgements are given by the narrator with "the miserable farce of governments" (64), "the rascally crucible of revolutions" (65); Charles Gould: "The words one knows so well have a nightmarish meaning in this country. Liberty, democracy, patriotism, government–all of them have a flavour of folly and murder" (408); Father Roman: "The working of the usual public institutions presented itself to him most distinctly as a series of calamities overtaking private individuals and flowing logically from each other through hate, revenge, folly, and rapacity, as though they had been part of a divine dispensation" (399). The skeptical Martin Decoud (see Part 1, Chapter 2 on his isolation) considers the Republic's political reality as representative of the entire continent and explains it in terms of tragicomedy and farce: "After one Montero there would be another, the lawlessness of a populace of all colours and races, barbarism, irremediable tyranny....America is ungovernable. Those who worked for her independence have ploughed the sea" (186).

Guzman Bento's reign brought the severest tyranny: he moved through the territory of Costaguana heading the Army of Pacification, accompanied by a number of chained prisoners (members of the opposition). From time to time the army would execute some prisoners "invading rural pueblos, devastating the haciendas of the horrid aristocrats...leaving behind a united land wherein the evil taint of Federalism could no longer be detected in the smoke of burning houses and the smell of split blood" (138). These dreary times are reflected in the stories of the principal characters. Among them were the afflictions of Dr. Monygham (370-375; see Part 1, Chapter 2 on his ethical estrangement) and Don José Avellanos (137-138).[78] Life in Costaguana is also characterized by lawlessness under this tyrant's successors:

> Everybody around...was being robbed by the grotesque and murderous bands that played their game of governments and revolutions after the death of Guzman Bento....The first casual colonel of the barefooted army of scarecrows that came along was able to expose with force and precision to any mere civilian his titles to a sum of 10,000 dollars; the while his hope would be immutably fixed upon a gratuity, at any rate, of no less than a thousand. (56)

Charles Gould's father, entrusted with the concession of the San Tomé mine, suffered from persecution by being systematically plundered under the pretext of royalty collection (53-58).

One of many coups d'état was carried out against the dictator Don Vincente Ribiera by the brothers Montero, and this coup forms the axis of the story in *Nostromo,* it is also the start of the criticism of the political model portrayed. This is evident from he way the narrator comments on the actions of ordinary participants in the events:[79]

> And first came straggling in through the land gate the armed mob of all colours, complexions, types, and states of raggedness, calling themselves the Sulaco National Guard, and commanded by Señor Gamacho. Through the middle of the street [they] streamed, like a torrent of rubbish.... (384; also 385)

Giorgio Viola shares this revulsion, viewing the riot as non-political (16), as an "outbreak of scoundrels and leperos, who did not know the meaning of the word 'liberty'" (21). The juxtaposition of the crowd to the Higuerota massif implies their insignificance: "the movements of the animated scene were like the passages of a violent game played upon the plain by dwarfs mounted and on foot, yelling with tiny throats, under the mountain that seemed a colossal embodiment of silence" (27).[80]

The ethos of the leaders of the revolt is presented in comic terms, too.[81] General Montero appears as "the exaggeration of a cruel caricature, the fatuity of solemn masquerading, the atrocious grotesqueness of some military idol" (122). Pedro,his brother and partner, is corrupt and has absurd views. He regards caesarism as the highest expression of democracy, the French Second Empire is in his idea of the political model most appropriate for Costaguana. This dishonest man craves for fame and wealth: he tries to imitate Duc de Morny, who profited from the appointments he held (387-388, 402-405). Sotillo, the Esmeralda garrison commander, is cowardly. He runs from his study when Captain Mitchell flings out an arm in an attempt to reach for the revolver (332). He is also foolish and conceited:

> he was carried away by the sound of fine words, especially if uttered by himself. He had no convictions of any sort upon anything except as to the irresistible power of his personal advantages. (285)
>
> 'He is the greatest imbecile that ever called himself a colonel in this country of evil,' growled Nostromo. (437)

But he is primarily a depraved, greedy individual:

> The only guiding motive of his life was to get money for the satisfaction of his expensive tastes, which he indulged recklessly, having no self-control. He imagined himself a master of intrigue, but his corruption was as simple as an animal instinct....Sotillo's ideas did not soar above the care for his personal safety and the chance of plundering the town in his charge.... (286-287)

His attitude toward the transported ingots exemplifies his character most conspicuously. His initial desire to get hold of them is politically motivated: "To gain possession of them would be a clear Monterist move; a sort of service that would have to be rewarded. With the silver in his hands he could make terms for himself and his soldiers" (287). Later, cupidity becomes the only principle of his life: it isolates him from events, absorbs him in a mad search for the silver, which he presumes is submerged in the port. Because he does not relieve the besieged Pedro Montero's army, Sotillo is largely responsible for the failure of the uprising and the defeat of his own regiment by Barrios's troops, who supported the Blanco (Gould's) party (484).

Condemnation of attempted coups d'état is complemented by the portrayal of their advocates as career-centered. Gamacho is an ex-criminal; he and Fuentes put themselves at the head of riot in Sulaco (227-228), and the leaders of the riot include other offenders:

> The man he [Fuentes] pitched upon to negotiate with Sotillo was a Notary Public, whom the revolution had found languishing in the common jail on a charge of forging documents. Liberated by the mob along with the other 'victims of Blanco tyranny,' he had hastened to offer his services to the new Government. (441)

The president of provincial assembly, Don Juste Lopez, vacillates, yields to the pressure of new forces and endeavors merely to save the form of parliamentary institutions at all costs (355, 366-367, 406).

The ethos of tyrants and revolutionaries is opposed to that of characters motivated by noble intentions, who aspire to exalted goals. They comprise the old Garibaldino Giorgio Viola:

> The spirit of self-forgetfulness, the simple devotion to a vast humanitarian idea which inspired the thought and stress of that revolutionary time, had left its mark upon Giorgio in a sort of austere contempt for all personal advantage. This man...had all his life despised money....It had been a habit of his mind to disregard to-morrow...it was a puritanism of conduct, born of stern enthusiasm like the puritanism of religion. (31)
> His austere, old-world Republicanism had a severe, soldier-like standard of faithfulness and duty, as if the world were a battlefield where men had to fight for the sake of universal love and brotherhood, instead of a more or less large share of booty. (313)

The domestic tradition of struggle against despotism is represented by Charles Gould's father and uncle: they stood for rational freedom and social order (64). Members of the Aristocratic Club also contributed a great deal to the establishment of Costaguana's independence and federation (97-98). Their leader is Don José Avellanos, the author of the unpublished book *Fifty Years of Misrule*. All his life he advocated "political rectitude" (137) and struggled with "the powers of moral darkness, whose stagnant depths breed monstrous crimes and monstrous illusions" (362).

However, the champions of absolutism and of violent revolution in *Nostromo* are primarily opposed to those who support the ethos of work for economic development as a precondition to law and order.[82] Among these are the National Central Railway builders (34, 36-37) and the O.S.N. establishment:

> as they seldom failed to account for the smallest package, rarely lost a bullock, and had never drowned a single passenger, the name of the O.S.N. stood very high for trustworthiness. People declared that under the Company's care their lives and property were safer on the water than in their own houses on shore. (10)

Law and order are served first by the San Tomé mine, whose

value in enriching people and ensuring peace[83] is emphasized most frequently:

> The San Tomé mine was to become an institution, a rallying point for everything in the province that needed order and stability to live. Security seemed to flow upon this land from the mountain gorge. (110)
> the mountain...seemed with its treasures to pour down the thundering ore shoots of the upper mesa, the gifts of well-being, security, and justice upon the toilers. (397; also 95)

People are bound by affection to their establishment, and they are aware of its beneficial influence on life in Sulaco:

> In a very few years the sense of belonging to a powerful organization had been developed in these harassed, half-wild Indians. They were proud of, and attached to the mine. It had secured their confidence and belief. They invested it with a protecting and invincible virtue as though it were a fetish made by their own hands. (397-398)

All this is mainly due to the administrator, Charles Gould, who uses the mine's wealth to achieve a revival of civilized politics in Costaguana:

> What is wanted here is law, good faith, order, security. Any one can declaim about these things, but I pin my faith to material interests. Only let the material interests once get a firm footing, and they are bound to impose the conditions on which alone they can continue to exist. That's how your money-making is justified here in the face of lawlessness and disorder. It is justified because the security which it demands must be shared with an oppressed people. A better justice will come afterwards. That's your ray of hope. (84; also 110, 115, 244-245, 521)

He reveals his devotion to the mine in his youthful resolution to accomplish idealistic visions (65-66, 74-75), his feelings of delight at its operation (104-105), his responsibility for it and its workers (209), his determination to blow it up rather than to give it over as booty to the mob (205-206, 365-366, 477). Thanks to Don Carlos the silver mine contributes to the economic development of the entire region. It is "imperium in imperio" (135, 244), becomes a factor in political considerations: "In fact, the mine, with its organization, its population growing fiercely attached to their position of privileged safety, with its amoury...the mine was a power in the land" (110; also 116, 388). El Señor Administrador gains extraordinary influence and

> seems to have the ear of every provincial authority apparently, and...he can wind all the hidalgos of the province round his little finger. (42)
> Gradually all of them discovered that, no matter what party was in power, that man remained in most effective touch with the higher authorities in Sta. Marta. (92; also 110-111)

The significance of the mine's potential is revealed when it supports the rule of Don Vincente Ribiera, who is the political spokesman for Gould's party:

> there was something in the faint whispers hinting at the immense occult influence of the Gould Concession. What was currently whispered was this–that the San Tomé Administration had, in part, at least, financed the last revolution, which had brought into a five-year dictatorship Don Vincente Ribiera, a man of culture and of unblemished character, invested with a mandate of reform by the best elements of the State. Serious, well-informed men seemed to believe the fact, to hope for better things, for the establishment of legality, of good faith and order in public life. (117; also 141-143)

During the Monterist upheaval Casa Gould becomes the opposition center. It brings together citizens determined to preserve the values glorified by the "King of Sulaco." Don José Avellanos, as the chairman of a Patriotic Committee, "displayed in the service of the endangered Ribiera Government an organizing activity and an eloquence of which the echoes reached even Europe" (136). He helps finance a regiment for the fight "in a contest for order, peace, progress" (137). He also contributes to arming Barrios's troops and sending them to oppose the rebels. Antonia Avellanos induces her cynical adorer Martin Decoud to expound the Blanco party's political faith (156-159, 175-177).

Decoud suggests that Sulaco be detached from Costaguana; he argues that the region is naturally secluded by its geography: "The Occidental Province should stand alone....The Occidental territory is large enough to make any man's country. Look at the mountains! Nature itself seems to cry to us 'Separate!'" (184).

The San Tomé mine, which is in Gould's opinion "big enough to take in hand the making of a new State" (380), plays the main part in this plan. The Administrator blackmails the ringleaders by threatening to blow up the silver mine if he is deprived of his office: this would cause the economic ruin of the republic (403). For an emergency his circle decides to conceal the reserves of silver in a safe place, where it can be saved for a crucial moment in the political struggle: "the existence of the treasure was of enormous importance. The mere knowledge that it had been saved from the Monterists would be a strong inducement for the Cayta troops to embrace the cause of the new State" (317; also 309). Dr. Monygham then plays his trump card: he focuses Sotillo's attention on the ingots, which have allegedly been sunk in the port, and this prevents the engagement of Sotillo's regiment in a crucial battle. Gould uses San Tomé money to pay Hernandez's outlaws, whose involvement makes a significant contribution to the Blancos' success. Ultimately Sulaco becomes the separatist state in "flourishing and stable condition" (354), and the repeated tale of Captain Mitchell (a town guide) turns the creators of Sulaco into legendary heroes.

The advocates of work for the development of commerce and industry are not spotless, although they are the antithesis to the spokesmen of despotism and military revolt. Their excellent ideas are corrupted in practice. Don Vincente Ribiera's dictatorship is not substantially different from his predecessors' régimes and it spawns guerilla activities.

> If it had not been for the lawless tyranny of your Government, Don Pépé [Emilia Gould says], many an outlaw now with Hernandez would be living peaceably and happy by the honest work of his hands....No wonder there are bandits in the Campo when there are none but thieves, swindlers, and sanguinary macaques to rule us in Sta. Marta. (109-110)

> [his] existence was a protest against the irresponsible tyranny of all parties alike, against the moral darkness of the land. The gloom of Los Hatos woods was preferable; a life of hardships in the train of a robber band less debasing. (353-354; also 217)

The Garibaldino Giorgio Viola cherishes the old-fashioned vision of his youthful idealism in isolation from the political actualities of Costaguana; he is portrayed slightly comically:[84]

> Even when he was cooking for the 'Signori Inglesi' ...he was, as it were, under the eye of the great man who had led him in a glorious struggle where, under the walls of Gaeta, tyranny would have expired for ever had it not been for that accursed Piedmontese race of kings and ministers. When sometimes a frying-pan caught fire during a delicate operation with some shredded onions, and the old man was seen backing out of the doorway, swearing and coughing violently in an acrid cloud of smoke, the name of Cavour–the arch intriguer sold to kings and tyrants–could be heard involved in imprecations against the China girls, cooking in general, and the brute of a country where he was reduced to live for the love of liberty that traitor had strangled. (23-24; also 20-21)

Decoud stresses that the conducts of Scarfe and Padre Corbelàn, for whom "The idea of political honour, justice and honesty...consists in the restitution of the confiscated Church property" (188-189), are motivated primarily by a desire to amass riches. He scorns Antonia's excitable declarations of love for her homeland (see Part 1, Chapter 2 on their reciprocal isolation); he feels that her attitude is conducive to narrow-mindedness, that patriotism is the justification for many barbarous deeds (176, 186-187). Even as an important member of Gould's group he distances himself from events. His patriotism is superficial, as his proposal for the autonomy of Sulaco is motivated by egoistical intentions: "But my true idea, the only one I care for, is not to be separated from Antonia....She won't leave Sulaco for my sake, therefore Sulaco must leave the rest of the Republic to its fate" (215).[85] The creation of this separatist state brings freedom, order and prosperity only to one province of the country (509). The Blanco party members are also censured for their performance during the critical time of Monterist upheaval. Hirsch's martyrdom is caused by Dr. Monygham, and is the price of preventing Sotillo's regiment from participating in the operation (438-439, 451-453). The grotesque characteristics of the army leaders are also applied to famous-for-"political-honesty" General Barrios (of Gould's circle) by emphasizing his boastfulness (160-162).[86]

Charles Gould is also an admirable character with a stigma.[87] There are many possible criticisms of the methods he uses to accomplish his undoubtedly laudable intentions where he bribes local notables, acts against his own declared principles by financing Ribiera's coup and dictatorship, pays Hernandez's guerillas and turns them into his private army. All of these are questionable acts; they follow the maxim that the end justifies the means. However, it is an exaggeration to claim that his involvement in the problems of the mine causes his ethical and psychological degeneration, a transformation from an idealistic capitalist into a slave of material interests and a tool of imperialists. He consciously uses the San Tomé establishment to achieve grand aims. Enterprise and initiative have made him largely independent from Holroyd, his financial backer, who desires to promote America's world expansion and his own concept of Christianity. Holroyd's aims, presented ironically, do not constitute the essence of Gould's ideas on Costaguana (77-78). Holroyd promises him freedom of action and warns him to hold back help in the event of troubles. This contradictory message pleases the Administrator: "to Charles Gould's mind these uncompromising terms were agreeable. Like this the mine preserved its identity, with which he had endowed it as a boy; and it remained dependent on himself alone" (82). Gould's zealous participation in public life isolates him from his wife (Part 1, Chapter 2). Initially she accepts her husband's aspirations (74-75, 106-107), but later, disappointed by his excessive enthusiasm for the mine, which is spoiling their marriage, she begins to disapprove of his activities (221-222, 244-245, 512, 520-522) even though she recognizes their beneficial results: "He was perfect–perfect [she thinks] ...It was a colossal and lasting success" (521). An important contribution to an adequate evaluation of the "King of Sulaco" is made by Martin Decoud and Doña Emilia, who condemn all political practices because they vitiate professed intentions: "There was something inherent in the necessities of successful action which carried with it the moral degradation of the idea" (521; also 177, 191). But only from such a perspective may El Señor Administrador's performance be regarded as ignoble.[88]

The image of the generally respected Nostromo–not merely as Capataz de Cargadores, who had the power to discipline (95-96), but who is a real leader of the people (185-186)–appears ambivalent as well. He is considered invaluable and indispensable by the Blanco party (e.g., 43-44). He achieves this distinction by fulfilling a number of extraordinarily dangerous and difficult missions they entrust to him. For example, he saves the overthrown dictator Ribiera from the enraged mob's vengeance (224-226); with Decoud's help he transports and conceals the silver (on his performance as mariner see Part 2, Chapter 4); he contributes significantly to the Monterists' defeat by bringing Barrios's army from Cayta to aid Gould's endangered supporters. Nostromo's conduct is motivated by a megalomaniac desire for adulation and popularity.[89] The proof of this can be seen in his attitudinizing during the fiesta, by which he hopes to increase the crowd's admiration (e.g., in the scene with his sweetheart Morenita) (127-130). In another case he gives money to a poor woman in order to gain praise (247). These motives are emphasized by the narrator (525), Antonia's fiancé (191, 226, 246, 248, 275, 300), and Teresa Viola (23, 256-257). This craving for fame is most conspicuous in his view of the silver transport commissioned by Gould: "Well, I am going to make it the most famous and desperate affair of my life–wind or no wind. It shall be talked about when the little children are grown up and the grown men are old" (265; also 259). Vanity determines the transformation of his attitude, represented metaphorically by his waking (411-414), and makes him reassume his real name–Captain Fidanza.

He realizes that Gould's defeat would cost him universal veneration, which would be his greatest loss: "But since it was no longer possible for him to parade the streets of the town, and be hailed with respect in the usual haunts of his leisure, this sailor felt himself destitute indeed" (415). He resents the principals for making him simply the one who executes commands, for underrating his heroism and merits. In particular, he feels that his role in the desperate expedition to the Great Isabel was not appreciated (426). Isolated and slighted in his honor, Nostromo surrenders to temptation and steals the ingots.[90] He secretly leaves them on the island and conceals Martin Decoud's death. Finally he becomes morally degenerate, dependent on the loot that overwhelms his entire personality, causing him turmoil and suffering (see also on the leading figure's self-imposed ethical isolation in Part 1, Chapter 5):

> the silver of San Tomé was provided now with a faithful and lifelong slave....
> He had made up his mind that nothing should be allowed now to rob him of his bargain....
> The treasure was putting forth its latent power.
> It troubled the clear mind of the man who had paid the price. (501-522)
> He yearned to clasp, embrace, absorb, subjugate in unquestioned possession this treasure, whose tyranny had weighed upon his mind, his actions, his very sleep. (529; also 460, 523-524, 526-527, 531, 544-545)

He professes his intention to marry Linda Viola so as to have a pretext for coming to the island and recovering the silver. Nor does he yield to his fianceé's sister, his true sweetheart Giselle, when she argues that they should move to another part of the country (see also Part 1, Chapter 2 on the pair's reciprocal amorous isolation). The plight of Capataz de Cargadores resembles that of "the legendary Gringos, neither dead nor alive, bound down to their conquest of unlawful wealth on Azuera" (526; also 263-264, 460, 531).[91]

Nostromo's embitterment turns into class hatred of his aristocratic-capitalistic "protectors":

> Had I not done enough for them to be of some account, *por Dios*? Is it that the *hombres finos*–the gentlemen–need not think as long as there is a man of the people ready to risk his body and soul? Or, perhaps, we have no souls–like dogs? (435)
> 'Ah! you are all alike, you fine men of intelligence. All you are fit for is to betray men of the people into undertaking deadly risks for objects that you are not even sure about. If it comes off you get the benefit. If not, then it does not matter. He is only a dog. Ah! *Madre de Dios*, I would–'He shook his fists above his head. (459; also 453-454, 469, 559-560)

He is influenced by the idealistic Garibaldino's outlook: "What he had heard Giorgio Viola say once was very true. Kings, minsters, aristocrats, the rich in general, kept the people in poverty and subjection; they kept them as they kept dogs, to fight and hunt for their service" (415; also 418). He undertakes actions against the existing social order; but then his riches again make him an idol of the populace (511).

Captain Fidanza, thereupon, systematically strengthens his position by financing the conspiracy against the rulers of separatist Sulaco. In this his comrades are portrayed harshly; their ringleader appears as a grotesque figure, analogous to the anarchists and extremists in *The Secret Agent* and *Under Western Eyes,* "an indigent, sickly, somewhat hunchbacked little photographer with a white face and a magnanimous soul dyed crimson by a bloodthirsty hate of all capitalists, oppressors of the two hemispheres" (528; also 562). His frame of mind is markedly different from that of truly revolutionary Giorgio Viola, who "would have understood nothing of his opening speech" (528). Such activity gives birth to unrest (555) which may lead to oppressions, which the ringleader anticipates by calling Dr. Monygham "a dangerous enemy of the people" (563). Even a coup to restore the traditional tyrannical government might result:

> they [members of secret societies] may raise the country with the new cry of the wealth for the people....There is no peace and no rest in the

> development of material interests...the time approaches when all that the Gould Concession stands for shall weigh as heavily upon the people as the barbarism, cruelty, and misrule of a few years back....It'll weigh as heavily, and provoke resentment, bloodshed, and vengeance, because the men have grown different. (511)

Such a pessimistic forecast is well founded. The current miners are not so strongly attached to their establishment as were their predecessors, who helped rescue the mine and its Administrator in the crucial time of the Monterist upheaval (511). The plot by fugitives from other regions of the country, supported by an underground proletarian movement, could mean the possibility of Sulaco's reunion with the remaining provinces of Costaguana and the loss of the fundamental political and economic blessings of autonomy.

Thus the victory of Gould's group does not put an end to political convulsions and the repeated absolutism, which are deeply rooted in the national experience. The pressure of this tradition is too strong to be overcome by a single triumph by the champions of (industrial) progress. Silver, the material base of their policy, now works against the values it had served before. It causes human tragedies and gives rise to unbridled cupidity. It even becomes a threat to law and economic growth, which it had helped to win.[92] So the history of Costaguana is determined by two tendencies, each supported by a distinct group of adherents: the representatives of the work ethos, who favor stability and developing the state, portrayed ambivalently though rather positively; censure concerns the army (its commanders included), who are responsible for coups d'état, domestic wars, despotism and persecutions.[93]

E. Damnation of Wars; The Martial Ethos

The central theme of *Gaspar Ruiz,* whose characters take part in struggles for independence between Republicans and Royalists, resembles the condemnation of military upheavals in *Nostromo*. The performance by politicians connected with the army is dealt with severely:

> Carreras, under the guise of politics and liberalism, was a scoundrel of the deepest dye, and the unhappy state of Mendoza was the prey of thieves, robbers, traitors, and murderers, who formed his party. He was under a noble exterior a man without heart, pity, honour, or conscience. He aspired to nothing but tyranny.... (SS 54)

Juxtapositing battles and monumental nature points up a grotesquery that echoes some of the activities of the Costaguana:

> A red and unclouded sun setting into a purple ocean looked with a fiery stare upon the enormous wall of the Cordilleras, worthy witness of his glorious extinction. But it is inconceivable that it should have seen the ant-like men busy with their absurd and insignificant trials of killing and dying for reasons that, apart from being generally childish, were also imperfectly understood. (19)

The antimilitarism of *Gaspar Ruiz* is, however, made stark by the impact of military operations upon civilians:

> That long contest, waged for independence on one side and for domination on the other, developed in the course of years and the vicissitudes of changing fortune the fierceness and inhumanity of a struggle for life. All feelings of pity and compassion disappeared in the growth of political hatred. And, as is usual in war, the mass of people, who had the least to gain by the issue, suffered most in their obscure persons and their humble fortunes. (3)

These disasters are caused by soldiers who act cruelly in spite of noble declarations, who are motivated by hatred and devoid of humanitarianism. They have become sadistic, inflicting pain on prisoners of war and deserters who have been sentenced to death:

> The sergeant [commanding an execution squad] was a humane man, and watched for any stir or twitch of limb [of the shotdown captives] in the merciful idea of plunging the point of his blade into any body giving the slightest sign of life. But none of the bodies afforded him an opportunity for the display of this charitable intention. (20; also 4-5, 7-8)

Citizens are plundered. Republicans shouting freedom confiscate a cow and some horses from Ruiz's parents (6), while "a detachment of Royalist troops coming to pacify the district, burnt the ranch, carried off the remaining horses and cattle, and having thus deprived the old people of all their worldly possessions, left them sitting under a bush in the enjoyment of the inestimable boon of life" (6). Doña Erminia's father's agony proves to be even more painful:

> [he] was...a man of property ruined by the revolution. His estates, his house in town, his money, everything he had in the world had been confiscated by proclamation, for he was a bitter foe of our independence. From a position of great dignity and influence on the Viceroy's Council he became of less importance than his own negro slaves made free by our glorious revolution. He had not even the means to flee the country, as other Spaniards had managed to do...wandering ruined and houseless, and burdened with nothing but his life.... (22)

Ruiz himself is victimized by the war: he is ill-treated and condemned to death as an alleged deserter. After avoiding undeserved execution for treason he is persecuted by both sides; Erminia's own story, too, illustrates the destructive influence of war upon people. Deeply embittered, she comes to direct her husband's vengeance:

> that woman...led Gaspar Ruiz into the practice of sanguinary treachery...by the subtle way of awakening and keeping alive in his simple mind a burning sense of an irreparable wrong...poured half of her vengeful soul into the strong clay of that man, as you may pour intoxication, madness, poison into an empty cup. (52)
>
> with a few whispered words she could change the expression of his face and revive his flagging animosity. (48; also 46)

On the eve of peace she instigates a rebellion that causes the further devastation of two provinces. The tragedy of Ruiz, who is a tool of political machinations, is symbolized by his upraising a cannon:

> He lay...on his breast under the darkly glittering bronze of his monstrous burden, such as no love or strength of man had ever had to bear in the lamentable history of the world. His arms were spread out, and he resembled a prostrate penitent on the moonlit ground. (62)

Finally, the combatants' behavior is depicted as universal: "At such times the heat of passionate convictions passing into hatred, removes the restraints of honour and humanity from many men and of delicacy and fear from some women" (24; also 3).[94]

Nevertheless, military actions do not always lead to depravity and inhumanity, for Gaspar Ruiz personifies a glorious martial ethos. He retains his dignity and high-mindedness amid the cruelty and bestiality of war.[95] He uses his tremendous strength honorably by bending the prison's iron bars enough to pass buckets of water to his fellow captives (15-17); he keeps his word by not trying to escape when escorted to the execution ground (17-18); as a rehabilitated Republican captain he saves the lives of prisoners of war (45). He does the same as a Royalist officer: in spite of the treacherous capture of his wife and child by the enemy, he is even eager to send food to besieged hostile troups (58-59). Another kind-hearted soldier, the narrator Santierra, seeks humane treatment and clemency for deserters (9-10), and he idealizes the Republican commander in chief as an excellent officer and considers him a just, compassionate, courteous, and brave man (43, 45).

Conrad's two Napoleonic works, *The Warrior's Soul* and *The Duel*, delineate similar wartime stereotypes. The first features an adjutant who approves when the Russians slay their starving, apathetic enemies to warm themselves up (TH 18). The protagonist of *The Warrior's Soul*, in spite of belonging to opposite sides, are generous and chivalrous toward each other. In Paris De Castel warns Tomassov of imminent imprisonment, enabling him to leave the country and fight in defense of his homeland. Tomassov has "the soul of a warrior. And what more desolate prospect for a man with such a soul than to be imprisoned on the eve of war; to be cut off from his country in danger, from his military family, from his duty, from honour, and–well–from glory, too" (16). During the fighting he reciprocates the favor: he fulfills the Frenchman's wish and shoots him to end his agony and humiliation (initially, this act causes Tomassov's ethical isolation because he is unjustly accused of putting a captive to death in cold blood–see Part 1, Chapter 2). "One warrior's soul paid its debt a hundredfold to another warrior's soul by releasing it from a fate worse than death–the loss of all faith and courage" (26). The young Russian reveals profound human feelings: he laments over the immensity of the calamities caused by the Moscow campaign. "His was fundamentally a fine nature. He grieved at the appalling amount of human suffering he saw around him. Yes, he was full of com-passion for all forms of mankind's misery in a manly way" (16). He refrains from killing soldiers of the retreating French army: "[he] sheathed deliberately his sword right in the middle of [a] charge" (17).[96] The leading characters of *The Duel* act just as generously; in spite of their having fought so many duels with each other, they help each other in battle (SS 212-213). After Napoleon's downfall D'Hubert saves Feraud from persecution and trials (224-229), and even nurses him, finally, in his senility.

Condemnation of war by portraying human suffering constitutes a significant theme in both these stories. The retreating soldiers of Napoleon bear the painful consequences of the campaign:

> It was an amazing and terrible sight....A crawling, stumbling, starved, half-demented mob...there were men walking on the outer edge so lost to everything but their misery that they never turned their heads to look at our charge....A smell of scorched rags and festering wounds hung in the air...it was like cutting down galvanized corpses that didn't care. (*The Warrior's Soul*, TH 3-4; also 1-2, 24-25, 3-4 other extracts; and *The Duel*, SS 211-215)

De Castel's fate exemplifies degeneration caused by battle. Prolonged, exhausting combat turns this pride of Paris salons into a miserable creature, devoid of all faith, hope, and courage: "Brilliant, accomplished, envied by men, loved by that woman–this horror–this miserable thing that cannot die" (TH 24; also 22-26).

Conclusion

The discussion of isolation and ethos has confirmed their pivotal importance as central motifs of Conrad's oeuvre. They are connected with the specific trends in literary and cultural traditions. Conradian presentation of life at sea is a continuation of Anglo-American adventurous fiction, especially of the sea (Stevenson, Marryat, Cooper). The works that involve "the white man's burden" have parallels with Kipling's writing. The portrayal of colonialism, anarchism, revolutionary movements, and despotism parallels contemporary discussions. Many of the fundamental traits of isolation derive from the works of Defoe, Byron, the literature of nineteenth-century France, and Polish Romanticism. Conrad's pessimistic view of reality resembles Hardy's philosophy of life. Yet significant elements of the Conradian ethos originate in the chivalric tradition (e.g., in the Polish ideals of honor, in the dictates of duty and faithful service stemming from Polish positivism, and in the system of values followed by the imperial British fleet.

Nevertheless, the diversity of influences do not result in an eclectic product. The glorification of life at sea conveyed in Conrad's texts transcends the scope of pre-Conradian marine writings to a considerable degree. His view of the white race's expansion is substantially different from Kipling's: Conrad's work is more objective and human, more profound both psychologically and morally.[1] Conrad's interpretations of imperialism, sedition, radicalism, and absolutism made a valuable contribution to the polemics of his time. His masterpieces do not reveal such extreme and unequivocal pessimism as Hardy's. His characters are left some hope for at least partial success in their tragic struggles.[2] But Conrad's greatest innovation consists in attaching basic importance to ethical issues and in universalizing situations in which isolation and a particular ethos are manifested. He regards isolation as inherent in man's predicament. The virtues displayed by seamen grappling with the elements have supraindividual significance and ensure success in any sphere. Images of colonizers and political activists reflect not merely concrete, historical attitudes but rather general models of social behavior. Conrad also espouses ideals that everyone may realize. His many heroes function not merely as schematic personifications of the norms and style of life of a certain community but as subtle and intricate individuals who are profoundly human.

Conradian configurations of isolation and ethos make his legacy relevent to our century.[3] He keenly perceived and strongly articulated loneliness, whether determined by the external world or by an individual's psychology. These visions have become a crucial component of twentieth-century cultural consciousness.[4] They have contributed to the foundation of existentialism, to the literature of solitude and its ethical consequences, for the works of such writers as T.S. Eliot, Graham Greene, J. Joyce, D. H. Lawrence, V. Woolf, E. Hemingway, W. Faulkner, F. Scott Fitzgerald, E. Pound, T. Wolfe, K. Hamsun, A. Camus, A. Malraux, F. Mauriac, A. de Saint-Exupéry, as well as K. Heuser, E. Jünger, J. Andrzejewski, T. Konwicki, and J. J. Szczepański.[5] Conrad's works depict colonization in a highly objective manner. He sees it both as the successful completion of a civilizing mission and as the looting and the extermination of indigenous peoples. He also reflects on dangerous sociopolitical tendencies: anarchism and terrorism (*The Secret Agent, The Informer, An Anarchist*), revolutionary extremism, tyranny, and military coups d'état (*Under Western Eyes, The Rovers, Nostromo*).

The essence of Conrad's outlook is found in the relationship between isolation and ethos, the two determinants of his characters' existence. These characters attempt to overcome their tragic loneliness by serving the values of a particular community,[6] but their endeavors do not lead to positive conclusions simply because such results are extremely hard to attain. Only a very few manage to overcome solitude and its consequences. This is very rare in cases of psychological isolation.

More characters are able to overcome sheer geographical separation:[7] Allistaun, Baker, Singleton and the mariners (except for James Wait and Donkin) in *The Nigger of the "Narcissus"*; the French Lieutenant and gunboat crew in *Lord Jim;* the *Judea* community in *Youth;* Marlow in *Heart of Darkness;* Van Wyk in *The End of the Tether;* MacWhirr, Lukes, Hackett and a part of the *Nan-Shan* company in *Typhoon;* the protagonists in *The Secret Sharer* and *The Shadow-Line;* Leggatt in *The Secret Sharer;* the sailors in *The Shadow-Line;* Carter in *The Rescue*. A majority of Conrad's characters are defeated in their confrontation with the forces of nature. They either fail to overcome isolation,[8] or make no attempt to change their predicament. These are Almayer and his wife in *Almayer's Folly;* Willems and Aissa in *An Outcast of the Islands;* James Wait and Donkin in *The Nigger of the "Narcissus";* the children in *The Idiots;* Kayerts and Carlier in *An Outpost of Progress;* the Herveys in *The Return;* Arsat in *The Lagoon;* the Malay helmsmen of the *Patna,* the fugitives from this steamer, Brown, Cornelius and Jewel in *Lord Jim;* young Marlow in *Youth;* the harlequin, the colonizers, Kurtz and his Intended in *Heart of Darkness;* the second mate and a part of the *Nan-Shan* crew in *Typhoon;* the *Borgmester Dahl* seamen and their superior in *Falk;* Yanko and Amy in *Amy Foster;* Hagberd in *To-morrow;* Charles and Emilia Gould, Antonia Avellanos and Martin Decoud, Giorgio, Linda and Giselle Viola, Nostromo and Monygham in *Nostromo;* the anarchists in *The Secret Agent, The Informer* and *An Anarchist;* Verloc, Winnie and Stevie in *The Secret Agent;* Paul Crocodile in *An Anarchist;* the Count in *Il Conde;* the revolutionaries in *Under Western Eyes;* Jocobus and Alice in *A Smile of Fortune;* Jasper Allen, Freya, and Nelson in *Freya of the Seven Isles;* Flora de Barral and Captain Anthony in *Chance;* Bauntz and Laughing Anne, Davidson and his spouse in *Because of the Dollars;* Burns, the second mate and the previous shipmaster in *The Shadow-Line;* Rita and George in *The Arrow of Gold;* the Traveres in *The*

Rescue; Lingard in *Almayer's Folly, An Outcast of the Islands* and *The Rescue;* Scevola in *The Rover;* the commanding officer in *The Tale* and Stephen in *The Sisters*. Finally, ending personal estrangement by suicide or another form of self-destruction can be hardly considered a success (Jim and Brierly in *Lord Jim,* Whalley in *The End of the Tether,* Rosumov in *Under Western Eyes,* Lena and Heyst in *Victory*, Jörgenson in *The Rescue*) even if it brings about a triumph of the cherished ideals (Jim, Lena, Heyst). Overcoming isolation through help from outside or confession hardly appears to be a true victory.[9]

Conrad does not unambiguously answer the question of how to be. He points the way–following a society's values–but simultaneously stresses the tremendous difficulty of achieving this goal. It is attainable by those few who are most persevering, most unyielding, and most capable of the maximum devotion. Therefore it is legitimate both to discern a pessimistic vision of the world and human existence in his literary output, and to interpret it as an affirmation of life and man.

Notes

Notes: Foreword

1. Its earlier versions were published in Polish: Krajka (49a) and Krajka (49). References to critical works comprise the author's name and the sequence number of a given item in the Bibliography (in parentheses), or, additionally, pages or the title of a pertinent chapter (in parentheses after the colon). Full data of all the publications referred to are given in the Bibliography.

2. Such an understanding of literary structure is depicted in a more detailed way in Krajka, Zgorzelski (50: 15-21).

Notes: Part 1: Isolation

1. Allen (1: 16, 301); Baines (104: 17-18); Blüth (114: 389-391, 395, 399-401); Chwalewik (131: 430); Dąbrowska (15: 113-114); Dyboski (147: 877-878); Fleishman (19: 4-5); Follett, Follett (158: 320-322); Gillon (23: The Incorrigible Don Quixote); Gillon (24: 154-155); Gillon (169: 42-44); Guerard (29: 73-74); Gurko (32: The Roots of Exile); Kocówna (214); Kołaczkowski (215: 242-243); Milbauer (250); Morf (55: 82-83); Najder (59: 200-201); Nettels (264: 267); Pettersson (67: 30); Retinger (71: 20-24); Sherry (81: 274-275); Staniewski (296: 52-53); Tarnawski (86: 31-32); Vincenz (321: 114-115); Watt (92: 4, 18-19, 23-24, 32-33, 70); Watt (327: 143-150); Zabierowski (98: 25-26, 41, 63-68).

2. Kennedy (205).

3. Gillon (23: 161).

4. Spoerri-Müller (83: 5, 8).

5. Hervouet (184: 201); Hervouet (185: 93-95, 107); Johnson (39: 15, 50); Kirschner (43: 184-185, 189-191); Wiley (94: 28-31, 80).

6. Gillon (23: 39-40, 85, 89-98, 125, 145); Mroczkowski (257: 16); Najder (59: 15-16); Zabierowski (98: 63).

7. Gillon (23: 162-172); Gillon (24: Conrad and Sartre); Lewis (227: 102-104); Seltzer (80: 116-119); Watt (327: 155-156).

Notes: Part 1, Chapter 1

1. Isolation at sea is mentioned by Bradbrook (117); Burgess (9: 132); Grabowski (27: 39); and Peirce (270: 74). Its more detailed delineation is given by Gillon (23: 99-104) and Spoerri-Müller (83: 21-23, 43-46, 65, 94-99).

2. All quotations and references to Conrad are located directly in the text and concern the following editions: *The Works of Joseph Conrad.* The Uniform Edition, vols. I-XXII (London, Toronto: J. M. Dent and Sons Ltd., 1923-28), and J. Conrad, *The Sisters* (New York: Crosby Gaige, 1928). The Arabic numerals indicate pages. The novels, collections of short stories, and essays are denoted by the following abbreviations: AF = *Almayer's Folly,* TU = *Tales of Unrest,* C = *Chance,* LJ = *Lord Jim,* MS = *The Mirror of the Sea,* PR = *A Personal Record,* NN = *The Nigger of the "Narcissus,"* TOS = *Typhoon and Other Stories,* N = *Nostromo,* OI = *An Outcast of the Islands,* SA = *The Secret Agent,* SS = *A Set of Six,* SL = *The Shadow-Line,* WT = *Within the Tides,* TLS = *Twixt Land and Sea,* UWE = *Under Western Eyes,* V = *Victory,* YNTOS = *Youth: A Narrative and Two Other Stories,* I = *The Inheritors,* Rom = *The Romance,* AG = *The Arrow of Gold,* NLL = *Notes on Life and Letters,* Re = *The Rescue,* Rov = *The Rover,* S = *Suspense,* Sis = *The Sisters,* TH = *Tales of Hearsay,* LE = *The Last Essays.*

3. Burgess (9: 34-36); Mroczkowski (58: 51-52); Roussel (73: 83).

4. Some Conradians point to the application of cosmic imagery in the shaping of marine seclusion in *The Nigger of the "Narcissus," Lord Jim, Youth,* and *The Shadow-Line:* Boyle (6: 39, 42, 46, 118); Daleski (13: 32-33, 81); De Voren Hoffman (16: 65); Guerard (30: 103, 106, 118); Komar (46: 12, 15, 21); Scrimgeour (285: 43); Spoerri-Müller (83: 21-22, 96), Watt (92: 96); Wiley (94: 45, 207-208); Yelton (97: 167).

5. Hewitt (36: 11-14, 70-71).

6. On Heyst's isolation on his island, see Whitehead (332).

7. Allen (103: 176); Daras (14: 109-110); Hewitt (36: 9-10); Karl (40: 174); and Orr (265: 117-118) highlight such a positioning of this area.

8. Tanner (85: 44-45).

9. Gillon (23: 104-108) gives a general portrayal of solitude in the tropics. Gillon (23: 104-108); Peirce (270); Verleun (91: X-XI); and Wiley (94: 35-36) mention the application of this kind of detachment to the shaping of characters in *Almayer's Folly, An Outcast of the Islands, An Outpost of Progress, The Lagoon, Lord Jim,* and *Heart of Darkness.*

10. It is remarkable that tropical isolation ultimately affects Willems's mistress Aissa (OI 248, 328). This is astonishing, since she is consequently

presented as an ally of the nature hostile to Willems.

11. However the narrator does not always identify his point of view with Karain's. The sovereign's exaggerated sense of the seclusion of his domain is frequently corrected by the narrative perspective of a European newcomer into this exotic region.

12. It is described in a "negative," typically naturalistic way, e.g., as "the enormous town slumbering monstrously on a carpet of mud under a veil of raw mist...[with] the streets without life and sound...shadowy houses...monotonous streets with unknown names where the dust of humanity settles inert and hopeless out of the stream of life" (SA 300; also 82, 135, 147). Nettels (60: 184-185) emphasizes the "enmity" of this urban colossus toward the characters of *The Secret Agent.*

13. Zgorzelski (348: 403, 406-407).

14. This is indicated by Gillon (23: 104) and Peirce (270).

15. The function of this motif is clearly different only in *Nostromo,* where it enhances the fictitious nature of the setting. The geographical isolation of Sulaco determines the economic backwardness of this province and its secondary role in the political life of the country (N 36-37). Most important, it becomes one of the principal arguments in Martin Decoud's campaign for turning Sulaco into an independent state and motivates activities directed toward accomplishing this goal (see Part 2, Chapter 5).

16. An essential differentiation between these two kinds of isolation consists primarly in the fact that on land a character's relation to his environment is ambivalent: he appears to be either a ruler of a domain that is completely subordinated to him, or a weak and lonely human being in contact with nature, which is powerful and indifferent to his tragedies and sufferings.

Notes: Part 1, Chapter 2

1. Geographical seclusion reveals occasionally a psychic shade of meaning, connected with an individual's perception of the pressure of surrounding nature; but it constitutes a nonessential aspect of solitude determined by outside factors.

2. On estrangement from European civilization in *An Outpost of Progress* and *Heart of Darkness,* see Szala (302: 23-25, 32).

3. On the accountant's estrangement and conduct, see Hawthorn (35: 180-181).

4. Hawkins (182: 80-82).

5. Gillon (23: 61-65); Hawkins (182: 76-77).

6. See the detailed discussions of this issue: Gillon (23: 61-62, 79-82);

Guerard (30: 140-141); Land (51: 79-83); Roussel (73: "Lord Jim": The Search for a New Aesthetic); Tanner (85); Urbisz (312: 294-297); Verleun (91); Wiley (94: 51-55).

7. On his loneliness, see Gillon (23: 60).

8. On the Russian's voluntary isolation, see Gillon (23: 60).

9. His solitude is delineated by Borowy (115); Gillon (23: 119-120); Hawkins (182: 73-75); Karl (40: 96-98); McLauchlan (246: 113-116, 120-121); Najder (59: 84-85); Pettersson (67: 57-59); Urbisz (312: 293-294); Watt (92: 37, 51-52, 63-67); Wiley (94: 35-38).

10. A similar elucidation of this image is presented by Ryf (74: 12-13); Watt (92: 55-56); and Yelton (97: 222).

11. This attitude is prefigured by his reaction to Reshid's marriage proposal concerning Nina: by treating it as a blow to his dreams and to the sense of a white man's dignity (AF 45-46).

12. On Almayer's tragic predicament, see Borowy (115). His life story acquires a universal quality, suggested primarily by the motto "Qui de nous / n'a eu sa terre promise, / son jour d'extase / et sa fin en exil"–the phrase "qui de nous," and by an allusion to the biblical motif of the Promised Land, which turn *Almayer's Folly* into a parable about a cycle of human hope, ecstasy, and defeat.

13. On Hagberd's estrangement see Krajka (219: 32-44).

14. However, the most tragic figure in *To-morrow* is Bessie Carvil, since only she is fully aware of the discrepancy between Harry's true self and his idealized image (TOS 269-270). The heroine's desperate plight consists, too, in the definitive collapse of the utopia of her own felicity, which is brought about by the young man's departure. Her wretched life, determined by the necessity of serving her blind father who tyrannizes her with his caprices, and listening to Hagberd's assurances of a lucky feature, is made permanent. She becomes painfully conscious that her dreams will never materialize: "She heard him at last, and, as if overcome by fate, began to totter silently back towards her stuffy little inferno of a cottage. It had no lofty portal, no terrific inscription of forfeited hopes–she did not understand wherein she had sinned" (274; also 277). On Bessie's grievous isolation see Krajka (219: 34-44); Osborn (63: 78-81).

15. On his influence see Daleski (141: 109-113, 116-118).

16. They are constantly depicted (frequently ironically) as the personification of evil and bestiality: Jones resembles a specter, Ricardo a wild cat, Pedro an ape; see Urbisz (313); Vidan (320: 655-659). Analogous characteristics concern Schomberg, their ally.

17. See the comments of both skeptics and the isolation resulting form

this attitude: Gillon (23: 129-130, 134-138); Guerard (30: 199-202); Hodges (37: 50-60, 173); Kaehele, German (199); Land (51: 192-194); Luyat-Moore (231); Marten (236); Newhouse (61: 120-125); Pawłow (269: 262-263); Penn Warren (271: XIV-XVI, XXIV-XXVII); Raval (69: 79-83); Ressler (70: 57-63); Roussel (73: 134-139); Schwarz (78: "Victory": Conrad's Indictment of Detachment); Secor (79: Heyst's World and the Perspective of Unreality); Urbisz (312: 297-299); Urbisz (313: 121-128); Vidan (320); Whitehead (332); Wright (95: 101-106).

18. Toker (311: 193).

19. On this character see Bancroft (3: 36-38); Bross (120: 40-41); Carter (130).

20. A similar illumination of symbolism in *Il Conde* is presented by Bross (120: 39-42); Schwarz (282); Wiley (94: 89-90); Wills (334).

21. This story also contains the conspicuous elements of tragicomedy and irony (Carter 130). The narrator frequently manifests his sarcastic treatment of the hypersensitive count: "I am sure that if he had been not too refined to do such a blatantly vulgar thing as dying from apoplexy in a café, he would have had a fatal stroke there and then. All irony apart" (SS 288; also 282-283). This time of action is displayed during the hero's leave taking: it gives rise, together with the mourning imagery, to black humor. A corresponding sense is conveyed by a local saying, which is in the motto, "Vedi Napoli e poi mori" (usually applied to tourists) in reference to the protagonist and his experiences. Its imperative form ("Come to Naples and die") directs Il Conde toward death, and the narator finds with spiteful satisfaction that he eventually "was going to his grave...by the *train de luxe*....As the four long, sombre coaches pulled out of the station I raised my hat with the solemn feeling of paying the last tribute of respect to a funeral *cortége*....*Vedi Napoli e poi mori!*" (289).

22. Jabłkowska (38: 116) and Ujejski (89: 147-150) interpret Stephen's attitude and views as an element of the Conradian artistic creed. He is largely a twin image of the writer himself because of leaving the Ukraine for the West to realize his vocation, his loneliness in alien environments, his numerous travels, his fascination with art, his nostalgia for his homeland. The autobiographical texture of *The Sisters*–see its discussion by Tarnawski (307: 129-132)–is also created by the figures of Rita, her sister, her uncle, her aunt, the priest, and the milieu of Spanish political emigration in France (they all appear in *The Arrow of Gold* as well).

23. Their conduct is highlighted by Gillon (23: 59-60); Hawthorn (35: 183-192); Hyland (193: 4-7); Kowalska (47: 55-56, 64-66); McLauchlan (247: 6-8, 12); Watt (92: 244-245). See also the discussion of shaping the women characters in *Heart of Darkness* in Geary (165).

24. A general elucidation of this kind of detachment is given by Baines (2: 441-443); and Urbisz (312: 302-303).

25. See its discussion in Baines (2: 265-267); Burgess (125: 121-123); Fraser (161); Gillon (23: 123-124); Guerard (30: 49-50); McLauchlan (245); Milbauer (250: 3-7, 12-17); Osborn (63: 70-73); Urbisz (312: 302-303).

26. Gillon (23: To Follow the Dream) discourses upon this type of solitude.

27. Both Heemskirk's outward appearance and conduct are repulsive (TLS 159-161, 164-165, 174, 187-188). The gunner who destroys Jasper's vessel at his command is a repellent figure as well (216-217).

28. Cox (12: 120-123, 129-133); Gekoski (22: 173-181); Gillon (23: 70-73, 129); Osborn (63: 153-156).

29. Gillon (23: 66-68).

30. Land (51: 18-20, 23); Lee (52: 129-132); McLauchlan (246: 116-122); Roussel (73: 38-43).

31. The two variants of the motif discussed are distinguished by Gillon (23: To Follow the Dream).

32. Gillon (23: 68-69).

33. Gillon (23: 68) indicates Rita's and George's mutual estrangement.

34. Baines (2: 387); Gillon (23: 72-74, 139); Pettersson (67: 164-166); Roussel (73: 159-167); Schwarz (78: 47-51, 53-54).

35. Gillon (23: 73-74, 138-140).

36. Roberts (276: 261-264). Wang, Heyst's servant, embodies the instinct of self-preservation too: he grows vegetables in the wilderness around the station (V 181-182). In a critical situation he arms himself with his master's revolver and hides with his own wife in her native village.

37. Similar explanations of the final scene in this novel are offered, e.g., by Vidan (320: 650-651); Whitehead (332: 99-106). Such a shaping of Lena reverses the classical situation of the chivalric romance, actually parodying it: "A thrill went through her at the sudden thought that it was she who would have to protect him, to be the defender of a man who was strong enough to lift her bodily" (V 309).

38. On the disparity of their views see Verleun (90: 61-74).

39. On their reciprocal seclusion see Gillon (23: 76, 120-122); Hawkins (182: 75-76); Lee (52: 122-124); Pettersson (67: 68-69); Roussel (73: 52-55).

40. Van Ghent (315: 235-237) connects this motif with the protagonist's loneliness and split personality. Goonetilleke (26: 65-67) and Lee (52: 106-107) indicate Jim's and Jewel's strangeness to each other.

41. Hawkins (182: 73-74); Lee (52: 121-122).

42. Gillon (23: 123-124); Milbauer (250: 14-17).

43. Roussel (73: 33-37) accentuates it, especially in reference to Hervey.

44. This self-centered performance is enhanced by the shape of the spatial setting in *The Return,* almost entirely enclosed by the walls of the room, with the high mirror, the pier glass, and the strips of glass on the doors of the wardrobes. All these combine to direct his sight and thoughts toward himself. See the explanation of this configuration by Dowden (18: 35-37). Focusing attention on the hero's character results from the design of *The Return* as a psychological short story (it was given this genre label both by Conrad in his Preface to *Tales of Unrest,* and by literary critics). In consequence of this the narration in *The Return* communciates mostly Hervey's thoughts and feelings, either directly in his utterances or indirectly, by means of narrative-dramatic language; and the fictional world is almost exclusively confined to the hero's psyche.

45. On this event and the couple's mutual estrangement, see Birdseye (113: especially 177); Gillon (23: 149-150); Hawthorn (35: 82); Wiley (94: 27-28).

46. See Hawthorn (35: 82); Land (51: 261-264, 268-269). See, as well, the comments by Urbisz (314) upon the characters of this novel, living in their dream worlds and alien to one another.

47. Gillon (23: 63-66), on the other hand, emphasizes her and Lingard's reciprocal love isolation.

48. Baines (2: 332-333, 336-337); Berthoud (5: 150-152); Cooper (11: 46, 53); Osborn (63: 103-105). Fleishman (19: 188-189, 193, 197-198, 203-204); Pettersson (67: 140-142); and Stallman (294: 236, 239-240) point to the separation of all characters in this novel from one another.

49. Its specific realization is discernible in *The Sisters*–in Rita's (a young provincial girl) solitude in the burgher milieu (Sis 67-68). It is interesting to speculate on how Conrad would have developed this situation if he had finished the novel.

50. See the argument by Schwarz (77: Conrad's Quarrel with Politics: The Disrupted Family in "Nostromo") concerning the destructive impact of the characters' involvement in political-economic matters on their relations with women in *Nostromo.*

51. See a broad discussion of this kind of insulation in Gillon (23: The Anatomy of Betrayal) and Gillon (167). Such a creation resembles to some extent a Byronic hero: see his delineatin in Dobrzycka (17: 43-45, 61); Thorslev (87: 149-152, 156-175, 181-182).

52. Haugh (34: "The Secret Sharer"); Lothe (54: "The Secret Sharer": Economic Personal Narrative); Zgorzelski, Krajka (349: 73-75) deal with

suspense as an element of the adventurous plot in *The Secret Sharer*.

53. On Leggatt's and his savior's estrangement, see Brown (121); Kowalska (48: 66-75). Much critical attention has been devoted to the protagonist's attitude and its psychological-ethical determinants. Conradians emphasize his distance from the ship and its crew in Zgorzelski, Krajka (349)–and, particularly, his identification with the newcomer: Brown (121); Dussinger (146); Eggenschwiler (149); Hoffman (190); Leiter (225: 159); Palmer (65: 225-228); Steiner (298); Zgorzelski, Krajka (349). Leggatt is interprted as the other, mysterious side of the narrator's personality: e.g., Dussinger (146); Haugh (34: "The Secret Sharer"); Hewitt (36: 72-76); Hoffman (190); Yelton (97: Homo Duplex: "The Secret Sharer"). For the embodiment of his evil features, see chiefly, Guerard (30: 21-29); Palmer (65: 222-229); or, contrarily, for the ideal of conduct he desires, Curley (138, 139); Graver (28: 150-158); Kowalska (48: 74-76); Schwarz (78: 1-10); Stallman (295); Ressler (70: 82-84, 88). Daleski (13: "The Secret Sharer") depicts an ambivalent portrait of the law breaker.

54. On his ethical detachment, see also Osborn (63: 173-174); Schwarz (78: 101-103); Williams (333); Wright (95: 94-96).

55. Osborn (63: 73-77); Tanner (306: 20).

56. In this story the hero's loneliness concurs with comic elements, which constitute a significant tendency of semantic organization.

57. See his delineation in Gillon (23: 81-82, 126-128); Haugh (34: 56-57); Van Ghent (315: 232, 235-237).

58. On Jim's isolation in Patusan see Hawkins (182: 76-80).

59. Jim's deathbed success makes him parallel to Lena in *Victory*. Presentation of the calamitous epilogue is furthered by the descriptions of nature, which is shaped by romantic convention, sympathizing with man sharing the same experiences (413); see Dowden (18: 69-70).

60. Johnson (196) draws a parallel between the principal characters in *Lord Jim* and *Karain*. Gillon (23: 122) and Osborn (63: 31-34) comment on Karain's detachment.

61. Karain's frame of mind is enhanced by the descriptions of the rainstorm, which make the predicament more overwhelming (TU 20-21). His extreme agitation and anguish are revealed in the way he tells hs tale–in the application of a highly dramatized mode of narration, abounding in short, broken sentences and pauses and words of high emotional intensity.

62. Conradians taking the psychological approach have disregarded this story, although it is worth a psycholoanalytical investigation.

63. See his presentation in Gillon (23: 122-123).

64. Zgorzelski (348) articulates the tragic and universal aspects of

Arsat's experiences. His torments are reflected in his way of relating the story with dramatized narration containing numerous short, emotionally loaded sentences, see Zgorzeiski (348: 406).

65. Razumov's pangs of conscience bring him close to the leading figure of *Crime and Punishment*, to which Conrad clearly alludes. Comparison and contrast with Dostoevsky's masterpiece constitutes a major chord in the research on *Under Western Eyes:* see Adams (102); Berman, Van Wagenen (109); Busza (127: 111-113); Gillon (168: 688-692); Kirschner (43: 252-264); Knapp Hay (44: 280-282, 308-309); Matlaw (240); Najder (59: 155-164).

66. Razumov's ethical detachment is dealt with extensively by critics, with emphasis mostly on the sufferings caused by his sense of guilt: Adams (102: 115, 117-118, 123-124); Berthoud (5: 174-183); Cooper (11: "Under Western Eyes"); Cox (12: "Under Western Eyes," "The Deaf Man"); Daleski (13: "Under Western Eyes"); Gillon (23: 126-128, 132); Guerard (30: 231-243); Haugh (34: "Under Western Eyes"); Hawthorn (35: 47-48); Kirschner (208: 5-10); Mayoux (241: 299-302); Ressler (70: "Under Western Eyes": Integrity Achieved); Rosenfield (72: "Under Western Eyes." The Mirror of a Double Quest); Roussel (73: 140-152); Tanner (304); Wright (95: 98-101); Zabel (343: 132-134, 143).

67. On Monygham and his ethical estrangement, see Berthoud (5: 115); Cooper (11: 106-107, 111-116); Cox (12: 81-82); Daleski (13: 139-142); Gillon (23: 128); Jabłkowska (38: 247); Land (51: 126); Osborn (63: 95); Pawłow (269: 263-265); Penn Warren (271: XI); Raval (69: 90-92); Ressler (70: 64-68); Toker (311: 193).

68. Berthoud (5: 125); Cooper (11: 127-133); Fleishman (19: 164, 175-176); Gillon (23: 132-134) point out his seclusion and remorse.

69. Gillon (23: 119-120); Urbisz (312: 293-294).

70. Dowden (18: 21-29); McLauchlan (246: 122-140); Nettels (60: 200-204); Roussel (73: 29-32), and Wiley (94: 38-44) highlight the strictures on the protagonist, who experiences growing moral deterioration.

71. On their estrangement from the crew, see Verleun (319).

72. Gillon (23: 106-108); Sherry (82: 345-349), and Watt (92: 140-141, 245) indicate Marlow's lone perception of the colonization in Africa and of Kurtz's activities.

Notes: Part 1, Chapter 3

1. We limit ourselves to considering only the most conspicuous, exemplary instances of solitude, disregarding those vaguely drawn, less

characteristic, and not quite convincing.

2. The register presented is simplified: it neither distinguishes the subspecies of the five basic kinds of separation surveyed nor differentiates between the cases cited according to their degree of distinctness and significance for the structure of the text.

3. They would have been much more numerous if we had treated lovers' (spouses') renunciation of the world and reciprocal detachment as distinct kinds and not successive phases of amorous estrangement. A similiar simplification was to regard the sea-mountainous and insular isolation of Nostromo, Decoud, Giorgio Viola and his daughters in *Nostromo* as isolation on land.

4. By tokens of the European civilization and illusions of a splendid future.

5. In the first half of this masterpiece.

6. In the second half of this masterpiece.

7. Through identification with the culprit and as his confidante.

8. Wyka (336: 72-73, 76, 91-94). On the other functions of narration in Conrad, see in Part 2, Chapter 4.

9. See especially Mroczkowski (58: 78-79) and Sherry (81: 281-282).

10. *Lord Jim* is generally interpreted as a novel about its main narrator's attemtps to elucidate the causes of the principal character's actions. See, in particular, De Voren Hoffman (16: Burlesque, Parody and Analogue in "Lord Jim": A Reading of the Novel); D'Hangest (143); Malbone (234); Mroczkowski (58: 60-61); Najder (59: 100, 103-104); Raval (69: Narrative and Authority: "Lord Jim"); Seltzer (286); Wright (95: 117-123).

11. Such apothegms appear in *Almayer's Folly* (AF 179), *An Outcast of the Islands* (OI 250), and *Heart of Darkness* (YNTOS 82, 157-158) as well.

12. This is highlighted principally by Cox (12: The Metamorphoses of "Lord Jim"); D'Hangest (143); Guerard (30: 161-164); Guetti (31: "Lord Jim": The Vitality of the Rhetoric); Mroczkowski (58: 106-107, 109, 127); Palmer (65: 42-43); Paris (268); Perry (272); Raval (69: Narrative and Authority: "Lord Jim"); Seltzer (80: 40-41, 68-69, 72-73); Seltzer (286); Stewart (84: 106-108, 115-116).

13. Darras (14: 83-84, 88).

14. According to Todorov (310), the quest for knowledge about Kurtz, which is impossible to attain, is the dominant theme of *Heart of Darkness*.

15. Similar care for verisimilitude is manifest in *The Partner* (WT 128) and in *The Inn of the Two Witches*, where the manuscript found serves as material for the story.

16. Bancroft (3: 64-71); Najder (59: 197); and Najder (261: 80-81)

claim that the motif of confession is typical of Conrad's literary output.

Notes: Part 2: Ethos

1. Follett (20: 18-23); Gekoski (22: Conrad's Moral World); Gillon (23: 99, 110, 162-172); Gillon (24: The Absurd and "Les Valeurs Ideales" in Conrad, Kafka and Camus; Conrad and Sartre); Paris (268: 218-219, 226, 236); Pettersson (67); Roussel (73); Seltzer (80: 96-97, 116); Watt (327: 139-141, 155). Such an attitude toward reality establishes a principal analogy between Conrad's masterpieces and Existentialism.

2. Baines (2: 441-443); Dąbrowska (15: 113-115); Drew (145: 227-229); Follett, Follett (158: 316-319); Gekoski (22: 6, 16, 21-22, 97-99); Gillon (23: 57-58); Guerard (29: 16); Guerard (30: 48-50); McCullough (242: 339); Newhouse (61: 139); Urbisz (312: 302-304); Wilson (335: 53, 76). Pettersson (67: especially 58-59, 69, 152, 166) points to the appearance of this idea only in the first phase of Conrad's output (through *The Secret Agent*).

3. This conviction, combined with the affirmation of certain values, distinguishes the outlook conveyed in Conrad's texts from Existentialist philosophy: Gillon (23: 162-172); Gillon (24: The Absurd and "Les Valeurs Ideales" in Conrad, Kafka and Camus; Conrad and Sartre); Tarnawski (86: Conrad and Sartre: Two Ethics Opposed); Watt (327: 155-156).

4. I use the term "ethos" as broader than "ethics," as encompassing the entirety of ideals and values (pertaining mostly to ethics, but also to customs and other spheres of life) that determine a group's culture and style of living: see Ossowska (64).

5. Critics formulate a similar view, considering solidarity to be the leading principle: Bancroft (3: in particular 15-21, 60, 73-88); Daleski (13: 41-43); Drew (145: 228-229); Fleishman (19: 56-57, 69-77); Follett, Follett (158: 322-328); Gillon (23: 100, 118, 134-135, 168); Gillon (24: 146, 157-158, 160); Gekoski (22: 6, 16-22, 70-71); Kowalska (216: 131-135); Paris (268: 219-220); Prorok (68: 78-83); Ryf (74: 40-46); Seltzer (80: 96-104); Stavrou (297: 80-86); Urbisz (312); Watt (92: 33); Watt (327: 151-156); Whitehead (332: 93, 99-100, 106); Zabel (344: 29-30); and Kisner (209: 85-88); and Pettersson (67: 38-41, 182-183, 186-188) who understand this concept more widely, as a sense of unity with the fellowship of mankind and its moral standards. Baines (2: 443); McCullough (242: 338-340); and Tucker (88: 52), on the other hand, highlight the internal conflict of Conradian characters between feelings of estrangement and the desire to join humanity. Spoerri-Müller (83: 68-75) indicates a different way of breaking out of isolation: through death or the transformation of mentality–forgetting the past

or overpowering "darkness" within and outside a psyche.

6. These circumstances, which typify the predicament of many Conradian characters, are emphasized by Burkhardt (10: 26-41, quoted after Mroczkowski, 257: 17); Daleski (13: 80-82, 105-106, 131, 179-182); Dąbrowska (15: 125-126); Gillon (23: 99-100, 103-104, 110-117, 136); Guerard (29: 52-54, 75); Karwacki (42: 38); Kisner (209: 85, 87); Moore (253); Moser (57: 14-16, 30); Mroczkowski (257: 17); Wain (323); and Zabierowski (99: 34). Mroczkowski (257: 17-18, 22, 26) points to the functioning of the notion of *Grenzsituation* in the works by the author of *Lord Jim* in reference to European political realities.

7. Watt (327: 145-150) indicates the identical line of development of Conrad's personality.

8. Baines (2: 441-443); Gillon (23); Moser (57: 30-35); and Urbisz (312) regard isolation as the primary reason for many individual's misfortunes and failures.

9. The biographical determinants of Conradian characters are indisputable: the writer's family traditions made him sensitive to the moral aspect of political activity, and his adult years on British ships to the ethical overtones of mariners' and colonizers' performance. The importance of such problems in Conrad's texts is stressed first and foremost by Cooper (11); Dąbrowska (15); Fletcher (155); Gekoski (22); Gillon (23: The Anatomy of Betrayal); Graver (28: The Major Stories); Komar (46); Kowalska (217); Najder (59: Nad Conradem; O "filozofii" Conrada); Najder (259); Najder (260); Ostrowski (266: 281-282); Palmer (65); Sherry (288); and Zabierowski (346: 112). The Conradian code of values is most frequently claimed to be founded upon honor and dignity–Dąbrowska (15: 124-128), Janion (194: 68-69, 77, 80), and Najder (260); faithfulness, conscientiousness, and responsibility–Berthoud (5: 16-22), Burgess (9: The Craft), Dąbrowska (15: 60-61, 70, 125, 148-158), Gurko (32: 39-40), Kowalska (216: 131-135), Najder (59: 15-19, 191, 195, 199), and Ujejski (89: 84, 90-91, 114-116); self-possession–Daleski (13); the cult of work–Bruss (8: 27-28), Burgess (9: 102-107), Fleishman (19: 72-75), Gaston (163), Kowalska (216: 131-135), and Watts (93: 59-67).

10. Some ethical qualities of the characters' actions emerge from the foregoing discussion of isolation. However, they pertain to individual relations, to attitudes asumed toward another human being. On the other hand, the following considerations focus on a depiction of ethos–on an intratextual evaluation of the patterns of behavior characteristic of a given society that lead to success or failure in overcoming loneliness.

Notes: Part 2, Chapter 4

1. Baines (2: 183-184); Gillon (23: 99-104). *A Personal Record* outlines a parallel between the mariners' solitary struggle and Conrad's creative process (PR 98-99); see Berthoud (5: 11-22).

2. Benson (108: 48); Gillon (23: 99, 101-103); and Wright (95: 47-48) point out this "privilege" of a shipmaster.

3. On James Wait's and Donkin's lines of action see Daleski (13: 36-42); Foulke (159: 119-122); Komar (46: 15-17); Lee (52: James Wait as a Symbol of the Burden in "The Nigger of the 'Narcissus'"); Parry (66: 67-70); Tanner (305: 407-408); and Tucker (88: 91-93).

4. See the unflattering description of him as an agitator by Fleishman (19: 130-131); Yates (338).

5. On their performance see Verleun (91: The Patna Perspectives). De Voren Hoffman (16: 54-61) highlights the portrayal of these characters in terms of caricature.

6. Gillon (23: 101).

7. On Burns's condemnable conduct and disadvantageous influence upon the captain, see Echeruo (148: 100-103). This superstition turns Burns into a grotesque figure, which introduces comic elements into this grandiloquent text.

8. On Mr. Burns's groundless hopes see Burgess (9: 125-126).

9. On Massy as a *schwarzcharakter* see McLauchlan (248: 57-58).

10. There are also other seamen in Conrad who deteriorate because of weak character, addiction, or external circumstances: Johnson in *Falk* (he goes utterly bad, living in a slum among natives); Schultz in *Freya of the Seven Isles* (a notorious drunkard and thief); and Rajah's yacht officer as mentioned by Captain Giles in *The Shadow-Line* (SL 13-14).

11. There are some exceptions to this: Freya in *Freya of the Seven Isles*, the wives of Captain Whalley in *The End of the Tether*, and Captain Harry Dunbar in *The Partner*.

12. A spouse's detrimental role is insinuated or overemphasized by misogynists. The chief mate Franklin in *Chance* asserts that Flora de Barral's presence on the *Ferndale* inhibits his superior's professional performance (C 302-33, 404-407). Nearly every word of his conveys antipathy toward her, but the falsity of this valuation is implied by Powell's and the narrator's ironic treatment of Franklin (403-407). Marlow in *Youth*, fascinated by an idealistic and escstatic vision of the mariners' calling, sneeringly depicts Captain Beard's rescue of his wife from danger (YNTOS 9).

13. See the argument by Burgess (9: The Land), though it is not always

convincing, about the injurious impact on seamen of land entanglements, and the comments on the superiority of the maritime existence over life on land in Part 2, Chapter 4).

14. The *Narcissus*'s crew's intrepid braving the fury of the elements is highlighted chiefly by Daleski (13: 36-43), Jones (198), and Kocówna (45: 216-228).

15. Berthoud (5: 26-27); Boyle (6: 50-54); Bruss (8: 33-36); Burgess (9: 89-90); Daleski (13: 39-43); Moser (57: 16-18); and Tanner (305: 416-418) articulate the steersman's exceptional steadfastness.

16. Burgess (9: 4, 87-88, 119), too, portrays him in this way.

17. For example, Guerard (30: 109-110) and Tucker (88: 91) emphasize this connotation.

18. Guerard (30: 295-296); Gurko (32: 86-91).

19. Berthoud (5: 26, 29); Burgess (9: 39-47); and Daleski (13: 30-31) indicate such shaping of a storm–the mariners' antagonist.

20. Exaggeration of their heroism results largely from Marlow's exaltation at perceiving the first marine experiences in terms of a youthful, idealistic vision of the profession (see Part 2, Chapter 4).

21. Zuckerman (350: 89-92).

22. Conrad points to the autobiographical aspect of the presentation of characters and events of this long short story as laudable (SL Author's Note X-XII).

23. Burgess (9:89).

24. Berthoud (5: 26-27, 35-37); Bruss (8: 31-33); and Michael (249: 97-98) indicate the glorious fulfillment of a captain's duties by Allistoun. Daleski (13: 40-41, 46-50) and Foulke (159: 111-119), on the other hand, compose an ambiguous portrait of this character.

25. Allen (103: 172-174); Burgess (9: 92-93); Gillon (23: 103); Guerard (30: 296-298); Gurko (32: 86-91); Hussey (192); Kocówna (45: 228-241); Moser (57: 17-18); Schwarz (77: 115-117); and Tarnawski (86: 98-100) view MacWhirr as irreproachable. Bruss (8: "Typhoon": Ironic Diminishing of the Pattern) takes the opposite stance.

26. This is highlighted by Burgess (9: 114).

27. Burgess (9:85) emphasizes his meritorious performance.

28. Bruss (123); Burgess (9: 134).

29. This is stressed by Burgess (9: 132-133).

30. This motif also pertains to the protagonist in *The Shadow-Line* (see on him in Part 2, Chapter 4) and to Powell in *Chance*, whose beginning of his luckily obtained post on board ship is equivalent to a start in adult life (C 29). The autobiographical aspect of initiation appears in *The Shadow-Line* (see

"Author's Note," and particularly SL X-XII), *The Arrow of Gold, Initiation,* and *The "Tremolino"* see especially the implied author's confessions (*Initiation,* MS 141-142, 148; *The "Tremolino,"* MS 155-157).

31. Chwalewik (132: 449); Komar (46: 12-13); Watt (92: 120).

32. Moser (57: 17-19).

33. In particular Allen (103: 172-174); Bruss (8: "Typhoon": Ironic Diminishing of the Pattern); Burgess (9: 98-99); Gurko (32: 86-91); Kocówna (45: 228-241); Morf (56: 247-248); Osborn (63: 66-67); Schuster (281); Tarnawski (86: 98-100).

34. This is stressed, too, by Marlow's sententious utterance in *Lord Jim,* where he recommends "belief in a few simple notions you must cling to it you want to live decently and would like to die easy" (LJ 43).

35. Karwacki (42: 34-35).

36. Berthoud (5: 30-38); Haugh (34: 6, 13-15, 18).

37. On the meanings of light and darkness in *The Nigger of the "Narcissus,"* see Gallagher (162: 56-58); Palmer (65: 67-70); and Watt (92: 95-96).

38. He is similarly viewed by Daleski (13: 43-46); Dowden (18: 52-54); Follett (20: 40-41); Gekoski (22: 61-62); Guerard (30: 109); Gurko (32: 68-79); Haugh (34: 3, 12); Komar (46: 16-17, 23); Miller (251); Parry (66: 70-72); Scrimgeour (285); Watt (92: 105-106); and Watt (326: 92-93).

39. Principally Boyle (6: "The Nigger of the "Narcissus"), Echeruo (148); Jones (198); Lowe-Evans (230); Michael (249); and Scrimgeour (285: 48-52) indicate such an influence.

40. Only Singleton does not surrender to the pressure (NN 41-42); this constitutes a factor in his unique status.

41. Boyle (6: "The Nigger of the "Narcissus"), Guerard (30: 107-114), and Haugh (34: 3, 6, 12-13, 18) regard him as a representation of the dark side of the *Narcissus* deckhands' personalities; Jones (198) and Lowe-Evans (230) are close to such a treatment.

42. Daleski (13: 35); Yelton (97: 160-161).

43. A parallel portrayal of the marine existence appears in *Falk:* its protagonist, practicing cannibalism on board, is desribed as a personification of the instinct of self-presevation (TOS 198-200, 223-224). In case of both the *Narcissus*'s and the *Borgmester Dahl*'s companies this "voice of nature" ensures self-defense. But whereas in *The Nigger of the "Narcissus"* it also prevents the sailors from yielding to faults, in *Falk,* on the contrary, it brings about surrender to them (on the principal character's conduct see Part 1, Chapter 2 and Part 2, Chapter 4). The tugboat commander's instinctive nature is persistently emphasized, e.g., in showing his relentless behavior toward the

captains dependent on him, his desire for Hermann's neice (224), in the description of the *Diana*'s abduction (170-171), or in comparing Falk to a centaur. Such an image is in tune with the depiction of his partner–an epitome of youthful energy and vitality–and with the description of the conversation and meal of the narrative situation members as resembling tales and meals of primeval people (145-146). The view of Falk and Hermann's niece outlined above is confirmed by Hewitt (36: 41-42); Karl (41: 512-513); Tanner (306: 22-23); Yaseen (96: 67); and De Voren Hoffman (16: 108-111), who stresses their comic traits.

44. It is symptomatic that the paralyzing impact of both outsiders is never disclosed in the course of the struggle with the storm, but only in the pauses between its particular stages. That is, when the vessel runs into danger, the deckhands instantly stop their mutiny, forget their grievances, and zealously work to save it (NN 124-125).

45. Considerations by Boyle (6: 124-133); Kisner (209: 88-90); and Wegelin (330) are close to this interpretation of MacWhirr's struggle with the storm.

46. See, especially, Lorch (229); and also Benson (108); Sherry (81: 287, 290); Tucker (88: 37); Vitoux (322: 84-85); and Watt (325).

47. The dedication of *The Shadow-Line*, as well as certain passages in "Author's Note," show that the experience described has a meaning contemporary to the creation of the novel, pertaining to the young English soldiers (the writer's son Borys included) who passed the threshold of manhood during battle in World War I.

48. Conrad (352) comprises some of them, Knowles (213) and Mroczkowski (255) discuss the rhetoric and functions of such comments.

49. Cox (12: 13); Follett (20: 42-47). On the bond between seamen see Berthoud (5: 14-16); Daleski (13: 41-43); Baines (2: 184); Gekoski (22: 63-64); Gillon (23: 99-104); Guerard (30: 104-105); Moser (57: 11-19); Watt (92: "The Nigger of the 'Narcissus'"); Watt (326: 97-99); Wright (95: Solidarity of Mankind).

50. A selection is included in Conrad (351).

51. Skutnik (291).

52. Craig (136); Fraser (21: "'The Lagoon,' 'Karain' and 'Lord Jim'"); Tarnawski (86: 27-31); Wyka (336: 59-60, 65, 94), and Zgorzelski (100: 4-15, 73-75, 78) deal with the techniques of "gaweda" ("told-tales") in Conrad's *Lord Jim*, and short stories.

53. Besides, *Lord Jim* abounds in insertions loosely connected both with the narrative present and the plot. There are also many tiny digressions during the narration that convey Marlow's thoughts and feelings and his interpreta-

tion of the particular aspects of the story. The tremendous number of different types of departures from the main presentation and the multiplicity of commentators–Marlow's informants–result in considerable complexity and make the narration superior to the events. On Marlow's atitude, story-telling strategies, and their functions in the novel, see Part 1, Chapter 3 and Part 2, Chapter 4.

54. In *The Brute* this tendency harmonizes with the use of maritime jargon by the narrator and his interlocutor.

55. In *The Partner* it assumes the form of a chat in which a master stevedore of the port of London discloses the *Sagamore*'s commander's history.

56. Parallel evocations are made by the speaking subject in *Karain*, as he appeals to the imagination of fellow mariners intimately connected with the Eastern Archipelago (TU 3).

57. These comments concern only the phonomena that strengthen this alliance. Conrad's narrative techniques fulfill other functions as well: e.g., getting to the truth about a character and his isolation (Part 1, Chapter 3); arguing for his concrete evaluation (Part 2, Chapter 4); stylization of the narration in "told-tale" form and enhancing the verisimilitude of related events–principally in *Gaspar Ruiz* and *The Warrior's Soul*–but also in *Il Conde*, *Under Western Eyes*, and *The Inn of the Two Witches*. in the last two it is combined with self-conscious writing (*The Tale*); shaping the narrator as a writer composing a text from hearsay (*The Partner*); digressive narrative highlighting the pesonal/autobiographical nature of a text (*The Mirror of the Sea*, *A Personal Record*).

58. Burgess (9: 107-111).

59. In *The Mirror of the Sea* Conrad extols sailing not only of the period directly preceding his creative years, but also of much earlier times: *The Nursery of the Craft* and *The "Tremolino"* evoke remote Mediterranean history, abounding in daring expeditions.

60. Dyboski (147: 865-866); Grabowski (27: 61-62, 65-66); and Ujejski (89: 256) indicate such a presentation.

61. Ujejski (89: 257-258).

62. Burgess (9: 52-63).

63. On this course of conduct see Burgess (9: 65-72); Dyboski (147: 865-866); and Grabowski (27: 61-66).

64. On their union see Liljegren (53: 7-9).

65. In *The End of the Tether*, *Freya of the Seven Isles*, and *The Partner* the captains' atachment to their ships is shared by their women. This contradicts some seamen's conviction that ties with them collide with sailors'

obligations. Whalley's and Harry Dunbar's wives create cosy hearths on board (YNTOS 172-173; WT 113), and Freya, "a ship-child, a sea-girl if ever there was one" (TLS 167), wants "to be mistress of the dear brig and sail about these seas" (162).

66. An original instance of this symbiosis appears in *Falk:* the protagonist and his tugboat are persistently described as a composite creature–a man-boat (TOS 162, 208). However, unlike other examples of the same, this image does not express a close emotional bond, but is connected with a system of symbolic meanings (see Part 2, Chapter 4).

67. Burgess (9: 65-66); Grabowski (27: 61, 65-66).

68. Occasionally a vessel is humorously called "old girl" by Conrad's seamen.

69. Personification does not express such feelings only in *The Brute,* where the craft is portrayed as a malicious monster that kills someone during each voyage. This makes it an object not of the seamen's love,but of their fear or even hatred.

70. Gurko (33: 173); Ujejski (89: 256-257).

71. In *The Mirror of the Sea* this trend is contrapuntal to the realistic narrative and descriptions.

72. Bruss (8); Burgess (9: 16-17, 72-80); Jabłkowska (38: 174-175, 179); Ujejski (89: 258-259).

73. Burgess (9: The Ships; The Craft) comments on behavior toward ships.

74. In Conrad's works there are also other youths who desire extraordinary adventurers: the Russian in *Heart of Darkness* (YNTOS 52, 126-127) and John Kemp in *Romance,* where the entire action of the novel implies a eulogy of the style of living he represents. See also the words of the narrators in *Chance* (C 31-32) and *Victory* (V 23).

75. De Voren Hoffman (16: 99-107) stresses his perception of the world to be presented in comic terms.

76. See the comments by Erdinast-Vulcan (150) on the opposition between the realms of romance and commerce in this story.

77. Conrad enlisted in the British Merchant Navy, obtained British citizenship, and wrote in English. These are the biographical data that contribute to the fact that traditional Polish Conradology considers betrayal of homeland as one of its principal themes. The writer's self-justification apperas in *A Personal Record,* where he argues that the Russian, German, or Austrian merchant services were out of the question for him. His reasons were patriotic and political (PR 121).

78. Berthoud (5: 41-42); Daleski (13: 43, 153); Grabowski (27: 63);

Guerard (30: 122-123); Jones (198: 161-162); Kowalska (217: 152-154); Najder (59: 175-177); Young (341: 109-110).

79. Tucker (88: 92) highlights this presentation.

80. Their appreciation from the point of view of the ironically portrayed settled characters is entirely dissimilar: the shipping office clerk regards Donkin as an intelligent man, and Singleton as "a disgusting old brute" (NN 169). Baker's brother-in-law, the leading tailor and politician in a little town, does not consider the *Narcissus*'s chief mate his peer (166-167).

81. Stability is also despised by individuals fond of adventure: Harry Hagberd in *To-morrow*, who reveals an inclination to maritime roaming and an abhorrence for the mode of existence represented by his father, and John Kemp in *Romance*, who wants to wrench himself from Kent's atmosphere and is later disappointed with the manner in which Mr. MacDonald and the other Jamaica planters live.

82. Burgess (9: 14-20).

83. On Conrad's deprecatory depiction of these judges see Lippe (228: 63-64).

84. See too Marlow's criticism of religion in *Heart of Darkness* for its not confronting difficult situations and problems in life, indeed for avoiding them (YNTOS 117).

85. Kowalska (48: 70-72); Zgorzelski, Krajka (349: 80-83).

86. This tendency is plain in *Romance* as well (John Kemp's victimization by inimical judges and public opinion), where it is subordinated to the melodramatic and adventurous design of the novel (see its final part, which abounds in caricatured descriptions of the officers of the law).

87. See Birdseye's (113: 172) and Chwalewik's (131: 436-438) comments on the condemnation of Victorian town dwellers' morality in *The Return*.

88. See on this issue in Jabłkowska (38: 255-260).

89. The description of the principal character and his father in *Prince Roman* as admirable is a depature from this tendency.

90. Burgess (9: 155) and Stallman (295: 285-288) highlight the existence of this category of individuals.

91. Tarnawski (86: Conrad, the Pole) considers betrayal and guilt as typical Conradian themes originating in the writer's Polish past. Gillon (23: The Anatomy of Betrayal) and Gillon (167) regards the attempt to expunge earlier betrayals or other offenses with honorable deeds as a specific feature of many Conradian characters, not only mariners.

92. Lee (52: 141-142) and Tanner (85: 30-31) point out such a presentation of the native members of the *Patna* crew, whereas Batchelor (4: 103-

104) and Burgess (9: 85-86) convey their ambivalent appreciation.

93. Burgess (9: 87) approves of Jörgenson's actions.

94. The portrayal of Peyrol as commendable is stressed by Burzyńska (126); Howarth (191); Jabłkowska (38: 274-278); Prorok (68: 107-109, 114-116); and Schwarz (28: 164-168).

95. The name "Ivy" is not accidental, since her needs enslave her father, twine round him like this plant. Whalley belongs among the Conradian shipmasters whose performance of professional duties is thwarted by family or land entanglements.

96. Folejewski (157); Gillon (23: 131); Hewitt (36: 28-30); and Osborn (63: 82-85) emphasize the ethical aspects of the protagonist's conduct, and McLauchlan (243) and Schwarz (283) focus on the universal dimension of his performance and the stratum of ideas. Land (51: "The End of the Tether"); McLauchlan (248); and Prorok (68: 93-96) view Captain Whalley in a positive way.

97. Burgess (9: 61-62, 91-92, 95-96) presents the opposite opinion: he stresses Whalley's improper attitude toward the craft and blames him largely for its sinking.

98. Daleski (13: 174-175, 180); Kowalska (48: 70-72); Ressler (70: "The Secret Sharer": Affirmation of Action); and Stallman (295: 285-286) articulate Leggatt's admirable conduct during the storm as redemptory–they view him in rather positive light.

99. See a nautical interpretation of this move by Evans (152) and Madison (233). Dilworth (144) views the motif of Koh-ring and the vessel's course in its vicinity in symbolic terms.

100. Burgess (9: 86); Kowalska (48: 78-87); Schwarz (78: 82-94); and Zuckerman (350) see his actions favorably.

101. Among many discussions of this issue, which is central to *The Shadow-Line* and *The Secret Sharer*, Benson (108); Burgess (9: 133-134); Curley (138: 81); Jaudel (195); and White (331) should be mentioned. According to "Author's Note," the writer initially intended to entitle this text "First Command."

102. Young Marlow's conduct in *Youth* (see Part 2, Chapter 4), contrary to Jim's, is not strictured. According to "Author's Note" in *Youth: A Narrative and Two Other Stories* (YNTOS Author's Note IX), this story was composed at the time of creaing *Lord Jim*. This coincidence strengthens the thesis about the correspondence of many motifs in both texts, e.g., the experienced seaman Marlow, the ecstatic attitude of his younger colleague.

103. Such causes of both these fiascos are indicated by Burgess (9: 100-101); Daleski (13: 88-95); Davidson (142: 26); Gillon (23: 61, 79-82, 96-97,

138); Moser (57: 21); Tanner (85: 29-30); Tarnawski (86: 69-70, 83); Verleun (91: 3-4); Watt (92: 310-311, 313); and Wright (95: 108-110).

104. Some critics highlight the protagonist's negative traits and interpret the novel as a critique of romantic egoism and daydreaming: Gillon (23: 61-62, 79-84, 93-94, 131-132); Hodges (37: 38-39); Karl (200); Malbone (234); Najder (59: 108-111); Nelson (263); Tanner (85); and Urbisz (312: 294-297). Ross (277) and Tarnawski (86: 72, 80, 84-87) represent an opposite viewpoint.

105. See especially, Watt (92: 313-314, 318, 322).

106. Baines (2: 251-252); Tarnawski (86: 74, 76); Watt (92: 338-346); Watt (329); and Wright (95: 113-115) approve of Tuan's conduct in Patusan after Brown's arrival and interpret his death as a moral victory. The opposite view is held, e.g., by Davidson (142).

107. Burgess (9: 101-102); Gillon (23: 83, 155-156); Guerard (30: 127-130); Kramer (220: 265); Kridl (221: 114-115, 259-260); Mroczkowski (58: 69-70); Palmer (65: 21, 26); Seltzer (80: 10, 11); Stewart (84: 107-110); Tanner (85: 25-26, 58-59); Watt (92: 310-311, 319).

108. Allen (103: 169-170); Boyle (6: 76-77); Daleski (13: 83-87, 94); Gekoski (22: 95-96); Guerard (30: 127); Bevan (111: 194-200); Kridl (221: 114-115, 259-260); Mroczkowski (58: 57-58, 62-64, 69-70); Schwarz (77: 87-88); Verleun (91: 50).

109. This idea is echoed in *Typhoon,* in the narrator's sententious comment: "These are the moments of do-nothing heroics to which even good men surrender at times" (TOS 51).

110. See, in particular, Bevan (111: 198); (Cook: 134); Mroczkowski (58: 88-90); Penn Warren (271: XXI-XXIII); Pettersson (67: 104-107); Schneider (279); Tarnawski (86: 84-87); Verleun (91: Evaluation in the Light of Eternity: Stein and Marlow); Watt (92: 322-331). Some other critics connect this tendency with the symbolism of butterflies and beetles, denoting, e.g., beauty, perfection, and lofty aspirations, as opposed to a dirty, earth minded existence: De Voren Hoffman (16: 82-89); Schneider (280: 47-50); Tanner (85: 40-42, 47-48, 52-56); Tanner (305); Verleun (91: Evaluation in the Light of Eternity: Stein and Marlow).

111. A reflection in *Well Done* and a confession in *Within the Tides* are in a similar, though more personal vein: "This is the common fate of mankind, whose most positive achievements are born from dreams and visions followed loyally to an unknown destination. (NLL 190; also WT Author's Note VII-VIII).

112. The image of Jim the idealist is a distinct allusion to the heroes of Polish Romantic literature–see Kridl (221: 251-267), or even an expression

of the Polish national spirit–see Knapp Hay (210). His attitude exerted considerable influence on the conduct of young Poles during World War II: see Młynarska (252); Szczepański (303); Zabierowski (345: 115-119); and Zabierowski (99: 32-36).

113. In *Heart of Darkness* Marlow similarly generalizes the truth about Kurtz.

114. Steinmann (299) points out the application of this method.

115. Batchelor (4: 88, 91-92); Berthoud (5: 75-78); Boyle (6: 69-70); Burgess (9: 60-61); Haugh (34: 58-66); Schneider (279: 431-432); Schneider (280: 47-49); Sherry (81: 47-48, 71-72, 75); Tanner (85: 21, 24, 41-42); Verleun (91: The Patna Perspectives). Mroczkowski (58: 55-56, 61-62, 69), on the other hand, asserts that this opposition magnifies Jim's responsibility and guilt.

116. Baines (2: 247-248); Batchelor (4: 88-90, 104-105); Boyle (6: 73-74); Gekoski (22: 100-101); Gillon (23: 126); Haugh (34: 66-67); Haugh (179: 138-139); Kowalska (47: 94-95); Land (51: 88-91); Ressler (70: 32-34); Ross (277: 50-51, 53, 60); Tarnawski (86: 83-84); Tucker (88: 22-24); Verleun (91: 33-44); Watt (92: 276-281, 285).

117. According to Berthoud (5: 85); Boyle (6: 71); Guerard (30: 160-161); Haugh (179: 139); Mroczkowski (58: 79-81); Ross (277: 50-51, 53, 60); Steinmann (299: 86-87); Tanner (305): 402-403); and Verleun (91: 58-62) this connection highlights the young seaman's excellence.

118. See, in particular, Bevan (111: 197-198); Kramer (220: 68); Pettersson (67: 106-107); and Steinmann (299: 87-89).

119. Verleun (91: 169-170) and Watt (92: 322) emphasize Stein's endorsement of Jim's attitude.

120. Fletcher (155: 20, 22-23); Karl (200); Malbone (234); Ressler (70: 36-38); and Steinmann (299: 87-89) interpret *Lord Jim* in terms of praise of "realistic" romanticism (personified, e.g., by Stein), as opposed and superior to the protagonist's extremism. An approval of this attitude is also conveyed in "Author's Note" to *Within the Tides:*

> the romantic feeling of reality was in me an inborn faculty. This in itself may be a curse but when disciplined by a sense of personal responsibility and a recognition of the hard facts of existence shared with the rest of mankind becomes but a point of view from which the very shadows of life appear endowed with an internal glow. And such romanticism is not a sin. It is none the worse for the knowledge of truth. It only tries to make the best of it, hard as it may be; and in this hardness discovers a certain aspect of beauty. (WT Author's Note VII-VIII)

121. Mroczkowski (58: 101-102, 109-110, 121, 128-129, 131); Nelson

(263: 54-55); Tanner (85: 47-48); Tanner (305: 403-404); Verleun (91: 112-127).

122. His decisive superiority over Brown is emphasized by Berthoud (5: 91-92); Burgess (9: 143-144); Kridl (221: 248); Mroczkowski (58: 116-126); Ross (277: 59-61); Steinmann (299: 90-92); Tanner (305: 404-407); and Verleun (91: 167-168).

123. Burgess (9: 144); Gillon (23: 146-147); Haugh (34: 74-75); Mroczkowski (58: 116-126).

124. Haugh (179: 138-139) and Verleun (91: 56) assert that comparisons of Jim to Bob Stanton and the French lieutenant do not imply clearly the main character's superiority or inferiority. Ross (277: 50-51, 53, 60) interprets both of them, and Boyle (6: 71-73) the second, in favor of the young visionary. On the other hand Guerard (30: 158-159); Ressler (70: 30-34); and Tanner (85: 35-36) argue that these confrontations imply his unpraisworthy image.

125. Beach (106: 359-364); Guerard (30: "Lord Jim," I-II); McCullough (242: 342-346); Schnackertz (75: 36-42); Watt (92: 286-304); and Watt (328: 20-31) elucidate this point.

126. See, especially, De Voren Hoffman (16: Burlesque, Parody, and Analogue in "Lord Jim": A Reading of the Novel); Hillis Miller (186); Hillis Miller (187); Najder (59: "Lord Jim"); Palmer (65: 33-37); Paris (268); Shires (289; Van Ghent (315: 237-243); and Watt (92: 269-304). Other critics claim that the multitude of opinions creates an equivocal image of the principal character; see, mostly, Guerard (30: "Lord Jim" I-II); Mroczkowski (58: "Lord Jim." A Novel of the Chase After Contrition); Palmer (65: 27); Ressler (70: "Lord Jim": Romantic Retreat); Roussel (73: 102-107); Ryf (74: 21-24); and Seltzer (286).

127. This thesis is also supported by Bellis (107); Dyboski (147: 880); Gekoski (22: "Lord Jim"); and Glassman (25: An Intelligible Picture. "Lord Jim"); Gossman, Whiting (174); Karrfalt (204); Kowalska (47: "Lord Jim"–próba poświadczenia własnej godności "poza szeregiem"), Pettersson (67: 101-109); Ross (277); Tarnawski (86: 69-87); Verleun (91); and Watt (92: 310-356).

128. These attempts seem to be additionally confrmed by the motto: "It is certain / my conviction gains infinitely / the moment another soul / will believe in it."

Notes: Part 2, Chapter 5

1. Lee (52).

2. Fleishman (19: Colonists and Conquerors).

3. Fleishman (19: 99-105); Lee (52: 18, 79, 90, 135-136).

4. In *The Rescue* Lingard's style of trading is followed by the natives of Wajo (particularly Hassim): they too treat it as "a romantic and an honourable occupation," demanding sagacity and courage, satisfying a desire for fascinating experiences (Re 67-68).

5. This atitude contrasts with skepticism, a crucial trait of Heyst's character (see Part 1, Chapter 2 on his self-inflicted estrangement). The Swede is prone both to apathy and involvement in others' affairs (V 77), which is evidenced by his help to Morrison and Lena. On his dual nature, see Daleski (141).

6. Grabowski (27: 43-44); Jabłkowska (38: 76, 179); Kettle (206: 64-65); Kocówna (45: Kolorowi i biali); Łann (232: 110-111). Achebe (101), and Singh (290) represent the opposite view: they claim Conrad's negative depiction of natives, colored by racial prejudice. An argument against this approach is given, e.g., by Hawkins (181).

7. Fleishman (19: 106-110); Lee (52: "One of Us"); and Prorok (68: 93-103) highlight the admirable features of Jim as colonizer.

8. This is stressed by Verleun (91: "The Inner Circle").

9. Lee (52: 75, 82, 86, 90-92) stresses the meritorious aspects of his performance.

10. The "Rajah-Laut" displays extraordinary credulity and benevolence (see *An Outcast of the Islands,* OI 13, 302; *The Rescue,* Re 10); he becomes the protector of many natives and whites: "in obedience to his benevolent instincts, [he] shaped stray lives he found here and there under his busy hand...had an inclination to set right the lives of other people...." (*An Outcast of the Islands,* OI 198-199). In *Almayer's Folly* he renders constant assistance to the protagonist and Mrs. Almayer (he saves her from death as a child, gives her a convent education, and arranges her marriage). In *An Outcast of the Islands* Lingard lends support to Willems (making him a clerk and trader, preventing him from committing suicide by sending him to Sambir), Joanna (he brings about her reconciliation with her husband, Willems), Aissa (he cares for her after her lover's death), and Jim–Eng. Lingard and Almayer intend to find gold: it is to be the material basis for the happy future of their favorite, Nina, when she goes to Amsterdam (*An Outcast of the Islands,* OI 193-194). And in *The Rescue,* the King of the Sea helps Hassim (by rescuing him from a siege and trying to enthrone him as the leader of the Wajo) and Jö rgenson (who, entrusted with temporary command of the *Emma,* gets a chance to regain self-respect).

11. Lee (52: 37, 85-86) portrays Morrison as commendable.

12. Fleishman (19: 84-85, 87-89, 99, 103-105) and Young (340) criticize the performance of Lingard as colonizer. This opinion is shared by Burgess (9: 146-151), Guerard (30: 69-70, 79), and Najder (59: 91-92), who claim that egoism and conceit underlie his apparent magnanimity. According to Gillon (23: 63-65), undertaking obligations to Edith Travers is the direct cause of his Waterloo. This fatal dependence is noticed by "Rajah-Laut's" friends, Immada (Re 234-235) and Jörgenson, who unsuccessfully try to change his conduct, and also by Lingard himself, when facing his downfall (450, 464-465). Mrs. Travers's role is reminiscent of the harmful impact of women on mariners (see Part 2, Chpater 4).

13. Boyle (6: 85-91); De Voren Hoffman (16: 115-118); Fodaski Black (156); Fraser (21: "'An Outpost of Progress' and 'The Secret Agent'"); Gillon (23: 104-106); Hilson, Timms (188); Kowalska (47: 16-18); Schwarz (77: 25-27); Wright (95: 131-134).

14. Fleishman (19: 82-85, 90-91); Goonetilleke (26: 53-56); Lee (52: 111-112); and Wright (95: 126-128) interpret his conduct in this way.

15. Watt (92: 65).

16. Karl (40: 100-106).

17. Cornelius's censurable traits are also emphasized by Marlow, who describes him as a repulsive figure–the mean, ignoble adversary of the high-minded Jim.

18. This story displays parallels with *Almayer's Folly:* e.g., Bamtz's and Almayer's inept commercial activities on inland outposts, and their patrons Davidson and Lingard.

19. Guerard (30: 80-81); Yelton (97: 223-224).

20. Fleishman (19: Colonists and Conquerors) and Knapp Hay (44: 138-139) indicate the loss of ties to civilization by the tropically isolated colonials in *Almayer's Folly, An Outpost of Progress,* and *Heart of Darkness* as the principal cause of their downfall.

21. Chwalewik (131: 434-435).

22. *The Congo Diary* presents a chronicle of some events of this voyage.

23. The Russian is the exception here. Yet, he is not an agent but rather an adventurer. His unselfishness results from youthful idealism and elation–Hawthorn (35: 193).

24. Marlow views the Central Station manager with obvious antipathy. He calls him "a flabby, pretending, weak-eyed devil of a rapacious and pitiless folly" (YNTOS 65), and emphasizes his mediocrity and lack of ability (73-74).

25. The whites' performance in Africa is characterized in *Geography and Some Explorers* as "the vilest scramble for loot that ever disfigured the

history of human conscience and geographical exploration" (LE 17).

26. Morf (56: 204-205); Watt (92: 222).

27. Hawthorn (35: "Heart of Darkness"); Mroczkowski (58: 21, 27-28, 32); and Watt (92: 218, 220-222, 224, 235-236) claim that this is one of the principal themes of this story.

28. Exploitation, mindless activity, and inhuman treatment of Negroes are given prominence in many critical studies of *Heart of Darkness:* see, especially, Brady (118); Chwalewik (131: 429, 432); Cox (12: 51-53); Dąbrowska (15: 117-119); De Voren Hoffman (16: 16-27, 42-45); Komar (46: 85-95); Kowalska (47: 46-49); Mroczkowski (58: 20-25); Nettels (60: 144-147); Parry (66: "Heart of Darkness"); Singh (290: 41-43); Watt (92: 218-223); and Watts (93: Marlow's Narrative, I-II).

29. Berthoud (5: 46-48).

30. On this category of metaphors, see Yousef (342: 25-27).

31. Fleishman (19: 106-107) and Lee (52: Kurtz's Infidelity to the "Idea" of the Burden in "Heart of Darkness") portray him as reprehensible.

32. His moral degeneration and absorption by wild nature are comprehensively discussed in the following studies: Baines (2: 225-230); Berthoud (5: 52-60); Broncel (119); Cox (12: 53-57); Daleski (13: 66-71); Dąbrowska (15: 119-120); Fleishman (19: 82, 89-91, 99); Gertzman (166); Gillon (23: 106-107); Guetti (176: 46-54); Jabłkowska (38: 94-97); Komar (46: 93-97); McLauchlan (247); Mroczkowski (58: 32-45); Najder (59: 118-122); Nettels (60: 204-207); Raval (69: 27-31); Watt (92: 163-168, 223-241); and Wright (95: Ingress to the "Heart of Darkness").

33. Kurtz is adored by the young Russian too. The adventurer is strongly impressed by his high-flown rhetoric, which he takes for truth: he feels that it broadens his mind. He discerns neither Kurtz's barbarity and cupidity nor idolatory. Nor does he notice the disparity between the other's professed ideals and actual performance. Instead, he is nearly as bewitched by Kurtz as the Africans (YNTOS 127-129, 132). Marlow's comment about the preeminent agent's ability to fascinate pimitive personalities includes the Russian, too–see Burgess (124: 192-193); Hawthorn (35: 192-194). It seems that such an attitude might be a reason for portraying the young adventurer as a harlequin. See extensive comments on this figure's function in Burgess (124); Helder (183); Verleun (318); Watts (93: 120-122); and Yoder (339).

34. The juxtaposition of Kurtz with the starving Negro crew members who refrain from attacking, killing, and eating the pilgrims, is particularly significant here.

35. Kurtz's symbolic picture of a blindfolded woman carrying a lighted torch in darkness expresses the same.

36. Dąbrowska (15: 123-124) and Raval (69: 34-36, 41) postulate extenuating circumstances in his case.

37. This deed is also motivated by a desire to preserve her subtle, idealized realm of illusions, love, goodness, and faith: see on such an attitude of Conradian heroines in Part 1, Chapter 2, Part 2, Chapter 4). Boyle (116); Bruffee (122); De Voren Hoffman (16: 27-35); Gertzman (166: 193-195); McLauchlan (247); Stewart (301: 326-330); Watt (92: 241-252); and Martin (238) present comprehensive remarks about this scene and the story teller's white lie.

38. Similar implications are conveyed by the ending of *An Outpost of Progress,* where the ship approaching Kayerts's and Carlier's station, bringing "Progress and civilization and all the virtues" is called an "exasperated and ruthless creature," and the society sending it a "rubbish heap" (TU 116).

39. The general significance of the actions of Kurtz and other whites in Africa is indicated by most of the critical comments concerning *Heart of Darkness,* and most comprehensively by Berthoud (5: 59-60); Brady (118); Chwalewik (133); Cook (135); Daleski (13: "Heart of Darkness"); De Voren Hoffman (16: 17-18, 49-51); Evans (153); Feder (154); Gertzman (166); Goonetilleke (26: 117-118); Guerard (30: 33-48); Hewitt (36: 17-27); Karl (203); Kisner (209: 90-93); Komar (46: Zegar moralności); Kowalska (47: "Jądro ciemności"–Noc piekielna [*Une Saison en Enfer*] Kurtza); McLauchlan (244); Mroczkowski (58: "Heart of Darkness". The Inmost Journey Retraced); Najder (59: 120-122); Peirce (270); Sherry (82: 340-345, 350); Stephens (300); Thale (308); Watt (92: 163-168, 189-196, 223-241); Watts (93); and Yarrison (337). Some other Conradians highlight the concrete historical aspect of the fictional world, i.e., as a reflection of Belgian policies in the Congo: Baun (105); Gray Willy (175); Hawkins (180); Jabłkowska (38: 82-94); Knapp Hay (44: 110-128); Watt (92: 135-168).

40. Chwalewik (131); Cook (135); Daleski (13: "Heart of Darkness"); De Voren Hoffman (16: 28-35, 45-51); Dowden (18: 71-84); Watts (93: Reflections on the Title); Yousef (342: 22-25).

41. See Lothe (54: 21-34) on this and other functions of the frame narration in *Heart of Darkness.*

42. Daleski (13: 52-53); Harkness (178); Kowalska (47: 45); Raval (69: 20-21); Ridley (273: 52); Stewart (84: 85).

43. These general ideas are in harmony with Marlow's attitude. He is the philosopher who assumes the lotus position to spin the yarn and meditate on it (YNTOS 50, 162).

44. Fleishman (19: 86, 97, 112-120, 125); Lee (52); Ostrowski (266: 280-281).

45. Their actions are censured in *Freya of the Seven Isles* (TLS 148-149, 154) and *The Rescue* (Re 75, 100-102) too.

46. Gillon (169: 47-48, 53); Gurko (32: 179-180); Gurko (33: 160); Morf (56: 217-218); and Mroczkowski (256: 178-179) point out their unfavorable depiction in his writings.

47. This issue is discussed mainly by Busza (128); Busza (129: 11-21); Fleishman (19: 15-20); Hodges (37: The Fatherland: "Prince Roman," the Polish Essays and "Lord Jim"); Jabłkowska (38: 284-295); Kocówna (45); Krzyżanowski (222); Leśnodorski (226); Morf (56: 95-96, 104-112, 225-233); Najder (59: 129-136); Retinger (71: 134-138, 168-174); Ujejski (89: Conrad i Polska); Zabierowski (98: 108-121); and Zeigler (347).

48. Blüth (114: 385-387); Dąbrowska (15: Na drodze uczynków); Hodges (37: 171, 196, 206-212); Howarth (191: 683-684, 695); Jabłkowska (38: 276-277); Knapp Hay (211); Morf (55: 180-186); Schwarz (78: 139-154); Schwarz (284: 164-168).

49. On his patriotism see Busza (129: 11-21) and Ressler (70: 138-140).

50. See the discussion of the elements of Polish literary and cultural tradition in *Prince Roman* in Busza (129).

51. Albeit this applies neither to *The Informer* nor to *The Inheritors*, which gives a satirical image of the British political scene (Churchill, Gurnard, and their factions).

52. On its depiction in *Romance* see Jabłkowska (38: 162-164).

53. Corresponding readings of this novel are offered by many critics who usually indicate elements of satire and irony in the presentation of nihilists, especially Baines (2: 334-336); Cooper (11: 27-36); Daleski (13: 157-164); Knapp Hay (44: "The Secret Agent"); Palmer (65: 104-121); Schrader (76: 92-98); and Stallman (294: 236-239).

54. Agitators appearing in other works are echoes of the characters in *The Secret Agent*. Donkin in *The Nigger of the "Narcissus"* instigates seamen to mutiny (see on him in Part 2, Chapter 6). After the voyage he gives up maritime toil and remains on land, living lazily and haranguing others about social injustice and workers' rights (NN 172). In Marlow's opinion Kurtz would be an excellent leader of an extreme party because of his persuasive voice and brilliant declamations (YNTOS 154).

55. Shadoian (287) examines the use of irony in the scene of Verloc's death. Such an attitude determines the depiction of many other characters as well. Examine, if you will, "a butcher boy, driving with the noble recklessness of a charioteer at Olympic Games" (SA 14); the cabman who resembles "Virgil's Silenus, who...discoursed of Olympian Gods to the innocent shepherds of Sicily" (166), and is the master of "the steed of apocalyptic misery"

(167), moving lean thighs "with ascetic deliberation," and "walking in stiff and forlorn dignity" (168); Winnie who "talked evenly at him [Verloc] the wifely talk, as artfully adapted, no doubt, to the circumstances of this return as the talk fo Penelope to the return of the wandering Odysseus" (183). "[having learnt about her brother's death, her] moral nature was subjected to a shock of which, in the physical order, the most violent earthquake of history could only be a faint and languid rendering" (255); Stevie, whose remains are compared to "an accumulation of raw material for a cannibal feast," "that heap of mixed things, which seemed to have been collected in shambles and rag shops," "the by-products of a butcher's shop" (86-88); policemen (84-85), and the representatives of the English upper class (214-217). That irony and its functions pervade *The Secret Agent* is indicated mostly by Gilmore (171); Fraser (21: "An Outpost of Progess" and "The Secret Agent"); Johnston (197: 57-65); Karl (40: 193-205); Karl (202); Knoepflmacher (212: 242-252); Lothe (54: "The Secret Agent": Ironic and Disillusioned Authorial Narrative); Najder (59: 144-145); Spector (293); Stewart (84: 175-179); and Tillyard (309).

56. The image of the street in which the Professor lives is in a similar vein (62). All pictures of the London setting accentuate ugliness. This accords with the nihilists' moral degeneratin and the misery of the inhabitants of the metropolis (on urban isolation in *The Secret Agent* see Part 1, Chapter 1). Cox (12: 92-96); Dowden (18: 112-123); Fleishman (19: 204-205); Morley (254: 60-62); Yaseen (96: 100); Yelton (97: 184-190).

57. On the Professor's ideology of nihilism see Raval (69: 113-121).

58. This attitude is emphasized by the majority of critical works, in particular Cooper (11: 20-26); Daleski (13: 164-170); Marsh (235: 60-63); and Palmer (65: 104-105, 109-111, 115-117).

59. *The Secret Agent* is a crime novel as well–see Ostrowski (267), Walton (324: 455-462). This is also clear in the shaping of both characters (offenders against and guardians of order) and events (the bomb bursting and killing its carrier, the investigation of the causes of this accident, the murder of Verloc, Winnie's tragic suicide). This creates permanent, occasionally strong, suspense (especially the final sections of chapters 7 and 9, which communicate facts directly preceding the shop owner's death). This genre convention is strengthened by the professional competition between the investigating policemen: each of them tries to authenticate the version of the story that suits his own aims.

60. This novel is interpreted by some critics as a symbolic vision of England's internal crisis and the moral nihilism of its people. See, in particular, Daleski (13: 153-157); Fleishman (19: The Symbolic World of

"The Secret Agent"); Fradin (160); Gose (173); Karl (202); and Schwarz (77: Language as Value in "The Secret Agent"); or of universal absurdity and the hopelessness of human existence–Morley (254).

61. Bross (120: 32-38).

62. Fleishman (19: 137-138).

63. Harry Gee's fondness for excessive advertising is commented on sarcastically. On his behavior see Fleishman (19: 138-140).

64. Knapp Hay (44: 269-276); Komar (46: Razumow, czyli krąg ostatni).

65. The later Conrad is interested in the psychology of women and the nature of the relations between the sexes. Evidence for this is in Peter Ivanovitch's frame of mind, in Sophia Antonovna's coquettishness, and in the puns she uses in her coversations with Razumov.

66. Dowden (18: 128-129) points out the application of this method.

67. Guerard (30: 243-246).

68. Berthoud (5: 169-185); Goodin (172); Hagan (177); Knapp Hay (44: "Under Western Eyes"); and Komar (46: 160-168), in particular emphasize the tragic aspect of his lot, and Karl (201) asserts that his biography, and not political problems, is central to the novel.

69. The narrative of Razumov's life story is permeated by suspense. This transforms *Under Western Eyes* into a crime novel. It initially pertains to Haldin's outrage and whether he will be caught. Later it is connected with the part played by the envoy in Geneva and the constant danger of his being unmasked. This danger is imminent in many of his comments, which border on self-denunciation. He also runs great risks in his talks with Sophia Antonovna, who is perceptive enough to see through him, e.g., UWE 227-229, 259-261.

70. The condemnation of absoltue monarchy in *Under Western Eyes* is viewed in such perspective by Berthoud (5: "Under Western Eyes"); Busza (127); Crankshaw (137: 95-98); Fleishman (19: 221-226); Gurko (32: The Russian Colossus); Gurko (33: 164-165); Knapp Hay (44: "Under Western Eyes"); Kołaczkowski (215: 235-236), Komar (46: Razumow, czyli krąg ostatni); Schleifer (278); Stewart (84: 185-194); and Tarnawski (86: 165-171). This tendency appears in *Autocracy and War* as well.

71. Many Conradians, particulary Schleifer (278), point out his role in distancing the implied reader from Russian reality.

72. The transports of idealism, so differently embodied by Razumov, Victor, and Nathalie, are represented by Spontini's sculpture "Flight of Youth." Gillon (170: 256-257) highlights the ironical effect of its juxtaposition with the principal character's plight.

73. Nathalie's views are criticized by Berthoud (5: 162-163), and

praised by Fleishman (19: 239-241).

74. This tendency is discussed in particular by Baines (2: 423-424); Hodges (37: 210-211); Howarth (191: 683-687); Laine (224); and Schwarz (78: 143-144).

75. Braun (7: 161-164, 186-219, 276-279); Fleishman (19: 167-171); Jabłkowska (38: 230-237); Mursia (258); Oliva, Portelli (62: 106-108); Sherry (82: 171-201); and Spatt (292) establish its approximate situation.

76. Bevan (110); Dąbrowska (15: 96-100, 107-110); Guerard (30: 189-199); and Hewitt (36: 132-136) highlight this aspect of ideas.

77. Berthoud (5: 95); Nettels (60: 153-154).

78. On unflattering delineation of Guzman Bento's rule see Curreli (140: 161-166).

79. Nettels (60: 153-156); Van Ghent (316: 55-57).

80. Orr (265: 117-122) views this mountain symbolically–as an ironic chorus on insignificant human activity.

81. Dąbrowska (15: 98); Guerard (30: 186-187); Nettels (60: 153-156); Verleun (90: The Monterists).

82. Their performance resembles that of Conradian colonizers striving to civilize conquered areas (see Part 2, Chapter 5). In this novel, however, the concern is with a community at a much higher level of socioeconomic development. Such performance acquires the primarily political significance of resistance to the tradition of uprisings and dictatorship.

83. Lee (52: 83-84, 104-105).

84. Penn Warren (271: XII-XIII).

85. Cooper (11: 116-123) stresses Decoud's less admirable traits.

86. Guerard (30: 187-189) describes the ambiguity of his portrayal.

87. Berthoud (5: 102-106); Lee (52: 83-84, 104-105); and Van Ghent (316) stress the virtuous aspects of Gould's conduct. Others, especially Baines (2: 304-309) and Dąbrowska (15: 105-107), emphasize the moral ambivalence of his image.

88. See the analysis of the characters of *Nostromo* from this point of view in Marten (237). Similar reflections appear in *Autocracy and War:* "it is the bitter fate of any idea to lose its royal form and power, to lose its 'virtue' the moment it descends from its solitary throne to work its will among the people. It is a king whose destiny is never to know the obedience of his subjects except at the cost of degradation" (NLL 86).

89. Berthoud (5: 113-115, 124); Jabłkowska (38: 167-168, 242); and Pawłow (269: 254-257) emphasize this trait, as well as parallels between Capataz de Cargadores and Manuel-del-Popolo in *Romance* (Rom 410-411).

90. This development of the action is foreshadowed by the title character's

possessions and the accessories of his dress. He has, for example, a decorative braid on his sombrero, buttons on his jacket and down the seams of his pants, ornaments on bridle and saddle, mare, whistle, ring, and key. These are his predilections for silver. See Dowden (18: 95-97).

91. Most publications point out the importance of this episode in anticipating the eventual fate of both protagonists. According to Van Ghent (317), the silver poses a test of character for the main figures in the novel (Nostromo, Gould, Monygham, Decoud), which they fail to pass. The key motif reveberates in the images of nature that form the setting of the final events: "the moonlight in the offing, closed as if with a colossal bar of silver the entrance of the Placid Gulf" (N 552); "the bright light of the horizon [was] overhung by a big white cloud shining like a mass of solid silver" (566).

92. The destructive role played by the silver and the material interests in the moral degeneration of individuals is emphasized by almost all Conradians, especially Berthoud (5: "Nostromo"); Billy (112); Boyle (6: 157-168); Cooper (11: "Nostromo"); Cox (12: 69-74); Dąbrowska (15: Prawdziwa rzeczywistość Conrada); Gekoski (22: "Nostromo"); Gillon (23: 150-152); Goonetilleke (26: Conrad's "Nostromo"); Hawthorn (35: Adventurers and Fairy Tales); Kettle (206); King (207); Knapp Hay (44: "Nostromo"); Nettels (60: 226-232); Parry (66: "Nostromo"); Raval (69: 74-79, 83-90, 92-97); Ressler (70: "Nostromo": Versions of Failure); Rivera (274); Roussel (73: "Nostromo": The Ironic Vision); Wiley (94: 98-106); and Yelton (97: 177-181); Fleishman (19: "Nostromo": Class Struggle as Tragedy); Kettle (206); and Pawłow (269) interpret the novel as a condemnation of capitalism from a Marxist point of view.

93. On the relationship of characters to historical processes depicted in this novel, see Roberts (275).

94. The narrator's reflections in *The Tale* (TH 67) are in a similar vein.

95. See Martin (239). Such a delineation of the protagonist justifies adding the subtitle "A Romantic Tale" to *Gaspar Ruiz*.

96. On his noble conduct see Kowalska (218: 3-4) and Schwarz (78: 98-101).

Notes: Conclusion

1. Darras (14: 3, 61-62); Gillon (23: 84); Jabłkowska (38: 71-75, 85-86); Kettle (206: 64-65); Lee (52: 18-19); Łann (232: 110-111); Ostrowski (266: 277); Watt (92: 157-159).

2. On the differences between the outlooks in the two author's canons, see Follett (20); Hoare (189: 131-132); Jabłkowska (38: 303-304, 309-310);

and Knoepflmacher (212: 241, 271).

3. Gillon (23: 158-159, 176); Najder (262: 25-27).

4. Baines (2: 443); Erné (151); Gillon (23: 58, 160, 176); Gillon (24: 154-155); Stavrou (297: 82).

5. Erné (151); Gawliński (164); Gillon (23: 159-160, 174-176); Jabłkowska (38: 227); Kulshrestha (223); Watt (92: 32).

6. In Watt's opinion (327: 154) this conviction distinguishes Conrad from many eminent contemporary writers and constitutes a major reason for the wide popularity of his novels and short stories.

7. Gillon (23: 102-103, 112-117); Kowalska (48: 75-76); Ryf (74: 43); and Urbisz (312: 301-302) highlight their achievement.

8. See Gillon (23: especially 111-118) who, however, presents conclusions different from mine.

9. This tabulation disregards many characters either episodic or insignificant in terms of the relation between isolation and ethos.

Bibliography of Critical Works*

BOOKS

1. Allen, J. *The Sea Years of Joseph Conrad.* London: Methuen and Co. Ltd., 1967 (1965).

2. Baines, J. *Joseph Conrad: A Critical Biography.* London: Weidenfeld and Nicolson, 1960 (1960).

3. Bancroft, W. W. *Joseph Conrad: His Philosophy of Life.* Boston: The Stratford Company Publishers, 1933.

4. Batchelor, J. *Lord Jim.* Unwin Critical Library, London: Unwin Hyman, 1988.

5. Berthoud, J. *Joseph Conrad: The Major Phase.* British Authors. Introductory Critical Studies, Cambridge: Cambridge University Press, 1978.

6. Boyle, T. E. *Symbol and Meaning in the Fiction of Joseph Conrad.* Studies in English Literature VI, The Hague: Mouton, 1965.

7. Braun, A. *Kreacja Costaguany. Świat południowoamerykański u Conrada.* Warszawa: "Czytelnik," 1989.

8. Bruss, P. *Conrad's Early Sea Fiction. The Novelist as Navigator.* Lewisburg, 1979.

9. Burgess, C. F. *The Fellowship of the Craft. Conrad on Ships and Seamen and the Sea.* Port Washington, N.Y.: Kennikat Press, 1976.

10. Burkhardt, J. *Das Erlebnis der Wirklichkeit und seine künstlerische Gestaltung in Joseph Conrads Werk.* Marburg: privately published, 1935.

11. Cooper, C. *Conrad and the Human Dilemma.* London: Chatto and Windus Ltd., 1970.

12. Cox, C. B. *Joseph Conrad: The Modern Imagination.* London: J. M. Dent and Sons Ltd., 1974.

---

* In the bibliography the following abbreviations of titles of periodicals are used: C–"Conradiana"; LEC–"L'Epoque Conradienne"; MFS–"Modern Fiction Studies"; NCF–"Nineteenth Century Fiction"; SSF–"Studies in Short Fiction"; TC–"The Conradian."

13. Daleski, H. M. *Joseph Conrad. The Way of Dispossession*. New York: Holmes and Meier Publishers, 1977.

14. Darras, J. *Joseph Conrad and the West. Signs of Empire*. trans. from French A. Luyat, J. Darras, London: The MacMillan Press Ltd., 1982.

15. Dąbrowska, M. *Szkice o Conradzie*. Warszawa: "Czytelnik," 1974 (1959).

16. De Voren Hoffman, S. *Comedy and Form in the Fiction of Joseph Conrad*. Studies in English Literature, vol. 49, The Hague: Mouton, 1969.

17. Dobrzycka, I. *Kształtowanie się twórczości Byrona. Bohater bajroniczny a zagadnienie narodowe*. Wrocław: Zakład Narodowy im. Ossolińskich. Polska Akademia Nauk, Komitet Neofilologiczny, 1963.

18. Dowden, W. S. *Joseph Conrad: The Imaged Style*. Nashville: Vanderbilt University Press, 1970.

19. Fleishman, A. *Conrad's Politics. Community and Anarchy in the Fiction of Joseph Conrad*. Baltimore: The Johns Hopkins Press, 1967.

20. Follett, W. *Joseph Conrad. A Short Study of His Intellectual and Emotional Attitude Toward His Work and of the Chief Characteristics of His Novels*. Garden City, N.Y.: Doubleday, Page and Co., 1966.

21. Fraser, G. *Interweaving Patterns in the Works of Joseph Conrad*. Studies in Modern Literature, no. 81, Ann Arbor: UMI Research Press, 1988.

22. Gekoski, R. A. *Conrad: The Moral World of the Novelist*. New York, 1978.

23. Gillon, A. *The Eternal Solitary. A Study of Joseph Conrad*. New York: Bookman Associates, Inc., 1960.

24. Gillon, A. *Conrad and Shakespeare and Other Essays*. New York: Astra Books. Twayne Publishers, 1976.

25. Glassman, P. J. *Language and Being. Joseph Conrad and the Literature of Personality*. New York: Columbia University Press, 1976.

26. Goonetilleke, D. C. R. A. *Developing Countries in British Fiction*. London: The MacMillan Press Ltd., 1977.

27. Grabowski, Z. *Ze studiów nad Josephem Conradem*. Poznań: Skład główny: Księgarnia Gebethnera i Wolffa, 1927.

28. Graver, L. *Conrad's Short Fiction*. Berkeley: University of California Press, 1969.

29. Guerard, A. J. *Joseph Conrad*. New York: New Directions, 1947.

30. Guerard, A. J. *Conrad. The Novelist*. Cambridge, Mass.: Harvard University Press, 1958.

31. Guetti, J. L. *The Rhetoric of Joseph Conrad*. Amherst: Amherst College Press, 1960.

32. Gurko, L. *Joseph Conrad: Giant in Exile*. New York: The MacMillan Co., 1962.

33. Gurko, L. *The Two Lives of Joseph Conrad*. New York: Thomas Y. Crowell Co., 1965.

34. Haugh, R. F. *Joseph Conrad. Discovery in Design*. Norman: University of Oklahoma Press, 1957.

35. Hawthorn, J. *Joseph Conrad. Narrative Technique and Ideological Commitment*. London: E. Arnold, 1990.

36. Hewitt, D. *Conrad. A Reassessment* (With a New Conclusion). London: Bowes and Bowes, 1975 (1952).

37. Hodges, R. R. *The Dual Heritage of Joseph Conrad*. Studies in English Literature, vol. 29, The Hague: Mouton, 1967.

38. Jabłkowska, R. *Joseph Conrad. 1857-1924*. Wrocław: Zakład Narodowy im. Ossolińskich. Polska Akademia Nauk, Komitet Neofilologiczny, 1961.

39. Johnson, B. *Conrad's Models of Mind*. Minneapolis: University of Minnesota Press, 1971.

40. Karl, F. R. *A Reader's Guide to Joseph Conrad*. New York: Farrar, Straus and Giroux, 1969 (1960).

41. Karl, F. R. *Joseph Conrad: The Three Lives. A Biography*. London: Faber and Faber, 1979.

42. Karwacki, R. *Temat morski. O prozie fabularnej dwudziestolecia międzywojennego*. Gdańsk: Wydawnictwo Morskie, 1975.

43. Kirschner, P. *Conrad: The Psychologist as Artist*. Biography and Criticism, Edinbourgh, 1968.

44. Knapp Hay, E. *The Political Novels of Joseph Conrad. A Critical Study*. Chicago: The University of Chicago Press, 1963.

45. Kocówna, B. *Polskość Conrada*. Warszawa: Ludowa Spółdzielnia Wydawnicza, 1967.

46. Komar, M. *Piekło Conrada*. Warszawa: "Czytelnik," 1978.

47. Kowalska A. *Conrad 1896-1900. Strategia wrażeń i refleksji w narracjach Marlowa*. Łódź: Zakład Narodowy im. Ossolińskich. Łódzkie Towarzystwo Naukowe, 1973.

48. Kowalska, A. *Conrad i Gombrowicz w walce o swoją wybitność*. Warszawa: Państwowy Instytut Wydawniczy, 1986.

49. Krajka, W. *Izolacja i etos. Studium o twórczości Josepha Conrada*. Wrocław: Zakład Narodowy im. Ossolińskich. Polska Akademia Nauk. Komitet Neofilologiczny, 1988.

49a. Krajka, W. *Kształty izolacji i etosu Conradowskich bohaterów*. Lublin: Uniwersytet Marii Curie-Skłodowskej, 1981–the earlier version of (49) Krajka.

50. Krajka, W. Zgorzelski, A. *On the Analysis of the Literary Text*. trans.

from Polish A. Blaim, Warszawa: Państwowe Wydawnictwo Naukowe, 1984.

51. Land, S. K. *Paradox and Polarity in the Fiction of Joseph Conrad.* New York: St. Martin' Press, 1984.

52. Lee, R. F. *Conrad's Colonialism.* Studies in English Literature, vol. 54, The Hague: Mouton, 1969.

53. Liljegren, S. B. *Joseph Conrad as a "Prober of Feminine Hearts". Notes on the Novel "The Rescue."* Essays and Studies on English Language and Literature, vol. 27, Uppsala, 1968.

54. Lothe, J. *Conrad's Narrative Method.* Oxford: Clarendon Press, 1989.

55. Morf, G. *The Polish Heritage of Joseph Conrad.* London: Sampson Low, Marston, 1930.

56. Morf, G. *The Polish Shades and Ghosts of Joseph Conrad.* New York: Astra Books, 1976.

57. Moser, T. *Joseph Conrad: Achievement and Decline.* Cambridge, Mass.: Harvard University Press, 1957.

58. Mroczkowski, P. *Conradian Commentaries.* Kraków: Jagellonian University, 1970.

59. Najder, Z. *Nad Conradem.* Warszawa. Państwowy Instytut Wydawniczy, 1965.

60. Nettels, E. *James and Conrad.* Athens, Georgia: The University of Georgia Press, 1971.

61. Newhouse, N. H. *Joseph Conrad.* ARCO Literary Critiques, New York: ARCO Publishing Co. Inc., 1969 (1966).

62. Oliva, R., Portelli, A. *Conrad. L'Imperialismo imperfetto.* Torino, 1973.

63. Osborn, A. *Joseph Conrad. A Study in Non-conformity.* London: Vision Press Ltd., 1962 (1959).

64. Ossowska, M. *Ethos rycerski i jego odmiany.* Warszawa: Państwowe Wydawnictwo Naukowe, 1973.

65. Palmer, J. A. *Joseph Conrad's Fiction. A Study in Literary Growth.* Ithaca, N. Y., 1968.

66. Parry, B. *Conrad and Imperialism. Ideological Boundaries and Visionary Frontiers.* London: The MacMillan Press Ltd., 1983.

67. Pettersson, T. *Consciousness and Time: A Study in the Philosophy and Narrative Technique of Joseph Conrad.* Äno: Äbo Akademi, 1982.

68. Prorok, L. *Inicjacje Conradowskie.* Kraków: Społeczny Instytut Wydawniczy "Znak," 1987.

69. Raval, S. *The Art of Failure: Conrad's Fiction.* Boston: Allen and Unwin, 1986.

70. Ressler, S. *Joseph Conrad: Consciousness and Integrity.* New York: New York University Press, 1988.

71. Retinger, J. H. *Conrad and His Contemporaries.* New York: Roy, 1943.

72. Rosenfield, C. *Paradise of Snakes. An Archetypal Analysis of Conrad's Political Novels.* Chicago: University of Chicago Press, 1967.

73. Roussel, R. *The Metaphysics of Darkness. A Study in the Unity and Development of Conrad's Fiction.* Baltimore: The Johns Hopkins Press, 1971.

74. Ryf, R. S. *Joseph Conrad.* New York, 1970.

75. Schnackertz, H. J. *Joseph Conrad. "Lord Jim,"* Muñchen: Wilhelm Fink Verlag, 1984.

76. Schrader, H. H. *Person und Wirklichkeit in Joseph Conrads politischen Romanen. Unter besonderer Berücksichtigung von "The Secret Agent."* Hamburg: Hamburg University, 1969.

77. Schwarz, D. R. *Conrad: "Almayer's Folly" to "Under Western Eyes."* Ithaca, N. Y.: Cornell University Press, 1980.

78. Schwarz, D. R. *Conrad: The Later Fiction.* London: The MacMillan Press Ltd., 1982.

79. Secor, R. *The Rhetoric of Shifting Perspectives: Conrad's "Victory."* University Park, Penn.: Pennsylvania State University, 1971.

80. Seltzer, L. *The Vision of Melville and Conrad. A Comparative Study.* Athens, Ohio, 1970.

81. Sherry, N. *Conrad's Eastern World.* Cambridge: Cambridge University Press, 1966.

82. Sherry, N. *Conrad's Western World.* Cambridge: Cambridge University Press, 1971.

83. Spoerri-Müller, R. *Joseph Conrad. Das Problem der Vereinsamung.* Winterthur: Verlag P. G. Keller, 1959.

84. Stewart, J. I. M. *Joseph Conrad.* Harlow: Longmans and Co. Ltd., 1968.

85. Tanner, T. *Conrad: "Lord Jim."* London: Edward Arnold Publishers Ltd., 1975 (1963).

86. Tarnawski, W. *Conrad the Man, the Writer, the Pole. An Essay in Psychological Biography.* trans. from Polish R. Batchelor, London: Polish Cultural Foundation, 1984.

87. Thorslev, P. L. *The Byronic Hero. Types and Prototypes.* Minneapolis: University of Minnesota Press, 1962.

88. Tucker, M. *Joseph Conrad.* New York, 1976.

89. Ujejski, J. *O Konradzie Korzeniowskim.* Warszawa: Dom Książki

Polskiej Sp. Akc., 1936 (trans. from Polish P. Duméril–Ujejski, J. *Joseph Conrad*. Collection Polonaise, Paris: Editions Edgar Malfère, 1939).

90. Verleun, J. *The Stone Horse. A Study of the Function of the Minor Characters in Joseph Conrad's "Nostromo."* Groningen, 1978.

91. Verleun, J. *Patna and Patusan Perspectives. A Study of the Function of the Minor Characters in Joseph Conrad's "Lord Jim."* Groningen: Bouma's Boekhuis B.V., 1979.

92. Watt, I. *Conrad in the Nineteenth Century*. London: Chatto and Windus Ltd., 1980.

93. Watts, C. *Conrad's "Heart of Darkness." A Critical and Contextual Discussion*. Milano: Mursia, 1977.

94. Wiley, P. L. *Conrad's Measure of Man*. Madison: University of Wisconsin Press, 1954.

95. Wright, W. F. *Romance and Tragedy in Joseph Conrad*. Lincoln: University of Nebraska Press, 1949.

96. Yaseen, M. *Joseph Conrad's Theory of Fiction*. Aligarh, 1967.

97. Yelton, D. C. *Mimesis and Metaphor. An Inquiry into the Genesis and Scope of Conrad's Symbolic Imagery*. Studies in English Literature, vol. 39, The Hague: Mouton, 1967.

98. Zabierowski, S. *Conrad w Polsce. Wybrane problemy recepcji krytycznej w latach 1896-1969*. Gdańsk: Wydawnictwo Morskie, 1971.

99. Zabierowski, S. *Conrad w perspektywie odbioru. Szkice*. Gdańsk: Wydawnictwo Morskie, 1979.

100. Zgorzelski, A. *O nowelach Conrada. Interpretacje*. Gdańsk: Wydawnictwo Morskie, 1984.

Articles and Essays

101. Achebe, C. "An Image of Africa," *Massachusetts Review* (1977 (1974/75), vol. 18, no. 4, pp. 782-794.

102. Adams, B. B. "Sisters Under Their Skins: The Women in the Lives of Raskolnikov and Razumov," *C* 1974, vol. 6, no. 2, pp. 113-124.

103. Allen, W. "Joseph Conrad," *Six Great Novelists (Defoe, Fielding, Scott, Dickens, Stevenson, Conrad)*, London: H. Hamilton, 1962 (1955), pp. 154-182.

104. Baines, J. "Joseph Conrad–Raw Material Into Art," *Joseph Conrad Korzeniowski. Essays and Studies (Studia i szkice)*, Warszawa: Państwowe Wydawnictwo Naukowe, 1958, pp. 11-18.

105. Baum, J. "The 'Real' 'Heart of Darkness'," *C* 1975, vol. 7, no. 2, pp. 183-187.

106. Beach, J. W. "Impressionism: Conrad," *The Twentieth Century Novelists. Studies in Technique*, New York: Appleton-Century, 1932, pp. 337-365.

107. Bellis, G. "Fidelity to a Higher Ideal. A Study of the Jump in Conrad's 'Lord Jim'," *Erasmus Review* 1971, vol. 1, no. 1, pp. 63-71.

108. Benson, C. "Conrad's Two Stories of Initiation," *PMLA* 1954, vol. 69, no. 1, pp. 46-56.

109. Berman, J., Van Wagenen, D. "'Under Western Eyes': Conrad's Diary of a Writer?" *C* 1977, vol. 9, no. 3, pp. 269-274.

110. Bevan, E. "'Nostromo': The Permanence of the Past," *C* 1978, vol. 10, no. 1, pp. 63-71.

111. Bevan, E. "Marlow and Jim: The Reconstructed Past," *C* 1983, vol. 15, no. 3, pp. 191-202.

112. Billy, T. "A Curious Case of Influence: 'Nostromo' and 'Alien(s)'," *C* 1989, vol. 21, no. 2, pp. 147-157.

113. Birdseye, L. E. "The Curse of Consciousness: A Study of Conrad's 'The Return'," *C* 1977, vol. 9, no. 2, pp. 171-178.

114. Blüth, R. M. "O tragicznej decyzji krakowskiej Konrada Korzeniowskiego (Parę myśli i uwag w związku z książką profesora Ujejskiego 'O Konradzie Korzeniowskim')," (1936), *Wspomnienia i studia o Conradzie*, ed. B. Kocówna, Warszawa: Państwowy Instytut Wydawniczy, 1963, pp. 379-405.

115. Borowy, W. "'Szaleństwo Almayera' (Czy tragedia małości?)," (1947), in cf. 114, pp. 406-413.

116. Boyle, T. E. "Marlow's 'Lie' in 'Heart of Darkness'," *SSF* 1964, vol. 1, no. 2, pp. 159-163.

117. Bradbrook, M. C. "Conrad and the Tragic Imagination," cf. 104, pp. 7-10.

118. Brady, M. C. "Conrad's Whited Sepulcher," *College English* 1982, vol. 24, no. 1, pp. 24-29.

119. Broncel, Z. "Pokusa nadczłowieka," *Conrad Żywy*, ed. W. Tarnawski, Londyn: B. Świderski, 1957, pp. 159-168.

120. Bross, A. C. "'A Set of Six': Variations on a Theme," *C* 1975, vol. 7, no. 1, pp. 27-44.

121. Brown, P. L. "'The Secret Sharer' and the Existential Hero," *C* 1971/72, vol. 3, no. 3, pp. 22-30.

122. Bruffee, K. A. "The Lesser Nightmare: Marlow's Lie in 'Heart of Darkness'," *Modern Language Quarterly* 1964, vol. 25, no. 3, pp. 322-329.

123. Bruss, P. S. "'Typhoon': The Initiation of Jukes," *C* 1973, vol. 5, no. 2, pp. 46-55.

124. Burgess, C. F. "Conrad's Pesky Russian," *NCF* 1963, vol. 18, no. 2, pp. 189-193.

125. Burgess, C. F. "Conrad's Catholicism," *C* 1983, vol. 15, no. 2, pp. 111-126.

126. Burzyńska, J. "Symbol i uogólnienie w 'Korsarzu' Josepha Conrada," *Studia Conradowskie*. Prace Naukowe Uniwersytetu Śląskiego no. 136, Katowice 1976, pp. 131-150.

127. Busza, A. "Rhetoric and Ideology in Conrad's 'Under Western Eyes'," *Joseph Conrad. A Commemoration*. Papers from the 1974 International Conference on Conrad, ed. N. Sherry, London: The MacMillan Press Ltd., 1976, pp. 105-118.

128. Busza, A. "The Rhetoric of Conrad's Non-fictional Political Discourse," *Annales de la Faculté des Lettres et Sciences humaines de Nice* 1978, no. 34, pp. 159-170.

129. Busza, A. "St. Flaubert and Prince Roman," *LEC* 1980, pp. 1-23.

130. Carter, E. "Classical Allusion as the Clue to Meaning in Conrad's 'Il Conde'," *C* 1971/72, vol. 3, no. 2, pp. 55-62.

131. Chwalewik, W. "O głównym motywie wczesnej twórczości Conrada." (1959), in cf. 114, pp. 427-438.

132. Chwalewik, W. "Conrad a tradycja literacka," in cf. 114, pp. 439-456.

133. Chwalewik, W. "A Note on the Play of Poetical Allusion in 'Heart of Darkness'," *Joseph Conrad Conference in Poland*. 5-12 September 1972. Contributions. Second Series, ed. R. Jabłkowska, Wrocław: Zakład Narodowy im. Ossolińskich, Polska Akademia Nauk, Komitet Neofilologiczny, 1979, pp. 25-33.

134. Cook, W. J. "'Lord Jim' as Metaphor," *C* 1969, vol. 1, no. 2, pp. 45-54.

135. Cook, W. J. "More Light on 'Heart of Darkness'," *C* 1971/72, vol. 3, no. 3, pp. 4-14.

136. Craig, R. "Swapping Yarns: The Oral Mode of 'Lord Jim'," *C* 1981, vol. 13, no. 3, pp. 181-193.

137. Crankshaw, E. "Conrad and Russia," in cf. 127, pp. 91-104.

138. Curley, D. "Legate of the Ideal," (1962) *Conrad. A Collection of Critical Essays*. A Spectrum Book, ed. M. Mudrick, Englewood Cliffs, N. J.: Prentice-Hall, 1966, pp. 75-82.

139. Curley, D. "The Writer and His Use of Material: The Case of 'The Secret Sharer'," *MFS* 1967, vol. 13, no. 2, pp. 179-194.

140. Curreli, M.. "Aspetti della Tecnica Narrativa nel 'Nostromo' di Conrad," *Studi dell' Istituto Linguistico* 1979, no. 2, Facoltà di Economia e

Commercio, Universitá degli Studi di Firenze, pp. 153-185.

141. Daleski, H. M. "'Victory' and Patterns of Self-Division," *Conrad Revisited: Essays for the Eighties*, ed. R. C. Murfin, Alabama: University of Alabama Press, 1985, pp. 107-123.

142. Davidson, A. E. "The Abdication of Lord Jim," *C* 1981, vol. 13, no. 1, pp. 19-34.

143. D'Hangest, G. "Sense of Life and Narrative Technique in Conrad's 'Lord Jim'," *Studies in Joseph Conrad.* Cahiers d'Etudes et de Recherches Victoriennes et Edouardiennes, ed. C. Thomas, no. 2, Montpellier: Université Paul-Valéry, 1975, pp. 129-160.

144. Dilworth, T.R. "Conrad's Secret Sharer at the Gate of Hell," *C* 1977, vol. 9, no. 3, pp. 203-217.

145. Drew, E. "Joseph Conrad," *The Modern Novel. Some Aspects of Contemporary Fiction*, Washington: Kennikat Press, 1967 (1926), pp. 221-240.

146. Dussinger, G. R. "'The Secret Sharer': Conrad's Psychological Study," *Texas Studies in Literature and Language* 1969, vol. 10, no. 4, pp. 599-608.

147. Dyboski, R. "Joseph Conrad (1857-1924)," *Sto lat literatury angielskiej*, Warszawa: "PAX," 1957, pp. 853-902.

148. Echeruo, M. J. C. "Conrad's Nigger," *The Conditioned Imagination from Shakespeare to Conrad. Studies in the Exo-cultural Stereotype*, London: The MacMillan Press, 1978, pp. 93-112.

149. Eggenschwiler, D. "Narcissus in 'The Secret Sharer': A Secondary Point of View," *C* 1979, vol. 11, no. 1, pp. 23-40.

150. Erdinast-Vulcan, D. "'A Smile of Fortune' and the Romantic Paradox," *TC* 1990, vol. 15, no. 1, pp. 1-11.

151. Erné, N. "Joseph Conrad i proza męskiej samotności,, (1948), trans. Z. Fonferko, in *Conrad w oczach krytyki światowej*, ed. Z. Najder, Warszawa: Państwowy Instytut Wydawniczy, 1974, pp. 365-384.

152. Evans, F. B. "The Nautical Metaphor in 'The Secret Sharer'," *C* 1975, vol. 7, no. 1, pp. 3-16.

153. Evans, R. O. "Conrad's Underworld" (1956), *The Art of Joseph Conrad. A Critical Symposium* (1960), ed. R. W. Stallman, Ann Arbor, 1965, pp. 171-178.

154. Feder, L. "Marlow's Descent into Hell" (1955), in cf. 153, pp. 162-170.

155. Fletcher, J. V. "Ethical Symbolism in Conrad," *College English* 1940, vol. 2, no. 1, pp. 19-26.

156. Fodaski Black, M. "Irony in Joseph Conrad's 'An Outpost of Progress',"

TC 1985, vol. 10, no. 2, pp. 132-134.

157. Folejewski, E. "'U kresu sił' (Ze studiów nad techniką atystyczną Conrada)," *Roczniki Humanistyczne* (1957 (1959), vol. 6, no. 6, pp. 127-135.

158. Follett, H. T., Follett, W. "Joseph Conrad," *Some Modern Novelists. Appreciations and Estimates*, London: George Allen and Unwin Ltd., 1919, pp. 312-338.

159. Foulke, R. D. "Creed and Conduct in 'The Nigger of the Narcissus'," *C* 1980, vol. 12, no. 2, pp. 105-128.

160. Fradin, J. I. "Conrad's Everyman: 'The Secret Agent'," *Texas Studies in Literature and Language* 1969, vol. 11, no. 2, pp. 1023-1038.

161. Fraser, G. "Conrad's Revisions to 'Amy Foster'," *C* 1988, vol. 20, no. 3, pp. 181-193.

162. Gallagher, M. P. "'The Nigger of the 'Narcissus'. Two Worlds of Perspective," *C* 1970/71, vol. 3, no. 1, pp. 51-60.

163. Gaston, P. L. "The Gospel of Work According to Joseph Conrad," *Joseph Conrad. Commemorative Essays*. Selected Proceedings of the International Conference of Conrad Scholars, San Diego, August 29-September 5, 1974, ed. A. Gillon, L. Krzyżanowski, New York: Astra Books (Twayne Publishers) 1975, pp. 202-209.

164. Gawliński, S. "Sytuacje conradowskie" in cf. 126, pp. 169-181.

165. Geary, E. A. "An Ashy Halo: Woman as Symbol in 'Heart of Darkness'," *SSF* 1976, vol. 13, no. 4, pp. 499-506.

166. Gertzman, J. A. "Commitment and Sacrifice in 'Heart of Darkness': Marlow's Response to Kurtz," *SSF* 1972, vol. 9, no. 2, pp. 187-196.

167. Gillon, A. "Betrayal and Redemption in Joseph Conrad," *The Polish Review* 1960, vol. 5, no. 2, pp. 18-35.

168. Gillon, A. "Polish and Russian Literary Elements in Joseph Conrad," *Proceedings of the Vth Congress of the International Comparative Literature Association*, Belgrade, 1967, ed. N. Banašević, Amsterdam, 1969, pp. 685-694.

169. Gillon, A. "Joseph Conrad: Polish Cosmopolitan," *Joseph Conrad: Theory and World Fiction*. Proceedings of the Comparative Literature Symposium. (January 23, 24, and 25, 1974), vol. 7, ed. W. T. Zyła, W. M. Aycock, Lubbock: Texas Tech University, 1974, pp. 41-69.

170. Gillon, A. "Conrad as Painter," *C* 1978, vol. 10, no. 3, pp. 253-266.

171. Gilmore, T. B. "Retributive Irony in Conrad's 'The Secret Agent'," *C* 1969, vol. 1, no. 3, pp. 41-50.

172. Goodin, G. "The Personal and the Political in 'Under Western Eyes'," *NCF* 1970, vol. 25, no. 3, pp. 327-342.

173. Gose, E. B. "Cruel Devourer of 'the World's Light': 'The Secret

Agent'," *NCF* 1960, vol. 15, no. 1, pp. 39-51.

174. Gossman, A. M., Whiting, G. W. "The Essential Jim," *NCF* 1961, vol. 16, no. 1, pp. 75-80.

175. Gray Willy, T. "The 'Shamefully Abandoned' Kurtz. A Rhetorical Context for 'Heart of Darkness'," *C* 1978, vol. 10, no. 2, pp. 99-112.

176. Guetti, J. "'Heart of Darkness': The Failure of Imagination," *The Limits of Metaphor. A Study of Melville, Conrad, and Faulkner*, Ithaca, N. Y.: Cornell University Press, 1967, pp. 46-68.

177. Hagan, J. "Conrad's 'Under Western Eyes': The Question of Razumov's Guilt and Remorse," *Studies in the Novel* 1969, vol. 1, no. 3, pp. 310-322.

178. Harkness, B. "The Young Roman Trader in 'Heart of Darkness'," *C* 1980, vol. 12, no. 3, pp. 227-229.

179. Haugh, R.F. "The Structure of 'Lord Jim'," *College English* 1951, vol. 13, no. 3, pp. 137-141.

180. Hawkins, H. "Conrad and Congolese Expolitation," *C* 1981, vol. 13, no. 2, pp. 93-100.

181. Hawkins, H. "The Issue of Racism in 'Heart of Darkness'," *C* 1982, vol. 14, no. 3, pp. 163-171.

182. Hawkins, H. "Conrad and the Psychology of Colonialism" in cf. 141, pp. 71-87.

183. Helder, J. "Fool Convention and Conrad's Hollow Harlequin," *SSF* 1975, vol. 12, no. 4, pp. 361-368.

184. Hervouet, Y. "Conrad's Relationship with Anatole France," *C* 1980, vol. 12, no. 3, pp. 195-225.

185. Hervouet, Y. "Conrad and Maupassant: An Investigation into Conrad's Creative Process," *C* 1982, vol. 14, no. 2, pp. 83-111.

186. Hillis Miller, J. "The Interpretation of 'Lord Jim'," *The Interpretation of Narrative: Theory and Practice*, ed. M. W. Bloomfield, Harvard English Studies, vol. 1, Cambridge, Mass.: Harvard University Press, 1970, pp. 211-228.

187. Hillis Miller, J. "'Lord Jim': Repetition as Subversion of Organic Form," *Fiction and Repetition. Seven English Novels*. Oxford 1982, pp. 22-41.

188. Hilson, J. C., Timms, D. "Conrad's 'An Outpost of Progress' or, the Evil Spirit of Civilization" in cf. 143, pp. 113-128.

189. Hoare, D. M. "The Tragic in Hardy and Conrad," *Some Studies in the Modern Novel*, London: Chatto and Windus, 1938, pp. 113-132.

190. Hoffman, C. G. "Punkt widzenia w 'Tajemnym wspólniku'," (1962), trans. from English M. Ronikier, in cf. 151, pp. 719-728.

191. Howarth, H. "The Meaning of Conrad's 'The Rover'," *The Southern Review* 1970, vol. 6, no. 3, pp. 682-697.

192. Hussey, W. R. M. "'He Was Spared That Annoyance'," *C* 1971/72, vol. 3, no. 2, pp. 17-25.

193. Hyland, P. "The Little Woman in the 'Heart of Darkness'," *C* 1988, vol. 20, no. 1, pp. 3-11.

194. Janion, M. "Conrad wobec dylematu polskiego romantyzmu," *Twórczość* 1978, vol. 34, no. 3, pp. 61-80.

195. Jaudel, P. "The Calm as Initiation: A Plural Reading of 'The Shadow-Line'," *LEC* 1988, ed. J. H. Stape, pp. 129-135.

196. Johnson, B. "Conrad's 'Karain' and 'Lord Jim'," *Modern Language Quarterly* 1963, vol. 24, no. 1, pp. 13-20.

197. Johnston, J. H. "'The Secret Agent' and 'Under Western Eyes': Conrad's Two Political Novels," *West Virginia University Bulletin* 1970, vol. 17, pp. 57-71.

198. Jones, M. P. "Judgement and Sentiment in 'The Nigger of the 'Narcissus'," *C* 1977, vol. 9, no. 2, pp. 159-169.

199. Kaehele, S., German, H. "Conrad's 'Victory': A Reassessment," *MFS* 1964, vol. 10, no. 1, p. 55-72.

200. Karl, F R. "Conrad's Stein: The Destructive Element," *Twentieth Century Literature* 1958, vol. 3, no. 4, pp. 163-169.

201. Karl, F. R. "The Rise and Fall of 'Under Western Eyes'," *NCF* 1959, vol. 13, no. 4, pp. 313-327.

202. Karl, F. R. "Conrad's Waste Land: Moral Anarchy in 'The Secret Agent'," *Four Quartets* 1960, vol. 9, no. 2, pp. 29-36.

203. Karl, F. R. "Introduction to 'Danse Macabre': Conrad's 'Heart of Darkness'," *MFS* 1968, vol. 14, no. 2, pp. 143-156.

204. Karrfalt, D. H. "Accepting Lord Jim on His Own Terms: A Structural Approach," *C* 1969/70, vol. 2, no. 1, pp. 37-47.

205. Kennedy, G. W. "Conrad and 'Robinson Crusoe'," *C* 1978, vol. 10, no. 2, pp. 113-122.

206. Kettle, A. "Joseph Conrad. 'Nostromo'," *Introduction to the English Novel,* vol. 2, Hutchinson University Library, London, 1972 (1953), pp. 62-74).

207. King, W. E. "Conrad's 'Weltanschauung' and the God of Material Interests in 'Nostromo'," *C* 1971/72' vol. 3, no. 3, pp. 41-45.

208. Kirschner, P. "Revolution, Feminism, and Conrad's Western 'I'," *TC* 1985, vol. 10, no. 1, p. 4-25.

209. Kisner, M. R. "The Lure of the Abyss for the Hollow Man: Conrad's Notion of Evil," *C* 1969/70, vol. 2, no. 3, pp. 85-99.

210. Knapp Hay, E. "'Lord Jim': From Sketch to Novel," *Comparative Literature* 1960, vol. 12, no. 4, pp. 289-309.

211. Knapp Hay, E. "Joseph Conrad's Last Epigraph," *C* 1969/70, vol. 2, no. 3, pp. 9-15.

212. Knoepflmacher, U. C. "'The Secret Agent': The Irony of the Absurd," *Laughter and Despair: Readings in Ten Novels of the Victorian Era*, Berkeley, 1973 (1971), pp. 240-273.

213. Knowles, O. "Commentary and Rhetoric: An Aspect of Conrad's Art," *C* 1973, vol. 5, no. 3, pp. 5-27.

214. Kocówna, B. "The Problem of Language," in cf. 127, pp. 194-198.

215. Kołaczkowski, S. "Józef Conrad (Korzeniowski)," (1925), in cf. 114, pp. 185-245.

216. Kowalska, A. "Człowiek i morze w twórczości Conrada-Korzeniowskiego," *Prace Polonistyczne* 1940-1946, vol. 4, pp. 117-137.

217. Kowalska, A. "Conrad–moralista," *Kultura i Społeczeństwo* 1959, vol. 3, no. 2, pp. 147-162.

218. Kowalska, A "One of the Shortest Masterpieces of Joseph Conrad. The Problem of Conrad's Autobiographical Works," *Bulletin de la Société des Sciences et des Lettres de Łódź* 1960, vol. 11, no. 5, pp. 1-9.

219. Krajka, W. "Aspekty dramatyczności w noweli 'Jutro'," *Nad tekstami Conrada*, ed. A. Zgorzelski, Gdańsk: Wydawnictwo Morskie, 1976, pp. 28-45.

220. Kramer, D. "Marlow, Myth and Structure in 'Lord Jim'," *Criticism* 1966, vol. 8, no. 3, pp. 263-279.

221. Kridl, M. "'Lord Jim' Conrada," *Przegląd Współczesny* 1929, vol. 28, no. 81, pp. 113-125, no. 82, pp. 247-269.

222. Krzyżanowski, L. "Joseph Conrad: Some Polish Documents'" (1958), *Joseph Conrad: Centennial Essays*, ed. L. Krzyżanowski, New York: Polish Institute of Arts and Sciences in America, 1960, pp. 111-143.

223. Kulsrestha, J. P. "'Isolatoes' and Exiles," *Graham Greene: The Novelist*, Delhi, 1977, pp. 18-55.

224. Laine, M. "Conrad's 'The Rover': The Rejection of Despair," *Queen's Quarterly* 1973, vol. 80, no. 2, pp. 246-255.

225. Leiter, L. H. "Echo Structures: Conrad's 'The Secret Sharer'," *Twentieth Century Literature* 1960, vol. 5, no. 4, pp. 159-175.

226. Leśnodorski, B. "Conrad i sprawa niepodległości Polski," in *Polska–Niemcy–Europa. Studia z dziejów myśli politycznej i stosunków międzynarodowych*, ed. A. Czubiński, Poznań: Uniwersytet im. A. Mickiewicza, 1977, pp. 351-357.

227. Lewis, R. W. B. "The Current of Conrad's 'Victory'," *Joseph Conrad. A Collection of Criticism*, ed. F. R. Karl, New York, 1975, pp. 101-119.

228. Lippe, H. "Reconsidering the Patna Inquiry in 'Lord Jim'," *TC* 1990, vol. 15, no. 1, pp. 59-69.

229. Lorch, T. M. "The Barrier Between Youth and Maturity in the Works of Joseph Conrad," *MFS* 1964, vol. 10, no. 1, pp. 73-80.

230. Lowe-Evans, M. "Conrad's James Wait: Prototype of Faulkner's Charles Bon," *C* 1989, vol. 21, no. 3, pp. 221-229.

231. Luyat-Moore, A. "La Reve et la Poétique de Conrad," *LEC* 1983, pp. 1-7.

232. Łann, E. "Joseph Conrad," (1962), trans. from Russian B. Kocówna, in cf. 151, pp. 93-123.

233. Madison, R. D. "The Secret Maneuver in 'The Secret Sharer'," *C* 1982, vol. 14, no. 3, pp. 233-236.

234. Malbone, R. G. "'How to be': Marlow's Quest in 'Lord Jim'," *Twentieth Century Literature* 1965, vol. 10, no. 4, pp. 172-180.

235. Marsh, D. R. C. "Moral Judgements in 'The Secret Agent'," *English Studies in Africa* 1960, vol. 3, no. 1, p. 57-70.

236. Marten, H. "Conrad's Skeptic Reconsidered: A Study of Martin Decoud," *MFS* 1972, vol. 27, no. 1, pp. 81-94.

237. Marten, H. "Drama and Theme in 'Nostromo': The Relationship of Nostromo, Dr. Monygham and Emilia Gould," *C* 1976, vol. 8, no. 1, pp. 27-36.

238. Martin, D. M. "The Function of the Intended in Conrad's 'Heart of Darkness'," *SSF* 1974, vol. 11, no. 1, pp. 27-33.

239. Martin, W. R. "Gaspar Ruiz: A Conradian Hero," *C* 1971/72, vol. 3, no. 3, pp. 46-48.

240. Matlaw, R. E. "Dostoevskij and Conrad's Political Novels," in *American Contributions to the Fifth International Congress of Slavists.* Sofia, September 1963, vol. 2: Literary Contributions, The Hague: Mouton, 1963, pp. 213-231.

241. Mayoux, J. J. "Joseph Conrad" (1961), trans. from French A. Iwaszkiewiczowa, in cf. 151, pp. 281-328.

242. McCullough, B. "The Impressionistic Novel. Joseph Conrad. 'Lord Jim'," *Representative English Novelists: Defoe to Conrad.* New York, London: Harper and Brothers Publishers, 1946, pp. 336-348.

243. McLauchlan, J. "Conrad's 'Three Ages of Man': The 'Youth' Volume," in cf. 163, pp. 188-201.

244. McLauchlan, J. "The 'Something Human' in 'Heart of Darkness'," *C* 1977, vol. 9, no. 2, pp. 115-125.

245. McLauchlan, J. "'Amy Foster'–Echoes from Conrad's Own Experience?" *The Polish Review* 1978, vol. 23, no. 3, pp. 3-8.

246. McLauchlan, J. "Almayer and Willems–'How Not to Be'," *C* 1979, vol. 11, no. 2, pp. 113-141.

247. McLauchlan, J. "The 'Value' and 'Significance' of 'Heart of Darkness'," *C* 1983, vol. 15, no. 1, pp. 3-21.

248. McLauchlan, J. "'The Empty Heavens': A Reading of 'The End of the Tether'," *LEC* 1988, ed. J. H. Stape, pp. 47-61.

249. Michael, M.C. "James Wait as Pivot: Narrative Structure in 'The Nigger of the 'Narcissus''," in cf. 169, pp. 89-102.

250. Milbauer, A. Z. "Joseph Conrad: Marginal Existence," *Transcending Exile. Conrad, Nabokov, I. B. Singer,* Miami: Florida International University Press, 1985, pp. 1-26.

251. Miller, J. E. "'The Nigger of the 'Narcissus': A Re-Examination," *Twentieth Century Interpretations of "The Nigger of the 'Narcissus'": A Collection of Critical Essays,* ed. J. A. Palmer, Englewood Cliffs, N. J.: Prentice-Hall, Inc., 1969, pp. 18-24.

252. Młynarska, M. "Lord Jim w powstaniu warszawskim," in cf. 119, pp. 262-266.

253. Moore, C. "Conrad and the Novel as Ordeal," *Philological Quarterly* 1963, vol. 42, no. 1, p. 55-74.

254. Morley, P. A. "Conrad's Vision of the Absurd," *C* 1969/70, vol. 2, no. 1, pp. 59-68.

255. Mroczkowski, P. "The Gnomic Element in Conrad," *Kwartalnik Neofilologiczny* 1959, vol. 6, no. 3, pp. 193-209.

256. Mroczkowski, P. "Joseph Conrad's International World of Men," *Kwartalnik Neofilologiczny* 1974, vol. 21, no. 2, pp. 171-191.

257. Mroczkowski, P. "Conrad the European," in cf. 126, pp. 13-29.

258. Mursia, U. "The Fictional State of Costaguana," *LEC* 1979, pp. 86-107.

259. Najder, Z. "Conrad," *Twórczość* 1955, vol. 11, no. 10, pp. 143-155.

260. Najder, Z. "Conrad and the Idea of Honor," in cf. 169, pp. 103-114.

261. Najder, Z. "Conrad and Rousseau: Concepts of Man and Society," in cf. 127, pp. 77-90.

262. Najder, Z. "Conrad in His Historical Perspective," *Critical Essays on Joseph Conrad,* ed. T. Billy, Boston: G. K. Hall and Co., 1987, pp. 19-28.

263. Nelson, C. "The Ironic Allusive Texture of 'Lord Jim': Coleridge, Crane, Milton and Melville," *C* 1972, vol. 4, no. 2, pp. 47-59.

264. Nettels, E. "Conrad and Stephen Crane," *C* 1978, vol. 10, no. 3, pp. 267-283.

265. Orr, L. "The Semiotics of Description in Conrad's 'Nostromo'," in cf. 262, pp. 113-128.

266. Ostrowski, W. "Problemy conradologii" (1957), *O literaturze angielskiej*, Warszawa: "PAX," 1958, pp. 253-299.

267. Ostrowski, W. "'Tajny agent' J. Conrada jako powieść kryminalna," *Prace Polonistyczne*, 1964 (1965), vol. 20, pp. 209-219 (trans. into English W. Ostrowski: "'The Secret Agent' as a Crime Novel," in cf. 133, pp. 137-148).

268. Paris, B. J. "The Dramatization of Interpretation: 'Lord Jim'," *A Psychological Approach to Fiction: Studies in Thackeray, Stendhal, George Eliot, Dostoevsky, and Conrad*, Bloomington, Ind.: 1974, pp. 215-274.

269. Pawłow, G. "The Theme of Alienation and Some Aspects of Presentation in Joseph Conrad's 'Nostromo'," *Godišnik na Sofijskija Universitet Fakultet po zapadui filologii*, 1967, vol. 61, pp. 245-278.

270. Peirce, W. P. "An Artistic Flaw in 'Heart of Darkness'," *C* 1969, vol. 1, no. 3, pp. 73-80.

271. Penn Warren, R. "Introduction," J. Conrad, *Nostromo*, New York: Random House, 1951, pp. VII-XXXIX.

272. Perry, J. O. "Action, Vision, or Voice: The Moral Dilemmas in Conrad's Tale-Telling," *MFS* 1964, vol. 10, no. 1, pp. 3-14.

273. Ridley, F. H. "The Ultimate Meaning of 'Heart of Darkness'," *NCF* 1963, vol. 18, no. 1, pp. 43-53.

274. Rivera, R. O. "The 'Silver of the Mine.' Conrad's 'Nostromo'," *Diliman Review* 1965, vol. 13, no. 2, pp. 199-204.

275. Roberts, A. "'Nostromo' and History: Remarkable Individuality and Historical Inevitability," *TC* 1987, vol. 12, no. 1, pp. 4-16.

276. Roberts. M. "Joseph Conrad and the Springs of Action: A Study of 'Victory'," *The Tradition of Romantic Morality*, New York 1973, pp. 259-287.

277. Ross, D. W. "'Lord Jim' and the Saving Illusion," *C* 1988, vol. 20, no. 1, pp. 45-69.

278. Schleifer, R. "Public and Private Narrative in 'Under Western Eyes'," *C* 1977, vol. 9, no. 3, pp. 237-254.

279. Schneider, D. J. "Symbolism in Conrad's 'Lord Jim': The Total Pattern," *MFS* 1966/67, vol. 12, no. 4, pp. 427-438.

280. Schneider, D. J. "The Dream and the Knitting Machine: Joseph Conrad's Symbolism," *Symbolism: The Manichean Vision. A Study in the Art of James, Conrad, Woolf and Stevens.* Lincoln, 1975, pp. 40-61.

281. Schuster, C. I. "Comedy and the Limits of Language in Conrad's 'Typhoon'," *C* 1984, vol. 16, no. 1, pp. 55-71.

282. Schwarz, D. R. "The Self-Deceiving Narrator of Conrad's 'Il Conde'," *SSF* 1969, vol. 6, no. 2, pp. 187-193.

283. Schwarz, D. R. "'A Lonely Figure Walking Purposefully': The

Significance of Captain Whalley in Conrad's 'The End of the Tether'," *C* 1975, vol. 7, no. 2, pp. 165-173.

284. Schwarz, D. R. "The Continuity of Conrad's Later Novels," in 141, pp. 151-169.

285. Scrimgeour, C. "Jimmy Wait and the Dance of Death: Conrad's 'Nigger of the 'Narcissus',''' in cf. 251, pp. 40-55.

286. Seltzer, A. J. "The Rescued Fragment: Elusiveness of Truth in Conrad's 'Lord Jim'," *Chaos in the Novel. The Novel in Chaos.* New York, 1974, pp. 80-91.

287. Shadoian, I. "Irony Triumphant: Verloc's Death," *C* 1971/72, vol. 3, no. 2, pp. 82-86.

288. Sherry, N. "The Essential Jim," in cf. 169, pp. 141-149.

289. Shires, L. M. "The 'Privileged' Reader and Narrative Methodology in 'Lord Jim'," *C* 1985, vol. 18, no. 1, pp. 19-30.

290. Singh, F. B. "The Colonialistic Bias of 'Heart of Darkness'," *C* 1978, vol. 10, no. 1, pp. 41-54.

291. Skutnik, T. "O semantyce kompozycji 'Zwierciadła morza'," *O kompozycji tekstu Conradowskiego*, ed. A. Zgorzelski, Gdańsk: Wydawnictwo Morskie, 1978, pp. 7-28.

292. Spatt, H. S. "'Nostromo's' Chronology: The Shaping of History," *C* 1976, vol. 8, no. 1, pp. 37-46.

293. Spector, R. D. "Irony as Theme: Conrad's 'The Secret Agent'," *NCF* 1958, vol. 13, no. 1, pp. 69-71.

294. Stallman, R. W. "Time and 'The Secret Agent'," (1959), in cf. 153, pp. 234-254.

295. Stallman, R. W. "Conrad and 'The Secret Sharer'" (1949), in cf. 153, pp. 275-288.

296. Staniewski, M. "Angielskość Conrada" (1929), in cf. 114, pp. 48-60.

297. Stavrou, C. N. "Conrad, Camus and Sisyphus," *Audience* 1960, vol. 7, no. 1, pp. 80-96.

298. Steiner, J. E. "Conrad's 'The Secret Sharer': Complexities of the Doubling Relationship," *C* 1980, vol. 12, no. 3, pp. 173-186.

299. Steinmann, T. "Lord Jim's Progression Through Homology," *Ariel* 1974, vol. 5, no. 1, p. 81-93.

300. Stephens, R. C. "'Heart of Darkness': Marlow's Spectral Moonshine," *Essays in Criticism* 1969, vol. 19, no. 3, pp. 273-284.

301. Stewart, G. "Lying as Dying in 'Heart of Darkness'," *PMLA* 1980, vol. 95, no. 3, pp. 319-331.

302. Szala, A. "Joseph Conrad (1857-1924)," *Problems of Civilization in*

the Novels of Conrad, Forster and Lawrence, Lublin: Maria Curie-Skłodowska University, 1978, pp. 19-64.

303. Szczepański, J. J. "W służbie Wielkiego Armatora," *Przed nieznanym trybunałem*, Warszawa: "Czytelnik," 1975, pp. 5-30.

304. Tanner, T. "Nightmare and Complacency: Razumov and the Western Eye," *The Critical Quarterly* 1962, vol. 4, no. 3, pp. 197-214.

305. Tanner, T. "Motyle i chrząszcze–dwie prawdy conradowskie" (1963), trans. from English H. Carroll-Najder, in cf. 151, pp. 395-418.

306. Tanner, T. "'Gnawed Bones' and 'Artless Tales'–Eating and Narrative in Conrad," in cf. 127, pp. 17-36.

307. Tarnawski, W. "The Sisters," *C* 1980, vol. 12, no. 2, pp. 129-134.

308. Thale, J. "Marlow's Quest" (1955), in cf. 153, pp. 153-161.

309. Tillyard, E. M. W. "'The Secret Agent' Reconsidered" (1961), in cf. 138, pp. 103-110.

310. Todorov, T. "Knowledge in the Void: 'Heart of Darkness'," trans. from French W. C. Putnam III, *C* 1989, vol. 21, no. 3, pp. 161-172.

311. Toker, L. "Parallel Experience in Conrad's 'Nostromo'," *C* 1989, vol. 21, no. 3, pp. 183-202.

312. Urbisz, K. "The Theme of Isolation in Joseph Conrad," *Zeszyty Naukowe Uniwersytetu Jagiellońskiego. Prace Historycznoliterackie* 1974, vol. 29, no. 362, pp. 291-305.

313. Urbisz, K. "'Zwycięstwo' J. Conrada: struktura i semantyka," in cf. 126, pp. 117-129.

314. Urbisz, K. "Semantyka przestrzeni i jej rola kompozycyjna w 'Ocaleniu'," in cf. 291, pp. 29-55.

315. Van Ghent, D. "On 'Lord Jim'," *The English Novel: Form and Function*, New York: Harper and Row, 1961 (1953), pp. 229-244.

316. Van Ghent, D. "Nostromo," in cf. 227, pp. 43-58.

317. Van Ghent, D. "Guardianship of the Treasure: 'Nostromo'," in *Joseph Conrad's "Nostromo,"* Modern Critical Interpretations, ed. H. Bloom, New York: Chelsea House Publishers, 1987, pp. 23-37.

318. Verleun, J. "Marlow and the Harlequin," *C* 1961, vol. 13, no. 3, pp. 195-220.

319. Verleun, J. "Donkin and Wait," *TC* 1981, vol. 6, no. 4, pp. 4-21: 1982, vol. 7, no. 1, pp. 4-20.

320. Vidan, I. "'Zwycięstwo' Conrada (Szkic o strukturze powieści)" (1958), trans. Z. Najder, in cf. 151, pp. 647-666.

321. Vincenz, S. "Conrad a konwencje," in cf. 119, pp. 114-128.

322. Vitoux, P. "Marlow: The Changing Narrator of Conrad's Fiction," in cf. 143, pp. 83-102.

323. Wain, J. "The Test of Manliness," *The London Magazine* November 1957, vol. 4, no. 11, pp. 23-26.

324. Walton, J. "Conrad, Dickens and the Detective Novel," *NCF* 1969, vol. 23, no. 4, pp. 446-462.

325. Watt, I. "Story and Idea in Conrad's 'The Shadow-Line'" (1960), *Modern British Fiction. Essays in Criticism,* ed. M. Schorer, New York: Oxford University Press, 1961, pp. 119-136.

326. Watt, I. "Conrad Criticism and 'The Nigger of the 'Narcissus'," in cf. 251, pp. 78-99.

327. Watt, I. "Joseph Conrad: Alienacja i zaangażowanie" (1964), trans. from English H. Caroll-Najder, in cf. 151, pp. 135-162.

328. Watt, I. "Pink Toads and Yellow Curs: An Impressionist Narrative Device in 'Lord Jim'," *Joseph Conrad Colloquy in Poland,* 5-12 September 1972. Contributions, ed. R. Jabłkowska, Wrocław: Zakład Narodowy im. Ossolińskich, Polska Akademia Nauk, Komitet Neofilologiczny, 1975, pp. 11-31.

329. Watt, I. "The Ending of 'Lord Jim'," *C* 1979, vol. 11, no. 1, p. 3-21.

330. Wegelin, C. "MacWhirr and the Testimony of the Human Voice," *C* 1975, vol. 7, no. 1, pp. 45-50.

331. White, J. F. "The Third Theme in 'The Secret Sharer'," *C* 1989, vol. 21, no. 1, pp. 37-46.

332. Whitehead, L. M. "'An Island Is But the Top of a Mountain': Isolation and Solidarity in Conrad's 'Victory'," *LEC* 1980, pp. 87-107.

333. Williams, P. "Story and Frame in Conrad's 'The Tale'," *SSF* 1968, vol. 5, no. 2, pp. 179-185.

334. Wills, J. H. "Adam, Axel, and 'Il Conde'," (1955), in 153, pp. 254-275.

335. Wilson, A. "The Great Theme in Conrad," *Susquehanna University Studies* 1953, vol. 5, pp. 51-84.

336. Wyka, K. "Czas powieściowy," *O potrzebie historii literatury.* Szkice polonistyczne z lat 1944-1967, Warszawa: Państwowy Instytut Wydawniczy, 1969, pp. 5-98.

337. Yarrison, B. C. "The Symbolism of Literary Allusion in 'Heart of Darkness'," *C* 1975, vol. 7, no. 2, pp.155-164.

338. Yates, N. W. "Social Comment in 'The Nigger of the 'Narcissus'," in cf. 251, pp. 103-108.

339. Yoder, E. K. "The Demon Harlequin in Conrad's Hell," *C* 1980, vol. 12, no. 2, p. 88-92.

340. Young, V. "Lingard's Folly: The Lost Subject" (1953), in cf. 153, pp. 96-108.

341. Young, V. "Trial by Water: Joseph Conrad's 'The Nigger of the 'Narcissus'," (1952), in cf. 153, pp. 108-120.

342. Yousef, T. "Imagery in Conrad's 'Heart of Darkness'," *TC* 1982, vol. 7, no. 1, pp. 22-32.

343. Zabel, M. D. "Introduction to 'Under Western Eyes'," (1963), in cf. 138, pp. 111-144.

344. Zabel, M. D. "Editor's Introduction," *The Portable Conrad* (1947), ed. M. D. Zabel, New York: Viking Press, 1979, pp. 1-47.

345. Zabierowski, S. "Recepcja 'Lord Jima' w Polsce w latach 1939-1961 (Zarys problematyki)," *Rocznik Komisji Historycznoliterackiej* 1968, vol. 9, pp. 115-139.

346. Zabierowski, S. "Pięć typów interpretacji 'Lord Jima'," (1974), in cf. 126, pp. 97-115.

347. Zeigler, S. L. "Borys Conrad's Visit to Poland: Some Reflections on the Nature and Significance of Conrad's Polishness," *C* 1970/1971, vol. 3, no. 1, pp. 61-67.

348. Zgorzelski, A. "Funkcjonalność struktur w 'Lagunie' Conrada," *Kwartalnik Neofilologiczny* 1969, vol. 16, no. 4, pp. 401-409.

349. Zgorzelski, A., Krajka, W. "Konwencje gatunkowe w 'Tajemnym wspólniku'," in cf. 219, pp. 67-88.

350. Zuckerman, J. "The Architecture of 'The Shadow-Line'," *C* 1971/72, vol. 3, no. 2, pp. 87-92.

Subsidiary Sources

351. Conrad, J. (Joseph). *O morzu. Wybór myśli*, ed. P. Dzianisz, Gdańsk: Wydawnictwo Morskie, 1974.

352. Conrad, J. (Joseph). *Myśli*, ed. T. Skutnik, Gdańsk: Wydawnictwo Morskie, 1974.

Index of Titles of Conrad's Works